AMERICAN LIBRARY CLASSIFICATION

AMERICAN LIBRARY CLASSIFICATION

With Special Reference to
the Library of Congress

LEO E. LaMONTAGNE

HAMDEN, CONNECTICUT
THE SHOE STRING PRESS, INC.
1961

To the LaMontagnes
especially,
Leopold J., 92, my father
Nora Lee, my wife
Margaret Ellen, my daughter

"The investigation of the truth is in one way
hard, in another easy. An indication of this is
found in the fact that no one is able to attain the
truth adequately, while, on the other hand, we do
not collectively fail, but every one says something
true about the nature of things, and while individually we contribute little or nothing to the truth,
by the union of all a considerable amount is amassed."

Aristotle

"... New nations in new lands, as contrasted
with old nations in old lands, tend to live in the present plus the future instead of the present plus the past."

James Truslow Adams

PREFACE

Originally planned as a brief history and description of the Library of Congress Classification and of its immediate antecedents — Cutter's Expansive Classification, Dewey's Decimal Classification, and the Halle Schema of Otto Hartwig — the scope and content of this work were changed several times during the writing.

Although much has been written of the development of library classification in the United States since 1870 the long "pre-history" of the process remained untold. The recording of these early American essays in theory and practice extended the scope of the work considerably. The history of American library classification which resulted seemed incomplete, however, without a history of the Old World systems which were its sources; the second change produced a brief history of classification in Western Thought from its origin in Ionia to its development in Colonial America. Unlike previous histories this summary treats classification as a unitary intellectual process rather than as discrete systems of the classification of knowledge, the classification of the sciences, and book classification, with and without notation. A third change produced an expanded history of classification in the Library of Congress and a more detailed description of the present Library of Congress Classification. Since change engenders change, another came about — an introduction to classification in general and to library classification in particular. This introduction which became the first chapter seemed necessary in order to make the work reasonably self-contained. The structure of the work quite obviously reflects these changes in scope and content.

The manuscript was completed nearly six years ago, but only material dealing with the Library of Congress has been brought up to date.

The final purpose which developed during the changes is to present a history and description of classification in general and of library classification

in particular, with special reference to the United States and to the Library
of Congress.

It is a pleasure as well as a duty to acknowledge the valuable contributions of Audrey A. Cook and Dorothy C. Norberg to this book — Mrs. Cook
for assistance in research and writing and for typing a difficult manuscript;
Miss Norberg for assistance in writing, in proofreading, and in preparing
the bibliography and index.

I want also to express my appreciation to Mr. John W. Cronin, Director of the Processing Department, for his continuing interest and encouragement.

LEO E. LA MONTAGNE

CONTENTS

AMERICAN LIBRARY CLASSIFICATION

CHAPTER I

Library Classification

American library classification has a long history but no historian. According to a tradition long taught and never questioned, classification entered American libraries in 1870 with the system William Torrey Harris devised for the library of the St. Louis public schools. Harris, a Hegelian, is said to have derived his system from Francis Bacon's divisions of knowledge; Melvil Dewey followed Harris, and his decimals ended the "dark age" of American librarianship. It is a sad commentary on librarians as historians that this myth of the origin of library classification and the assumption of a previous state of bibliographic chaos have so long survived and that American classification can, as a consequence, be divided into "prehistoric" and "historic" eras – before and after 1870.

Actually, the history of American classification extends over two and a half centuries, a long period in the life of a young country. But long as the period is, it is short in the history of a process which goes back over six millennia. Man's attempts to classify, to introduce order into the arrangement of his books and the records describing them, have been many and varied. From the "brick books" of Mesopotamia and the papyri of ancient Egypt to the books, microfilms, microprints, and audio-visual material of the present, many systems have been devised and applied. Cicero's dictum, "Ordo est maxime qui memoriae lumen affert, " has indeed been followed, and there has been no limit to man's ingenuity in devising methods to create that order. There was consequently no consistent unilinear development such as is found in other areas of culture. As Savage observes,

> The truth is that the chief processes in library administration undergo periodical occultations. They emerge again the brighter for their eclipse, and shine upon us for a time, and fade again into obscurity. We lose ideas, regain them, fight against them, yield to them, and forget them once more. [1]

Library classification is but a part of a larger process of classification which goes back to the dawn of man's thinking. Man uses classification in all his affairs as unwittingly as Molière's M. Jourdain used prose.

> Ages before the logician, or any one else who deals with systems, had a hand in the matter, the necessities of common life had been at work prompting men to group the things which they observed. All names imply the recognition of groups, and a great number of names imply a subordination of groups, so that at the earliest stage to which we can transfer ourselves we find that we are already in possession of a rudimentary classification; and that we cannot even talk or think about the things without an appeal to this. [2]

Things acquire names and meaning just as objects indistinguishable in a fog become, as the sun burns away the fog, trees – then pines, oaks, maples.

Plato, a great inventor of the sciences, was the first to give a formal description of the process, which, as Aristotle records, he learned from his teacher Socrates. In the Phaedrus, written ca. 370 B. C. , he sought to vindicate philosophy against the false claims of the rhetoricians, to reform rhetoric, and to expound a new method of philosophy – the method of dialectic. Speaking for Plato, Socrates explains to his sole interlocutor, Phaedrus, the principles or procedures involved:

> Collection – "That of perceiving and bringing together in one idea [form] the scattered particulars, that one may make clear by definition the particular thing which he wishes to explain; ... "
>
> and   Division – "That of dividing things again by classes, where the natural joints are, and not trying to break any part, after the manner of a bad carver [butcher]. "[3]

Here are the seeds – definition, division, and classification – of a new science, Logic. The human mind perceives that unity exists amid a bewildering diversity, that the objects of thought are not isolated but related in varying degrees by characteristics they share in common. The mind groups them into classes which it names and defines, divides the terms formally, and creates other classes and systems of classes. Plato's pupil Aristotle wrote the first treatises on the subject, which in Byzantine times were combined in the Organon – the instrument of knowledge.

It has been traditional to divide classifications into natural and artificial, or, the classes discovered by man and those invented by him. It is assumed that the first are based upon traits inherent in objects while the second depend upon traits which man selects to organize material for a special use. Logicians frequently use the plant world as an illustration: the taxonomic arrangement of systematic botany is natural, while the classifications used in economic botany are artificial because they are based upon use rather than kinship. While the division has some merit, it is the human mind that must select the principle of classification, "natural" or "artificial."

"The general aim of all classification is, of course, to give us clear ideas, definite, well-ordered knowledge, control over facts, increase of power in retaining and communicating our knowledge about them."[4]

The process (and product) of classification can be schematized as follows:

Universe of classification (Entities to be arranged)

Purpose of classification, from which derives the

Basis of classification (Trait, characteristics, etc.)

Classification (Structure)

Logicians have developed rules for classification. Originally devised for formal division rather than classification, they represent in practice an ideal rather than a method. In fact, one logician went so far as to state that "... the confusion between the practicality of empirical classifications (to be tested by their applicability) and the absoluteness of division based on logical principles, is perhaps the most fruitful source of philosophic error."[5] The most useful rules are:

1. The classification must be exhaustive – provide for all entities in the universe being classified.

2. The divisions should be mutually exclusive.

3. At each stage in the process only one principle, the fundamentum divisionis, should be employed.

The following examples illustrate the application of classification to widely differing universes.

Universe: domestic dogs

Purpose: grouping for breeding, showing, using, etc.

Basis: use, real or assumed

Classification: sporting dogs (pointers, retrievers, spaniels, etc.)
                 sporting dogs (hounds)
                 working dogs
                 terriers
                 toys
                 non-sporting

Over a hundred distinct breeds are grouped in the six divisions of this classification which is used by the American Kennel Club. To a geneticist with no fondness for dogs this "practical" classification might appear absurd, for only among the terriers is there any relationship of descent. But for those concerned with dogs the classification is a "natural" one. The zoologist, on the contrary, is concerned with the position of the dog in relation to other animals. He bases his "natural" classification principally on similarity of structure and probable relationship:[6]

Phylum Chordata (Animals possessing notochords)
  Subphylum Vertebrata (Chordates with vertebral columns)
    Class Mammalia (Vertebrates with mammary glands)
      Order Carnivora (Mammals that eat flesh)
        Family Canidae (Carnivores that walk on their toes)
          Genus Canis (Canidae with round pupils)
            Species lupus Linnaeus [timber wolf]
          [Species familiaris – dog]

The classification devised by anthropologists for the grouping of "peoples," tribes, and other units on the basis of their cultural similarities or dissimilarities is an interesting application to highly complex material. It should be noted that culture to the anthropologist (and other social scientists) means the complex whole of man's speech, knowledge, beliefs, arts, crafts, laws, etc. Applied to American Indians, a structure like the following appears:

Universe: Indians of North America

Purpose: knowledge of prehistory

Basis: systemic patterns of culture

Classification: culture area   North Pacific Coast
                 sub-area   Northern
                                     Vancouver Island
                 tribes   Kwakiutl
                                     Nootka
                                     Bellacoola
                                     Southern (Oregon and Washington)

                                     Southwest
                                     Plains

As the following example, that of position classification, is somewhat

complicated, let us begin with definitions.

Title III
Section 301. For the purposes of this Act, the term —

(1) "position" means the work, consisting of the duties and responsi-
    bilities, assignable to an officer or employee;
(2) "class" or "class of positions" includes all positions which are
    sufficiently similar, as to (A) kind or subject-matter of work,
    (B) level of difficulty and responsibility, and (C) the qualifica-
    tion requirements of the work, to warrant similar treatment
    in personnel and pay administration; and
(3) "grade" includes all classes of positions which (although differ-
    ent with respect to kind or subject-matter of work) are suffi-
    ciently equivalent as to (A) level of difficulty and responsibili-
    ty, and (B) level of qualification requirements of the work, to
    warrant the inclusion of such classes of positions within one
    range of rates of basic compensation, as specified in title VI. [7]

Universe: positions

Purpose: standardization of duties, responsibilities, qualifica-
                 tions and compensation
Basis: duties and responsibilities

Classification: Classes   Grades[8]

                 Clerk-Typist   GS 3
                 Stenographer   GS 4
                 Editorial assistant   GS 5
                 Abstractor-Bibliographer GS 6
                   (Trainee)
                 Legal Analyst   GS 7
                   etc.

The relativity of classification to purpose is clearly illustrated in the

systems devised for the classification of diseases, injuries, etc. A classifi-

cation designed for the compilation of statistics differs widely in structure

and specificity from one prepared for the description and recording of cli-

nical and pathological observations. The system employed in Standard

<u>Nomenclature</u> <u>of</u> <u>Diseases</u> <u>and</u> <u>Operations</u> is based upon two elements, topo-
graphy, the part of the body concerned, and etiology, the cause of the disor-
der. But since it is concerned with <u>individual</u> <u>occurrences</u>, the system is
ill-suited for the classification of <u>groups</u> <u>of</u> <u>cases</u>, which are the material
of statistics. Statistical classifications, therefore, comprise a smaller number of divisions for the entire range of morbid conditions and are usually
based upon several factors, including etiology, anatomy, age, and onset of
disease.

The universes of knowledge we have schematized above provide practical samples of the whole classificatory method. In broad terms, the object
of classification is to introduce order into our thinking and into the arrangement in space of the physical things we use in our daily living. When libraries came into existence classification was called upon to assist in the work
of organization. This was of course inevitable, for

> Nothing can represent chaos more completely than a disor-
> derly, unrelated mass of books, unless it is a mass of pamphlets,
> cuttings, prints, photographs and the other ana of civilized life.
> Anyone who has tried to find something in the lumber room of a
> library which has been merely a place where things are collected
> in the hope that some day someone will arrange them, understands
> the waste of effort and the futility involved in disorder.[9]

Applied to books and other library material, classification provides a systematic subject arrangement of

1. The books on the shelves

2. The entries describing them in shelflists, catalogs, and bibliographies.

The basis of library classification by subject is the assumption, confirmed
by the experience of generations of librarians, that books on the same, or related, subjects will frequently be used together. Richardson wrote:

> If we come down to the real fact why we put books or cards
> [entries] together according to subjects in a library, we find that
> it is to get together those books or cards which will be most used
> together.... Libraries are not gotten together as a museum to
> exhibit what we have called the fossils of knowledge. It is a ma-
> chine got together to instill that knowledge into men's minds. The

books are collected for use; they are administered for use; they are arranged for use; and it is use which is the motive of classification. [10]

Classification, however, is but a part of the process of organizing books for use. Organization may be defined as the arranging and coordinating of parts, physical or mental, into a systematic whole. The organization of any collection – minerals, merchandise, art objects, ideas, or books – involves the identification, description, and location of its parts or units. Since books are composite entities, physical in form, but mental in content, they must be identified, described, and located both as physical things and as units of knowledge. They must be identified and described bibliographically by author, title, imprint, collation, and notes of various kinds. In addition, their contents must be made accessible and their location assigned so that they may be readily found. The entries containing this information are organized into catalogs in sheaf, book, or card form.

Historically, catalogs have been organized on various bases: author, subject (first classed and later alphabetical), and, finally, the amalgam of authors, titles, and subjects into a "theoretical" single alphabet called the dictionary catalog. During the nineteenth century, before a laudable zeal for the standardization of entries led to a standardization of catalogs, American librarians, unlike their successors, tailored their catalogs to their collections and the needs of their users. There were author catalogs and classed catalogs, and divided catalogs were common. Depending upon the predilection of the librarian, the main catalog comprised full entries in classified order with an author or descriptive catalog composed of briefer entries attached, or the main catalog was, conversely, an author catalog of full entries with an added analytical or classified index or catalog of brief entries.

Although early American classification was applied both to books and to entries, more importance was attached to classed catalogs than to classed books. It was not until after the development and widespread adoption of the Decimal Classification that physical location became the dominant purpose

of library classification. This was ironic, for Dewey constructed his system
for cataloging purposes; its use in shelving books was a by-product. A
classed catalog is one in which the entries are arranged in the order of a
system of classification. Like other catalogs it may be in book or card form.
The arrangement of the books on the shelves may, or may not, follow the
classification used in the catalog. Free of the limitations imposed by the
fact that books as physical things can occupy only one position in space at a
time, classification provides a deeper subject analysis when applied to entries in catalogs than to books. The depth of the analysis is limited only by
the needs of the library, its classification, the competence of its staff – and,
important today as always, its budget. In addition to the classed catalog proper, two auxiliary tools are required, an author catalog and a subject index.
A combined system which Clement W. Andrews introduced into the John Crerar Library of Chicago in 1896 still offers many interesting possibilities.
The catalog contained the parts described above but the index also served as
a partial alphabetical subject catalog. Entries were made "under headings
which collect material separated in the classed catalogue because of its relations to broader subjects and also under those which separate material
collected in the classed catalogue. "[11]

The "locating" of books, their arrangement on shelves, and the devices
used to correlate entries and books have been as diverse as the catalogs
listing and describing them. [12] They have been arranged by size, in accession order, and by subject; press, alcove, and shelf marks provided their addresses. But, contrary to an opinion somewhat widely held, books were rarely (in American libraries) shelved with no regard for their contents. More
often, alcoves, bookcases, and shelves were alloted to subjects – a system
known as fixed location because the class numbers were assigned to the
physical quarters the books occupied. More flexible and satisfactory is the
"relative" or "movable" plan which Thomas Jefferson used. When his library
was moved from the "book-room" at Monticello to Washington, first to Blodget's

Hotel and later to the Capitol, the arrangement of his books was not affected. Jefferson had numbered the divisions of knowledge, not their quarters. In Washington, as at Monticello, the books in Chapter 8 Chemistry stood between those in Chapter 7 Agriculture and Chapter 9 Surgery. Charles A. Cutter described the differing systems in these words:

> The old method may be compared to the line in the directory which states that a man lives at 129 Grace Street; the method proposed may be compared to the army register, which says that he is captain of Company C, 5th Regiment, M. V. M. Let the regiment be marched all over the country, yet the soldier is easily found by his position in it. If the citizen moves to a new street, a new directory is needed, but the army register does not have to be altered whenever the regiment is quartered in a different town. Similarly, books may be found by their position in a certain class, though the class itself be transferred from one alcove to another, or from one building to another. [13]

Contemporary book classifications (in the English-speaking world) are based upon the principle of relative location. There is evidence, however, of a return to the fixed location plan, for librarians are ever "original."

Let us now consider briefly the material from which library classifications are constructed and their organization. What is the raw material of library classification? At present, strangely enough, there is some confusion on this point. Most writers on the subject, even classifiers themselves, work with systems constructed with terms from a single language – English or French or German, etc. The exceptions to the vernacular are usually the latinized terms found in the nomenclature of systematic botany and zoology. As a consequence, writers and classifiers sometimes confuse concepts and terms, ideas and objects, with their names. The widespread acceptance of the dictionary catalog with its subject component of subject headings, which in general are arranged in the fortuitous order of the alphabet, has added to the confusion.

Classification is concerned with conceptual organization; its order is therefore independent of the terms employed and of the semantics and syntax of individual languages. The classification of 🐕 is unaffected whether it is called "bow-wow," "dog," "chien," "Hund," "כֶּלֶב," or any one

of the many names by which it is known. When, however, terms are the product of a classificatory process, as in the nomenclature of systematic botany
and zoology, the conventionalized (and internationalized) terms indicate but
do not determine the classification, e. g. Canis familiaris. It is this relative
freedom from semantic problems that makes classification (even if a Uto-
pian international language were developed) the most effective instrument
for the international organization of knowledge. The following extract from
the trilingual Système de classification des sciences agricoles[14] illustrates
this freedom:

F	CULTURE DES PLANTES EN GÉNÉRAL	PLANT PRODUC- TION IN GENERAL	ALLGEMEINER PFLANZENBAU
522	Méthodes de l'ensemencement	Sowing methods	Ausfuhrung der Saat
5221	Époque de l'ensemencement	Time of sowing	Saatzeit
5222	Quantité de semences à employer	Seed quantity	Saatmenge
5223	Profonduer du semis	Depth of sowing	Saattiefe
5224	Distance du semis	Distance of sowing	Saatweite
5225	Semis à la volée	Broadcast sowing	Breitsaat
5226	Semis en lignes	Drilling	Reihensaat
5227	Semis en poquets	Pocket drilling	Dibbelsaat
523	Plantation	Planting	Pflanzung
5231	Époque de la plantation	Time of planting	Pflanzzeit
5232	Profondeur	Depth of planting	Pflanztiefe
5233	Distance des plantes	Distance of plant- ing	Pflanzweite
5234	Pepinières	Nurseries	Pflanzschulen. Baumschulen.
5235	Repiquage	Transplanting	Auspflanzen
524	Assolements (point de vue technique) v. a. E 346	Crop rotation tech- nical aspects)	Fruchtfolge (vom pflanzenbaulichen Standpunkt)

Three indexes, French, English, and German, lead users from the vernacular
terms, arranged alphabetically, to the concepts in the systematic schedules.
They differ from each other both in arrangement and specificity.

Ensemencement	F52
--Epoque	F5221
--(Sylviculture)	K253

Sowing	F52
--and planting machines	Q34
--Depth of	F5223
Saattiefe	F5223
Saatweite	F5224
Saatzeit	F5221

Because of their relative independence of language, classification and notation were made the bases of several interesting attempts to develop a means of international communication after the Reformation had brought about the decline of Latin as a universal language. The German philosopher Gottfried Leibniz and the English clergyman John Wilkins, among others, contemplated a philosophical construct which would become a universal language because it was philosophical. In his De Arte Combinatoria (Leipzig, 1666) and Historia et Commendatio Linguae Charactericae Universalis (Amsterdam and Leipzig, 1765), Leibniz merely hinted at such a language, but Wilkins elaborated his in great detail in An Essay towards a Real Character, and a Philosophical Language (London, 1668). He began his project with a systematic classification of the objects of thought and communication. To these fundamental concepts he added a system of notation, probably derived from early shorthand symbols, and, finally, a system of sounds for the symbols.

While library classification is concerned with concepts, not words, it is with concepts in organized systems. The construction of a library classification involves the assembly and integration into a comprehensive system, based upon some theory of the order of the sciences, of the branches of knowledge and the subdivisions developed in each by specialists in the subjects. Fundamentally the process is one of discovery rather than of invention. Existing classifications are the product of trial and error, of research and experiment. Many of the disciplines, like philosophy and law, are old; some, like sociology and aeronautics, are new. But old or new, the subject matter in each field has been divided and classified. These classifications provide an organization of material for continuing study and research; they also serve as the basis of exposition for those who write about or teach the subjects. One discipline differs from another discipline in its principles of division and classification and in the nature and fixity of its divisions. Some are relatively constant while others are in a state of flux, reflecting the "studies, " their age and maturity, and the degree of systemization they have achieved. It is these conceptual systems, or subsystems, with which library classifiers, and perhaps all classifiers, build, for no system is ever created de novo. Each system maker builds upon the work of preceding classifiers; each finds that much of the classification has already been done cumulatively throughout the years and the centuries.

It is true that a unanimity of opinion concerning the divisions and their order does not always exist, especially in the newer branches of learning. It is also true that the objects of knowledge and the specialties which deal with them frequently do not coincide. There are overlapping and twilight zones, and fission and fusion of subjects. Thus the divisions of knowledge are not discrete, unrelated segments; they are parts of an organic whole: man's description and interpretation of his universe and himself. As one scholar observed:

> It has become impossible to catalogue a scientific library without innumerable cross-references and reduplications, and it is more and more plain that science must be regarded as a single organized body, no part of which is complete in itself.
> So it comes about that the student of geology soon finds himself trespassing on the grounds of the astronomer (in cosmology), the chemist (in mineralogy), the physicist (in geophysics), and the biologist (in palaeontology). The biologist wanders into the fields of chemistry (in biochemistry) and physics (in cytology and neurology), and the astronomer into that of physics (in astrophysics). The psychologist sometimes considers himself a biologist, the physicist a mathematician, and the archaeologist an anthropologist. Thus the final paradox is that the more you specialize in a scientific subject the less you specialize in science. [15]

Add to the sciences the humanities and the technologies, and the problem of the organization of knowledge becomes far more complex. More twilight zones, overlapping, and cross division appear. All these the classifier must solve on the basis of theory or the practical needs of a library or libraries.

He may select one place and refer from alternate places; he may also make alternative provisions so that each library may select the classes which best suit its needs. Special library classifications organize specialties or areas or fields of knowledge. They differ from general systems in organization, which is oriented from their special point of view, and also, frequently, in specificity. In actual classing, the library's interests, even if of secondary importance, determine the class.

Librarians have long made a distinction between knowledge and literature — between books read for information and those read for pleasure. The classes devoted to knowledge are known as subject classes while those assigned to Polite Letters, Belles Lettres, and Literature are called form classes, which are generally regarded as additions to a classification of knowledge. Form (poetry, oratory, drama, etc.) rather than subject was presumed to provide the basis of classification. Some librarians, particularly earlier ones like Brunet, did classify literature on the basis of pure form, e. g. , Orateurs orientaux, Poètes anglais et écossais; but most systems, even the Decimal Classification, at least subordinated form to the language of the literature and the period in which works were written. Form as a primary principle of classification would lead to the very antithesis of order — chaos. The term has been much overworked: Sophocles is a subject, and so is his Oedipus Rex. Curiously, the distinction between form and subject has rarely, if ever, been carried over to the other disciplines which depend upon the aesthetic avenues of apprehension, sight and hearing. In music and the fine arts form is fully as important as it is in literature: Beethoven's Eroica and Da Vinci's Mona Lisa certainly have less "information value" than, for instance, Chaucer's Canterbury Tales. But in all these classes there is an inevitable overlapping of "form" and subject; poetry and drama become subjects when studied as forms of literature rather than as expressions in the form of poetry or drama. A history of Elizabethan drama has the dramatic form as subject, while Marlowe's Tamburlaine the Great is a work in dramatic form which in its turn becomes a subject in Emil Hubener's Der Einfluss von Marlowe's Tamburlaine auf die zeitgenossischen und folgenden Dramatiker.

The problem of the order of the sciences has preoccupied man's mind from their very beginning. The solutions to the problem have been as many and varied as the philosophers and scientists who created them, as we shall see in the chapters that follow. The liberal arts, the philosophies – physical, metaphysical, and moral – the "artes illiberales or mechanici, " and the disciplines, sciences, arts, and technologies which have derived from them have been classified on the basis of many theories – of genesis, filiation, and dependence. The known and the knower, the universe and man, have served as principles of order. The characterization of authors by Callimachus in the library at Alexandria in the third century B. C. as poets, orators, etc. , and by librarians of the Middle Ages as theologici, philosophici, etc. , provided a grouping and ordering for the books of those periods. The mental faculties, Memory, Imagination, Reason; the university faculties, Theology, Jurisprudence, Medicine, and the Liberal Arts; matter, mind and matter, mind; evolution in its various interpretations; the scientific and educational consensus – all these and more have determined the order of man's studies. And, if a past that reaches back six millennia provides any clue to the future, it seems improbable that any one order will ever be universally accepted.

Classifications have often been compared to maps, especially since Francis Bacon made his "small globe of the intellectual world" in 1605. The analogy is apt, for as maps represent the divisions of the surfaces of the earth, classifications represent the divisions of knowledge. They differ, however, in their modes of representation: the physical oceans, land masses, and countries can be delineated graphically, but knowledge, being abstract, can be expressed only in terms – the names of its divisions and subdivisions. The written or printed statement of these terms is known as a classification schedule. Both maps and schedules show the whole and its parts, the parts in relation to the whole – microcosms of macrocosms. The orientation value of classification in showing students the relations of individual studies to the whole of knowledge was emphasized by many earlier classifiers. It is obvious that orientation is far more needed today when men are divided vertically by specialty and not, as formerly, horizontally by class.

It is impossible to describe, even briefly, within this chapter the processes and logical considerations involved in developing a system of classification. The way leads from an outline of the main classes in the order determined upon, through synopses of subclasses and divisions, to detailed schedules (or tables), auxiliary schedules (or tables), and finally to notation and index. Theory and practice, coordination and subordination, "gradation in specialty, " cross division and its alternatives – these present some of the problems which must be solved. Competent discussions of the process will be found in Henry E. Bliss's works, especially The Organization of Knowledge in Libraries and the Subject-Approach to Books, [16] and in W. C. Berwick Sayers' A Manual of Classification for Librarians and Bibliographers. [17]

The terms (class names, captions) used in schedules should conform as closely as possible to current usage in the various disciplines. Popular, technical, and non-English words all have their places in classification schedules. It should be noted that since classification is less confined by words than are subject headings there is greater latitude in the selection of terms. In subject heading work it is necessary to select a single term (not always a simple task) and to make see references from synonyms, even partial synonyms, and varying structural forms to the term selected. Classification imposes no such limitations: it is possible to use synonyms, partial synonyms, popular, technical, and foreign terms as captions or definitions whenever advisable. Semantic change, which constitutes an annoying and expensive problem in subject headings, where tracing is alphabetical, is a minor problem in classification, since the tracing is based on notation. There are no cards to change; only the terms in the schedules and indexes and on guide cards.

Definition in some form is frequently necessary to insure consistent interpretation of terms in the construction and application of classification. In many instances the context defines the terms: realism in literature, realism in philosophy; marketing in economics, marketing in home economics. In other cases more explicit definitions or notes are needed.

During the process of assembling the divisions of knowledge, systemizing, and recording them in schedules, the classification must at all stages be applied to books. It is in books that the divisions of knowledge are recorded; it is through books that new divisions are made known. Moreover, the idiosyncracies of books, or rather of authors and publishers, frequently make it necessary to provide for subjects in relationships and combinations which philosophers could never have foreseen. The question might well be raised at this point: since both philosophers and librarians construct classifications, how do their systems differ (if indeed they do)? Unfortunately, the differences between the two have been highly exaggerated by both philosophers and librarians. Logicians like Jevons[18] deny that books can be classified, while historians of classification, among them Shields[19] and Flint,[20] casually dismiss the systems of librarians as mere pigeonholes of bookish people. The few librarians who have delved into history usually postulated a fundamental difference between the two. They divided systems into those which had or did not have notation and those with or without philosophical bases, thus separating the "theoretical" from the "practical." The result of these arbitrary divisions by philosophers and librarians is that the history of classification remains untold. But the gulf between the two kinds of system makers was never so wide as the historians describe. And no philosopher or scientist or group of them has even approximated the classifications developed by modern librarians — with the assistance, however, of philosophers, scientists, and other specialists. The philosophers were generally content to organize the main divisions of knowledge, forgetting or overlooking their many subdivisions, their twilight zones, and cross divisions.

The application of classification in libraries is concerned, not with the mere philosophical schematization of knowledge, but with the practical arrangement of books and entries on the basis of the subjects they contain or represent. Since library classification deals with physical things as well as abstract knowledge, it is necessary to add certain devices to a knowledge classification to adapt it to library use.

Historically the first, and still one of the most important, is the addition of a class for books which are polygraphical or too broad in scope to be included in the subject classes proper. Known variously as General, Generalia, Miscellany, or Polygraphy, the class which in the past frequently followed the subject divisions, like Jefferson's "Chapter 44 Authors who have written on various branches, Polygraphical, " now ordinarily precedes them. The comprehension of the class, which varies from system to system, usually includes general periodicals, encyclopedias, society transactions, collections, indexes, and similar material. Some systems also include in the class subjects of a pervasive character like education, library science, logic, and "general" science or knowledge.

However diverse in content, books follow common modes of organization. It is possible, therefore, to provide, either in the schedules or in tables, general patterns of subarrangement. Similar in the physical organization of their contents are periodicals, encyclopedias, society transactions, etc., which in relation to the various subdivisions of a class are polygraphical, resembling the material of the generalia class. Other books are alike in internal form or mode of treating subjects: history, theory, general works, relations, etc. The provisions made for these recurring subdivisions vary greatly. Early systems were almost completely enumerative, while the later ones, beginning in 1906 with James Duff Brown's "Categorical Tables, "[21] tended toward less enumeration and more construction of schedules from common subdivisions. Ranganathan[22] compares enumerative classifications to tourist conversation books, which are composed of ready-made phrases and

sentences. Constructive systems, of which his Colon Classification is the
most extreme example, are, on the contrary, like dictionaries from which the
classifier must construct (the "meccano feature") classes as he needs them.

The parts of the classification thus far briefly described provide for
books on all the divisions and subdivisions of knowledge, for books too general to be included in them, and for those possessing common patterns of
organization, external and internal. Other necessary additions provide, either in the schedules themselves or in supplementary tables, for geographical,
historical, and linguistic subdivisions. Since both the objects of knowledge
and the studies into which it is organized can be described in time and space,
it is important to provide temporal and spatial subdivisions for them. Various devices are used to separate older from more recent works, the history
of subjects, and subjects treated locally.

Books of a theoretical or descriptive character (general works) mir-
ror in time the status of the "subject" they treat. It is convenient, therefore,
to divide them by periods corresponding as closely as possible to stages in
the development of the individual specialties. In addition to their convenience
to readers, the use of such divisions makes it a simple matter to weed out
obsolete material. In some systems the treatment is usually ad hoc adapted
to the subject, e. g. , Pre-and Post- Linnaean in Natural History, or a somewhat arbitrary division into works before and after 1800. Other systems
make no provisions for this kind of subdivision.

The problem of the classification of the history of individual subjects
has been solved in several ways. It was formerly the practice of librarians
to treat their history classes as form classes, including in them the histories of nearly all subjects. Natural history was frequently excepted, although
after Bacon's time even this subject was made a subdivision of history. Later,
librarians began the policy of collocating the history of a subject with the
subject – a practice followed by contemporary systems. These classifications provide historical subdivisions either under the subjects in the full

schedules or in auxiliary tables applicable to all or parts of the various classes.

Both the objects of knowledge and their studies are treated geographically and chronologically. Conventional practice calls for the subordination of place to topic: the rule is an excellent one — if followed with discretion as all rules of practice should be. Rigid adherence to the principle, however, for instance in the social sciences, provides for the needs of the "comparative" reader to the detriment of those interested in the institutions of individual countries. Cutter solved this problem neatly by reversibility, e. g., W36 Art - Italy or 36W Italy - Art. Geographic subdivisions may be provided under the subjects in the schedules, in auxiliary tables, or by applying the subdivisions used in geography and history.

Another adjustment to practical needs in library classification is the addition of linguistic subdivisions to the schedules. While the subdivision of books on the basis of language is not new, it is becoming more important as libraries receive, catalog, and service books in languages early librarians knew only by name or which they classed as specimen texts of the language. The division is a purely practical one which enables readers to select or reject material on the basis of their linguistic competence.

When books or their parts, and the entries representing them, are classified, it is necessary to correlate them with the classification applied. This is effected by notation — the addition of symbols to the schedules. Notation is a system of graphic symbols which denote and stand for the classes, their divisions, and subdivisions, and fix the order of their arrangement. These symbols serve as a means of reference to the classes, providing links between the terms (class names) systematically ordered in the schedules and alphabetically arranged in the index. They also determine the arrangement of books on the shelves and their entries in the shelflist and classed catalogs. Notation is wholly extrinsic to the classification; it is a device which is added after the schedules have been developed. It bears the same relation to the theory and structure of classification that street names and numbers do to city plans. In contemporary library classification, however, the symbols indicate the classes and their position in the classification rather than the physical location of books. The symbols provide the addresses of the various classes of knowledge and make catalogs into directories of man's knowledge.

Traditionally, notations have been divided on the basis of their homogeneity into pure and mixed: those composed of one kind of symbol and those composed of more than one. The Decimal Classification with its Arabic numerals illustrates the first, and the Library of Congress Classification, which combines letters with numbers, the second. Whatever the kind of notation employed, the symbols used should possess certain qualities of which the following are the most important:

1. <u>Simplicity</u>. The symbols should be restricted to those commonly known, chiefly to letters and figures. Arbitrary signs like + , □ , △ , and others used by Lloyd Smith[23] should be avoided.

2. <u>Orderliness</u>. Since notation serves to fix the systematic order of the classes, the system of symbols should follow a known or readily learned sequence. The letters A, B, C, etc., and the numbers 1, 2, 3 follow a well-defined order; signs like those mentioned above do not.

3. <u>Brevity</u>. While the classification should not be circumscribed by the notation into the oft-quoted Procrustean bed, the symbols should be as brief as possible for economy in reading, memorizing, and marking them on books and cards. Simplicity and orderliness also contribute to this economy of reading, learning, and writing.

4. <u>Mnemonics</u>. Aids to the memory in acquiring and retaining the meanings of the symbols are few. The most obvious, and least effective, is the use of the initial letters of subjects, e. g. C Chemistry, F Fine Arts, N Natural Sciences, which was tried by several system makers. Whatever their mnemonic value, symbols of this kind can produce only structural chaos; names disperse, they do not collocate their underlying referents. The principal

aid to memory is the use of constant symbols for common, or recurring, sub-divisions, either in the system as a whole or in its parts.

5. <u>Expansibility</u>. Library classifications reflect the changing world of knowledge, past, present, and future — the old and the new. The notation should therefore be flexible enough to provide for the logical expansion of the system in all of its parts.

To supplement the notation thus far described, symbols are needed to provide for the arrangement of the individual books within classes — in Bliss's apt expression, "internal notation." Although several different ar-rangements have been used, among them chronology, accession number, and size, the most widely used is the alphabetical by author. Charles A. Cutter, in connection with his Expansive Classification, devised a method of book marks, or numbers, which makes the shelving and locating of books a simple matter. The combination of the class and book number (internal notation) form the call number which individuates each book in a library. Added to all entries describing the book and marked on its spine or cover, the call number thus links the book with the records describing it and assures the easy location of the book and return to its place.

To provide an alphabetical approach to a classification it is necessary to add an index, which is a list in alphabetical order of the terms used in the schedules and their notation. The symbols of the notation refer to the position the terms occupy in the systematic order of the schedules. A good index includes not only the terms actually used but synonyms or varying forms of terms (old as well as new, if necessary), species of genera, and the enumeration of other parts of wholes too numerous to be included in the schedules. There are two kinds of indexes: the specific, which indicates only one place, and the relative, which lists under the various topics their subdivisions, aspects, and relations. The following excerpts illustrate the two types of index:

Brown's Subject Classification		Bliss's Bibliographic Classification	
Absorption (Biol.)	E 033	Absorption by gases,	BGK
-- Light	C 107	-- -- liquids,	BGM
Abstinence (Food)	H 107	-- -- solids,	BGQ
-- (Drink)	G 787	-- of gases by liquids,	BGM
Abstracting	M 162	-- -- liquids by solids,	BGQ
Abstraction	J 160	-- -- radiation,	BFD
Abubeker, Caliph	Q 266	-- spectra,	BFN
Abyssinia	O 510	Technology of, Chemical,	CTP
-- Church	K 448	Abstraction (Ideation),	IFK
Acacias	E 611	Abstraction (Logic),	ALI

In the late nineteenth century, when knowledge was far simpler than it is to-day, the value of an index was somewhat exaggerated. This led to what Bliss has called "the subject-index illusion": that an index can make a classification, however imperfect, into an efficient instrument. It should be obvious that an alphabetical index leads to subjects but does not organize them any more than the dispersive headings in our dictionary catalogs do. In practical book classing the index should be used with great caution.

The shelflist, which is a record of books as they stand on the shelves in the order of the classification used, constitutes, in Margaret Mann's words, "a key" to call numbers. [24] It guarantees the uniqueness of each call number so that the right call number brings the right book. This classed record also guides the classifier in his daily work and, especially if equipped with added entries (cross references) for subjects or aspects of subject which the main entry does not cover and for individual works collectively classified, serves the purposes of a classed catalog in a reasonably satisfactory way. The shelflist not only complements the dispersive dictionary catalog but can be correlated to supplement it when subject headings and classification are in approximate correspondence. In history, for instance, the subject heading structure closely parallels that of classification, e. g. , Venezuela - History - 1810-1830, for which period L. C. Classification provides the number F2324. The following examples used by Haykin [25] illustrate the process in other subject fields.

Geology - Uruguay.

> For works devoted exclusively to this subject as a whole, see, in addition to those cited under this heading, the following number in the shelflist:

QE249

Skating.

> For works on this subject, see, in addition to those cited under this heading, the following number in the shelflist:

GV849

The shelflist also makes it possible to prepare "class lists" and bibliographies, to survey a library's resources and its lacunae in the various areas of knowledge. And finally, the shelflist constitutes the inventory record of a library's collections.

To summarize library classification, Bliss's description, although succinct, is excellent if too much importance is not attached to his personal interpretation of "the educational and scientific consensus. "

> A good classification is a structural survey of the fields of knowledge, thought, and interest; it is a synthetic organization of the special subjects of study and their analytical details. It is constructed on a basis of general classes in an order consistent with the scientific and educational systems. On this basis it proceeds by coherent division and gradation of subjects and by subordination of specific and again analytically more specific subjects, collocated, wherever feasible, by intrinsic relations or interests. Where requisite, interrelated subjects are systematically referred to chosen and to alternative allocations. And to all this complex system of subjects the index is the alphabetic reference by means of the notation. Thus good classification as a structural organization serves the functional organization of knowledge. [26]

Its components are

1. The classification schedules, written or printed statements, of the

    system, comprising

    a. An outline of the system as a whole

    b. Synopses, or outlines, of the main classes and divisions

    c. The main schedules (or tables)

    d. Auxiliary tables (or schedules) of recurring form, geographic,

    historical, linguistic, and subject subdivisions

e. A notation

f. An index

2. Classified books on the shelves

3. The shelflist, or record of the books as they stand on the shelves, and

4. A classed catalog, if classification is to be fully exploited.

There are many canons or criteria of classifications, theoretical and practical, against which systems may be evaluated. The most important are the following: A good general classification:

1. Provides in specific detail for all knowledge, past and present, in a system of logically integrated coordinate and subordinate classes and divisions;

2. Is adaptable to special viewpoints and uses by means of alternative arrangements;

3. Is logically receptive (hospitable) to the knowledge of the future;

4. Has an orderly notation of simple symbols which possesses the flexibility to receive new knowledge; and

5. Has an alphabetical key to its contents in a detailed index.

The systems described in the following pages exemplify in varying theories, structures, and details the general principles and methods of library classification described in this chapter. The increasing complexity of the systems mirrors both greater publishing activity and the expansion of man's knowledge and activities.

THE "OLD" L. C. CLASSIFICATION

CHAPTER II

Jefferson As Classifier

When Colonel Peter Jefferson died in 1757 he left forty-two books —
in addition to other property, real and personal — to his oldest son Thomas,
then fourteen. After the loss of these books and most of the others he had
added to them, in the fire which destroyed Shadwell on February 1, 1770,
Thomas Jefferson began the development of a library which numbered 2,640
volumes by the spring of 1783 and 6,487 when it became the property of Congress in 1815.

Jefferson's love of books has been described on many pages, but not
all the words written express this love better than the simple "I cannot live
without books" which he wrote to John Adams after parting with his library
in 1815. Jefferson thanked Adams for introducing George Ticknor and Francis Gray, of Boston, who were to assist him in "reprocuring some part of
the literary treasures which I have ceded to Congress to replace the devas-
tations of British Vandalism at Washington. " He added, ". . . but fewer will
suffice, where amusement, and not use, is the only future object. "[1] When
Jefferson died in 1826 his last library contained nearly a thousand volumes.

Jefferson's interest in books was not purely personal. He advised his
friends and aided at least two institutions, the young Library of Congress and
the University of Virginia, in forming libraries; he was also one of the most
prominent early American classifiers. To a mind like Jefferson's, encylo-
pedic in its interests, practical and methodical in all things, the problem of
order, of classification, must have come early. Jefferson made two separate
ventures in the organization of knowledge, the first for the selection and arrangement of his books, the second in connection with his plans for the reorganization of the College of William and Mary [2] and the organization of the
University of Virginia. [3] They reveal a strange dualism in Jefferson, the

classifier, which resulted in the creation of classifications so different that
they might well have been the products of different minds. It is difficult to
reconcile the Jefferson of the Rockfish Report of 1818, or even of the earlier
Bill of 1779 for the reorganization of William and Mary, with Jefferson, the
librarian.

As a book collector, Jefferson, early in life, adopted Bacon's classification with some of d'Alembert's modifications, made a few changes of his
own, and was content with the system ever after. Even as late as 1824 he
wrote that if he were to recompose this classification he would add Ideology
_ nothing more. [4] To Jefferson, as to many others, Bacon's classification, if
not particularly accurate, "was a comprehensive and attractive, sketch of the
intellectual world, indicating in a striking way, difficult to forget, not only
what provinces had been acquired by the human mind, but where, and in what
manner, new conquests were still to be made. "[5]

Jefferson, the philosopher and university founder, however, was not satisfied with a classification based upon the faculties of the mind. Keenly aware
of the organization of the knowledge of his time and of the way that knowledge
should be taught, this Jefferson adapted his classification to the educational
needs of the period. Although circumscribed in his efforts by the number of
possible professorships, he was unhampered by the super-categories of history, philosophy, and poetry into which Bacon and d'Alembert had forced all
knowledge. As a consequence, Jefferson's classifying activities in the educational field are fresher and more original than are his essays in the classification of books.

In 1779 Jefferson proposed that the College of William and Mary be organized on the basis of eight professorships:

> ... to wit, one of moral philosophy, the laws of nature and of
> nations, and of the fine arts; one of law and police; one of history,
> civil and ecclesiastical; one of mathematics; one of anatomy and
> medicine; one of natural philosophy and natural history; one of the
> ancient languages, oriental and northern; and one of modern lan-
> guages.

Each "professorship" was subdivided as follows:[6]

I.
- Ethics,
  - Moral Philosophy.
  - Law of Nature.
  - Law of Nations.
- Fine Arts,
  - Sculpture.
  - Painting.
  - Gardening.
  - Music.
  - Architecture.
  - Poetry.
  - Oratory.
  - Criticism.

II. Law.
- Municipal.
  - Common Law.
  - Equity.
  - Law Merchant.
  - Law Maritime.
  - Law Ecclesiastical.
- Oeconomical.
  - Politics.
  - Commerce.

III. History.
- Civil.
- Ecclesiastical.

IV. Mathematics
- Pure.
  - Arithmetic.
  - Geometry.
- Mixed.
  - Mechanics.
  - Optics.
  - Acoustics.
  - Astronomy.

V.
- Anatomy.
- Medicine.

VI.
- Natural Philosophy.
  - Chymistry.
  - Statics.
  - Hydrostatics.
  - Pneumatics.
  - Agriculture.
- Natural History.
  - Animals – Zoology.
  - Vegetables – Botany.
  - Minerals – Mineralogy.

VII. Ancient Languages
- Oriental.
  - Hebrew.
  - Chaldee.
  - Syriac.
- Northern.
  - Moeso Gothic.
  - Anglo Saxon.
  - Old Icelandic.

VIII. Modern Languages.
- French.
- Italian.
- German.

Missionary for Indian History, &c.

With few variations Jefferson was consistent in this scheme of classification. From the bill of 1779 his theory can be traced through his letters to Dr. Joseph Priestley in 1800, his letter to Peter Carr of September 7, 1814, the 1817 Bill for Establishing a System of Public Education, [7] and the Rockfish Report.

The first Jefferson, whose problem was not university organization but the selection and arrangement of his library, followed a different pattern of organization. It is with this Jefferson and his classification that we are primarily concerned, for the arrangement of his books in forty-four chapters determined the classification of the Library of Congress for nearly a century.

In Jefferson's time there were two basic kinds of catalogs, the alphabetical, in which the entries were arranged by author or title, and the classified, in which the arrangement was according to the subject content of the books. It is not surprising that Jefferson should have disdained the alphabetical and selected the classified. He described his theory of cataloging to George Watterston, who was Librarian of Congress when Jefferson's library became the property of the Congress:

> two methods offer themselves, the one Alphabetical, the other according to the subject of the book. the former is very unsatisfactory, because of the medley it presents to the mind, the difficulty sometimes of recollecting an author's name, and the greater difficulty, where the name is not given of selecting the word in the title which shall determine it's Alphabetical place. the arrangement according to subject is far preferable, altho' sometimes presenting difficulty also. for it is often doubtful to what particular subject a book should be ascribed. this is remarkably the case with books of travels, which often blend together the geography, natural history, civil history, agriculture, manufactures, commerce, arts, occupations, manners etc. of a country, so as to render it difficult to say to which they chiefly relate. others again, are polygraphical in their nature, as Encyclopedias, Magazines etc. yet on the whole I have preferred arrangement according to subject; because of the peculiar satisfaction, when we wish to consider a particular one, of seeing at a glance the books which have been written on it, and selecting those from which we expect most readily the information we seek. [8]

Jefferson's first essay in book classification is found in the selection of books he made for Robert Skipwith in 1771. [9] He divided knowledge into

      Fine Arts
      Criticism on the Fine Arts
      Politicks, Trade
      Religion
      Law
      History, Antient
      History, Modern
      Natural Philosophy
         Natural History, etc.
      Miscellaneous

The order of the divisions is fortuitous but they reveal the source and the major divisions of Jefferson's later book classifications. The trifurcate division of man's knowledge into History, Philosophy, and Poesy is the work of Francis Bacon, whom Jefferson numbered along with Newton and Locke in his "trinity of the three greatest men the world had ever produced."[10] It is not surprising, therefore, that he should have felt attracted to Bacon's divisions of knowledge. Many years later, however, Jefferson rejected Bacon's "origination of this division" and attributed it to the Abbé de Charron:

> it has been proposed by Charron, more than 20 years before in his book de la Sagesse. B. 1. c. 14. and an imperfect ascription of the sciences to these respective faculties was there attempted. this excellent moral work was published in 1600.[11] Ld. Bacon is said not to have entered on his great works until his retirement from public office in 1621.[12]

Although Bacon had used the arrangement in his <u>Advancement of Learning</u>, first published in 1605, his divisions had long been a part of man's intellectual equipment. The story of Jefferson's classification begins with Bacon but is continued in the work of d'Alembert, whose order it followed rather than that of Bacon. It is therefore necessary to turn from seventeenth-century England to eighteenth-century France for the origin of Jefferson's main divisions.

On November 17, 1717, d'Alembert, an infant only a few hours old, "débile et presque mourant," was found on the steps of the church of Saint-Jean-Lerond in Paris. Baptized at the request of a "commissaire de police" he became Jean Lerond, and only later d'Alembert. The illegitimate son of the Chevalier Destouches, general of artillery, and Mme. de Tencin, he was raised by the wife of a glazier named Rousseau. When the Chevalier Destouches died in 1726 he left his son an annuity of 1,200 francs. After graduating from the Collège des Quatre-Nations, to which the influence of his father's family had gained him entrance, d'Alembert studied law, became an avocat, then turned to medicine. He liked neither of these professions, for his real interests were in mathematics and philosophy. In 1740 he was admitted to the Académie des Sciences and the following year published his Traité de Dynamique. Five years later his Réflexions sur la Cause Générale des Vents won a prize from the Berlin Academy. This brought d'Alembert to the attention of Frederick II of Prussia, who offered him the presidency of the Academy in 1752. D'Alembert refused this honor as he did, later, the requests of Catherine of Russia that he become tutor to her son. He was made a member of the Académie Francaise in 1754 and later became its perpetual secretary, succeeding Voltaire as leader of the philosophical party. D'Alembert died in Paris on October 29, 1783.

In 1750 d'Alembert became associated with Dénis Diderot in the compilation of the Encyclopédie, ou Dictionnaire Raisonné des Sciences, des Arts et des Métiers, and the following year he published the Discours Préliminaire de l'Encyclopédie in which he set forth the plans of the compilers. The Discours contained two essential parts: the genealogy and classification of knowledge, and a history of the arts and sciences from the Renaissance to 1750. Only the first part is of concern to the present study.

D'Alembert acknowledged his debt to "l'immortel chancelier d'Angleterre, Francois Bacon" for providing the basis of the classification he developed. He added, however, that the sciences had made great progress since Bacon's time and, as a result, different roads must be followed. D'Alembert chose to follow the metaphysical order of the operations of the mind rather than the historical order of Bacon. His main divisions therefore departed from the order Bacon had adopted and provided the sequence History, Philosophy, Fine Arts, or

l'Histoire, qui se rapporte à la mémoire;
la Philosophie, qui est le fruit de la raison; et
les Beaux-Arts, que l'imagination fait naitre.

The general distribution of beings into spiritual and material beings furnishes the subdivisions of the three great branches of knowledge. At the head of
spiritual beings is God, who by reason of His nature, and of man's need to
know Him, stands first. Below Him are certain created spirits of whose existence Revelation has informed man. Man, composed of a soul and a body,
linked to both the spiritual and material, comes next, followed by the material
universe we know as Nature.

History which concerns God is composed of revelation or tradition, and
yields Sacred and Ecclesiastical History. The History of Man has two objects,
his deeds and his knowledge, and is consequently Civil or Literary. Natural
History has three subdivisions: the history of the normal development of ce-
lestial bodies, animals, vegetables, etc.; the history of "monstres," when nature departs from her usual course; and finally the history of the arts or the
uses which man makes of nature. These are the divisions of History which
collect the raw material of philosophy.

Philosophy, the product of man's reason, comes next, and at the beginning stands Ontology, or General Metaphysics, which comprises the principles
common to all sciences. The science of God, Theology, has two branches: Natural and Revealed Theology, depending upon the source of the knowledge —
man's unaided reason or Revelation. The science of Man deals with the soul
and its operations. The study of the nature of the soul, which derives in part
from Theology, is called Pneumatology, or Special Metaphysics. The operations of the soul are two fold: the discovery of truth and its communication
which is Logic, and the practice of virtue which is Ethics. Logic comprises
the arts of thinking, of retaining, and of communicating. Ethics includes individual ethics, economics, and politics. The science of nature, which deals with
matter, comprises two main divisions, Physics and Mathematics, the first concerned with the properties of material things, the second with quantity. As
certain properties are common to all bodies it is necessary to subdivide
Physics into General Physics, or Metaphysics of bodies in general, and Special

Physics, which is concerned with individuals. Quantity, the study of which is

the object of Mathematics, can be divided into Pure Mathematics, Mixed Math-

ematics (Mechanics, Statics, Dynamics, etc.), and Physico-mathematics.

Special Physics follows the divisions given in Natural History.

The branches born of the Imagination – the Fine Arts – are Painting,

Sculpture, Architecture, Poetry, Music, and their several subdivisions. These

might well be brought under the heading Painting, since the Fine Arts are

concerned with painting and differ only in the methods employed, or, even un-

der Poetry, using the term in its pristine sense of invention or creation.

D'Alembert originally planned to follow Bacon's fundamental division

of knowledge according to its source into Revealed Theology and Human

Knowledge but abandoned it "... parce qu'elle a paru plus ingénieuse que

solide." He said that in Philosophy "... nous ne devons nullement à Bacon,"

and added that variations in this branch were many and radical and only phi-

losophers, of whom there were few, could express judgment on the arrange-

ment.

It was from this tradition that Jefferson derived his classification, not

as a mere copyist but as an independent thinker. Fundamentally the goals of

all three men were practical: Bacon's, to survey knowledge – to ascertain

what had been done and what remained to be done; d'Alembert's, to provide

a framework for a systematic encyclopedia; and Jefferson's, to devise divi-

sions of knowledge to assist him in selecting books and in keeping them in

order. But, unlike Bacon and d'Alembert, Jefferson was little given to theo-

rizing on classification. His distrust of metaphysics and his practicality led

him to an instrumental theory of the process.

> Nature has, in truth, produced Units only thro' all her works.
> Classes, orders, genera, species, are not of her work. her crea-
> tion is of individuals. no two animals are exactly alike; no two
> plants, nor even two leaves or blades of grass; no two crystalli-
> sations. and, if we may venture, from what is within the cogni-
> sance of such organs as ours, to conclude on that beyond their
> powers, we must believe that no two particles of matter are of
> exact resemblance. this infinitude of Units, or individuals being
> far beyond the capacity of our memory, we are obliged, in aid of

that, to distribute them into masses, throwing into each of these all the individuals which have a certain degree of resemblance; to subdivide these again into smaller groupes, according to certain points of dissimilitude observable in them; and so on, until we have formed what we call a system of classes, orders, genera, and species. [13]

He would have heartily endorsed Shepherd's assertion that "Classifications impose a definiteness on nature which has no counterpart in the real world ..."[14] Jefferson would go even further and force the disciplines into divisions of his own choosing on the basis of their usefulness.

Metaphysics have been incorporated with Ethics, and little extention given to them. for, while some attention may be usefully bestowed on the operations of thought, prolonged investigations of a faculty unamenable to the test of our senses, is an expense of time too unprofitable to be worthy of indulgence. [15]

This is a far different theory from that of Bacon or d'Alembert, both of whom made provision for Metaphysics, or the principles and axioms which were the source of all knowledge. Jefferson's insistence upon the practical, the useful, is emphasized as he continues:

Geology, too, has been merged in Mineralogy, which may properly embrace what is useful in this science, that is to say, a knowledge of the general stratification, collocation and sequence of the different species of rocks and other mineral substances, while it takes no cognisance of theories for the self-generation of the universe, or the particular revolutions of our own globe by the agency of water, fire, or other agent, subordinate to the fiat of the Creator. [16]

Through the years Jefferson developed six book classifications, or perhaps it would be more exact to state that he developed one classification which he modified five times.

In cataloging and shelving his books Jefferson was, in his own words, a "collocationist." He voiced his concern over the physical arrangement of his books in a note to James Ogilvie.

the key [to the library at Monticello] is at present in the hands of mr. Dinsmore, at the place, who on sight of this letter will consider you as at all times authorised to have access to the library, & to take from it any books you please. I will only ask the favor of you to keep a piece of paper on one of the tables of the room, & to note on it the books you have occasion to take out, and to blot it out when returned. the object in this is that should I want a book at any time when at home, I may know where it is. the arrangement is as follows. 1. Antient history. 2. Modern do. 3. Physics. 4. Nat. hist. proper. 5. Technical arts. 6. Ethics. 7. Jurisprudence.

8. Mathematics. 9. Gardening, architecture, sculpture, painting, music. 9. Poetry. 10. Oratory. 11. Criticism. 12. Polygraphical. you will find this on a paper nailed up somewhere in the library. the arrangement begins behind the partition door leading out of the Book room into the Cabinet, & proceeds from left to right round the room; then entering the Cabinet it begins at the Eastern angle, & goes round that room. The presses not having been sufficient to contain the whole, the latter part of Polygraphics was put into the kind of closet at the first entrance of the book-room. as after using a book, you may be at a loss in returning it to it's exact place, & they cannot be found again when misplaced, it will be better to leave them on a table in the room. my familiarity with their places will enable me to replace them readily....[17]

The outlines of the systems of Bacon and d'Alembert given below are

not complete; they are abridgments of the schemes sufficiently detailed to

illustrate the origin of Jefferson's classification. Bacon's divisions[18] are

derived from Spedding's edition of his works, those of d'Alembert from the

Discours préliminaire.[19] Jefferson's classification is the one used in the

1815 Catalogue of the Library of the United States.

BACON

HUMAN KNOWLEDGE: "information derived from the sense"
  History
    Natural: deeds and works of nature
      Generations: normal developments
      Pretergenerations: abnormal developments, monsters, etc.
      Arts: mechanical and experimental history
    Civil: deeds and works of man
      Sacred or Ecclesiastical
      Civil proper
      Learning and the arts
      Appendices: words of men — Speeches, Letters, Apophthegms
  Poesy
    Narrative
    Dramatic
    Parabolical
  Philosophy
    Primary philosophy: fundamental principles and axioms
    Natural theology
    Natural philosophy
      Speculative: inquisition of causes
        Physic: efficient and material causes
        Metaphysic: formal and final causes
      Operative: production of effects
        Mechanic: Physic
        Magic: Metaphysic
    Mathematics
      Pure: Geometry and Arithmetic
      Mixed: Astronomy, Cosmography, Machinery, etc.

    Human philosophy
      Philosophy of Humanity (Individual man)
        Mind and Body
        Body
          Medicine: Health
          Cosmetic: Beauty
          Athletic: Strength
          Voluptuary: Arts
        Soul
          Psychology
          Logic
            Art of Inquiry or Invention
            Art of Examination or Judgment
            Art of Custody or Memory
            Art of Elocution or Tradition
          Ethics
      Civil philosophy (Man in society)
        Conversation: Comfort against solitude
        Negotiation: Assistance in business
        Government: Protection against injuries
          Economics
          Law
THEOLOGY: "information derived from revelation"
  History
  Poesy
  Philosophy

D'ALEMBERT

HISTORY
  Sacred
  Civil
    Civil proper
    Literary
  Natural
    Normal developments
    Abnormal developments: monsters, etc.
    Arts, crafts, manufactures
PHILOSOPHY
  General Metaphysics. Ontology
  God
    Natural theology
    Revealed theology
  Man
    Pneumatology. Soul (Psychology)
    Logic
      Art of Thinking: Logic proper
      Art of Retaining: Memory, writing, printing, etc.
      Art of Communicating: Grammar, rhetoric, etc.
    Morality
      Ethics
      Jurisprudence: Economics, Politics, Commerce, etc.
  Nature
    General physics: Metaphysics of bodies
    Mathematics
      Pure: Arithmetic and Geometry
      Mixed: Mechanics, Astronomy, Optics, etc.

Physico-Mathematics
General physics
Special physics
    Zoology: Anatomy, Physiology, Medicine, etc.
    Physical astronomy
    Meteorology
    Cosmology: Geology, Hydrology, etc.
    Botany: Agriculture, Gardening
    Mineralogy
    Chemistry
FINE ARTS
  Poetry
  Music
  Painting
  Sculpture
  Architecture (Civil)
  Engraving

JEFFERSON (1815)

Books may be classed according to the faculties of the mind employed
on them: these are –

| I. MEMORY | II. REASON | III. IMAGINATION |

Which are applied respectively to –

| I. HISTORY | II. PHILOSOPHY | III. FINE ARTS |

	Chapter
I. HISTORY	
Civil	
Civil Proper	
Antient	1
Modern	
Foreign	2
British	3
American	4
Ecclesiastical	5
Natural	
Physics	
Natural Philosophy	6
Agriculture	7
Chemistry	8
Surgery	9
Medicine	10
Natural History Proper	
Anatomy	11
Zoology	12
Botany	13
Mineralogy	14
Occupations of Man. Technical Arts	15
II. PHILOSOPHY	
Moral	
Ethics	
Moral Philosophy	16
Law of Nature and Nations	
Jurisprudence	
Religious. Religion	17

It is the custom today to criticize historic classifications from the

point of view of the theory and knowledge of the twentieth century. Such cri-

ticism is largely pedantic and worthless — classifications should be evaluated in relation to the intellectual climate in which they originate. While contemporary criticisms of the various schemes are rare, we are fortunate in having one of Jefferson's system, the work of Judge Woodward, a friend of Jefferson and a fellow classifier. Woodward's penetrating analysis of classification and his criticism of Jefferson's system deserve a wider audience than the rarity of his work[20] makes possible.

> Mr. Jefferson had long been sensible that his literary collections ought, at some day, to become the property of the nation. He had made arrangements for that event, when his earthly concerns should be closed, but the destruction of the national library induced him to make the intervening sacrifice; and the congress of the United States have availed themselves of the valuable acquisition. His classification of the works accompanies them; and either already has been, or, no doubt, soon will be, published, under the authority of congress. Thus this distribution of human knowledge may, for the present, be considered, in some degree, as a national one.

> Books, it is observed by Mr. Jefferson, may be classed according to the faculties of the mind employed on them. These are, first, the memory, secondly, the reason, and thirdly, the imagination; which are applied, respectively, first, to history, secondly, to philosophy, and thirdly, to the fine arts.

> History is divided into civil and natural. Civil history is either civil proper, or ecclesiastical. Civil history proper is ancient or modern. Ancient history forms the first department which is called a chapter, and numbered; the total of the specific departments or chapters amounting to forty-four. Modern history comprizes the three chapters of foreign, British, and American. Ecclesiastical history forms a single and entire chapter.

> Natural history has three ramifications; physics, natural history proper, and the occupations of man. Physics comprize five chapters; natural philosophy, agriculture, chemistry, surgery, and medicine. Natural history proper relates either, to animals, to vegetables, or to minerals; affording the four chapters of, anatomy, zoölogy, botany, and mineralogy. The occupations of man form the fifteenth and last chapter of history, under the title of technical arts.

> The second province, philosophy, is divided into moral and mathematical. Moral philosophy is separated into, ethics, and jurisprudence. Ethics comprize two chapters; those of, moral philosophy, and the law of nature and nations. Jurisprudence is either, religious, municipal, or œconomical. Religious jurisprudence occupies a single and entire chapter, under the title of religion. Municipal jurisprudence is divided into domestic and foreign. Domestic municipal jurisprudence comprizes five chapters; equity, common law, law merchant, law maritime, law ecclesiastical. Foreign municipal jurisprudence forms a single chapter, under the title of foreign law. Œconomical jurisprudence comprizes the two chapters of, politics, and commerce; and closes the branch of moral philosophy.

> Mathematical philosophy is divided into two parts; pure

mathematical philosophy, and physico-mathematical philosophy.
Arithmetic, and geömetry, compose the two chapters of the first.
The several subjects of, mechanics, statics, dynamics, pneumatics,
phonics, and optics, constitute a single chapter. Astronomy follows
as another, succeeded by geögraphy; and closing the branch of mathematical philosophy.

The fine arts, constituting the third and last province, amount
to eight. These are; architecture, gardening, painting, sculpture,
music, poetry, oratory, and criticism. Architecture forms a chapter; gardening, painting, and sculpture a second; and music a third.
Poetry has ten divisions. Epic and romance are the first two, and
occupy each a chapter. Pastorals, odes, elegies, the three which
next succeed, are comprized in one chapter. Didactic poetry, tragedy, comedy, follow; and occupy each a chapter. The two last, dialogue and epistles, are contained in one chapter; and close the
branch of poetry. Oratory comprizes, logic, rhetoric, and orations;
which form a single chapter. Criticism has three parts, theory,
bibliography, and languages, each constituting one chapter; and closing the province of the fine arts. The last and forty-fourth specific
department, or chapter, is extraneous of the provinces; consisting
of authors who have written on various branches, under the title of
polygraphical. The whole is represented in a neat and concinnous
table.

This table was twice, by permission, copied; at Washington,
November the thirtieth 1801, and at Monticello, May the nineteenth
1814. It contains some variations. In the first, politics and commerce are two distinct heads or chapters. In the second, they are
but one. In the first, in the place of natural philosophy, stands cosmology. In the first, the fine arts are arranged, gardening, architecture, sculpture, painting; in the second, architecture, gardening,
painting, sculpture. In the first, gardening, painting, sculpture, are
distinct heads or chapters. In the second, those three form one.
In the first, music is divided into theoretical and practical, and the
latter into vocal and instrumental, making three chapters. In the
second, music, as a general term, is one chapter. In the first, poetry is divided into narrative, dramatic, and didactic. The first includes epic, romance; the second tragedy, comedy, pastorals, odes,
elegies, dialogue; the third satire, epigram, epistles. The whole
number of specific departments or chapters, in the first, is forty-
six. There is, in the first, a note, annexed to moral philosophy;
remarking that in classing a small library one may throw under
this head books which attempt what may be called the natural history of the mind, or an analysis of its operations; and that the term
or division of metaphysics is rejected, as meaning nothing, or something beyond our reach, or what should be called by some other
name.

As this system is founded on that of D'Alembert, which is itself derived from Lord Bacon, it will be only necessary to advert
to its deviations from the one, or the other, of those; or from both.
It is distinguished from both in this particular. It brings out the
subjects of human knowledge into forty-four or forty-six distinct
heads, which may almost be termed sciences, counted and numbered,
and ingeniously concatenated, with an English name for every subject, and that the most usual, and perfectly intelligible; though the
boundaries of mechanics, statics, and dynamics, would appear ob-
scure. There is but a single attempt at nomenclature, and that is

not a happy one. The mechanic arts are distinguished from the fine
arts, by the name of, technical arts. Whoever will undertake to contrast the table of Mr. Jefferson against the emanation of the sciences, of Lord Bacon; or the systéme figuré des connoissances hu-
maines, of D'Alembert; will find a perfect chaos in the two latter,
and a clear and lucid exhibition in the classification of Mr. Jefferson. Mr. Jefferson arranges civil history before natural; in which
he deviates from Lord Bacon, and corresponds with D'Alembert;
but arranges civil history before ecclesiastical; in which he differs
from D'Alembert, and corresponds with Lord Bacon. His specification of civil history is much more luminous and clear than that
of either D'Alembert, or Lord Bacon. Mr. Jefferson transfers the
physics, of D'Alembert, from his third branch of the second province, and places it in the second branch of the first province; de-
viating in this also from Lord Bacon. This, it is conceived, is a
manifest deterioration. The position assigned by Lord Bacon is
better than that given by Mr. Jefferson; and D'Alembert's alterations on Lord Bacon are manifest and indubitable improvements.
The whole province of philosophy is altered by Mr. Jefferson. Lord
Bacon and D'Alembert beautifully divided it, as relating to, God,
man, and, nature. Mr. Jefferson divides it into moral and mathematical. Mathematical philosophy is now, it is believed, first introduced as a scientific denomination. D'Alembert had, very correct-
ly, made mathematics the first branch of natural philosophy; preceding physics. Both adopt the branch physico-mathematics, or
mixt mathematics; which, it is conceived, will always be productive
of confusion. Mathematics constitute but an auxiliary or instrumental science; and, to whatever they may be applied, are, themselves,
distinct.

Moral philosophy is singularly divided, by Mr. Jefferson, into ethics and jurisprudence. Religion comes out to be nothing
more than a part of jurisprudence, and is the commencement of
that branch, while commerce is the termination of it; and, in strict
language, it may be doubted if either the first or the last subject,
if either religion or commerce, are parts of jurisprudence. Governments have, indeed, acted upon them; but both, and more particularly the first, have a substantial existence, entirely independent of the incidental circumstance of their being acted upon by
governments. The passage, by the legislature of Virginia, of Mr.
Jefferson's immortal "act for the establishment of religious freedom;" constitutes, it is believed, the first instance, in the history
of the human race, of a government formally disclaiming the right
of interfering with religious sentiment. Religion, therefore, even
in this respect, that of being acted upon by governments, ceases;
at least in our country, so far as the state and general governments leave it free, which they almost perfectly do; from forming
any part of jurisprudence.

It may be farther remarked of Mr. Jefferson's system, and
which may be fully accounted for, from the circumstance of its
being intended only for the arrangement of a library, and not directly as a classification of human knowledge; that many of the
terms must include more than they would strictly import. Thus
arithmetic must include algebra, logarithms, and fluxions; since
they are not elsewhere mentioned. History must include biography, and antiquities; and the extensive department of voyages and
travels. Chronology must be a part of some other science; and in
the same manner meteorology, and some other subjects. They do

not appear, nor is it easy to say where they are contained. There must be a reiteration in the chapter of natural philosophy, being the sixth, and those parts of the physico-mathematical sciences contained in the twenty-seventh; nor will a reference to the authors and works included in those chapters tend to render their boundaries more definite; and it would have been far better that natural history proper should have preceded natural philosophy. The separation of agriculture and botany is unquestionably right; but that of gardening from agriculture, and its association with architecture and painting, agreeably to the views of Lord Kames, is more dubious. Romance, comedy, dialogue, epistles, are not necessarily poetry; and indeed it was observed by Mr. Jefferson that poetry was hard to be defined. An edition of the elements of Euclid, in the Arabic language, is classed under criticism; and it is remarked that books in rare languages are classed under that head, not according to their subject matter, but philologically, as specimens of the language in which they are written. Some of the chapters are very barren. The ninth, surgery, contains but seven works. Others are very fertile. The twenty-fourth, politics and commerce, contains a large proportion of the library. [21]

CHAPTER III

Jefferson and the Library of Congress

In the spring of 1815, ten wagons carrying the library of Thomas Jefferson left Monticello for the new city of Washington. By a margin of ten votes in the House of Representatives, the books of the third President, more than 6,000 in number, had been acquired by the Nation to replace the 3,000 volumes of the Library of Congress which had been lost when British soldiers burned the Capitol on the night of August 24, 1814. With the books from Monticello came a new concept of congressional librarianship and a new system of classification. In the future the Library was to contain many classes of books which, until 1814, had been excluded as unnecessary to the legislative process. And these new books, and all that would be added to them, were to be classified systematically, both in catalogs and on the shelves.

The first catalog of the Library of Congress, published in 1802, [1] listed in ten pages the contents of the eleven hair trunks and a map case which had crossed the Atlantic on the ship <u>American</u> in the winter of 1800. As was not uncommon in those days, the books were listed by size with little regard for authors or subjects. The entries were numbered consecutively, and the number of volumes and their estimated value were recorded – 740 volumes worth about $2,200. The second catalog, published in 1804, followed the same arrangement.

When John Beckley, the first Librarian of Congress, died in 1807, Patrick Magruder, a native of Maryland and a former Congressman from that State, succeeded him as Clerk of the House of Representatives and Librarian of Congress. The first catalog published by Magruder, that of 1808, was arranged by size like its predecessors, but there were some modifications. To Maps and Charts, Plans were added; following these came sections listing State Laws, Journals of the House of Representatives of the United States,

Reports of Committees of the House, Executive Reports and Papers, Receipts

and Expenditures, Bill Books of the House, and, finally, Gazettes. Physical

format was, even in 1808, yielding to classification by subject and bibliograph-

ic form.

In 1812, an era of classed catalogs began that was to continue for a half

century. The catalog of that year, the last to be issued before the burning of

the Capitol in 1814, provided eighteen classes for the 3,000 volumes to which

the Library had grown. These classes were:

1. Sacred History
2. Ecclesiastical History
3. Civil History, including Chronology, Biography, Antiquities, etc.
4. Geography and Topography, Voyages and Travels
5. Law
6. Ethics, or the Moral System in General, Theology and Mythology
7. Logic, Rhetoric and Criticism
8. Dictionaries, Grammars and Treatises on Education
9. General and Local Politics, Political Economy, etc.
10. Trade and Commerce
11. Military and Naval Tactics
12. Agriculture, Rural Economy, etc.
13. Natural History, Natural and Experimental Philosophy, etc.
14. Medicine, Surgery and Chemistry
15. Poetry and the Drama, Works of Fiction, Wit, etc.
16. Arts and Sciences, and Miscellaneous Literature
17. Gazettes
18. Maps, Charts and Plans

This classification was derived from the Bacon-d'Alembert scheme used

in the 1789 catalog of the Library Company of Philadelphia. Whether the

transition from an arrangement by format to a classified arrangement was

the work of Magruder, or was due to the presence of Representative Samuel

Latham Mitchill of New York on the Joint Committee on the Library cannot

be determined.

Mitchill, who had studied chemistry in Edinburgh under the old master,

Joseph Black, was an early exponent of the antiphlogistic doctrine of Lavoi-

sier. He later became professor of chemistry, natural history, and philoso-

phy in Columbia College, New York. A man of wide scientific interests, he

founded, with Edward Miller and Elihu H. Smith, in 1797, the quarterly Medi-

cal Repository, perhaps the first American scientific journal. Mitchill's in-

terest in classification and the system he developed for natural history are described in this journal. [2]

Magruder resigned as Librarian in January 1815, and President Madison appointed George Watterston to succeed him on March 21, 1815. Watterston had long thought that the arrangement of the old Library was "incorrect and injudicious," and a month after assuming office he wrote to Jefferson to ask his opinion on the arrangement of libraries. In reply Jefferson stated his preference for a classified rather than an alphabetical arrangement and briefly described his classification. He continued:

> You will recieve my library arranged very perfectly in the order observed in the Catalogue, which I have sent with it. in placing the books on their shelves, I have generally, but, not always, collocated distinctly the folios, 4tos. 8vos. & 12mos. placing with the last all smaller sizes. on every book is a label, indicating the chapter of the catalogue to which it belongs, and the order it holds among those of the same format. so that, altho' the Nos. seem confused on the catalogue, they are consecutive on the volumes as they stand on their shelves & indicate at once the place they occupy there. Mr. Millegan, in packing them has preserved their arrangement so exactly, in their respective presses, that on setting the presses up on end, he will be able readily to replace them in the order corresponding with the catalogue, and thus save you the immense labor which their re-arrangement would otherwise require.
>
> To give to my catalogue the conveniences of the Alphabetical arrangement, I have made at the end an Alphabet of Authors' names, and have noted the chapter, or chapters, in which the name will be found. where it occurs several times in the same chapter it is indicated by one or more perpendicular scores, thus | | | |, according to the number of times it will be found in the chapter. where a book bears no author's name, I have selected, in it's title, some leading word for denoting it alphabetically. this member of the catalogue would be more perfect if, instead of the score, the number on the book were particularly noted. this could not be done when I made the catalogue, because no label of numbers had then been put on the books. that alteration can now be readily made, and would add greatly to the convenient use of the Catalogue. [3]

No classification remains long unchanged; each succeeding librarian either "improves" upon it or replaces it. And Jefferson's was no exception. The Catalogue of the Library of the United States, which appeared in the late fall of 1815, pleased neither Jefferson nor the Congress. Watterston had made changes toward what he thought was simplification by eliminating subdivisions under some of the chapters. Under Chapter 2 Modern History: Foreign, Jefferson had provided the following divisions and subdivisions:

Southern: General Works — Italy, Rome, Florence, Naples, Venice, Spain, Portugal, France.

Northern: General Works — Lapland, Russia, Poland, Hungary, Sweden, Denmark, Prussia, Germany, Flanders, United Netherlands, Switzerland, Geneva.

Turkey, Asia, Africa.

Watterston retained these divisions and subdivisions in the chapter heading but arranged the titles in one alphabet. This was a curious deviation in view of the fact that he followed similar subdivisions which Jefferson had made in Chapter 29 Geography — General, Europe, Asia, Africa and America. Jefferson did not like the simplification and wrote to Watterston from Monticello on March 2, 1816:

> you ask how I like the arrangement within the chapters? of course, you know, not so well as my own; yet I think it possible the alphabetical arrangement may be more convenient to readers generally, than mine which was sometimes analytical, sometimes chronological, & sometimes a combination of both. [4]

The opinion of the Library Committee was more lengthy:

> Your committee are persuaded, that however ingenious, scientific, philosophical, and useful such a catalogue may be in the possession of a gentleman who, as was the case with the former proprietor of this, now the library of Congress, has classed his books himself, who alone has access to them, and has become from long habit and experience as perfectly familiar with every book in his library, as a man who has long lived in a city is familiar with every street, square, lane, and alley in it, still this form of catalogue is much less useful in the present state of our library, consisting chiefly of miscellanies, not always to be classed correctly under any particular head, than a plain catalogue in the form which had been adopted for the formation of the catalogue of the old library, ... [5]

Forgotten was the fact that the last catalog of the "old Library," that issued by Librarian Magruder in 1812, had been arranged in eighteen classes.

Other critics, however, praised the classified arrangement. Mr. Mackenzie, editor of the Canadian York Colonial Advocate, wrote that the Library was "remarkably well arranged, each description of books being kept by themselves. The catalogues, too, are upon a new and I think useful principle in large Libraries, which not only facilitates your finding any author you want, but also other works treating upon similar subjects. "[6]

The Washington City Chronicle's editorial of July 11, 1829, was laudatory but qualified by aesthetic misgivings:

> It is, ... perhaps, the best that has yet been introduced. It is, indeed, scientific; and by keeping all works upon the same subject together and under one head, it affords facilities that no other mode hitherto adopted has been found to yield. This classification is, however, not so well calculated for display as the common mode of arranging according to size, because one division being often much less than another, large volumes are sometimes placed above smaller ones, or chasms are left in the shelves which are not agreeable to the eye. But the subject being kept apart, each can with more facility be consulted. This arrangement, it will be seen, requires a knowledge of science and languages on the part of him who has to arrange, because it is necessary that the contents of each volume should be known before it can be correctly classed....
> To render this arrangement ... more complete it would be proper to make some additional subdivisions, as Biography, ancient and modern, Archaeology, Conchology, &c.

The first major changes in the classification occurred in the chapters devoted to Law. Jefferson's library had been rich in general works on the law and in the law of Virginia, but it was lacking in the constitutions, statutes, and court reports of other states. Now that it had become a national library, these lacunae were filled, and the classification was changed to provide for the new material.

Jefferson 1815		Library of Congress 1830	
Chapter			
18	Equity	18	Common Law 1. Commentaries, Treatises, Entries, Conveyancing 2. Criminal Law, Trials 3. Military Law, Courts Martial
19	Common Law	19	Common Law – Reports 1. British Reports 2. American Reports Supreme Court of the United States Circuit Courts of the United States General Digests of Reports Courts of Maine, New Hampshire, etc.
20	Law – Merchant	20	Equity Treatises and Reports
21	Law – Maritime	21	Law – Ecclesiastical Treatises and Reports
22	Law – Ecclesiastical	22	Law – Merchant, and Maritime Treatises and Reports

23	Foreign Law	23	Civil Law – Statutes, etc.

23   Civil Law – Statutes, etc.
    1. Civil Law, Codes, etc.
    2. British Statutes
    3. Laws of the United States
       and of the Several States,
       etc.
        United States
        State of Maine, New
        Hampshire, etc.

Conchology was added, perhaps to comply with the request of the critic who in the Washington City Chronicle had noted its absence. It was added to the caption of Chapter 14 Mineralogy in which Jefferson had classed Da Costa's Elements of Conchology. In the Technical Arts, Chapter 15, several new subdivisions appeared. Canals, which Jefferson had placed under Navigation, were made independent, and Rail Roads, Roads, and Smelting appeared. Gas Lighting for Peckston on Gas Lighting, 8vo; London, 1823, Fishing for the Complete Angler, by Isaac [sic] Walton, 8vo; London, 1822, and Sporting for the American Turf Register, vol. 1, 8vo; Baltimore, 1829-'30, were other additions. Two titles made it necessary to add Ventilating. Warming. ; a new division, Chapter 45, for State Papers, Laws, Journals, &c. , appeared at the end.

The catalog of 1840 contained but few changes. Michigan had become a State, and a new Territory, Florida, was added. Chapter 45, State Papers, etc. , disappeared and in Chapter 15 Water Works, Painting, Varnishing, etc. , Cements and Mortars were added. Under Aerostation, Cavallo's History and Practice of Aerostation, 8vo; London, 1785, one of Jefferson's books, was still the sole entry. The entries under Rail Roads doubled and the books under Canals increased.

The following decade was one of quiescence and the catalog of 1849 revealed few changes. Many new titles were added to the Library but the general structure and divisions of the classification were not altered. Chapter 45 reappeared, this time for Newspapers. Two books by Alfred Vail, American Electro-Magnetic Telegraph; with the Reports of Congress, and a Description of all Telegraphs known, Employing Electricity or Galvanism, 8vo;

Philadelphia, 1845, and Description of the American Electro-Magnetic Tele-

graph, now in Operation between the Cities of Washington and Baltimore, 8vo;

Washington, 1845, made it necessary to add Electro-Magnetic Telegraph as

a subdivision of Chapter 15. Knight, T. A. : Treatise on the Culture of the

Apple and Pear, and on the Manufacture of Cider and Perry, 12mo; London,

1802, remained the only volume under Cider and Perry.

In 1861 John Silva Meehan, who succeeded Watterston as Librarian in

1829, compiled the last of the classed catalogs to be published by the Library.

The reclassification which preceded publication of the catalog involved many

changes. The number of chapters shrank to forty, but in some areas, notably

in the humanities and social sciences, the alterations were radical. In the

chapters originally based upon the Imagination the following changes occurred:

1849	1861
32 Music	32 Music
33 Poetry – Epic	33 Poetry
34 Romance – Tales, Fables, Fictions, etc.	34 The Drama
35 Pastorals, Odes, Elegies, etc.	35 Fiction
36 Didactic	36 Dialogues and Epistles
37 Tragedy	37 Logic and Rhetoric
38 Comedy	38 Bibliography and Criticism
39 Dialogue – Epistolary	39 Language
40 Logic – Rhetoric – Orations	40 Polygraphical
41 Criticism, Theory	
42 Criticism, Bibliography	
43 Criticism, Languages	
44 Polygraphical	

Chapter 16. 2 Law of Nature and Nations became Chapter 24 between

Law and Politics. Arithmetic was merged with Geometry in Chapter 26 leav-

ing 25 vacant for the following expansion in the Social Sciences:

25	Politics
25. 1	Colonies
25. 2	Colonies – American Revolution
25. 3	Commerce, Industry, Statistics
25. 4	Crime and Punishment, Police, Pauperism, Charities
25. 5	Elections
25. 6	Finance, Weights and Measures
25. 7	Government
25. 8	Legislation
25. 9	Political Economy
25. 10	Registers and Directories
25. 11	Secret Societies
25. 12	State of Nations, and State Papers

Photography makes its appearance among the Technical Arts in Chapter 15, and in the same group Lithography is added to Engraving.

President Lincoln removed Meehan from office on May 24, 1861, and appointed John G. Stephenson to replace him. In September, Ainsworth Rand Spofford became his first assistant and the era of the classed catalog was over. Stephenson was frequently absent from the Library and the burden of his duties fell upon Spofford. The Civil War was being fought and except for occasional members of Congress few readers entered the Library. Spofford therefore had time, although he had but two assistants, to prepare the annual lists of new accessions and to compile a complete catalog of the Library's holdings. This catalog, [7] published in 1864, was the first general catalog to be printed by the Government Printing Office.

Spofford expressed his theory of cataloging and his distrust of classification in a prefatory Note:

> To consolidate all these catalogues into a single volume, and to facilitate reference by reducing the multifarious alphabets of former general catalogues to one alphabetical arrangement, is the object of the present volume.
> All former general catalogues of this Library have been arranged upon a system of classification prepared by Thomas Jefferson, and based upon Lord Bacon's division of knowledge. This classification, however well adapted, in some respects, to a small library, like that of Mr. Jefferson when adopted in 1815 as the basis of the present collection, is wholly unsuited to the necessities of readers consulting a large library. It was never designed by its author as a bibliographical system, but rather as a scientific arrangement of the various branches of human knowledge. No further illustration of its defects need be given than the fact that in the last catalogue of the Library of Congress the titles are distributed through a series of one hundred and seventy-nine distinct alphabets, arranged in an arbitrary sequence, and without an index. Few readers have the leisure and fewer still the inclination, to study the intricacies of such a system of classification. In abandoning it for a more simple method, the officers of the Library are assured that they have consulted the convenience as well as the wishes of Congress, and of other frequenters of the Library.
> In the arrangement of any catalogue of books, the chief desideratum, next to accuracy of description, is facility of reference, and to this end all minor considerations should be sacrificed. This volume embraces the present contents of the Library, arranged in all cases under the names of the authors, when known . . .

This catalog provided the first direct approach to authors and their works in the history of the Library. The librarian's memory replaced the written record, and for the difficulty of finding entries was substituted the difficulty

of finding books. The kind of memory Josiah Quincy describes in Figures

of the Past might suffice. Mr. Quincy and John Randolph were discussing

oratory in the latter's lodgings at Dawson's on Capitol Hill. The Senator

from Virginia quoted a passage from Burke which Quincy could not remem-

ber. He asked where he could find it and Randolph replied: "Go to the Con-

gressional Library, look in the third alcove, on the right-hand side, third

shelf from floor, fifth volume on the shelf, page 336, about halfway down. "[8]

Quincy made a memorandum of the direction and found the passage exactly

where Senator Randolph had placed it.

Late in 1864 Dr. Stephenson resigned and Spofford succeeded him. A

new era in the history of the Library opened — one in which it was to grow

into a national library both in the size and content of its collections and in

the quality of its services. The new era, however, was not to be one wholly

favorable to classification. Spofford was well aware of the necessity of clas-

sification "to bring order out of confusion, "but he thought that close classi-

fication failed by attempting too much. Books and not knowledge were the

objects of practical library classification and there was little need to waste

time in wrangling about the topic, for:

> No sooner does some sapient librarian, with the sublime confi-
> dence of conviction, get his classification house of cards construc-
> ted to his mind, and stands rapt in admiration before it, when there
> comes along some wise man of the east, and demolishes the fair
> edifice at a blow, while the architect stands by with a melancholy
> smile, and sees all his household gods lying shivered around him. [9]

Despite Spofford's conservatism, the classification of the Library was

altered and expanded during his librarianship. Major structural changes

were made, and the number of chapters, reduced to forty by Meehan, again

reached Jefferson's forty-four. Form classes, geographic and subject sub-

divisions numbering in the thousands were introduced, as well as various

devices for reducing the number of authors in the alphabetical arrangement

under the major divisions.

Broadly, the classification was changed to ten major groups: History; Science and Technology; Religion; Law; Political Science and Economics; Philosophy, Education, and Sociology; Geography; Art; Literature, Bibliography, and Languages; and Polygraphy. From a logical point of view the systematic sequence of these groups left much to be desired, but a closer collocation of related subjects resulted.

A new chapter, 2 1/2, was established to provide for archeology and other auxiliary sciences of history, which in the 1861 catalog had been dispersed in Chapters 1 to 4. Biography, previously scattered throughout History, was assigned form classes like the following:

4   American History
$4B_1$ Biography, General
$4B_2$ Individual
$4B_3$ Genealogy

Chapter 5 Ecclesiastical History was transferred to Chapter 16 immediately preceding Chapter 17 Theology, and was replaced by Mathematics from Chapter 26. In Chapters 5 to 15 were grouped Science and Technology, material formerly as far away as Chapters 26-28. Chapter 6 Natural Philosophy — Physics, Geology, and Meteorology was divided into 6 Geology and 7 Physics. Agriculture, formerly in Chapter 7, was now found in 14 following Botany in Chapter 13. From Chapter 28 Astronomy was brought to Chapter 8, moving Chemistry to 9, replacing Surgery, which was combined with Medicine in Chapter 10. Anatomy was transferred from Chapter 11 to Chapter 12 Zoology, leaving 11 for Natural History. Mineralogy in Chapter 14 was transferred to 6 Geology, and Conchology, added long before to Mineralogy, now found a resting-place in Chapter 12 Zoology.

In the Technical Arts many new divisions were made. Roads and Railroads were separated, and Rubber, Rural Sports, Servants, and Silk appeared. Bullfights, Cosmetics, Cold Storage, Massage, Petroleum products, Ping Pong, Refrigerating, Submarine Telegraphy, and Electroplating were also introduced for the first time. The chapters devoted to Law remained relatively static.

Chapters 25 through 28 were changed and expanded to the following:

25.1   State of Nations and State papers
25.2   Colonies
25.3   Statistics, Commerce
25.4   Political economy
25.5   Elections
25.6   Finance
25.7   Science of Government
25.8   Legislation
25.9   Directories
25.10 Politics

26.1   Mental Philosophy
26.2   Logic
26.3   Ethics
26.4   Phrenology
26.5   Physiognomy
26.6   Education

27.1   Sociology
27.2   Family, Marriage, Sex, etc.
27.3   Charities, Crime and Punishment, etc.
27.4   Secret Societies
27.5   Slavery

28   Mythology, Mysticism, etc.

The Fine Arts and Literature remained unchanged, but Logic was divorced from Rhetoric in Chapter 37 and moved to 26.2. Writing, Printing, and Bookbinding were transferred to Chapter 38, a consolidation of bibliography and the book arts which would later result in Class Z Bibliography and Library Science, the first of the modern Library of Congress schedules.

An amusing instance of the "biographical element" which inevitably pervades classification activity is found in the classing of Landscape Gardening. Jefferson had originally placed the subject in the Fine Arts, Chapter 31 Gardening, Painting and Sculpture, following Chapter 30 Architecture. For this he was criticized by Judge Woodward, who attributed the classification to the bad influence of Henry Home, Lord Kames. Meehan retained Jefferson's arrangement, but Spofford moved the material to Chapter 14 Agriculture. Even in classification, de gustibus non est disputandum.

Four new chapters were added:

41 Essays and Miscellanea
42 Ana, Wit, Humor, etc.
43 Smithsonian Collection
44 Periodicals, Serials, Newspapers

In addition to these major organizational changes, over ten thousand divisions and subdivisions were developed by 1897. These divisions and subdivisions derived their notation from the numbers assigned to the shelves for the Library in the Capitol during the reclassification which preceded the publication of the 1861 Catalogue. The class numbers which resulted were a curious combination of movable and fixed-location symbols. Chapter 15 was Technology wherever located; but within the class, 9456, one of the shelves devoted to Technology, was the shelf on which books on Inter-ocean canals were placed. As the years passed, however, the shelf number became associated with the subject and ceased to be a mere indication of physical location. The arrangement of the first six chapters was:

	Chapter	Shelves
1.	General History	2433-2507
2.	Foreign History	2012-2923
3.	British History	3750-3895
4.	American History	3030-3464
5.	Mathematics	1560-1640
6.	Geology	4340-4495

Thus the shelf sequence was Mathematics, Foreign History, General History, American History, British History, and Geology. How the system was used in actual practice is illustrated by the examples given below.

A book on the Panama Canal carried the class number

15   Technology
9456 Inter-ocean canals

following

15   Technology
9453 Canal and River improvements [in general]

Geographic subdivisions were used:

15	Technology
9443	Railroads. General
9444	Railroads (American)
9450	Railroads (Foreign)

Under Chapter 2 was

Africa – History & Travels	
Whole	2540
South	2544
Basutoland	2545 B
Cape Colony	2545 C
Natal	2545 N
Transvaal	2545 T

Hence the class number for a book on the Transvaal, $\frac{2}{2545}$ T.

Cross references were used to indicate the preferred classification.

When the subject was in the same chapter, references like the following
were made:

Chapter 7 Physics	
Statics	See Mechanics
Chapter 31 Fine Arts	
Modeling	See Sculpture
Chapter 15 Technology	
War (Art of)	See Army. Military science, etc.

When the class number fell in another chapter, specific class references
were made:

Chapter 10 Medicine	
X-rays	7. 1443-4 [Physics]
Chapter 17 Theology	
Episcopacy	16. 1192 [Church History]
Chapter 30 Architecture	
Ventilation	15. 9426 [Technology]

Various devices were used to break up the alphabet in classes where
many entries could be expected:

Chapter 10 Medicine
General and systematic A-B 1340; C 1341;
D-K 1342; L-Pa 1343; Par-Z 1344

Thus, Brown's _Principles of Medicine_, $\frac{10}{1340}$, and Parks, _Principles of
Medicine_, $\frac{10}{1344}$.

Three elements of notation sometimes appeared in expanding areas. The class number for Bimetallism was 25. 6. 2. The first two elements, 25. 6, were for Finance; similarly, Monopoly was 25. 3. 2351, the first two elements denoting Commerce.

On the linen pages of the old classification schedule, [10] used until the progressive reclassification of the collections, typed and manuscript additions recorded the progress of knowledge during the late nineteenth century. These pages, in chapter arrangement, but with the divisions and subdivisions partly in systematic arrangement and partly in the alphabetical form of an index, reflect the subjects of the books added to the Library: Spanish war [Spanish American] 4. 3220; Delsartism 31. 10805-06; German war [Franco-Prussian] 2. 2812; Crimean war 2. 2155; Stereo-chemistry 9. 4573; Mental healing 10. 4295; Psychiatry 10. 4295; Cold storage 15. 9572; Dynamo 15. 9430; Manicure and Massage 15. 9407; Epworth League 17. 1740; Interstate Commerce Commission 25. 3. 2343; Eastern question 25. 10. 5347; Vocophy 26. 5. 5495; Red Cross Association 27. 3. 5582; Chromolithography 31. 10841; Volapuk 39. 10965; Last words 42. 6535; Mafia 27. 3. 5605; Freedmen 27. 5. 5616; Saxophone 32. 10093; Oleomargarine 15. 9411.

Hidden for years in the pages of the old schedule was a yellowed sheet bearing the message:

> Same book in 2 places.
> Ditt.
> Merton H. (Holmes N)
> Descriptive mentality
>
> $\frac{28}{5635}$
>
> $\frac{26.5}{5495}$
>
> D. H.

Thus had D. H. [David Hutcheson, Superintendent of the Reading Room from 1897 to 1907] called to the attention of the classifiers the age-old problem — one title, one class, and that the right one. In this case, Palmistry 28 or Physiognomy 26?

The end of the century was approaching, and the new Library building

for which Spofford had fought valiantly since 1872 was nearing completion.
Plans were being made to move the Library from the cramped quarters in
the Capitol it had occupied for nearly a century. The Congress, aware of the
importance of the move, directed the Joint Committee on the Library to "inquire into the condition of the Library of Congress," to make such recommendations as it deemed desirable, and to report a plan for its organization,
custody, and management. Hearings were held between November 20 and
December 7, 1896; among the librarians called by the Committee to advise
it were a future Librarian of Congress, Herbert Putnam, and two eminent
librarians who had had considerable experience with classification, Melvil
Dewey and William Torrey Harris. The classification of the new Library
was one of the many problems discussed.

"The organization of the library is a subjective one, and not governed
by any Procrustean system of classification," stated Librarian Spofford. He
objected to minute classification because it could not, in his opinion, be applied to books. A treatise on diseases of the heart and lungs would fall in
two places, heart and lungs. "You can not tear the book to pieces to satisfy
logical classification." He also was opposed to the complicated notation
which he thought close classification would bring and which would break the
system down "by its own weight." Moreover, it would take the staff a long
time to learn the system and to label and mark the books, and memory would
be unduly taxed.

Representative Quigg of New York, who carried on most of the questioning, did a thorough job. Spofford had to describe the "subjective system" in
general and all the parts in detail — nearly twenty printed pages of testimony
before it was over. Melvil Dewey, from the New York State Library, and
Herbert Putnam, Librarian of the Boston Public Library, supported a classification system based on the principle of relative location.

> MR. PUTNAM: I have experienced difficulty with "fixed location." It
> would be worth thousands of dollars to us if we could
> have thrown over the idea of a fixed location and adop-
> ted one of relative position. I presume it would be

> impossible for you to adopt outright any system. The principle you could adopt, but the particular classification would have to be modified. [11]

Earlier in the hearings Spofford had expressed his opinion on the question of change.

> REPRESENTATIVE QUIGG: Now, applying that system, your purpose in fitting up the new library is to continue this subjective system, is it not?

> MR. SPOFFORD: In the main, yes. It is just as Daniel Webster said, "an established usage has two advantages over any innovation – in the first place it is established, and in the second place it is understood." I do not mean that this would apply to a system not reasonable or not practically demonstrated to be serviceable. Those two conditions being concurrent, it, in my opinion, fully establishes the best way of arranging a library; for, in the reorganization of the collection, my object would be to find the books as rapidly as possible.[12]

On June 30, 1897, President McKinley nominated John Russell Young as Librarian of Congress. The Senate confirmed the nomination, and the following day Young took the oath as the seventh Librarian of Congress. Spofford became his first assistant. One of Young's most pressing duties was the selection of a chief for the new Catalogue Department. He appointed James Christian Meinich Hanson, head cataloger of the University of Wisconsin Library. When Hanson reported for duty on the first of September, he did not find the situation particularly encouraging, as he described years later.

> There were between 750,000 and 800,000 volumes in sore need of recataloguing and reclassification, great quantities of new books pouring in, no shelf list or official catalogue, no furniture or equipment, and a force consisting of three holdovers from the old régime, respectively fifty, sixty-eight, and seventy-six years old, wedded to the old system and wholly out of touch with recent library development. Moreover, ordering and binding were considered part of the duties of the Catalogue Division, eleven positions out of the seventeen provided were still to be filled, and the Division had been assigned to a long, narrow room seventy yards distant from the card catalogue stored in cramped and poorly lighted trays inside the circular desk at the center of the reading room.[13]

The new chief immediately turned his attention to the selection of a competent staff. Hanson later recalled that an eager horde of would-be librarians swooped down upon Congress, the President, and the Library. He added, "There were needy journalists, clergymen without a call, teachers unable to

teach, unsuccessful authors, actors without engagements, college and university graduates whose mental development must have been arrested soon after graduation, and the usual assortment of lame ducks from states east and
west. "[14]

Among the applications on file in the chief clerk's office were those of
three former associates of Hanson, competent catalogers and classifiers.
Hanson made recommendations, but they were returned with a curt note that
"merit and experience" had been the determining factors in the appointment
of heads of departments, and "from now on it would be the duty of the librarian to give heed to the wishes of Congress. " Undismayed, Hanson renewed
his efforts and after several months secured the appointment of Charles Martel, of the Newberry Library in Chicago, as his first assistant and chief classifier. Martel, whom Hanson later called "Chief Architect of the Library's
Classification System, " entered the Library's services on December 1, 1897.

The problem of classification was immediately given consideration. On
December 6, 1897, Young reported to the Congress, "How far it may be necessary to amend this [Subjective Classification], in addition to the changes
introduced by my predecessor, and especially in a library with subdivisions
like our own, it would be premature to say. " The quest for a solution began.
The following chapters describe the background of the quest and the solution
of the problem.

BACKGROUND OF DECISION: "PRE-HISTORY"

CHAPTER IV

The Old World

The story of classification begins over 2,500 years ago in Ionia, on the shores of Asia Minor, meeting place of East and West. After the Dorian invasions of the eleventh century B. C. had destroyed the Aegean culture of the Bronze Age, it was the Ionians who preserved the spirit of the old civilization. From the cultural seeds saved in Ionia, "the cradle of Western Thought, " came a new Greek civilization. Earliest of Greek philosophers, the Ionians speculated on their society and the universe in which they found themselves. For the authoritarian group or collective philosophies which had preceded them, they substituted free inquiry. The first philosophers, Thales, Anaximander, and Anaximines, sought something permanent in an ever-changing world – an <u>Urstoff</u> that persisted through the process of change. Ionian interest in art and science as well as in cosmology led to the development of a system of education which emphasized the whole man.

Ionian influence led to the establishment of two schools in southern Italy. At Kroton, Pythagoras, a native of Ionia, founded the first, both a religious community and a school, in the second half of the sixth century B. C. The second school, attributed to Xenophanes of Colophon but more likely the work of Parmenides, was established at Elea. The philosophers of these schools as well as Heraclitus, Empedocles, Anaxagoras, and others continued to seek answers to the questions the early Ionians had raised – questions far more important than the answers given.

During the sixth century B. C. the Athenians imported the Ionian system of encyclopedic education. A century later the new teachers, the Sophists, added professional studies and emphasized training in Rhetoric. Unlike the earlier Greek philosophers, the Sophists were professional teachers, encyclopedists or polymaths, little given to speculation. They were interested in the

subject, man, rather than in the object, the cosmos. In time, however, the rel-
ativism and skepticism of Sophism led to its decline, bringing the name into
disrepute; in Plato's words they were "shopkeepers with spiritual wares."[1]

Counted among the Sophists by his contemporaries was Socrates (470?-
399 B. C.) who, like them, was interested in education and the problems of
human conduct. Unlike the Sophists, however, Socrates considered himself a
learner who sought through dialectic or conversation (the Socratic Method)
to find true knowledge and universal and stable norms of ethics. Aristotle
attributed to him two improvements in method, "inductive arguments and universal definition, both of which are concerned with the starting point of
science."[2]

Socrates was born about 470 B. C., the son of Sophroniscus and Phae-
narete of the Antiochid tribe and the deme of Alopecae. Robust of body, he
wore the same garment winter and summer; he walked barefoot even on a
winter campaign. In his early twenties Socrates turned from cosmological
speculation to man, a subject that was to occupy him the rest of his life. He
married Xanthippe, famous or infamous for a shrewish character which her
picture in Plato's Phaedo does not bear out. During the Peloponnesian War
Socrates distinguished himself for bravery at the siege of Potidaea in 431/30 B.C.
and later at the defeat of the Athenians by the Boeotians. It was his moral
courage, however, not his physical courage, which led him to his death.

As a member of the πρυτάνεις, or Committee of the Senate, Socrates
refused, in 406 B. C., to agree to a joint trial of eight commanders for negli-
gence at Arginusae. In his opinion a joint trial would not only be contrary to
Athenian law but would yield a hasty sentence. Two years later he refused to
participate in the arrest of Leon of Salamis whom, for the sake of his property, the Oligarchs intended to kill. In 400/399 the leaders of the restored de-
mocracy brought Socrates to trial for failure to worship state-approved gods,
for introducing new religious practices, and for corrupting the young. On
these flimsiest of unproved charges he was convicted and condemned to death.

Socrates could have escaped death by proposing an alternative penalty, by going into voluntary exile, or by escape, but such courses were contrary to his principles. Plato describes his last day on earth in the Phaedo. Socrates drank of the hemlock and lay dying; he spoke his last words: "Crito, we owe a cock to Aesculapius. Pay it therefore and do not neglect it."[3]

One of the greatest philosophers of all time, Plato was born in Athens, or Aegina, in 428/7 B.C. Member of a distinguished Athenian family, Plato was urged by relatives to enter political life, but the excesses of the Oligarchy of 403/4 turned him from a political career. In 388/7 he founded the Academy in Athens, the first European university, where not only philosophy but also mathematics, astronomy, and the physical sciences were studied. Plato died in Athens in the year 348/7, "uno et octogesimo anno scribens est mortuus."[4]

Plato, a pupil of Socrates who wrote nothing, was a prolific writer. He made the first attempt at philosophical systemization; while he did not explicitly state the divisions of his philosophy, his pupil Aristotle divided his master's work into Dialectic (Philosophy), Ethics, and Physics. Plato's synthesis in the Republic of Athenian and Spartan theories of education led him to the following curriculum and classification:

    Gymnastics
    Music (and literature and other elementary studies)
    Mathematical sciences
        Arithmetic
        Geometry
        Astronomy
        Harmonics (Mathematical theory of music)
    Dialectic, an all embracing philosophy

No classification ever devised was as influential as the system Plato's pupil Aristotle developed. Son of Nichomachus, who was physician to Amyntas II, King of Macedonia, Aristotle was born in Stagira, Thrace, in 384/3 B.C. For twenty years he was associated with Plato in the Academy. After Plato's death Aristotle left Athens to found a branch of the Academy at Assos in Asia Minor. In 343/2 he became tutor to the son of King Philip of Macedon, Alexander the Great. Returning to Athens in 335/4 Aristotle founded a new school, the Lyceum, also known as the περίπατος either because the members carried on their discussions while walking back and forth in the covered ambulatory or because a large part of the instruction was given there. After the death of Alexander the Great in 323 Aristotle fled from Athens to Chalcis in Euboea to escape prosecution for his political opinions. With the fate of Socrates in mind, Aristotle said that he fled to prevent the Athenians from sinning a second time against philosophy.

Like many of his successors, Aristotle prepared no clear chart of his classification; rather, it must be assembled from several of his works and as a result differing schemes are produced. The chief difficulty, and one about which there has been considerable controversy, is whether his main divisions were Theoretical and Practical, or Theoretical, Practical, and Poetic (productive). Actually he used both, even in a single work. In the Topics, for instance, he gives the divisions Theoretical, Practical, and Poetic in books VI and VIII but only Theoretical and Practical in book VII. The latter division is also found in the Metaphysics where he says "The end of speculative science is truth, while the end of practical science is action."[5] The Greeks made a clear distinction between πράττειν and ποιεῖν : the first meaning action for its own sake; the second, action which produced an effect. In Latin "actio" and "effectio" are corresponding terms. Aristotle's divisions were:

    Analytics (Methodology and Logic, later Organon)
    Theoretical (Speculative)
       Physics or Natural Philosophy
       Mathematics
       Theology or First Philosophy (later Metaphysics[6])
    Practical
       Active
         Ethics
         Politics
            Economics
            Rhetoric
    Poetic, or productive

The first definitive use of classification in a library was in the city founded by Aristotle's pupil, Alexander the Great. Although there is evidence that early libraries were systematically arranged, existing records of the

classification used are fragmentary and their interpretation controversial.
The history of library classification therefore begins in Alexandria in the
famous Alexandrian Library founded by Ptolemy Soter in the early years of
the third century B. C.

The first classifier was Callimachus of Cyrene (ca. 305-ca. 240 B. C.),
a teacher and poet turned librarian. His classed catalog of the Alexandrian
Library, the Pinakes, or "Tables of all those who were eminent in any kind
of literature and of their writings, " has been called "the first great library
catalogue of western civilization. "[7] In 120 Pinakes, or Tables, Callimachus
listed the corpus of extant Greek literature. From existing fragments and
from references in Greek writers it is possible to determine the following
main divisions:

Poetry	Prose
Non-dramatic	History
Epic	Oratory
Elegiac	Philosophy
Iambic	Medicine
Melic	Law
Dramatic	Miscellany
Tragedy	
Comedy	

No records of other classes have been found, but it is probable, judging from
the literature of the time and the nature of the library, that Mathematics and
Natural Science should be added to these divisions. [8] Following this early
Alexandrian classification we have little knowledge of library classifications
for a period of well over a thousand years.

After Aristotle's death two new schools of philosophy came into existence — the Stoic, founded by Zeno in 308 B. C. , and the Epicurean, founded by
Epicurus in 306 B. C. They continued the old traditions but, like the Sophists,
placed far more emphasis upon conduct (Ethics) than Speculation (Logic and
Metaphysics). The Stoics developed an influential triadic division of knowledge which was substantially the one Aristotle attributed to Plato.

Logic (guidance of man's mind)
    Dialectic (reasoning)
    Rhetoric (expression)

Physics (to explain the universe)
  Cosmology
  Theology
Ethics (guidance of man's conduct)
  Morals
  Politics

The first systematic treatment or encyclopedia of all knowledge was made by a Roman, Marcus Terentius Varro (116-27 B. C.), contemporary and friend of Cicero. Varro's work, Disciplinarum libri ix, long lost, served to carry existing knowledge into the Christian Era. The nine books contained: I. Grammar (language and literature) II. Dialectics III. Rhetoric IV. Geometry V. Arithmetic VI. Astrology VII. Music VIII. Medicine and IX. Architecture. The first seven books foreshadowed the liberal arts of the Middle Ages. Varro's encyclopedia influenced Pliny the Elder (ca. 23-79 A. D., who compiled an encyclopedic Natural History which summarized nearly all the knowledge of the period. In the third century Gaius Julius Solinus, Latin grammarian and compiler, based his Collectanea rerum memorabilium on Pliny's work. A revised and interpolated edition with the title Polyhistor appeared in the sixth or seventh century.

Philo of Alexandria, known as Philo Judaeus (ca. 30 B. C.-45 A. D.), mediator between Hellenistic philosophy, Christianity, and Neo-Platonism, considered philosophy and profane learning the handmaids of theology. This opinion, adopted by the two Gregories, Clement of Alexandria and St. John Damascene, was widely held during the Middle Ages.

Under Augustus and his immediate successors Alexandria, which had again become a center of learning, sent scholars to Rome to teach the traditional disciplines. Ammonius Saccus numbered among his students in Alexandria Longinus, the grammarian, Origen, and Plotinus. Origen (185-254 A. D.) fled from persecution in Alexandria to Caesarea, where he established a school in which the curriculum comprised geometry, physics, astronomy, philosophy, ethics, and a new subject, the Holy Scripture. Plotinus (203/4-269/70), who wrote nothing until he was 50 years old, then produced a series of philosophical essays for the pupils in his seminars. These were collected and arranged in six books of nine chapters, hence the name Enneades, by Porphyry, a student and biographer of Plotinus. In the work of this great thinker culminated Neo-Platonism, which fused philosophy, religion, and mysticism. The spiritual idealism of Plotinus exercised considerable influence upon St. Augustine.

The question of classification, to which little thought had been given in the first three centuries of the Christian Era, reappears in the work of St. Augustine, greatest of the Latin Fathers. Born in Tagaste in the Province of Numidia on November 13, 354 A. D., Augustine became teacher, philosopher, and theologian. In 396 he became Bishop of Hippo, a position he held until his death on August 28, 430, during the siege of the city by the Vandals.

Augustine adopted the Platonic division of Philosophy into Natural, Rational, and Moral but superimposed Aristotle's dichotomy of speculative and practical.

Plato	Aristotle
Natural philosophy (or Physics) ⎱ Rational philosophy (Logic) ⎰	Speculative
Moral philosophy (Ethics)	Practical

He introduced a similar division into the liberal arts which clearly distinguished for the first time arts and sciences, the trivium and quadrivium of succeeding centuries.

Augustine planned to compile a compendium of all knowledge as Varro had done four centuries before. After he retired as teacher of rhetoric in Milan to prepare for Christian baptism he completed a treatise on grammar and, years later, works on logic, rhetoric, music, geometry, arithmetic, and philosophy. But the project as a whole was never completed; his increasing interest in religion turned his mind from secular learning. Augustine's work played an important part in determining Western education, philosophy, and classification from the sixth to the twelfth century.

The artes liberales next appeared in the Liber de nuptiis Mercurii et Philologiae, or Disciplinae, of Martianus Capella of Carthage. Written sometime between the sack of Rome by Alaric in 410 A. D. and the Vandal conquest of North Africa in 429, this work, a mixture of prose and poetry, contains nine books. The opening allegory, in two books, describes the marriage of Mercury to Philologia. The remaining books celebrate the seven bridesmaids, Grammar, Dialectic, Rhetoric (the later trivium), and Geometry, Arithmetic, Astronomy, and Music (the later quadrivium). For eight centuries this strange satura was popular in translations and revisions.

Aristotle's divisions reappear in the sixth century in the work of Boethius, well known as the author of De Consolatione Philosophiae. Boethius (ca. 480-524), the last of the Romans and the first of the Scholastics, held the office of consul under Theodoric, King of the Ostrogoths. Accused and convicted of treason, he was sent to prison in Ticinum (Pavia), where he was executed in 524. He translated into Latin the Organon of Aristotle and wrote works on arithmetic, music, geometry, and astronomy which had considerable influence in the Middle Ages. The first known use of the term "quadrivium" is found in his De Arithmetica. Boethius' divisions of philosophy into Theoretical and Practical or Speculative and Active and their subdivisions appear in his In Isagogen Porphyrii Commenta and De Trinitate.

Later in the sixth century Cassiodorus Senator (ca. 477-565/70), a pupil of Boethius who also held high office under Theodoric, continued the tradition of the artes liberales. After retiring from public life to found the monastery of Vivarium in Bruttium, Cassiodorus wrote for his fellow monks the Institutiones Divinarum et Saecularium Lectionum, a summary of all knowledge. The first part of the treatise was devoted to sacred literature; the second, De Artibus ac Disciplinis Liberalium Litterarum treated the seven liberal arts: the scientiae sermocinales (Grammar, Dialectic, and Rhetoric) and the scientiae reales (Arithmetic, Geometry, Music, and Astronomy). Cassiodorus' compendium was widely used as a textbook for centuries.

Isidorus Hispalensis (560?-636), Archbishop of Seville in the Visigothic Kingdom, was another important link between antiquity and the Middle Ages.

He wrote an encyclopedia, the Originum seu Etymologiarum Libri XX, which began with etymology, dealt with the seven liberal arts, and covered geography, law, medicine, and natural history as well. Popular during the early Middle Ages, the work could be found in every monastery library of importance.

With the decline of civilization on the continent at the end of the seventh century, the artes found a refuge in the British Isles, first in Ireland, then in England. The Venerable Bede (674-735), priest and monk of Jarrow, and his friend and pupil, Egbert, later Archbishop of York, who made the school of York the leading educational center of England, transmitted the ancient learning. From York, Alcuin (735-804) carried the learning preserved in the British Isles back to France and Western Europe during the Carolingian Renaissance. At Charlemagne's Palace School, as well as at other schools, the basic curriculum was the trivium (grammar, rhetoric, and dialectic) and the quadrivium (arithmetic, geometry, astronomy, and music). Alcuin's poem, The Bishops and Saints of the Church of York, gives a survey of the subjects taught at the cathedral school of York in the middle of the eighth century. They included the trivium, grammar and rhetoric (logic strangely was missing) and the quadrivium, music (oddly including law), astronomy, geometry (plus geography), and arithmetic. Last, and "above all," were the sacred writings, not yet a specialized study.[9]

Alcuin treated philosophy in his De Dialectica where, in answer to a question put by his interlocutor Charlemagne, he states its divisions: Physics, Ethics, and Logic — the Platonic and Stoic triad. Later he indicated the subdivisions of each:

```
Physics
    Arithmetic
    Geometry
    Music
    Astronomy
Ethics
    Prudence
    Justice
    Fortitude
    Temperance
Logic
    Dialectic
    Rhetoric
```

He also applied his three main divisions to the Holy Scriptures, substituting
Theology for Logic.

Rhabanus Maurus (ca. 776-856), a pupil of Alcuin at Fulda and Tours,
who became Archbishop of Mainz, composed his De Clericorum Institutione
for the instruction of the clergy. In three books he dealt with things religious
and with the seven liberal arts. His encyclopedia De Rerum Naturis, which
showed no more originality than his first work, was derived from Isidore,
Bede, and Augustine. A typical product of the Carolingian Renaissance, Rhabanus Maurus, Praeceptor Germaniae, had real enthusiasm for learning but,
like most of his encyclopedic predecessors, little originality.

While the Carolingian Renaissance conserved and disseminated existing knowledge, it did nothing to add to the store. There was little, if any,
speculation during the period; Philosophy, almost abandoned since the time
of Boethius, was merged with Dialectic. The seven liberal arts and religion
encompassed all knowledge. In the ninth century, however, Joannes Scotus
Erigena (ca. 810-877) restored Philosophy to the dominant position it had occupied in the thinking of Plato, Aristotle, Augustine, and Boethius.

Born in Ireland and educated in an Irish monastery, John Scotus, like
Alcuin, went to the Continent and taught in the Palatine School of Charles the
Bald. His most important work, the De Divisione Naturae, probably written
between 864 and 866, comprised five works in the dialogue form popular at
the time. Nature to John Scotus was coextensive with all reality; and philosophy and theology were one. He divided knowledge into four branches:

    Practical philosophy, or Ethics
    Physical, or Natural philosophy
    Theology
    Rational philosophy, or Logic

Following St. Augustine he made the liberal arts subservient to philosophy, as
preparatory studies. Unfortunately, the work of Scotus exerted little influence.

The great Moslem philosopher and physician, Avicenna, or Ibn Sīnā
(980?-1037), adapted Aristotle's classification to his own needs in the al-
Shifā, known in the Middle Ages as the Sufficientiae. His divisions were:

```
Logic (Propaedeutic to philosophy)
Speculative Philosophy
   Physics
   Mathematics
   Theology
      First Theology (Ontology and Natural Theology)
      Second Theology (Islamic Theology)
Practical Philosophy
   Ethics
   Economics
   Politics
```

The development of the studia generalia, and later the universities, led

to specialization in the higher faculties of law, medicine, and theology. In-

creasing interest in learning found expression in attempts to develop classi-

fications of existing knowledge. One of the most interesting is the work of

Hugo of St. Victor (1096-1141), German mystic philosopher and theologian,

who merged in his Didascalicon the triadic division of the Stoics with the

system of Aristotle. His classification provided:

```
Logic (preamble to science)
   Grammar
   Dialectic
   Rhetoric
   "Sophistic"
Science
   Theoretical
      Theology
      Mathematics (number)
      Music (proportion)
      Geometry (extension)
      Astronomy (movement)
      Physics (intrinsic nature)
   Practical
      Ethics
      Economics
      Politics
Mechanics (illiberal arts)
```

Dominicus Gundissalinus (12th century), Archbishop of Segovia, based

his De Divisione Philosophiae upon Alfarabi's De Scientiis and the writings

of Ammonius, Isaac Israeli, Avicenna, Boethius, Isidore of Seville, and the

Venerable Bede. He provided the following divisions:

```
Propaedeutic sciences
   Grammar (including History)
   Rhetoric
Logic (Arabian instrumentum)
Philosophy
   Theoretical
      Physics (medicine, agriculture, navigation, etc. )
```

        Mathematics (quadrivium)
        Metaphysics and Theology
    Practical
        Politics
        Economics
        Ethics

The <u>Sacerdos</u> <u>ad</u> <u>Altare</u> <u>Accessurus</u>[10] of the twelfth century, ascribed to Alexander Neckam, contains a list of text books in the order of the liberal arts and the higher faculties of medicine, law, and theology. Haskins considered it to be an unofficial list of the books used in the schools of Paris in the twelfth century.

St. Bonaventure, the "Seraphic Doctor" (1221-1274), based his classification upon a clear-cut distinction between theology and philosophy. Theology begins with God; philosophy ends with Him. In his <u>De</u> <u>Reductione</u> <u>Artium</u> <u>ad</u> <u>Theologiam</u> he divided human knowledge, which proceeded from the <u>internal</u> <u>light</u>, as follows:

    Natural:
        Physics
        Mathematics
        Metaphysics
    Rational:
        Grammar
        Logic
        Rhetoric
    Moral:
        Ethics
        Economics
        Politics

Robert Kilwardby (d. 1279), noted Dominican master at Oxford and Cardinal Archbishop of Canterbury, united the classification of Hugo of St. Victor with that of the Arabian School of Toledo (Gundissalinus). His work, <u>De</u> <u>Ortu</u> <u>et</u> <u>Divisione</u> <u>Philosophiae</u>, marked an improvement upon that of Gundissalinus. Baur[11] described Kilwardby's work as the most remarkable classification of the sciences to appear in the Middle Ages.

    Philosophia rerum divinarum
        Physics
        Mathematics
        Metaphysics
    Philosophia rerum humanarum
        Practical
            Ethics
            Mechanical arts
        Logic

    Sermocinales
       Grammar
       Logic
       Rhetoric

The high point of medieval classification is in the work of St. Thomas

Aquinas, called <u>Doctor Angelicus</u>. St. Thomas was born in the castle of Roc-

casecca near Naples in 1224 or 1225. When he was five years of age his

father, the Count of Aquino, placed him in the Benedictine Abbey of Monte

Cassino as an oblate. He later attended the University of Naples and in 1244

entered the Dominican Order. St. Thomas devoted his life to study, teaching,

and writing. He died on March 7, 1274, at the Cistercian Monastery of Fossa-

nuova between Naples and Rome. His most influential work was the <u>Summa</u>

<u>Theologica</u> in which he summarized all knowledge.

The classification of St. Thomas recalls the divisions of his teacher, St.

Albert the Great, and those of Aristotle. Like other classifiers, Thomas Aqui-

nas varied the order of his divisions on occasion. The following outline con-

tains his major classes:

    Theology
    Logic (Instrument of Knowledge)
    Philosophy
       Speculative
         Mathematics
            Pure: Arithmetic and Geometry
            Applied: Music and Astronomy
         Natural Science, or Physics
         Theology i. e. Metaphysics
       Practical
         Moral
            Individual Ethics
            Economics i. e. Domestic Ethics
            Politics
         Mechanical Arts
    Liberal Arts (Preparatory subjects)

Girolamo Savonarola (1452-1498), better known as reformer than phil-

osopher, turned his attention to classification in his <u>Opus Perutile de Divisi-</u>

<u>one Ordine ac Utilitate Omnium Scientiarum</u> (Veneti, 1534). Based upon Aris-

totelian theory, his system comprised the following divisions:

    Philosophy
    "Realis"
       Practical
         Mechanical

> Moral
>> Ethics
>> Economics
>> Politics
> Speculative
>> Natural
>>> Astronomy
>>> Music
>> Mathematical
>>> Arithmetic
>>> Geometry
>> Metaphysics
> "Rationalis"
>> Logic
>> Rhetoric
>> Poetics

It is interesting to compare a few early library catalogs with the classification systems thus far described to show to what extent the classification of knowledge had developed into plans for practical application to collections of books by the end of the fifteenth century. The examples given are taken from Dorothy Norris' history of cataloging. [12]

The Priory of Christchurch, a Benedictine foundation at Canterbury, had a catalog compiled not later than 1170. Written on four leaves at the end of a manuscript of Boethius' _Music_ _and_ _Arithmetic_, it contained the following classes:

> Grammar
> Rhetoric
> Music
> Philosophy
> Poetry
> Astronomy
> Miscellaneous
> Logic, Dialectic, and Law

Miss Norris writes that the catalog is obviously merely a fragment since it contains not a single Bible.

A second catalog of this same library, compiled between 1313-1331, contained a few more classes and a different arrangement:

> Theology
> Chronicles, Martyrologies, Monastic Rules
> English books
> Books kept in the cloisters
> Passionals, Lectionaries
> Grammar
> Rhetoric
> Dialectic

Philosophy
Arithmetic and Music
Physic

The Friars Eremites of the Augustinian Order at York compiled a catalog of their library in 1372. The 646 titles of the library, fairly large for the time, were entered in the following classes:

Bibles
Scholastic history
Texts of the Bible with commentaries
Commentaries (Postille)
Concordances
Patristic and later church writers (Originalia)
History of the people
Books on the Sentences
Indexes
Logic and philosophy
Prophecy and superstition
Astronomy and astrology
Civil law
Canon law
Works by foreign writers
Grammar
Rhetoric
Medicine
History and chronicles
Sermons
Arithmetic, music, geometry, perspective

On Christmas Eve, 1418, a catalog of the Peterhouse Library, Cambridge, was drawn up. Following the Statutes, the books were entered according "to what faculty they belong" in the following divisions:

Theology
Natural philosophy
Metaphysics
Moral philosophy

Astronomy
Alchemy
Arithmetic
Music
Geometry
Rhetoric
Logic
Grammar
Poetry
Chronicles
Medicine
Civil Law
Canon Law

Just as these early catalogs illustrate the application of divisions of knowledge to book arrangement, the first encyclopedias also show a similar influence.

Gregor Reisch (d. 1525), prior of the Carthusians at Freiburg and confessor to Emperor Maximilian I, compiled the first German encyclopedia, the <u>Margarita</u> <u>Philosophica</u>. Both the place and date of the publication of his work are uncertain: Heidelberg, 1496, or Freiberg, 1503. Reisch's compendium was popular and published in numerous editions. Stephen Hawes not only based his didactic poem, <u>The</u> <u>Passetyme</u> <u>of Pleasure</u> (1509), upon Reisch's work but even copied three woodcuts of the Freiberg edition.

Reisch's work contained twelve books, which recorded, in the following divisions, the knowledge of his time – from the liberal arts to Philosophy and Theology:

    Grammar
    Dialectic
    Rhetoric
    Arithmetic
    Music
    Geometry
    Astronomy
    Natural History
        Principles
        Origins
    Vegetative and sentient powers
    Rational Psychology
    Moral Philosophy
        Philosophy proper
        Theology

Not satisfied with the pedagogic order he followed in his book, Reisch added, on the page following the table of contents, a more philosophic arrangement of the sciences. He divided Knowledge into Theoretical, or Speculative, and Practical, a plan obviously derived from that of Hugo of St. Victor. Reisch's chart provided the following order:

    Theoretical (Speculative)
    "Realis"
        Metaphysical
            Divine
            Human
        Mathematical
            Arithmetic
            Geometry
            Music
            Astronomy
        Physical (Natural history and philosophy)
    Rational
        Grammar
        Rhetoric
        Logic

```
Practical
  "Activa"
    Ethics
    Politics
    Economics
  "Monastica"
  "Factius" (Mechanical arts)
```

Konrad Gesner (1516-1565), Swiss-German naturalist and writer, "The German Pliny," used a classification in his four-volume Bibliotheca Universalis[13] which Edward Edwards, noted British librarian, called the first bibliographical system. Gesner's system, however, was but a minor rearrangement of the elements contained in those just described. His divisions of knowledge first appeared in 1548 in the "Ordo Librorum Huius Operis," of the Pandectarum, which formed the second volume of the Bibliotheca Universalis. In this work the twenty-one divisions, or "books," are given in simple tabular form following the title page. A more elaborate table grouped these divisions but did not appear until 1549, when the Partitiones Theologicae, third volume of the great work, was published. Gesner's system follows on page 80.

Johann Heinrich Alsted (1588-1638), a German theologian, arranged his Encyclopaedia[14] in seven broad divisions. He further subdivided into thirty-five books to provide for all the knowledge of the early seventeenth century. His plan provided:

I. Preliminary disciplines: Intellectual habits and classification, origin and study of the arts

II. Philology: Dictionaries, grammar, rhetoric, logic, oratory, and poetry

III. Theoretic philosophy: Metaphysics, pneumatology, physics, arithmetic, geometry, cosmography, astronomy and astrology, geography, optics, and music

IV. Practical philosophy: Ethics, economics, politics, and education

V. The superior faculties: Theology, jurisprudence, and medicine

VI. Mechanical arts (general): Mathematical mechanical arts, agriculture, gardening, animal care, baking, brewing, pharmacy, metallurgy (and mining), physical mechanical arts, printing, etc.

VII. Mixed arts: Mnemonics, history, chronology, architecture, etc. [15]

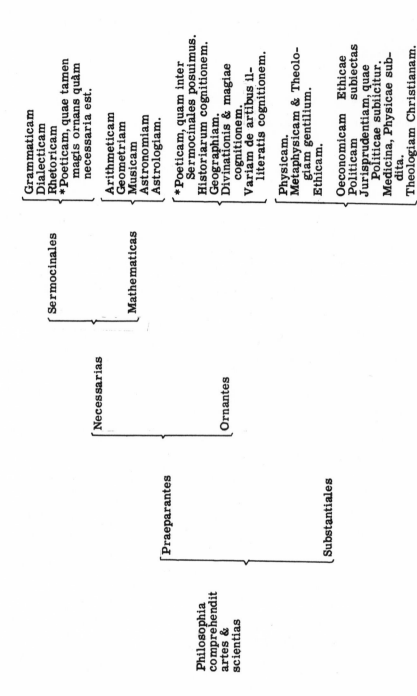

Philosophia comprehendit artes & scientias

Praeparantes

  Necessarias

    Sermocinales
- Grammaticam
- Dialecticam
- Rhetoricam
- *Poeticam, quae tamen magis ornans quàm necessaria est.

    Mathematicas
- Arithmeticam
- Geometriam
- Musicam
- Astronomiam
- Astrologiam.

  Ornantes
- *Poeticam, quam inter Sermocinales posuimus.
- Historiarum cognitionem.
- Geographiam.
- Divinationis & magiae cognitionem.
- Variam de artibus il-literatis cognitionem.

Substantiales
- Physicam.
- Metaphysicam & Theologiam gentilium.
- Ethicam.
- Oeconomicam Politicam Jurisprudentiam; quae Politicae subiicitur. } Ethicae subiectas
- Medicina, Physicae sub-dita.
- Theologiam Christianam.

Alsted's work illustrates the dependence of each succeeding classification designer on the work of his predecessors. The <u>artes liberales</u> of Varro, Aristotle's "Theoretical and Practical," the Faculties, Theology, Jurisprudence, and Medicine are here in a slightly new arrangement.

As this stream of development in the classification of knowledge is followed further, one philosopher is found to have had a more direct influence on American library classification. This was Francis Bacon. Bacon was born in London on January 22, 1561, son of Sir Nicholas Bacon, Lord Keeper of the Great Seal, and Anne Cooke, daughter of Sir Anthony Cooke, tutor to Edward VI. He was educated at home and entered Trinity College, Cambridge, when he was twelve years old. In 1576 he began the study of law at Gray's Inn but left the same year to go to Paris with Sir Amyas Paulet, Queen Elizabeth's ambassador to France. Bacon remained in France until the sudden death of his father in 1579 brought him back to England and Gray's Inn. He was admitted to the bar in 1582 and two years later secured a seat in the House of Commons, where he took an active part in debate until he went to the House of Lords. Bacon became counselor to the Earl of Essex, who tried to have Bacon, still in his thirties, made Attorney-General, but the Queen appointed Sir Edward Coke to the vacancy in 1595.

Under Elizabeth, Bacon's advancement in the public service was slow, but after the accession of James he became successively King's Counsel and, in 1607, Solicitor-General. In 1613 he was appointed Attorney-General and in 1617 obtained the Great Seal with the title of Lord Keeper. A year later he became Lord Chancellor and was created Baron Verulam.

Bacon was made Viscount St. Albans on January 27, 1621. Three days later Parliament met, and his political enemies, of whom he had more than a few, accused the Viscount of bribery in accepting gifts from litigants in his court. Although the gifts were customary at the time, Bacon was found technically guilty and removed from office. A commonplace book of Rawley's records Bacon's comment on the decision, "I was the justest judge that was in England these fifty years. But it was the justest censure in Parliament that was these two hundred years." Bacon retired to Gorhambury. He died on Easter Sunday, April 9, 1626.

Philosopher as well as statesman, Bacon early became concerned with classification. "I have taken all knowledge to be my province," he wrote to Lord Burghley in 1592. In 1605 he published his famous Advancement of Learning, summarizing, in the closing paragraph of this classification and survey of knowledge, what he had attempted to do: "Thus have I made as it were a small globe of the intellectual world, as truly and faithfully as I could discover; with a note and description of those parts which seem to me not constantly occupate, or not well converted by the labour of man." By destiny, if not design, the Advancement was to form part of Bacon's ambitious project to regenerate man's knowledge by a new method of science. [16]

Bacon was sixty when he published, in 1620, the Novum Organum, intended to be the second part of the Instauratio Magna, which he did not live to complete. In this work he referred readers to the Advancement of Learning as representing the first part, the classification and survey of knowledge. This was merely an interim reference, however, for Bacon, growing old, hastily revised and expanded the work, had it translated into Latin, and published it in 1623 as De Augmentis Scientiarum. The second book of the Advancement, dealing with classification, was expanded to eight.

Bacon's classification has been frequently garbled and misinterpreted. The fault is in part Bacon's, for he used many terms (physics, metaphysics, magic, causation, etc.) in nontraditional senses. To this difficulty must be added his style, which his mother described as "enigmatic folded writing." In addition, most of his biographers and critics have been literary men with no great knowledge of philosophy. Add to these difficulties the fact that his classification, the so-called "Partitiones Scientiarum," must be extracted from paragraph and chapter headings and from the text in which the sequence of divisions frequently varies, and there is little wonder that Bacon has been misunderstood.

Bacon first divided man's knowledge, [17] on the basis of the source
from which it was derived, into:

1. Human knowledge: "information derived from the sense," and

2. Theology: "information derived from revelation."

These differ both in matter and in the manner of conveyance; "they are like
different liquids poured into the same vessel, the human mind." Human knowledge begins with sensation, which is the door of the intellect. Only individuals affect sensation but the sense impressions of these individuals, their
images as it were, fix themselves in memory. The human mind then reviews
them "and thereupon either simply rehearses them, or makes fanciful imita-
tions of them, or analyses and classifies them. Wherefore from these three
fountains, Memory, Imagination, and Reason, flow these three emanations, History, Poesy, and Philosophy; and there can be no others." Bacon also applied
these subdivisions to Theology and thought that no others were needed:

1. Sacred history, including prophecy, which is history "before the
   event,"

2. Parables, which are "a divine poesy," and

3. Doctrines or Precepts, which form "a perennial philosophy."

In Human Learning, or Knowledge, history records the deeds and works
of Nature and of Man and gives rise to Natural History and Civil History.
Founded upon the conditions of nature, Natural History reflects its threefold
state: free, erring, or moulded by the hand of Man. Its divisions therefore are
the History of Generations, of Pretergenerations, and of Arts or Mechanical
and Experimental History. Civil History records the deeds and works of men,
and may rightly be divided into Sacred or Ecclesiastical, Civil History proper, and the History of Learning and the Arts. There are in addition certain
appendices to History which deal with the words of men, as History itself deals
with their actions: Orations, Letters, and Apophthegms.

The second principal part of Learning is Poesy, feigned history or fables, which is divided into Narrative, Dramatic, and Parabolical. Narrative

Poesy is a mere imitation of History, which "might pass for real, only that it commonly exaggerates things beyond probability." Dramatic Poesy is "History made visible, for it represents actions as if they were present, whereas History represents them as past." Parabolical Poesy is "typical History, by which ideas that are objects of the intellect are represented in forms that are objects of the sense." Verse as a character of speech or style belongs with the Arts of Speech in Philosophy. [18]

> All History, excellent King [James], walks upon the earth, and per-
> forms the office rather of a guide than of a light; whereas Poesy
> is as a dream of learning; a thing sweet and varied, and that would
> be thought to have in it something divine; a character which dreams
> likewise affect. But now it is time for me to awake, and rising
> above the earth, to wing my way through the clear air of Philoso-
> phy and the Sciences. 19

"The knowledge of man is as the waters. Some waters descend from above, and some spring from beneath." It can therefore be divided into Divinity (Sacred or Inspired) and Philosophy. Philosophy has three objects: God, Nature, and Man, but common to all, "mother of the rest," is the universal science, "Philosophia Prima" or "Sapience," which comprises the basic principles and axioms of all knowledge.

The knowledge, or rudiment of knowledge, of God which man obtains by the light of nature and the contemplation of His creatures yields Natural Theology, or Divine Philosophy. The doctrine concerning Angels and Spirits, good and evil, forms an appendix to the division.

The second division of Philosophy is concerned with Nature and can be divided into two parts: the Speculative (the Inquisition into Causes) and the Operative (the Production of Effects). These resemble the mine and the furnace and make two occupations of natural philosophers, the miner and the smith, "The one searching into the bowels of nature, the other shaping nature as on an anvil." Physic, concerned with Efficient and Material Causes, and Metaphysic, with Formal and Final Causes, constitute the Speculative division. Corresponding to these in the Operative division are Mechanic, concerned with Efficient and Material Causes, and Magic, with Formal and Material

Causes. Following Natural Philosophy is its great Appendix, Mathematic, which is subdivided into Pure and Mixed.

The third main division of natural knowledge deals with Man. It comprises the Philosophy of Humanity, which is concerned with Man Segregate, and Civil Philosophy, which is the study of Man Congregate and in Society. Mind and Body form the divisions of the Philosophy of Humanity, but before considering the divisions it is necessary to constitute a general science, the Nature and State of Man composed of those things which are common to the body as well as to the soul. The studies concerned with the Body of Man are based upon four goods: Health, Beauty, Strength, and Pleasure, which yield the divisions Medicine, Cosmetic, Athletic, and Voluptuary.

Human Philosophy, relating to the Soul, is first divided into the Doctrine concerning the Breath of Life (the rational soul), and the Doctrine concerning the Sensible or Produced Soul. The Doctrine of the Soul is next divided, according to the use and objects of its faculties, into Logic and Ethic. Logic comprises the Arts of Discovering, of Judging, of Retaining, and of Transmitting – the arts of understanding and communicating. Ethics, or moral knowledge, is divided into the Exemplar or Platform of Good, and Georgics, the Culture of the Mind. Bacon's last division, Civil Knowledge, is subdivided according to the three summary actions of Society, or the kinds of good which men seek in society: Conversation, comfort against solitude; Negotiation, assistance in business; and Empire or Government, protection against injuries.

"Now let us come to that learning which the two former periods have not been so blessed as to know, namely, Sacred or Inspired Divinity, the most noble Sabbath and port of all men's labours and peregrinations. " However, Bacon never divided Revealed Theology beyond the History, Poesy, and Philosophy he mentioned at the beginning; he devoted his book on theology to a survey of three areas where he found deficiencies.

Although Bacon's classification was widely influential it was rarely adopted in its original form. And strangely enough the systems which derive

from Bacon failed to preserve his first division of knowledge into Divine
and Human, but, instead, classified Revealed with Natural Theology.

This, then, is the partial story of the stream of classification which
eventually reached the shores of the New World in the latter part of the seventeenth century. Limitations of time and space have precluded a more detailed account of the development of all the systems which drew from edu-
cators, from philosophers, and from early librarians, the methods of presenting the subject resources of libraries.

CHAPTER V

New World Pioneers

The classifications used in early American libraries were part of the tradition of library organization which the colonists brought with them from the Old World. Some of these systems were quite simple, one even humorous, but they represented the attempts of pioneer American librarians to introduce order into the arrangement of their book collections. If the divisions of their schemes seem broad and few, it must be remembered that the divisions of the knowledge of the eighteenth century were broad and few, as were the contents and number of the books containing that knowledge. But, however simple, these systems have more than an antiquarian interest, for they continued the old patterns of library order which led to the classifications we use in the twentieth century.

1693 Samuel Lee.

The earliest book classification published in the United States was in a sales catalog issued in 1693 by Duncan Campbell, a Boston bookseller. It was The Library of the Late Reverend and Learned Mr. Samuel Lee. The catalog[1] "created quite a sensation in the literary circles of New England, " for it contained a thousand well selected and diversified titles.

Lee was born in London in 1625, the only son of Samuel Lee, a well-to-do London haberdasher. He prepared for college at St. Paul's School, then entered Oxford University in 1640 at the age of fifteen. In 1648 he received the degree of Master of Arts and became a fellow of Wadham College. Cromwell gave him the living of St. Botolph's, Bishopsgate, where he remained "until silenced and ejected in 1682. " Lee sailed for New England with his family in 1686 and settled in Bristol, Rhode Island, where he founded the "First Church" and was its first pastor. Cotton Mather said of Lee that "hardly ever a more Universally Learned Person trod the American Strand. "[2]

After the accession of William III to the throne of England, Lee decided to return home. He sailed with his family from Boston on the _Dolphin_. When the ship neared the Irish coast after a stormy passage, it was seized by a French privateer. Lee's family was permitted to return to England, but he was held as a prisoner in St. Malo, France. He died in December 1691 at the age of sixty-four, victim of a "prison fever" induced by depression, solitude, and the rigors of winter.

The catalog of Lee's library listed his books by language, size, and subject – from Biblia Polyglatta, under "Latin Folio's Divinity," to Frazius de Hist: Animalium, under "Miscelany Books Latin Octavo's." The subject divisions were:

1. Divinity
2. Physical Books
3. Philosophy
4. Mathematical, Astrological and Astronomical
5. History
6. School Authors
7. Juris Prudentia
8. Miscelany

1697 Thomas Bray.

The first classification used in American libraries was the classification of religious topics contained in the Bibliotheca Parochialis of the Reverend Thomas Bray, published in London in 1697.

Bray was born at Marton, in Shropshire, England, in 1656. After graduation from All Souls College, Oxford, in 1678, he entered the ministry, where his ability so impressed Bishop Compton of London that he named him Commissary of the Anglican Church in Maryland. The new Commissary became interested in libraries when he found that the only clergymen he could recruit for service in Maryland were too poor to buy books. Perhaps the example of the Reverend Thomas Rawlet, who bequeathed his library to his native town, Tamworth, for the use of the clergy, led Bray to develop a system of parochial libraries. The first library, comprising 1,005 volumes, was sent to Annapolis, Maryland, in 1697. Through Bray's efforts 34,000 volumes were shipped to the British Colonies to establish libraries from Newfoundland to Georgia. Bray died in London in 1730, but his activities were continued by "Dr. Bray's

Associates for founding clerical libraries and supporting negro schools."

Bray's classification of religion, which was quite detailed, comprised

ten main divisions and many subdivisions. His main divisions were:

    I.   Upon the Divine Existence and Providence.
    II.   Upon Natural Religion.
    III. Upon the Scripture.
    IV. To prove the Truth, and to understand the Design of Christianity.
    V.   For Bodies of Divinity.
    VI. Upon the Doctrine of the Covenant of Grace.
    VII. On the Means enabling us to perform the Covenant.
    VIII. Sermons.
    IX. Controversies.
    X.   Ministerial Instructions.

Of greater interest and importance, however, was the more worldly

classification which served as the basis of the arrangement of the "Regis-

ter"[3] of books Bray sent to Trinity Parish, New York, in 1698. This was his

"Compleat Scheme of the severall Sciences or Parts of necessary and Use-

full Knowledge."[4] Bray first divided knowledge on the basis of its source, in-

to divine and "humane," but, like many of his predecessors, added Metaphys-

ics and Pneumatology to the science of God. Then, as if not fully convinced,

he divided the human sciences into the traditional two groups: 1) those con-

cerned with Things, and 2) those concerned with Words. His complete system,

omitting the many subdivisions he made in Theology, provides:

Divine
   Theology
   Metaphysics
   Pneumatology

Humane
   Things
     Ethics
     Economics
     Politics
     Law
     History
       Geography
       Voyages
       Travels
     Physiology
     Natural Philosophy
     Medicine
     Chemistry
     Pharmocopy
     Anatomy
     Chirurgery

        Mathematics
        Trade and Commerce
    Words
        Grammar
        Rhetoric
        Poetry
        Logic

Although Bray's classification followed Lee's by four years, it is of more interest in that it was the first scheme actually used in an American library.

1723 Harvard College.

The 400 volumes which the Reverend John Harvard bequeathed to Harvard College in 1638, two years after its founding, had grown to 3,500 before a catalog of the library was published. As early as 1667 the college laws provided for the compilation of a catalog in three parts:

> First in the order as they are placed & disposed according to the affixed catalogue. Secondly, In one continued Alphabet setting down the Authors name & what of his works are in the Library & where. Thirdly, The Names of the Severall Donors of ye Books with the Books given by them. [5]

At least two early manuscript catalogs were compiled, but it was not until April 1722 that the Harvard Corporation voted to have a catalog printed to transmit to friends of the college abroad. Upon Joshua Gee, librarian of the college (1721-22), fell the task of preparation.

Gee was born in Boston on June 29, 1698, the son of a prominent shipbuilder of the same name. He graduated from Harvard in 1717 and took his A. M. in course. On December 18, 1723, Gee was ordained pastor of the Old North, or Second, Church in Boston, where he became the colleague of the Reverend Cotton Mather. He remained at this church until his death on May 22, 1748.

Gee spent five months in the compilation of his catalog but left the library before his work was published. It was printed the following year in a small quarto volume of 106 pages, with the title Catalogus Librorum Bibliothecae Collegij Harvardini quod est Cantabrigiae in Nova Anglia (Bostoni Nov-Anglorum: Typis B. Green, Academiae Typographi. MDCCXXIII). [6] This is probably the first public library catalog printed in the British Colonies of America. Actually it comprises three catalogs: "Librorum in Folio, Catalogus;" "Librorum in Quarto, Catalogus;" and "Librorum in Octavo, Duodecimo, &c, Catalogus. " In each the titles are arranged in an order that is only roughly alphabetical. At the left of each entry Gee indicated its location: bookcase, shelf, and book number. The pluteis, or bookcases, were called "classes, " a term which had come into use in the University Library, Cambridge, England, in 1584, superseding the older "stall. " Gee's classification provided the following divisions:

    Theology
    Jurisprudence
    Civil History
    Natural History
    Philosophy
    Natural Philosophy (Physics)
    Philology
    Mathematical sciences: mathematics, optics, navigation, etc.
    Medicine

In England, the same year, Conyers Middleton, Academiae Proto-Bibliothecarius of Cambridge University, presented to the authorities a new system of classification[7] comprising eight divisions:

    Theology
    Profane History
    Civil Law
    Philosophy (propriè dicta)
    Mathematics
    Natural History
    Medicine
    Humane Letters

The similarity of the divisions, if not their sequence, indicates that Gee and Middleton adopted, as most classifiers do, the divisions of knowledge common in their time.

1730?   Mr. Procter's Et Cetera.

"This Day is Published a Catalogue of the valuable Library, the Property of the Estate of the late Hon. William Byrd, Esq.; consisting of near 4000 volumes, in all Languages and Faculties, contained in twenty three double presses ... and the Executrix will treat with those who are inclined to purchase the Whole. "[8] And so began the dispersal of one of the finest libraries of Colonial America. [9]

William Byrd II, born in Virginia in 1664, was sent to England at an early age to be educated. He returned to the Colonies in 1696 and was elected a member of the Virginia Assembly. Byrd went back to England to act as agent for Virginia but returned to America after the death of his father, in 1704, to succeed to his estate. He built Westover, one of the finest existing examples of Georgian architecture in America, on the north side of the James, 25 miles from Williamsburg. His library occupied a full wing of the main house, its walls lined with black walnut cases filled with 3,625 volumes. Byrd died in 1744 and his estate passed to his son William Byrd III. When the third William died in 1777 his widow was forced to sell the library to provide for her eight children.

The legend "J. Stretch fecit" appears on the original copy of the Catalogue, but the order of the books is probably that which William Procter[10] devised for their shelving at Westover. Procter, a Scotchman, was librarian, secretary, and tutor at Westover. And at least once, when he had complained of a lack of candles to read by at night, he became to his employer "Most hypochondrack Sir"; Byrd wrote him, "I have your complaints last night which you drew up into the Form of a letter to save your Blushes."[11]

Whatever virtues the melancholy Procter possessed as secretary and tutor he lacked in his third capacity, that of librarian. His classification provided the following:

1. History, Voyages, Travels, etc.
2. Law, Tryals, etc.
3. Physick, etc.
4. Entertainment, Poetry, Translations, etc.
5. Divinity, etc.
6. French Books, Chiefly of Entertainment
7. Classicks and Other Latin and Greek Authors

Despite the et ceteras there was an eighth division for "Unclassified," which contained books on most of the preceding subjects.

1731 Samuel Johnson.

The first edition of Samuel Johnson's essay in the classification of knowledge, which was to culminate in the Noetica of 1752, was published anonymously

in The Present State of the Republick of Letters for May 1731. [12] It had been
forwarded to the journal by "P. N." who wrote, "I make bold to send you here
a Scheme for a general Partition of the Sciences, drawn up by a Friend of
mine, which seems to me very well calculated to give the Youth a good general Notion of the Nature, Order, and Use of the Sciences." A second and enlarged edition was distributed to the students of Yale College with T. Clap's
1743 Catalogue of the Yale Library, [13] thus giving birth to the belief that the
classification was Clap's work. In 1752 the third revision, called Noetica, [14]
left the presses of B. Franklin and D. Hall, at the "New-Printing-Office, near
the Market," in Philadelphia. In the same year it was combined with a second edition of Ethices Elements under the title Elementa Philosophica, [15]
and in 1767 with another of Johnson's works. [16]

Johnson was born in Guilford, Connecticut, on October 14, 1696, the son
of Deacon Samuel Johnson. He received an A. B. from the Collegiate School
in Saybrook (Yale College) in 1714. When the school moved to New Haven two
years later, Johnson became a tutor, although but eighteen years old. He became pastor of the Congregational Church at West Haven but left to become
a member of the Church of England. After his ordination by the Bishop of Norwich in 1723 he became minister at Stratford — the only Church of England
minister in Connecticut. In 1750 Benjamin Franklin urged him to become
president of the new college that was being established in Philadelphia. Johnson refused, but later became the first president of King's College (Columbia
University) in 1753. He resigned after ten years to resume parochial duties
in Stratford, where he died on January 6, 1772, in his seventy-sixth year.

When Bishop Berkeley, then Dean of Derry, came to America in February
of 1729 and lived for two and a half years at Newport, Rhode Island, Johnson
sought an introduction, "that he might converse with so extraordinary a genius
and so great a scholar." He later corresponded with the Bishop, but although
indebted to him intellectually, Johnson remained an independent thinker. It was
to Berkeley, Bishop of Cloyne by that time, that Johnson dedicated the Noetica,

prefacing it with a quotation from the Bishop's <u>De Motu</u>:

> <u>Quod</u> <u>si</u> <u>cuique</u> <u>scientiae</u> <u>provincia</u> <u>sua</u> <u>tribuatur</u>, <u>limites</u> <u>assignen-</u>
> <u>tur</u>, <u>principia</u> <u>&</u> <u>objecta</u> accurate <u>distinguantur</u>, <u>quae</u> <u>ad</u> <u>singulas</u>
> <u>pertinent</u>, <u>tractare</u> <u>licuerit</u>, <u>majore</u>, <u>tum</u> <u>facilitate</u>, <u>tum</u> <u>perspicuitate</u>.

> [Allot to each science its own province; assign its bounds; accurate-
> ly distinguish the principles and objects belonging to each. Thus it
> will be possible to treat them with greater ease and clarity.] [17]

Johnson briefly described his purpose:

> THIS little Tract I have introduced with a short <u>General</u> <u>View</u>
> of the whole <u>System</u> of <u>Learning</u>, wherein young Students may at once
> behold, as it were in Miniature, the Objects, Boundaries, Ends and
> Uses of each of the Sciences; their Foundation in the Nature of
> Things; the natural Order wherein they lie, and their several Rela-
> tions and Connections, both with Respect to one another, and to the
> general End, viz. <u>our</u> <u>Happiness,</u> pursued thro' them all.

Like Bray he found that all knowledge could be divided into Things and Words.

> LEARNING implies the Knowledge of every Thing useful to
> our Well-being and true Happiness in this Life, or our supreme
> Happiness in the Life to come. And as our <u>Happiness</u> consists in
> the Enjoyment of <u>Truth</u> and <u>Good</u>, by the right Exercise of our Un-
> derstandings, Affections, Wills and active Powers, it must take in
> every Thing that relates both to <u>Theory</u> and <u>Practice</u>, i. e. both to
> <u>Science</u> and <u>Art</u>; for <u>Science</u> is the Knowledge of Truth considered
> speculatively, and <u>Art</u> is the Knowledge of Truth considered as di-
> rective of our Practice for the attaining our true Good or Happi-
> ness. And all the various Parts of Learning may be reduced to
> these two, <u>Philology</u>, or the Study of <u>Words</u> and other Signs, and
> <u>Philosophy</u>, or the Study of the <u>Things</u> signified by them.

The following is an example of Johnson's method of subdivision and reasoning:

> <u>Ethics</u> explain the Laws of our Duty as we are Men
> in general, and which indeed are the eternal and immutable
> Laws of Right that equally bind all intelligent Creatures.
> But as we cannot well subsist without being combined into
> particular <u>Societies</u>: And as Societies are of two Kinds; the
> one founded in Nature, <u>viz.</u> <u>Families</u>, the other in Compact,
> <u>viz.</u> <u>Civil</u> <u>Governments</u>: Hence spring two other Branches of
> <u>Moral</u> <u>Philosophy</u>, viz. <u>OEconomics</u>, which relate to the Regu-
> lation of <u>Families</u>; and <u>Politicks,</u> which treat of the Consti-
> tution and good Government of <u>Cities</u>, <u>Kingdoms</u> and <u>Repub-</u>
> <u>licks</u>. And as good <u>Policy</u> provides for every Thing that
> may contribute to the publick Good and Happiness of Man-
> kind, it does, in Effect, comprehend and sum up the whole
> of <u>Philosophy</u>. And, lastly, as it provides for the Happiness
> of Men, both <u>Temporal</u> and <u>Spiritual</u>, both with Regard to
> this Life, and that which is to come, it must consist of two
> great Branches, <u>viz.</u> <u>Civil</u> and <u>Ecclesiastical</u> <u>Policy</u>. And
> the Facts in the <u>Moral</u> <u>World</u> are related in <u>Biography</u>, and
> in <u>Civil</u> and <u>Ecclesiastical</u> <u>History</u>. The whole may be seen
> in one View in the following Table.

CYCLOPAEDIA, is the whole Circle of Learning, or the Knowledge of every Thing that may contribute to our Happiness, both in Theory and Practice, and consists of two Parts.

I. Philology, or the Study of Language or Signs, called also Humanity, and the Belles Lettres, and is,

- 1. General, or common to all Kinds of Speaking, in
  - 1. Grammar, of pure Language.
  - 2. Rhetorick, of figurative Speech.
- 2. Special, of particular Kinds of Speaking or Writing, as
  - 1. Oratory, which treats of Eloquence.
  - 2. History, which relates real Facts.
  - 3. Poetry, which describes Things in an elevated Manner, whether real or imaginary; and to all these belongs the Art of Criticism.

II. Philosophy, or the Study of Wisdom, being the Knowledge of Things, together with Practice correspondent thereto, in both which consists our Happiness. All Things or Beings are,

- 1. Bodies, or sensible Things, which constitute the natural World, the Knowledge of which is, in a large Sense, called Physicks, or Natural Philosophy, and is,
  - 1. General, of the common Affections of Bodies, Number and Magnitude, in Mathematicks, including Arithmetick and Geometry.
  - 2. Special, of all particular Things in the natural World: Particularly,
    - 1. Natural History, which gives an Account of Facts in all Nature.
    - 2. Mechanicks, of the Laws of Motion.
    - 3. Geology, of this terraqueous Globe, and all Things in it, inanimate and animate. And,
    - 4. Astronomy, of the Heavens and Stars, and the whole Mundane System.
    - Under each of which Heads there are many practical Matters.
- Or,
- 2. Spirits, or intelligent moral Beings, which constitute the intelligent or moral World, the Knowledge of which, in a large Sense of the Words, may be called Metaphysics, and Moral Philosophy, and is,
  - First, Speculative, or what relates to the Knowledge of intellectual Beings.
    - 1. In General, the Noetics or Logic, including both Ontology and Dialectic of the Conduct of the Mind in Thinking or Reasoning.
    - 2. In Special, Pneumatology, of the several Kinds of created Intelligences.
    - 3. Theology, of the Deity, the Father and Lord of them all.
  - Second, Practical, or what relates to Life and Conduct, in our several Capacities, personal and social.
    - 1. Ethics, of the Conduct of our Temper and Behaviour in general, in order to Happiness.
    - 2. OEconomics, of the Conduct of Families. And,
    - 3. Politics, of the Government of States, Civil and Ecclesiastical; to which relate Biography, and Civil and Ecclesiastical History.

The critical Mr. Woodward observed:

> If we may now be permitted to traverse the Atlantic, we shall
> find that, at the very same time that D'Alembert was, in France, en-
> gaged in devising improvements on the system of Lord Bacon; an
> attempt was making, in America, to produce a system entirely original.
> . . . .
> No partiality for my country, or my countrymen, but a sin-
> cere veneration for truth, induces the declaration; that of all the
> systems which have hitherto appeared, whether in ancient times, or
> in modern days, that of Dr. Johnson is esteemed the best. The anal-
> ysis is wonderfully close. It is astonishing how much is comprized
> in the system, and in how small a space, and with what correct ar-
> rangement. The whole is marked with one of the singular qualities
> of the American character, sound unerring good sense. No licen-
> tiousness, of principle or of imagination, will be discovered; no van-
> ity, no pedantry, no affectation. Neither the system, nor the author,
> such was the humility of our country, ever attained any celebrity;
> and, yet, the system is infinitely preferable to that of Lord Bacon,
> with all the improvements effected by D'Alembert. The unassum-
> ing American mind, operating with its native clearness and dignity,
> takes a flight beyond the proudest genius of Britain, and of France.
> Dr. Johnson entitles his short system "a general scheme for
> the partitions of the sciences, according to the natural order of
> things; or, a synopsis of all the parts of learning."
> For learning in general; implying the knowledge of every
> thing, whether speculative or practical, which is conducive either
> to our present felicity, or to our future happiness; he adopts,from
> the Greeks, the term cyclopaedia.
> To know, and to practise, these are the two ingredients of
> our happiness; and constitute the essential means without which
> the great end cannot be pursued.
> The distinction between sciences and arts, characterized
> by perplexity and inutility, is entirely neglected; and knowledge
> is regarded as holding, throughout, its speculative and its practi-
> cal parts in inseparable combination.
> All human knowledge is then reduced to two grand and cap-
> ital departments. The first of these is that of the belles lettres.
> The second is that of philosophy.
> The department of the belles lettres, or of philological arts
> and sciences, is divided into general and special. Grammar is
> correctly placed at the portal of the temple of science. The appli-
> cation of language to the gratification of taste, the investment of it
> with embellishment and beauty, elegantly, next occupy the attention.
> The alliance of rhetoric and grammar, which are common to all
> kinds of speech and of composition, closes the division of general
> philology. Four interesting, and well deduced, and well defined
> sciences, limit the range of special philology. These compose the
> fine and attractive family of eloquence, history, poetry, criticism.
> Six particular and specific sciences have the common base of hu-
> man language, and exhaust the great province or department of
> philology, or belles lettres; the knowledge and study of words, as
> instruments and means, to be applied, in the hands of man, in order
> to understand the nature of things.
> Philosophy; the second great province or department of hu-
> man learning, embracing the knowledge of things, and a corres-
> pondent rectitude of action; is divided into natural philosophy and
> moral philosophy. Truth and wisdom are the results produced.
> The natural and the moral world, material and intellectual beings,
> constitute the whole universe.

Arithmetic is here, again, with equal propriety, placed at the portal; and is allied to geömetry. They compose mathematics; and are precedent to mechanics, to physics, and to astronomy. These three latter sciences take in the whole material universe, and exhaust the natural world.

Metaphysics and ethics are the two branches which arise from the intellectual and moral world. Logic, pneumatology, and theology, compose the first; and ethics proper, oeconomics, and politics, the last. Seventeen important and conspicuous specific sciences are deduced, admirably concatenated, and judiciously named. Viewed as a whole, the system of the reverend Dr. Johnson transcends in solidity, and in beauty, every scientific edifice of antiquity; and all the structures of Bacon, of Locke, and of D'Alembert.[18]

Had Woodward not overlooked the whole Middle Ages he would have seen at once that Johnson's scheme was another variant in an old tradition.

1743 Yale College.

"I Have here with considerable Labour and Pains, prepared a Catalogue of the Books in the Library under proper Heads that so you may Readily know and find any Book, upon any particular Subject, " reads T. Clap's "Advertisement To the Students of Yale-College, " in his 1743 catalog of the library.[19]

Thomas Clap was born in Scituate, Massachusetts, June 26, 1703, the son of Deacon Stephen and Temperance Clap. Four years after his graduation from Harvard at the age of nineteen, Clap became minister of the Congregational Church in Windham, Connecticut. In 1739 he was appointed rector of Yale College (under the charter of 1745, president), a position he held for twenty-six years. Clap wrote on religion and astronomy and collected material for a history of Connecticut. He died in New Haven on January 7, 1767.

Clap counseled the students:

The Introduction to Philosophy[20] will give you a General Idea or Scheme of all the Arts and Sciences and the several things which are to be known and learnt: and this Catalogue will direct you to many of the best Books to be read in order to obtain the Knowledge of them. And I would advise you, my Pupils, to pursue a Regular Course of Academical Studies in some Measure according to the Order of this Catalogue. And in the First Year to Study principally the Tongues, Arithmetic and Algebra; the Second, Logic, Rhetoric and Geometry; the Third, Mathematics and Natural Philosophy; and the Fourth, Ethics and Divinity. Other less principal Studies may be occasionally intermix't with these. Above all have an Eye to the great End of all your Studies, which is to obtain the Clearest Conceptions of Divine Things and to lead you to a Saving Knowledge of GOD in his Son Jesus Christ.

The classification, which ranged from Language to Divinity, with some miscellaneous topics at the end, derives from Samuel Johnson. Clap, however, rearranged Johnson's order and introduced new subdivisions, chiefly under Divinity. His classification contained the following divisions:

    Languages
    Logic
    Rhetoric
    Oratory
    Poetry
    Mathematics
    Natural Philosophy
        Botany or Agriculture
        Zoology or Animals
    Antient Philosophy, Natural and Moral
    Anatomy, Physick and Chyrurgery
    Pneumatology
    Metaphysicks
    Geography
    History [including "Ecclesiastical Histories"]
    Antiquities
    Voyages and Travels
    Lives of Famous Men
    Chronology
    Ethics, or Essays on Morality
    Divinity
    Law-Books
    Works on Various Kinds of Subjects
    Particular Treatises on Various Subjects
    Miscellaneous Essays
    Political Essays
    Plays and Books of Diversion

The entries in each division were made without too much regard for the alphabet, and opposite each its location was given: "The First Number signifies the Teer, the Second the Box; and the Third the Number of the Book: Where there is a Fourth, it signifies several Volumes or Duplicates. And where there are Two or more Setts of Numbers they signify the same Sort of Books in divers places."

Just as Jefferson's classification reveals his special interests, so does Clap's classification indicate his — mathematics and astronomy. He is said to have made the first orrery, an early form of planetarium, in America. John Worthington (1719-1800), a tutor, assisted Clap in his "considerable Labour and Pains."

The classifications thus far described reveal that American library classification, like the culture of which it forms a part, was both derivative and original. Jefferson revamped d'Alembert's modification of Bacon's radical and illogical divisions of knowledge; Johnson's essay followed the conservative and realistic tradition which throughout the centuries had been modified and expanded by philosophers and specialists to adapt it to man's increasing knowledge; Gee's divisions parallel those of Conyers Middleton; and even Mr. Procter's scheme created some order despite its cross divisions and "et ceteras."

CHAPTER VI

Simplicity and Complexity

Although classifications are based upon existing divisions of knowledge, arranged according to contemporary patterns of organization, many permutations are possible. It is the librarian, with his individual training and predilections, however, who creates the final order. Some librarians are content to adopt existing systems, some must adapt, but there are also those who must create new schemes. All three are seen in the present chapter, from the simple to the complex.

1764 The Redwood Library.

When George Berkeley visited Newport, Rhode Island, in June 1729, he found a prosperous city, fourth largest in New England, undergoing a cultural awakening. Newport's ships brought back the best products of the presses of England, and of Geneva and Amsterdam as well. These books were read and discussed, handed down as heirlooms from father to son. Berkeley found the love of learning so great that he determined to establish in Newport the college he had originally planned for Bermuda. When the necessary funds could not be found, Berkeley, discouraged, sailed home to England in the autumn of 1731.

During the last year of the Dean's stay in Newport, the Literary and Philosophical Society was founded there. The origin of the society had often been ascribed to Berkeley, but the facts do not support the contention.[1] That he was a member and found "congenial companions" among the other members, one of whom was the Reverend Samuel Johnson of Stratford, is reasonably certain. From this debating society, as from Franklin's Junto, an important library was destined to grow, the result of the generosity of a "merchant prince" of the town, Abraham Redwood.

Redwood (1709-88) was born in Antigua, the son of Captain Abraham Redwood, who owned extensive sugar plantations on the West Indian island.

When he was two years old, his father brought him to Philadelphia, where he was educated. The death of his brother left Redwood in possession of the family estate in Antigua, "Cassada Garden, " when he was sixteen years old. Two years later he married Martha Coggeshall, of Newport, and settled there. Redwood became a member of the debating society and made it a generous gift of money when the members decided to establish a public library. The charter of the library, first read at a meeting in Newport on the last Wednesday of September 1747, records his generosity:

To all to whom these presents shall come, Greeting.

> Whereas, Abraham Redwood, Esquire, hath generously engaged to bestow five hundred pounds sterling, to be laid out in a collection of useful books suitable for a Public Library proposed to be erected in Newport aforesaid, and, having nothing in view but the good of mankind, hath chosen to make his donation as lasting and diffusive as possible ...[2]

A catalog[3] of the books, which had been purchased in London by John Thomlinson, Esq., was published in 1764. The librarian at the time was the Reverend Ezra Stiles (1727-95), clergyman and scholar, who later became president of Yale College.

The arrangement of the books in the catalog was a curious combination of size and subject; only the octavos were classified.

Books in Folio
Books in Quarto
Books in Octavo
   Classicks
   History
   Divinity and Morality
   Physick (Medicine)
   Law
   Natural History, Mathematics, etc.
   Arts, Liberal and Mechanical
   Miscellanies, Politics, etc.
Books in Duodecimo

Stiles's arrangement reflects, although in a different order, the divisions used in the catalog of Samuel Lee's library.

1789 Library Company of Philadelphia.

Benjamin Franklin's proposal to the members of the Junto, assembled in "Pewter-Platter Hall, " Philadelphia, that they pool their books led to the

establishment of the Library Company of Philadelphia in 1731. Franklin relates in his <u>Autobiography</u> that the pooling plan failed.

> The number [of books] was not so great as we expected, and tho'
> they had been of great use, yet some inconvenience for want of
> care of them, the collection, after about a year, was separated
> and each took his books home again.

Failure did not deter Franklin, who then proposed a subscription library
which he later called "the mother of all North American subscription libraries, now so numerous. "

One hundred pounds was collected from the members of the Junto and
others who joined in the worthy enterprise. In the spring of 1732 Thomas
Hopkinson sailed for England with a bill of exchange and a list of desiderata.
The new books reached Philadelphia late in October 1732 and were placed on
shelves in "Pewter-Platter Hall. " Not long after, a catalog was prepared,
which Franklin published as "Presents" for the members. A protégé of
Franklin, Louis Timothée, a French refugee from Holland, became the first
librarian of the company but left in 1733 to become the second printer in
South Carolina. Franklin himself succeeded him.

Although the original one hundred pounds was collected without too
great effort, later applicants for membership in the society sometimes found
it difficult to raise forty shillings for a share. Money was scarce and hard to
come by in those days, even Scotch pennies and doubtful moidores. As a substitute, payments in kind were sometimes accepted by the directors for the
company's shares. Among these payments were personal services, stuffed
snakes, a dead pelican, and Indian chiefs' robes of skin. Matthew Clarkson's
offering of fossils caused the company difficulty because a committee appointed to assess their value thought its members too lacking in a knowledge of
fossils to accomplish their task.

Printed catalogs of the library, in which the books were arranged by
size without regard to subject, were issued from time to time between 1733
and 1772, but they were frequently criticized because they afforded no subject
approach to the library's collections. It was decided, therefore, to issue a new

catalog in classified form. This catalog was published in 1789 in Philadelphia by Zachariah Poulson, Jr., who was then librarian of the company. It is probable that he compiled as well as printed the catalog because no other name has been connected with its preparation. If Poulson was the cataloger responsible for the work, he may have determined the future of American library classification.

Poulson, one of the most colorful characters of early Philadelphia, was born in that city on September 5, 1761. His father and grandfather, emigrants from Denmark, were both printers; young Zachariah in turn learned the trade in the printing-houses of Joseph Cruikshank and James Humphreys. In 1785 he became librarian of the Philadelphia library company, which he continued to serve for fifty-nine years, twenty-one of which were spent as librarian. In 1788 he opened his own printing house, and in 1800 he bought Claypoole's American Daily Advertiser, the first daily newspaper published in America. For the next two decades Poulson not only brought the Advertiser profit and prestige, but he also continued his services for the Library Company of Philadelphia and was a leader in many philanthropies. At the time of his death, July 31, 1844, he was president of the Philadelphia Society for Alleviating the Miseries of Public Prisons and a senior member of the board of the first fire insurance company in America. He was equally interested in the Society for Promoting the Abolition of Slavery.

The "Advertisement" to the 1789 catalog describes it:

> In conformity to the general delineation of human science, laid down by Bacon, and afterwards illustrated and enlarged by D'Alembert, the books have been divided into three classes, corresponding with the three great divisions of the mental faculties – Memory, Reason and Imagination.
> It has been attempted to render the subdivisions of the several classes sufficiently ample, to combine only those which proceeded from a common source, and could not be separated without difficulty, and to adapt the arrangement rather to the science than the subject. [4]

The titles of this 1789 catalog are entered by size under each subdivision. An index of authors follows the classed catalog. The classification contains the following divisions:

MEMORY
    I.   Sacred History
   II. Ecclesiastical History
  III. Civil History – including Biography, Antiquities, Military
           and Naval History, and Civil History properly so called
  IV. Natural History in all its branches
   V. Voyages and Travels
  VI. Geography and Topography, with Maps, Charts and Plans

REASON
     I. Theology
    II. Mythology
   III. Ethics; or the Moral System in general
   IV. Grammars, Dictionaries, and Treatises on Education
    V. Logic, Rhetoric and Criticism
   VI. General and local Politics
  VII. Trade and Commerce, Treatises on Annuities and Insurance
 VIII. Law
   IX. Metaphysics
    X. Geometry
   XI. Arithmetic and Algebra
  XII. Mechanics
 XIII. Astronomy, Astrology and Chronology
 XIV. Optics, Pneumatics, Hydrostatics, Hydraulics, Phonics, and
           Gnomonics
  XV. Navigation and Naval Architecture
 XVI. Civil Architecture
 XVII. The Military Art
XVIII. Heraldry
 XIX. Anatomy, Medicine and Chemistry
  XX. Agriculture and Gardening
 XXI. Arts and Manufactures
 XXII. Experimental and natural Philosophy, and elementary
           Treatises on the Arts and Sciences

IMAGINATION
   I. Poetry and the Drama
  II. Works of Fiction, Wit and Humor
 III. The Fine Arts

1793 <u>T. M. Harris</u>.

When Thaddeus Mason Harris, A. M. , was librarian of Harvard College
in 1793, he was surrounded by the largest collection of books in America. He
had made it a constant practice to read <u>all</u> the English reviews and thought it
not presumptuous to make a choice of books for those less fortunately situated.
He therefore compiled a catalog for a <u>small</u> and <u>cheap</u> library adapted to the
taste and circumstances of common readers. The <u>Catalogue</u>[5] contained 276
entries for approximately 700 volumes, worth perhaps $1,500 in the money of
the period.

Harris was born in Charlestown, Massachusetts, on July 7, 1768, the son of William Harris, a schoolmaster who became a captain in the Colonial Army. After the death of his father in 1778, Thaddeus worked on farms and at carpentry. He prepared for college in the household of Dr. Ebenezer Morse, of Boylston. When his mother opposed his going to Harvard, he became a maker of saddle trees for a time. But, clinging to his idea of a Harvard education, he entered the school when he was fifteen years old and worked his way through as a waiter in the commons hall. After graduation in 1787 he taught school for a year in Worcester. He then received an offer to serve as secretary to George Washington, but an attack of smallpox prevented his accepting the position.

Harris returned to Harvard to study theology and was licensed to preach in 1789. From 1791 to 1793 he was librarian of Harvard, where he developed his catalog. During the next four decades he devoted most of his time to preaching, writing, and travel. Ordained as pastor of the church in Dorchester in 1793, he retained that pastorate for forty-three years. Among his many publications were a four-volume Minor Encyclopedia (1803), a Natural History of the Bible (1793 and rewritten in 1820), and the Biographical Memorials of James Oglethorpe (1841). He also assisted Jared Sparks in preparing the twelve-volume Writings of George Washington (1834-37). From 1837 until his death in 1842, Harris was librarian of the Massachusetts Historical Society.

Nathaniel Hawthorne, while American Consul in Liverpool in 1856, told of meeting Doctor Harris in the Boston Athenaeum. He saw him almost daily, "a small, withered, infirm, but brisk old gentleman, with snow-white hair," almost always with a newspaper, usually the Boston Post, "which was the leading journal of the Democratic party in the northern states."

One evening a friend said to Hawthorne:

"Did you hear that old Doctor Harris dead?"

"No," said I, very quietly, "and it cannot be true; for I saw him at the Athenaeum to-day."

"You must be mistaken," rejoined my friend. "He is certainly dead!" and confirmed the fact with such special circumstances that I could no longer doubt it.

The next day Hawthorne mounted the steps of the Athenaeum thinking within himself,

> "Well, I shall never see old Doctor Harris again!" With this
> thought in my mind, as I opened the door of the reading-room,
> I glanced towards the spot and chair where Doctor Harris usual-
> ly sat, and there, to my astonishment, sat the gray, infirm figure
> of the deceased Doctor, reading the newspaper as was his wont!
> His own death must have been recorded, that very morning, in
> that very newspaper! I have no recollection of being greatly dis-
> composed at the moment... Probably, if ghosts were in the habit
> of coming among us, they would coincide with the ordinary train
> of affairs, and melt into them so familiarly that we should not be
> shocked at their presence. At all events, so it was in this instance...
> I have forgotten how the ghost of Doctor Harris took its de-
> parture from the Athenaeum on this occasion, or, in fact, whether
> the ghost or I went first. This equanimity, and almost indifference,
> on my part — the careless way in which I glanced at so singular a
> mystery and left it aside — is what now surprises me as much as
> anything else in the affair. 6

For weeks after, Hawthorne continued to see Dr. Harris as frequently as before his death, regarding "the venerable defunct no more than any other old
fogies who basked before the fire, and dozed over the newspapers."

Harris' classification closely resembles the one Poulson used in the
1789 catalog of the Library Company of Philadelphia. It may well have been
derived from it. Harris, like Poulson, altered considerably the original Bacon-
d'Alembert tradition that Jefferson followed more closely. Harris made the
following divisions and subdivisions:

MEMORY
     I.   Sacred History
    II. Ecclesiastical History
   III. Civil History, including Biography
   IV. Natural History
    V. Voyages and Travels
   VI. Geography and Topography

REASON
     I.   Theology
    II. Mythology
   III. Ethics
   IV. Grammars and Dictionaries
    V. Logic, Rhetoric, and Criticism
   VI. General and Local Politics
  VII. Law
 VIII. Metaphysics
   IX. Arithmetic, Geometry, and Algebra
    X. Natural and Experimental Philosophy, including Astronomy
   XI. Chymistry
  XII. Agriculture
 XIII. Arts and Manufactures

IMAGINATION
I. Poetry and the Drama
II. Works of Fiction
III. Fine Arts
IV. Miscellanies

1816 <u>A</u>. <u>E</u>. <u>B</u>. Woodward.

In 1816 two classifications were published, one American, one English
— the first destined for oblivion, the second for some slight fame. The former
was the "Catholepistemia" of Judge Woodward;[7] the latter, the Chrestomathia
of Jeremy Bentham. And, perhaps strange to say, the one which achieved
fame was of less interest than the one which was forgotten.

Woodward was born in November 1774 in New York City, where baptis-
mal records reveal that he was christened Elias Brevoort Woodward. But
between christening and graduation from college he acquired the forename
Augustus, for it was as Augustus Brevoort Woodward that he received the
degree of Bachelor of Arts from Columbia College in 1793. He studied law
and was admitted to the bar in Georgetown, Maryland, in 1797. Woodward
then practiced law and engaged in land speculation in the District of Columbia until President Jefferson appointed him Chief Justice of the Supreme
Court of the Territory of Michigan in 1805.

Woodward reached Detroit in July, less than three weeks after the town
had been completely destroyed by fire. The Chief Justice was responsible
for having the new city laid out according to L'Enfant's plan for the Nation's
Capital, and Woodward Avenue commemorates his contribution. Woodward
was the only official who did not flee the city when General Hull surrendered
Detroit to the British in 1812. Consequently there devolved upon him the difficult task of representing the citizens before the British commander, Colonel Proctor.

While in Michigan, Woodward drafted the act establishing the "Cathole-
pistemiad," or University of Michigania, later the University of Michigan. He
served as justice until 1824, when he was legislated out of office by a change
in territorial government. President Monroe later made him a Federal judge

in the Territory of Florida, where he died in Tallahassee in 1827.

Woodward was keenly aware of the difficulties he faced in adding another to the long list of man's classifications of knowledge. "The knowledge which the human race are capable of acquiring upon this earth appears, at the first view, too multifarious to be susceptible of arrangement." Undaunted, however, he went on to develop a classification which, despite the Greek terminology (used also by Bentham), is of considerable interest. He planned

> To ascertain, upon correct principles, the general departments, or provinces, to which all human knowledge ought to be assigned; to divide those respective general departments, or provinces, into their appropriate classes; to subdivide the several classes into distinct orders; to dilate every order into specific and individual sciences; and to apply to the whole a definite, and a classical, nomenclature; – these are the objects of the present enterprize. [8]

Such was the goal Woodward set for himself. How well he achieved it is attested by A System of Universal Science, which left the presses of William Fry of Philadelphia late in 1816. Richard Rush, at the time Attorney General of the United States, wrote: "Such a man ought to have every opportunity of displaying himself before the world, where alone the verdict upon his new system can be made up. "[9] Rush asked to be considered a subscriber to the volume then in the press and said of a meeting with Woodward two years before, "There was a boldness and grandeur in the conception which, in my eyes at least, bore evidence of a mind of unusual enterprise, and I feel persuaded, that Mr. Woodward is a man of large research. "

Like many before and after him, Woodward realized that before a classification could be developed it was necessary to survey the progress and advancement of the human mind in all countries, at all times; and to describe all systems and classifications of knowledge ever developed. When these steps had been completed, he could develop and explain his own classification and nomenclature of the sciences. And lastly, he would show its usefulness to mankind in the development and diffusion of knowledge, including its use in the establishment and development of libraries and the foundation of an American National Institute, "embodying in one concurrent channel all the learning

and talents, all the erudition and genius, in the United States of America, for the
honor of our particular nation, and for the general benefit of the human race. "

Woodward's survey of learning and classification began with a review
of antediluvian science and ended with his criticism of a scheme sent him by
Abbé Mango of Sicily and the views of the Reverend Samuel B. Wylie on classification. He devoted two hundred and forty pages to the survey; and then:

> It will now be in course to explain those divisions of human
> knowledge, and that classification and nomenclature of the sciences,
> which it was the main object of the present discussion to develope.

Woodward first turned his attention to the laws of classification, which
he found to be:

1. A system should be comprehensive and include every part of human
   knowledge.

2. The analysis should be correct, and the principles of division consistently applied.

3. Subjects closely allied by nature should not be widely separated by
   art.

4. Subjects widely separated in nature should not be forcibly brought
   together by science. (Converse of the third law)

5. Elementary subjects should precede the more complex.

6. The boundaries of all divisions should be definite.

   Corollary 1. Reiterations must be avoided: the same science
   should not appear in two places.

   Corollary 2. The same subject should not be scattered and dissi-
   pated through a number of divisions. (Converse of Corollary 1)

7. The same natural priority which some subjects in the different
   branches claim to others should characterize not only the several
   parts but the system as a whole.

8. A correct and appropriate nomenclature is indispensable, for, "The
   nomenclature is the dress of the divisions, and should be adapted
   to its subject and season. Never so light and thin as to display the

nude anatomy, never so thick and cumbrous as to conceal and deform the symmetry of the limb and the elegance of the shape. "

9. Interminable subdivision ought to be avoided.

After Woodward had formulated his laws of classification, he proceeded to develop his own system — or systems — for there actually were two. The first organized knowledge from the point of view of "a being superior to man," while the second was arranged for man "with a reference to the means by which he obtains it. " The problem of nomenclature caused him some concern; he thought the terms employed should be specific, brief, euphonious, and universal. He finally decided that "Every radical term shall be selected from the Greek language. "

Woodward first divided "Catholepistemia" (Universal Knowledge) into three great provinces:

1. Hylica: The sciences dealing with matter,

2. Hylennoeica: The sciences dealing with matter and mind, and

3. Ennoeica: Those concerned with the mind.

Each province was subdivided into classes, the classes into orders, and orders into sciences. The first province, Hylica, was subdivided into two classes — Mathematica: number, and Physica: material objects. Hylennoeica had three classes — Anthropoglossica: language arts, Anthropodynamica: the sciences which are derived from "human power" exercised over matter, matter and mind, and mind (medicine, economics, industry, etc.), and Diegetica: the sciences which proceed from the application of language to human power, the historical sciences. The last class, Ennoeica, comprised the mental and spiritual disciplines.

The classification just described is given in full on the opposite page in tabular form because of its historic interest and rarity. [10] The English terms are the closest modern equivalents of Woodward's Greek coinage.

CATHOLEPISTEMIA (UNIVERSAL SCIENCE)

Hylica (Matter)
  Mathematica (Mathematics: Number and Space)
    Arithmetica (Number)
      Arithmia (Arithmetic)
      Analysia (Algebra)
    Geömetrica (Space)
      Geömetria (Geometry)
      Goniametria (Trigonometry)
      Ancylometria (Algebraic Geometry)
  Physica ("Matter in itself")
    Physiognostica (Natural History)
      Geögnosia (Geography)
      Oryctognosia (Paleontology)
      Phytognosia (Botany)
      Zoögnosia (Zoology)
    Physiosophica (Natural Philosophy [Physics])
      Stereosophia (Solids)
      Hydrosophia (Fluids)
      Aërosophia (Gases)
      Photosophia (Light)
      Electrosophia (Electricity)
      Magnetosophia (Magnetism)
    Uranica (Astronomy)
      Astronomia (Astronomy)
    Chymica (Chemistry)
      Chymia (Chemistry)

Hylennoëica (Mind and Matter)
  Anthropoglossica (Language and Literature. Arts of Speech)
    Grammatica (Grammar [Philology])
      Grammatia (Grammar)
      Anthropoglossia (Language)
    Dialectica (Dialectics)
      Logiotetia (Logic)
      Rhetoria (Rhetoric)
    Callilogica (Literature)
      Callilogia (Prose)
      Poësia (Poetry)
      Euphradia (Oratory)
      Diacrisia (Criticism)
  Anthropodynamica (Arts and Sciences)
    Iatrica (Medicine)
      Anatomia (Anatomy)
      Zoönomia (Physiology)
      Therapeutria (Materia medica)
      Anthropiatria (Medicine, proper)
      Chirurgia (Surgery)
      Maïeutria (Obstetrics)
      Zoötomia (Comparative Anatomy)
      Zoïatria (Veterinary medicine)
    Oëconomica (Power over matter)
      Geörgia (Agriculture)
      Chirotechnia (Manufactures)
      Callitechnia (Fine Arts)
      Emporia (Trade. Commerce)
      Politoëcia (Political Economy)

Ethica
   Ethosophia (Moral Philosophy)
   Themistia (Law)
   Politarchia (Government)
   Ethnonomia (International Law)
  Polemitactica (Military Science)
   Pezotaxia (Infantry)
   Hippotaxis (Cavalry)
   Barytotaxia (Artillery)
   Sthenotaxis (Fortification)
   Erismatotaxia (Staff)
   Stratotaxia (Organization)
   Polemitaxia (Art of War)
   Nautotaxia (Naval Warfare)
 Diegetica (Historical Sciences)
  Geöcosmica (Geography)
   Chroniotetia (Chronology)
   Geöcosmia (Geography)
  Historica (History)
   Hodöeporia (Voyages and Travels)
   Biotetia (Biography)
   Historia (History, proper)
   Archǽotetia (Antiquities)

Ennóeica (Mind)
 Ennóeica (Mind)
  Psychica (Psychology)
   Zoönóeia (Animal Psychology)
   Anthroponóeia (Human Psychology)
  Pneumatica (Spiritual Beings)
   Pneumatia (Angels, etc.)
   Theotetia (Theology)
  Eusebica (Religion)
   Ethnilatria (Non-Christian Religions)
   Hebrǽosebia (Judaism)
   Evangelia (Christianity)
   Eleutheria (Philosophy of Religion)

In his second classification, the "Encatholepistemia,"[11] Woodward began with the "instruments of science," Language and Mathematics, which formed the province Hetaerica, or auxiliary sciences. These were followed by the positive sciences which relate to the objects of sensation: Physica, Anthropodynamica, and Diegetica; they formed the province Aesthetica. The sciences relating to mind remained unchanged in the province Ennoeica.

Woodward ended his work:

> The fourth part of this investigation; relative, principally, to an American National Institute; must necessarily be deferred. The supreme court of the Territory of Michigan commences its annual session on the sixteenth day of September; and there remains barely time for the performance of the journey.
> A. E. B. Woodward.

Philadelphia, August 31st, 1816

Here, and not on the title page, is found the name of the author. The fourth part never was written.

In attempting to evaluate what Woodward tried to do and what he accomplished in a period when books were relatively scarce and the distances between libraries long in America, it is difficult not to be too enthusiastic. In an older country where libraries were more abundant, Bentham's attempt at a synthesis did not begin to compare with Woodward's survey and classification of all knowledge. Strangely enough, Shields[12] does not mention Woodward, nor, for that matter, does Robert Flint in his oft-quoted Philosophy as the Scientia Scientiarum.

Eight years after the publication of Woodward's work, Jefferson, then eighty-one, wrote from Monticello to acknowledge receipt of a copy, "it will be a monument of the learning of the author and the analysing powers of his mind. " He added, "your idea of making the subject matter of the sciences the basis of their distribution is certainly more reasonable than that of the faculties to which they are addressed. " Jefferson closed with,

> my mind unwillingly engages in severe investigations. it's energies indeed are no longer equal to them. being to thank you for your book, it's subject has run away with me into a labyrinth of ideas no longer familiar; and writing also has become a slow and irksome operation with me. I have been obliged to avail myself of the pen of a grand-daughter for this communication. I will here therefore close my task of thinking, hers of writing, and yours of reading, with assurances of my constant and high respect and esteem.[13]

Woodward's interest in classification continued throughout his life. Only a few months before his death he sent Jefferson an analysis of Bentham's classification and "twelve seeds of the indigenous orange of Florida."[14]

1821 Harvard College.

Although Harvard College Library was one of the first to introduce library classification into the United States (1723), it apparently did not give serious consideration to the publication of a classed catalog until the nineteenth century. The last printed catalog of the library, that of 1790, had listed books and pamphlets separately under alphabetical subject headings. The

headings were obviously class names from a previous, unpublished catalog.
When the need for a new catalog became imperative in the early 1800's, various plans were considered, among them the compilation of a classed catalog
based upon the French system of Jacques-Charles Brunet. But when Joseph
Green Cogswell became librarian in 1821, he arranged the library, not according to Brunet's system, but according to the German scheme used in the University of Gottingen.

Cogswell, who later gained renown as the founder and first director of
the Astor Library in New York City, was born on September 27, 1786, in Ips-
wich, Massachusetts. He graduated from Harvard in the class of 1806 and returned there to receive his A. M. in 1814. For the next five years Cogswell
traveled and studied in Europe. The University of Gottingen awarded him a
Ph. D. degree in 1817. Following his two-year librarianship at Harvard,
Cogswell turned to school teaching until he became John Jacob Astor's companion and adviser in 1837. His association with the Astor Library, which he
persuaded Astor to build and endow instead of erecting a monument to George
Washington, lasted until a few years before his death on November 20, 1871.

Cogswell became interested in library work while he was a student at
Gottingen. He described his training in the German library to his friend,
George Ticknor, who had accompanied him to the university.

> I have made two experiments with Benecke in the library,
> and rejoice that I now get an hour of very valuable instruction,
> for one which was worth nothing at all. He takes the library
> first according to the arrangement on the shelves, and goes
> through the whole with me in that way, giving minute accounts
> of all the divisions and subdivisions, and of the practical appli-
> cation of the principles of classification and distribution. After-
> wards he will do the same with the catalogues. [15]

When Cogswell applied the Gottingen plan at Harvard in 1821, Ticknor,
at the time Smith Professor of the French and Spanish Languages and Literatures, praised his work, particularly the systematic catalog.

> The library is now in fine order. It is arranged on the
> same plan with that at Gottingen, though, for want of books, the
> subdivisions are much fewer at present, and the Catalogues are
> made out in the same way, so that all possible future additions
> will require no alteration in any part of the system. [16]

The system of classification used in the Gottingen library while Cogswell was there had been installed as part of a grand cataloging program by
Christian Gottlob Heyne (1729-1812). [17] Heyne was a noted classical scholar
who is said to have been the first to have made a scientific study of mythology.
He had gone from Dresden to Gottingen in 1763 and remained there as teacher and librarian until his death. Heyne's influence on German librarianship
was great: "Das Gottinger System erlebte damals einen Triumphzug durch
die deutschen Lande."[18]

The classification was the work of Dr. Georg Matthia, professor of medicine on the university faculty. It was published as "Project, wie eine offentliche Bibliothec in die bequemste gemeinnutzige Ordnung zu bringen."[19] In
his "Project" Matthia briefly surveyed existing classifications and then developed his own on the basis of the university faculties, Theology, Law, Medicine, and Philosophy. The last division, as usual, contained all the subjects
not incorporated in the previous three. Under each of these main divisions
Matthia made many subdivisions applicable to the knowledge and books of the
eighteenth century.

Cogswell's variation of this scheme provided the following arrangement: [20]

1. Theology
     Bibles, etc.
     Other

2. Philosophy
     1. General
     2. Metaphysics and logic
     3. Ethics, Politics, Statistics
     [4]
     5. Jurisprudence
     6. Medicine
     7. Natural History

3. History
     Ancient
     Modern

4. Literature
     1. Bibliography and Literary History
     2. Grammar
     3. Philology
     [4]
     5. Rhetoric, Oratory, and Epistolary writings
     6. Greek and Latin Literature
     7. Poetry and the Drama
     8. Other works of Fancy and Fiction

The Gottingen system has erroneously been attributed to Bacon's classification of knowledge on the basis of the faculties of the mind, memory, imagination, and reason. Its genesis, however, was in the university faculties — not the mental faculties. While Cogswell's system did not prevail at Harvard, it continued an interest in systematic catalogs that resulted in the catalog Benjamin Peirce prepared in 1830.

1824 American Philosophical Society.

The American Philosophical Society was formed in 1769 by the union of two of Benjamin Franklin's creations, a society of the same name founded in 1743, [21] and the Junto of 1727, known after December 1766 as the American Society for Promoting and Propagating Useful Knowledge. Thomas Jefferson served as president of the society from 1797 to 1814. Fifty-five years after its foundation, the society published a catalog in which it expressed the hope ". . . to raise a National Library, for the promotion of the study of the different branches of human knowledge. "[22]

The committee charged with the preparation of the catalog began its work with two objects in view — one, that members might find books with ease, and two, that students might see at a glance all that the library possessed in the subjects of their researches. The committee decided to experiment by compiling a catalog unlike any library catalog, foreign or American, which its members had ever seen. If the experiment failed, the growth of the library within a few years would require a new catalog which could avoid the faults of the experimental one they had prepared.

The main divisions of the classification used were:

    I.   Memoirs and Transactions of Scientific and Literary Institutions
    II.   Astronomy
    III. Mathematics
    IV.   Natural Philosophy
    V.   Chemistry
    VI.   Natural History
    VII. Rural and Domestic Economy
    VIII. Medicine and Surgery
    IX.   Religion
    X.   Moral Sciences
    XI.   Jurisprudence
    XII. Biography

Subdivisions were provided in accordance with the need of the subject.

Those for IV. Natural Philosophy, for instance, were:

1. General Treatises
2. Electricity and Magnetism
3. Meteorology and Pneumatics
4. Optics
5. Hydrostatics and Hydraulics
6. Coins, Weights and Measures
7. Machines and Instruments – Steam Engine
8. Miscellaneous

Since no uniform method of arrangement within the classes could be found, the committee thought it best, despite the novelty, to adapt the arrangement of the titles to the nature of the subject. Memoirs and transactions of societies were entered in the order of the names of the places in which they were established. Historical documents and books and pamphlets on local and occasional politics were arranged by date, while the books in Medicine were grouped alphabetically by name of disease. When no particular arrangement was required, the order of the authors' names was followed. At the end was a "List of the names of authors, translators, and editors, mentioned in this catalogue, With references to the pages where their works are to be found. "

From the simple, practical divisions used in the Redwood Library to the highly abstract system Judge Woodward developed represents a considerable journey, not in time, but in human thought. Within his master framework of "matter, mind and matter, mind, "Woodward organized man's knowledge in an order that presaged the evolutionary theories of Comte and Spencer later in the nineteenth century. While ever-present since Jefferson introduced them into this country are the ubiquitous divisions of Francis Bacon – illogical but perennially attractive.

CHAPTER VII

A New Arrival – Brunet

Sometime in the seventeenth century a new system of classification began its slow development. An offshoot of the tradition described in Chapter IV, it grew to maturity in Europe, chiefly in France, where a long line of capable bibliographers successively refined the scheme. It was inevitable that this system, known as the Brunet, should have been introduced into the United States, where librarians were continuing a long search for more efficient classifications. In varying forms the new system offered strong competition to the divisions of Bacon and d'Alembert. But for a minor historical incident, American libraries today might be arranged according to its pattern.

1826 Charleston Library Society.

Seventeen years after Franklin founded the Library Company of Philadelphia, a group of "seventeen young gentlemen" of Charleston, South Carolina, raised a small fund to "collect such new pamphlets and magazines as should occasionally be published in Great Britain." This was the beginning of the Charleston Library Society. Two attempts to incorporate the society failed because the Governor of the Colony, James Glen, refused to sign bills which had been passed by both Houses of the Assembly. In 1754 Glen, withdrawing his opposition, signed a charter which was confirmed by the Crown on June 24, 1755.

The library grew rapidly until the Revolution "suspended all schemes of improvement." In the great fire of January 15, 1778, which destroyed nearly half of Charleston, only 185 of the more than 5,000 volumes of the library were saved. At the end of the war the society reorganized, but many of its members were dispersed and many were dead. Steadily, if slowly, the society increased its collections: from 4,500 volumes in 1808 to nearly 12,000 in 1826.

In 1823 the society appointed a committee "to inquire into the propriety

and expediency of preparing a new Catalogue of its books and the principles
on which a Catalogue should be constructed. . . . " The committee, in practice,
apparently was Stephen Elliott.

Elliott was born in Beaufort, South Carolina, on November 11, 1771. He
graduated from Yale in 1791. As a member of the State Legislature of South
Carolina from 1793 until 1812 he was active as a committee member and author of bills. Two of these were the Free School Act of 1811 and a bill establishing the Bank of the State of South Carolina. Elliott was the first president of this bank, serving until his death in 1830. With Hugh Swinton Legaré
he founded the Southern Review, to which he contributed many articles. Elliott was also the author of A Sketch of the Botany of South Carolina and Georgia (2 vols., 1821-24).

In the preface to A Catalogue of the Books belonging to the Charleston
Library Society, published in 1826, the "committee" recommended that the
Catalogue comprise

    1st, A systematic, and
    2dly, An alphabetical arrangement of the books which belong to
          this Society.

Elliott then described his classification, which is worth quoting in ex-
tenso. With the exceptions of Johnson and Woodward, it is the most logical of
early American essays in the subject.

    All Literature proceeds from the understanding. Its sources
    are in the mind. It derives its power from the human intellect, and
    to its intellect it addresses its researches, it communicates its
    discoveries, it imparts its knowledge. Whatsoever has been de-
    vised by man, whatsoever has been revealed from on high, has been
    communicated and must be comprehended through the powers of
    the understanding. It may not then be improper in an arrangement
    or classification of literature to commence with the inquiries which
    have been directed to those faculties from which literature had its
    origin, and without which it could have no existence.
        If the first division of literature should comprehend the in-
    quiries of rational man into his own nature, into those causes and
    principles which have made him rational and have in truth enabled
    him to make this inquiry; the next should be directed to that Power
    from whom these faculties have been derived; to Him who is the
    origin of all that we possess or know, of all that we pursue or per-
    form. The researches which have been made into the nature and
    attributes of the Deity, the ordinances, dispensations and duties
    which result from the relation of man to his Creator, the forms

under which he has been worshipped, and the errors with which
that worship has been clouded, will necessarily be included in
this division.

From the duties which man owes to his Creator, the transition is natural to those which he has to perform to his fellow beings. The first and most obvious are to the persons immediately
connected with him in the intimate relations of domestic life. In
savage or civilized society, among the wanderers of the desert or
the congregated multitudes of populous cities, the obligations of
private and personal morality are studied and sanctioned; and the
mutual duties of husband and wife, of parent and child, perhaps
also of master and servant, form a part of that code which has resulted almost inevitably from the nature and condition of human
existence. The doctrines and systems of ethics, the speculations
on the passions and emotions of man, should form another great
division of human literature.

A wider range of inquiry arises when detached and isolated
families become accidentally associated, or by natural increase
have extended into regular societies. It then becomes important
to investigate the principles and structure of the government that
unites them, the propriety and efficacy of the laws that guard them,
and the operation of those establishments that promote or retard
their welfare. The science, therefore, of government, jurisprudence and political economy, and the examinations which have
been made of the policy of different governments in their domestic administration, or in their relations with other governments,
will form another class in the distribution of literature.

Connected with these researches are the inquiries which
have been made into the pursuits and employments of man in
society, the illustrations which have been given of his inventions
and discoveries. This wide and comprehensive division embraces
the occupations and improvement of man through the whole period of his temporal existence. From the rude and simple arts which
were necessary to his physical existence; from the wild and coarse
amusements that beguiled the leisure of savage or pastoral society;
from the emblematic devices of ignorant and unlettered ages; to
the unnumbered improvements of the present day; to the diversified and ever changing pursuits of social life; to the sublime speculations of cultivated and aspiring talent; to the discoveries which
have made man the master of the material world. All that the
teeming and prolific mind engenders whilst brooding in solitude,
or exercised by the relations of civilized society; all that the active enterprize and persevering labour of man has performed,
must find a station among the records of the literature, the arts
and science of an enlightened age.

But neither the improvements of the human race, nor even
the associations from which these improvements have generally
sprung, were uniform or simultaneous. The increase and dispersion of the human race, their re-union in societies, their inventions and discoveries have all been progressive. In reviewing
these events, it has been necessary to determine the period of
each and every remarkable incident which has occurred in the
progress of these temporary or permanent establishments, the
date of each great revolution among nations or in governments,
of each invention in art, or discovery in science, and of every
change in the moral or physical world: To trace and describe
distinctly the progress, duration and decline of each nation or
community of individuals, to examine the location of societies
and nations on the globe, and to delineate the natural and artificial

divisions which have been made on its surface. To illustrate these great branches of Chronology, History and Geography, may be added the collateral aid derived – 1st, from the history of those individuals who have become distinguished amidst the revolutions of the world; who have merited commemoration as the improvers or benefactors of society; and even of those who have been merely remarkable from peculiarities of fortune or of character. 2dly, From the adventures and observations of individuals who have visited and explored the different divisions of the globe. 3dly, From the documents which have been published by governments or by statesmen. 4thly, From the monuments which remain of ancient ages, exhibiting the progress and improvement of the arts in different nations and at different periods; and, finally, from the history of the arts and sciences themselves, or of the human mind.

From this outline the following general distribution of literature may be deduced.

Literature treating

1st.   Of Man in his intellectual capacity. On the Philosophy and Discipline of the Human Mind.
2d.   Of Man in relation to the Deity. Theology.
3d.   Of Man in relation to his fellows. Ethics.
4th.   Of Man in relation to Society. Government, Jurisprudence and Politics.
5th.   Of the pursuits, the improvements and discoveries of Man in Society.
6th.   Of the History of Man in Society.

Each of these divisions was subdivided, many of them minutely. One of the most interesting is the fifth division, in which Elliott collocated man's arts and sciences. Natural History, for example, contains the following subdivisions:

3. General Treatises on Natural History
4. On the Natural History of Particular Countries
5. Treatises on the Mineral Kingdom
    1. Geology
    2. Mineralogy and Metallurgy
6. Treatises on the Vegetable Kingdom – Botany
7. On Agriculture
8. On Gardening
    *On Landscape and Picturesque Beauty, as connected with Ornamental Gardening
9. Treatises on the Animal Kingdom – Zoology
    1. General Treatises
    2. On the Mammalia
    3. On Ornithology
    4. On the Amphibiae
    5. On Invertebral Animals
10. Amusements connected with Zoology
    1. The Chase and the Turf
    2. Horsemanship
11. On the Management and Diseases of Quadrupeds
12. On Medicine
    1. Treatises on Anatomy & Physiology
    2. On Health and Longevity

　　3. General Treatises on Medicine
　　4. On Particular Diseases and Remedies
　　5. On the Diseases of Particular Climates and Professions
　　6. On the Materia Medica
13. Chemistry
　　1. General Treatises
　　2. Treatises on particular subjects
14. Electricity, Galvanism, Magnetism

The titles were entered alphabetically, by author or title, under each class with the exception of History, where the arrangement was chronological. Each item had a book number, and since these numbers were assigned in the sequence of the classification, the arrangement was a true book and not a shelf classification. An index of authors and titles with their book numbers followed the systematic catalog.

It is probable that Elliott was indebted to the system perfected by Jacques-Charles Brunet,[1] but his classification shows considerable originality. It is interesting to compare this product of a mind trained in botany with the system developed in 1862 by the geologist, J. Peter Lesley.

1830 Harvard College.

Brunet's system entered Harvard (and for practical purposes, the United States) in 1830, when the Harvard Library issued another in its series of catalogs. It was originally planned to prepare an alphabetical catalog in which the books would be described in the words of their respective titles, "to use the peculiar, and often uncouth, orthography found in each work, whether in the English or in any other language ..." As the work progressed, however, "a strong desire was felt to provide some expedient which should make it answer the purpose of a classed catalogue; and it was thought that this might be done by means of a systematic index." Into the index, which formed the third volume of the catalog, Librarian Benjamin Peirce introduced Brunet.

Peirce was born in Salem, Massachusetts, on September 30, 1778, the son of Jerahmeel and Sarah (Ropes) Peirce. After graduating from Harvard in 1801, he returned to Salem to work with his father in the India trade. Peirce represented Salem in the General Court of Massachusetts; in 1811 he was a senator from Essex County. But neither the India trade nor politics

gave Peirce much satisfaction. In 1826 he returned to Harvard to succeed
Charles Folsom as librarian of the college. Peirce died on July 26, 1831, at
the age of fifty-two.

The classification Peirce adopted has a long history. It was variously
known as the French System, or the System of the Paris Booksellers. Jacques-
Charles Brunet, however, gave the system its classic form and the name it
bears today. In this form the classification played an important part in the
arrangement of libraries and bibliographies in Europe and in the United States.

Brunet was born in Paris on November 2, 1780, the son of Thomas Brunet, a man of peasant stock who had left a home "chargé d'enfants" in Morigny
(Normandy) to seek his fortune in Paris. The elder Brunet tried many occupations before finally settling into the book trade. Jacques-Charles received
a good elementary education, but when he was about twelve years old his
father's business suffered as a result of the Revolution of 1789, and he stopped
his formal schooling to help in his father's shop. He very early showed a
love for bibliography, compiling several catalogs for his father. The older
man soon realized that his son's heart would never be in the more practical
side of the book business.

Brunet made his debut as a bibliographer anonymously, with an original work designed as a supplement to the Dictionnaire bibliographique ...
des libres rares of Cailleau and Duclos (1790). The work was so well received that it determined the lifelong career of the novice in bibliography. In
1810 he published, at his father's establishment, his Manuel du Libraire et de
l'Amateur de Livres (3 vols.). This publication met a real need and was a
great success. Two more editions quickly followed: the second in 1814 (4 vols.)
and a third (4 vols.) in 1820, which contained 30,000 entries.

By this time Brunet had taken over the management of his father's establishment, but when his father died in 1824 he withdrew from the business
to devote his time to bibliography. Around 1830 there was a change in the
reading taste of the public, and Brunet deferred the preparation of a new edition

of the Manuel, contenting himself with the publication of a supplement, Nou-
velles Recherches Bibliographiques (Paris, 1834, 3 vols.), and several other
books in the bibliographic field.

His Manuel, however, was always of paramount interest to him, and in
1843-44 he published a much enlarged edition, the fourth (5 vols. gr. in-8). Already an octogenarian, Brunet lived to see the publication of the fifth and last
edition of his book (1860-65, 6 t. en 12 part.), a prodigious work of "patience,
exactitude, and erudition, " an unrivalled monument to the bibliophile. Brunet's Manuel was financially profitable, bringing him 400,000 francs on the
first four editions alone, a sum almost unheard of in such a "profession."
Brunet was awarded the cross of the Legion of Honor in 1845, and in 1848 and
1849 he was a member of a national committee on the organization of libraries. When he died, November 14, 1867, he left the Institut de France an annuity
to provide triennial prizes of 3,000 francs to be awarded to one or more of
the best works in bibliography.

The Reverend Thomas Frognall Dibdin, English bibliographer of the period, gives a colorful picture of Brunet, whom he visited in 1818:

> This distinguished bibliographer, rather than bookseller,
> lives hard by — in the Rue Gît-Le-Coeur. He lives with his father,
> who superintends the business of the shop. The Rue Gît-Le-Coeur
> is a sorry street — very diminutive, and a sort of cropt copy — to
> what it should have been, or what it might have been. However,
> there lives JACQ. CH. BRUNET, FILS: a writer, who will be known
> to the latest times in the bibliographical world. He will be also
> thanked as well as known; for his Manuel du Libraire is a per-
> formance of incomparable utility to all classes of readers and
> collectors. You mount up one pair of stairs: — the way is gloomy,
> and might well lead to a chamber in the monastery of La Trappe.
> You then read an inscription, which tells you that "in turning the
> button you pull the bell. " The bell sounds, and Mons. Brunet, Pere,
> receives you — with, or without, a silken cap upon his head. He sits
> in a small room, sufficiently well filled with books. "Is the Son at
> home?" "Open that door, Sir, you will find him in the next room."
> The door is immediately opened — and there sits the son, surround-
> ed by, and almost imprisoned in, papers and books. His pen is in
> his hand: his spectacles are upon his nose: and he is transcribing
> or re-casting some precious little bit of bibliographical intelli-
> gence; while, on looking up and receiving you, he seems to be "full
> of the labouring God! " In short, he is just now deeply and uninter-
> mittingly engaged in a new and third edition of his Manuel. The
> shelves of his room almost groan beneath the weight of those wri-
> ters from whom he gathers his principal materials. "Vous voilà,

Mons. Brunet, bien occupé!;" "Oui, Monsieur, cela me fait autant de plaisir que de peine."[2]

The paternity of the Brunet system has long been disputed. English and French writers have made a mystery of its origin. The mystery, however, resulted from the methodological error of trifurcation mentioned in the Preface. The recombination of the divisions of knowledge of the seventeenth century by French bibliographers produced a system which differed only superficially from many of those previously described.

In its French form the system was published for the first time in 1678 in Jean Garnier's Systema Bibliothecae Collegii Parisiensis Societatis Jesu.[3] Although Garnier's name did not appear on the title page, he lists himself as fifth in a new series of librarians and author of the classification: "Quintus, P. Joannes Garnerius, hujus Systematis author." Adrien Baillet (1649-1706), a contemporary of Garnier, is undoubtedly responsible for the questioning of Garnier's authorship, for after praising the classification he said: "Some claim that he had done no more than to lend his name to the real author of the scheme."[4] Baillet, however, gives no reason for his statement.

Jean Garnier (1612-81), librarian of the Jesuit College of Clermont, yielding in part to the insistence of friends who had asked him to publish the catalog of the library, hoped that publication would assist other librarians and that they in turn would assist him by pointing out the defects in his work.

In Garnier's opinion a good classification should:

1. Follow the order of nature, or at least not run counter to it.

2. Provide a place for every book.

3. Give users a better knowledge of bibliography.

4. Make it possible to find books easily and quickly.

To these norms there is little that we of today can add.

Like many other systems, Garnier's classification is seldom given accurately; reliance upon secondary sources often results in garbled versions. In Caput III Garnier divides the general library into four principal parts[5] and toward the end of the brief chapter lists them as $\theta\epsilon o\lambda o\gamma\acute{\iota}a$, $\phi\iota\lambda o\sigma o\phi\acute{\iota}a$, ἰστορία, and εὐρομία — Theology, Philosophy, History, and Jurisprudence.

The second subdivision, Philosophy, contained nearly all of what would today be called Arts and Sciences, in addition to Philosophy proper. Following Philosophy proper was Mathematics embracing Mathematics proper, Astronomy, Divination, Music, Civil Architecture, Navigation, etc. The other subdivisions were Medicine, Philology, Rhetoric, Poetry, and Literary Criticism. There were many subdivisions adapted to the requirements of the several subjects. [6]

In 1679, a year after Garnier's pioneer essay, there was published in Paris the Catalogus Bibliothecae Thuanae ... tum secundum Scientias & Artes à Clariss. Viro Ismaele Bullialdo Digestus .... The classification used by Ismael Boulliau (Bouilleaud or Bouillaud) in arranging de Thou's library was similar to that of Garnier:

Garnier 1678	Boulliau 1679
Theology	Theology
Philosophy	Jurisprudence
History	History
Jurisprudence	Philosophy
	Belles Lettres

There are many likenesses between the two systems, but there are also many differences. Garnier had put Ecclesiastical History under History; Boulliau made it a subdivision of Theology, which coincides with today's practice. Belles Lettres, a main division in Boulliau's plan, is in Garnier's last four subdivisions of Philosophy. Garnier, like Bacon, placed Natural History in History, Boulliau in Philosophy. These are but a few of the many differences. Obviously both men had drawn from a common source of arrangement, the faculty organization of the universities, the arrangement of treatises, and other patterns of knowledge organization of the period. Each had adapted these methods to his own needs and created classifications which were alike and yet unlike. For few classifications are completely original; they are more often recombinations of existing elements and patterns of organization.

Succeeding French bibliographers, among them Gabriel Martin, Prosper

Marchand, Guillaume Francois Debure, his cousin Guillaume Debure, and Jean Francois Née de la Rochelle, modified and refined the pattern.

Although French bibliographers played a dominant role in developing the system, its use was not confined to France. Matthia's work was in the same tradition, as were some other German systems, notably that of philosopher Leibniz, which appeared as Idea Bibliothecae Publicae Secundum Classes Scientiarum Ordinandae (Leipzig, 1718). As early as 1709 Giusto Fontanini had used the system in Italy. In England, Thomas James, who compiled the first catalog (1605) of the Bodleian Library, which had opened in Oxford in 1602, based his work upon the four faculties of Theology, Medicine, Law, and Arts. Conyers Middleton (1723) reflected the tradition, as well as John Radcliffe in his 1791 catalog of the Chetham Library. Adam Clarke also presented a plan based upon the five "primitive" classes in his The Bibliographical Miscellany (1806). Thomas Hartwell Horne presented the system in 1814 in his Introduction to the Study of Bibliography. Later the plan served as the basis of the Outlines for the Classification of a Library which he presented to the trustees of the British Museum in 1825. He also used it in his methodically arranged catalog of the Library of Queen's College, Cambridge, published in 1827. In Edinburgh, George Sandy used the classification in his 1805 Catalogue of the Library of the Writers to His Majesty's Signet.

Brunet's version of the old tradition made its first appearance in 1810 in the third volume of his Manuel: Table Méthodique en Forme de Catalogue Raisonné. In the early editions there were over six two-column pages of subdivisions arranged in this sequence:

    Theology
    Jurisprudence
    Sciences and Arts
    Belles Lettres
    History

The following translation of the main topics of the synopsis is made from the second edition.

THEOLOGY
    I. Holy Scripture
    II. Sacred Philology
    III. Liturgies
    IV. Councils
    V. The Fathers
    VI. Theologians
    VII. "Singular beliefs"
    VIII. Religions of the Jews and Gentiles
    IX. Oriental Religions
    X. Deists. Sceptics. Atheists

JURISPRUDENCE
    I. Introduction: General Works
    II. Law of Nature and Nations
    III. Civil and Criminal Law
    IV. Ecclesiastical and Canon Law

SCIENCES AND ARTS
    Introduction: General Works
  SCIENCE
    I. Philosophy
    II. Logic
    III. Metaphysics
    IV. Ethics
    V. Economics
    VI. Political Science
    VII. Political Economy
    VIII. Physics
    IX. Chemistry
    X. Natural History
    XI. Medicine (Including Pre-clinical Sciences)
    XII. Mathematics and Dependent Sciences
    XIII. Appendix to the Sciences: Occult Sciences, Alchemy, Spagyric
        Medicine, Astrology
  ARTS AND CRAFTS
    Dictionaries and General Works
    I. Memory: Writing and Printing
    II. Fine Arts
    III. Mechanical Arts and Crafts
    IV. Gymnastics: Horsemanship, Dancing, etc.
    V. Amusements

BELLES-LETTRES
    Introduction
    I. Grammar. Philology
    II. Rhetoric
    III. Orators
    IV. Poetry
    V. Poets
    VI. Drama
    VII. Mythology
    VIII. Prose Fiction
    IX. Wit and Humor
    X. Criticism
    XI. Polygraphs
    XII. Dialogues
    XIII. Letters

HISTORY
   Introduction: Historiography, etc.
 I. Geography
 II. Voyages
 III. Chronology
 IV. Universal and Modern History
 V. History of Religions and Superstitions
 VI. Ancient History
 VII. Byzantine History
 VIII. Modern History
 IX. Chivalry. Heraldry. Genealogy
 X. Antiquities
 XI. Literary History
 XII. Bibliography
 XIII. Biography
 XIV. Historical Extracts

Each division was subdivided according to the nature of the subject, e. g.

 XI. Medicine
   1. History and Biography
   2. Dictionaries. Collections
   3. General Treatises
   4. Greek Physicians or Medicine
   5. Latin Physicians or Medicine
   6. Arabian Physicians or Medicine
   7. Modern Physicians or Medicine
   8. Anatomy
   9. Physiology
   10. Hygiene
   11. Dietetics
   12. Pathology
   13. Internal Medicine. Practice of Medicine
   14. Forensic Medicine
   15. Materia Medica
   16. Collections
   17. Surgery
   18. Pharmacy and Pharmacopoeias
   19. Veterinary Medicine

Brunet's provisions for America in History were broad even for the period

(1814):

   1. General History
   2. Peru, Chile, Paraguay, Brazil, and Cayenne
   3. Mexico, California, Florida, Louisiana, and the United
     States
   4. Antilles

This in brief was the system Peirce introduced into the Harvard Library in 1830. He added a sixth class for Works Relating to America, which contained added entries for books classified in American History, Voyages and Travels, Politics, etc. Numerous other changes were made to adapt Brunet's system to the needs of an American library.

Peirce's system comprised the following classes and divisions:

CLASS I.

THEOLOGY

    I. Holy Scriptures
   II. Natural Religion
  III. Evidences of Revealed Religion
  IV. Scripture Histories, Biblical Dictionaries, Concordances, Harmonies
    V. Critical Theology
  VI. Dogmatic, Controversial, and Practical Theology
 VII. Paraenetic Theology
     1. Sermons, Pastoral Letters, Charges
     2. Sermons on the Fifth of November, and Thirtieth of January
       [On the Gun-Powder Plot, and on the Execution of Charles I.]
     3. Massachusetts Election Sermons
     4. Massachusetts Convention, and Dudleian Lecture, Sermons
     5. Ordination and Installation Sermons
     6. Funeral Sermons
     7. Fast and Thanksgiving Sermons
VIII. Fathers of the Church
  IX. Ecclesiastical History
   X. Jewish Antiquities, History, and Literature
  XI. Miscellaneous Divinity
 XII. Various Religions and Superstitions

CLASS II.

JURISPRUDENCE, GOVERNMENT, AND POLITICS.

    I. Law of Nature and Nations, Treaties, &c.
   II. Civil Law
  III. Canon and Ecclesiastical Law
  IV. Statute, Common, and Chancery Law
    V. General and Miscellaneous Law (including Feudal, Maritime, and
       Commercial Law, &c.)
  VI. Government and Politics
 VII. Political Economy, Finance, Money, Trade, Commerce

CLASS III.

SCIENCES AND ARTS.

    I. Philosophy
     1. General Works
     2. Logic and Metaphysics
     3. Moral Philosophy
     4. Education, Elementary Works for Youth, &c.
   II. Mathematics
     1. General Works
     2. Arithmetic, Algebra, Fluxions
     3. Geometry; Practical Mathematics
  III. Physics
     1. General and Miscellaneous Works
     2. Astronomy
     3. Mechanics, Hydrostatics, Pneumatics, Optics, Meteorology
     4. Chemistry, Electricity, Galvanism, Magnetism

IV. Natural History
    1. General Works and Miscellaneous Natural History
    2. Zoology
    3. Botany, Agriculture, and Gardening
    4. Mineralogy and Geology
V. Medicine
    1. Anatomy, Physiology, and Surgery
    2. Physic
VI. Fine and Useful Arts
VII. Encyclopaedias, Journals, Publications of Learned Societies

CLASS IV.

BELLES LETTRES.

I. Bibliography
II. Literary History
III. Grammar and Lexicography
    1. General Works
    2. Works on the Greek and Latin Languages
    3. Works on the European Languages, except the Greek and Latin.
    4. Works on the Oriental and Other Languages
IV. Rhetoric and Criticism
V. Greek Authors
VI. Ancient Latin Authors
VII. Translations of Greek and Latin Authors
VIII. Poetry
    1. Treatises on Poetry
    2. Epic, Lyric, Didactic, and Pastoral Poetry
    3. Dramatic Poetry
IX. Works of Fiction and Humor, Apophthegms, Proverbs, Dialogues
X. Orations, Addresses, Speeches
XI. Oriental Literature
XII. Periodical Works, Registers, Directories, Gazettes
XIII. Miscellaneous Authors

CLASS V.

HISTORY.

I. Antiquities, Mythology, Numismatics, Heraldry, Genealogy
II. Geography, Topography, Statistics
III. Voyages and Travels
IV. General History and Chronology
V. Ancient History
VI. Modern History of Continental Europe
VII. British History
VIII. Asiatic, African, and Other History
IX. American History
X. Biography and Personal Narratives

CLASS VI.

WORKS RELATING TO AMERICA.

After its introduction into Harvard, Brunet's scheme spread rapidly;

within a generation it had been adopted by libraries from the Atlantic to the

Pacific. When William P. Curtis, librarian of the Mercantile Library Company of St. Louis, prepared the first catalog of that institution he chose the Harvard catalog of 1830 for his model and adopted Brunet for the classified section. [7]

Four years later the influence of his catalog carried Brunet to the West Coast, to the San Francisco Mercantile Library, only six years after Captain John B. Montgomery of the U. S. sloop of war Portsmouth had raised the American flag in the plaza which now bears the name of his ship. Within a quarter of a century after Benjamin Peirce introduced Brunet into Harvard the system had spread from Boston to San Francisco and from Salem, Massachusetts, to Richmond, Virginia. From 1830 on, it was Bacon versus Brunet in American libraries.

CHAPTER VIII

"Miscellaneous"

For the title of this chapter the writer is indebted to Mr. Procter, compiler of the catalog of Byrd's library at Westover. Mr. Procter's word is accurate for no other term fits as well. The old strains of classification continue, but new and original systems appear. They attest to the keen interest and ingenuity of American librarians in the organization of their libraries. No comparable period – a single generation – in the Old World exhibits so many diverse systems, so much originality.

1835 Library Company of Philadelphia.

Brunet's system drove Bacon's divisions of knowledge from Ben Franklin's library early in the nineteenth century. George Campbell, librarian of the institution from 1806 to 1829, installed the grand divisions of Religion, Jurisprudence, Sciences and Arts, Belles Lettres, and History, and prefaced them with a class for Bibliography. He added many subdivisions to provide for the 44,000 books which constituted the library at that time. Campbell's catalog was not published until 1835.[1] Samuel Austin Allibone, noted American bibliographer and librarian, said that on the whole it was the best printed catalog he had ever seen.

The long history of cataloging and classification – the old controversy between author and classed catalogs and, if classed, which system – was recapitulated within less than a half century in this one library. In 1789 Zachariah Poulson employed the system of Bacon and d'Alembert. In 1807 a change was made to an author catalog; only anonymous works and pamphlets were still "classed scientifically." The classed catalog returned in 1835, but Brunet, not Bacon, determined the order of the sciences. Poulson and Campbell were prototypes of the classificatory individualists who appeared after the foundation of the American Library Association in 1876.

Campbell was born in Philadelphia on March 28, 1783, son of George Campbell, an Irish lawyer who had migrated there in 1765. Young George was admitted in 1803 to the Philadelphia Bar, of which his father was a member. Shortly after, he was elected to the Common Council of the city but soon found law and politics little to his liking. Campbell abandoned both to devote his life to music and literature. In 1806 he succeeded Zachariah Poulson as librarian of the Library Company of Philadelphia. Campbell served in this position until 1829, "during which long period he was never once prevented by sickness from attending his daily duties, a circumstance almost unprecedented in the annals of a salary officer."[2] He continued his association with the library as its secretary from 1836 to June 11, 1855, the date of his death.

A great lover of music, Campbell was one of the founders of the historic Musical Fund Society of Philadelphia in 1820, serving as secretary for the group for nearly thirty years. An oil portrait of him by Thomas Sully is now in the society's possession.

Campbell made many changes in Brunet's system in addition to providing the separate class for Bibliography, previously mentioned. A successor of Campbell, Lloyd Smith, who expanded the classification and provided it with a notation, is usually credited with the system.[3]

As an example of Campbell's method of subdivision, the section of his scheme for the natural sciences (in Class III Sciences and Arts) is given.

Natural Philosophy, General Treatises, Systems, &c.
Electricity, Galvanism, Magnetism, Meteorology, Pneumatics
Chemistry
Natural History, General works
Natural History of different Countries, &c.
Geology, Volcanoes, Earthquakes, Waters, &c.
Mineralogy, Metals, Mines, Fossils
Botany, General works
Zoology: Animals, Birds, Fishes, Insects, Shells, &c.
Medicine, General and Miscellaneous works
Treatises on Health, Diet, Regimen
Theory and Practice of Medicine
Diseases incident to various Places, Professions, &c.
Treatises on particular Diseases
Anatomy and Physiology
Surgery and Obstetrics
Materia Medica: Pharmacopoeias, Dispensatories

Mathematics, General and Miscellaneous works
Arithmetic, Algebra, Fluxions
Geometry, Surveying, Trigonometry
Logarithms, Mathematical Tables, and Instruments
Calculations of Probabilities, Life Annuities
Mechanics: Hydrostatics, Descriptions of Machines, Steam Engines, &c.
Astronomy, Astronomical Tables, Atlases, Instruments, &c.
Treatises on the Calendar
Almanacs, Ephemerides
Optics: Light, Vision, &c.

1838 New York Society Library.

The development of the New York Society Library and its catalogs illustrates a rapid transition from a rudimentary to a more sophisticated classification within twenty-five years. The society was founded in 1754 by "a set of gentlemen" who subscribed, in a few days, nearly six hundred pounds. Seven hundred volumes of "new, well-chosen books" were purchased. In 1772 George the Third granted the society a charter which was signed by William Tryon, Governor of the Colony.

The library had increased to nearly 13,000 volumes when its first catalog of any importance was published in 1813. John Forbes, a native of Aberdeen, Scotland, who had been brought to the United States in childhood by his widowed mother, compiled the catalog. At the age of nineteen Forbes became librarian of the society in 1794 and continued in this position until his death in 1824. He arranged his entries in the following divisions:

Theology, Ecclesiastical History, Sacred Criticism, Religious
   Controversy
Classic Authors, Greek and Latin
Ethicks, Logic, and Metaphysics
Mathematics, Natural and Experimental Philosophy, Astronomy,
   Chemistry, and the Arts
Natural History, Botany, Agriculture, &c.
Civil and Military History, Antiquities, Mythology, Chronology,
   Biography, and Memoirs
Politics, Legislation, Political Economy, Commerce, and Revenue
Geography, Topography, Voyages and Travels
Education, Dictionaries, Grammars, Philology, Belles-Lettres,
   and Criticism
Poetry and Drama
Fictitious Writings, Novels, Romances, and Fables
Medicine and Surgery
Architecture, Civil, Military, and Naval
Magazines, Reviews, Translations of Learned Societies, and Newspapers
Miscellanies
Pamphlets, &c.

The University of Pennsylvania used a similar system as late as 1829.

In 1838 another catalog[4] was published. It was the work of Philip Jones Forbes, a son of John Forbes. Entering the services of the library in 1824, young Forbes succeeded his uncle, Burtis Skidmore, as librarian in 1828. He served until May 1855, when strained relations with the board of trustees forced his resignation. His catalog comprised an Alphabetical Catalogue, which contained full descriptions of the books, and an Analytical Catalogue of brief entries in systematic order. A modification of the Brunet system determined the order. The 1838 classification follows on pages 136 and 137.

1841   Park's Pantology.

Roswell Park wrote his Pantology[5] to serve as a "guide book, to those who are seeking to explore the vast expanse of human knowledge. " His primary object was to develop a Natural Classification of knowledge; his second, to give a brief summary of the knowledge classified. He hoped that the classification would serve as a Model for Libraries by bringing together books relating to the same subjects, either in the catalogs, or on the shelves.

Park was born in Lebanon, Connecticut, on October 1, 1807. He graduated from West Point in 1831, the highest ranking man in his class. After resigning from the Army (Corps of Engineers) in September 1836, Park served for the next six years as professor of natural philosophy and chemistry at the University of Pennsylvania. He left the university in July 1842 to prepare for the ministry of the Protestant Episcopal Church. Park was the first president of Racine College, Racine, Wisconsin, and an original member of the American Association for the Advancement of Science. He died on July 16, 1869.

Park became interested in classification while a student at West Point and presented an essay on the subject to the Dialectic Society of the Military Academy in the spring of 1829. [6] He developed his Pantology while he was teaching at the University of Pennsylvania. To Park, as to Woodward, mind and matter form the subjects of man's ideas; body and spirit are the only

SYNOPSIS

of the

ANALYTICAL CATALOGUE

N. B. A few titles of books lately added to the Library, occur in the
Analytical, which are not given in the Alphabetical Catalogue; but which refer
to a <u>Supplement</u> to be published hereafter.

Theology.
- I. Sacred Writings, Philology and Criticism
- II. Ecclesiastical History and Law
- III. Natural Theology and the Evidences of Christianity
- IV. Miscellaneous

Law. Statute, Common, Mercantile and Military

Science.

Universal. Mental and Moral Encyclopedias
- I. Metaphysics, Ethics and Logic
- II. Education

Political.
- I. Government and National Law and Politics
- II. Political Economy, Currency, Commerce, Statistics and Public Documents

Exact.
- I. Arithmetic and Mathematics
- II. Astronomy

Natural.
- I. Natural Philosophy
- II. Chemistry
- III. Natural History
- IV. Anatomy, Medicine and Surgery

Arts.

Mathematical. Engineering, Art of War and Navigation
Natural. Agriculture, Gardening and Veterinary
Fine.
- I. Drawing, Painting, Engraving and Music
- II. Architecture – Civil and Naval
Miscellaneous. Mechanical, Chemical, Domestic, &c.

Belles Lettres.

Elementary and Theoretical.
- Dictionaries and Grammars
- Rhetoric, Oratory, Poesy, Philology and Criticism

Proper.
- I. Poetry and Drama – English and American
- II. Do.   do. foreign and translated
- III. Romance and Facetiae – English and American
- IV. Do.   do. foreign and translated
- V. Literary Essays. Letters and Orations – English and American
- VI. Do.   do. foreign and translated
- VII. Greek and Latin Classics and translations

Geography, Topography, Voyages, and Travels.
- I. Universal, (including Gazetteers and Collections)
- II. Europe, (including Great Britain and Ireland)
- III. Asia and Africa
- IV. America – North and South
- V. Australia and Polynesia

History.	I. Introductions, Historical Dictionaries and Universal History II. Mythology, Chronology, Antiquities and Heraldry III. Greece and Rome IV. England, Scotland and Ireland V. Europe VI. Asia and Africa VII. America – North and South
Biography.	I. General and Dictionaries II. English, (including Scottish and Irish) III. Foreign IV. American
Transactions	Memoirs and Transactions of Literary and Scientific Institutions – Foreign and American
Periodical Works.	I. Registers, Reviews and Magazines – British and Foreign II. Do. do. American III. American and Foreign Newspapers
Polygraphy.	I. The collected Works of Miscellaneous Writers – English and American II. Do. do. Foreign
Bibliography.	Catalogues of Books – Foreign and American
Pamphlets.	Classified. I. Unclassified II. Theological III. Political IV. Statistical and Politico-Economical V. On Medicine and Natural History VI. Addresses and Orations VII. Poetical, Critical and Philological VIII. On Education IX. Historical and Biographical X. Moral XI. On Law and Reports of Trials XII. On Slavery and Indian Affairs XIII. On Prison Discipline XIV. On Arts and Internal Improvement XV. Miscellaneous
Novels.	

modes of existence which can be known. All knowledge can therefore be reduced to four great provinces:

1. Psychonomy, including the Laws of Mind, or intellectual sciences.

2. Ethnology, or the Study of Nations, geographically and historically.

3. Physiconomy, or the Laws of the Material World.

4. Technology, or the Study of the Arts which relate to material objects.

Park subdivided these provinces into four departments, each of which comprised several branches of knowledge. As guides to a natural method in arranging the departments and branches, he used four leading principles:

1. The order of dependence.

2. The order of time.

3. The order of place.

4. The order of resemblance.

Acknowledging his indebtedness to Judge Woodward, Park criticized him for using names derived from the Greek, "so new, and burthensome to the memory, as to prevent their ever coming into general use." Inconsistently, however, Park went on to develop similar names for his divisions and subdivisions, such as:

Idiophysics ($\iota\delta\iota\circ\varsigma$, special or particular, and $\varphi\upsilon\sigma\iota\varsigma$, nature) – Natural History.

Chreotechnics ($\chi\rho\epsilon\circ\varsigma$, necessity or utility, and $\tau\epsilon\chi\nu\eta$, art) – Useful Arts.

Machetechnics ($\mu\alpha\chi\eta$, battle, and $\tau\epsilon\chi\nu\eta$, art) – Arts of War.

Hoplistics ($\delta\pi\lambda\alpha$, arms or weapons) – the branch of Machetechnics relating to the arms, ammunition, equipage, and provisions, required for military operations.

Callotechnics ($\kappa\alpha\lambda\circ\varsigma$, beautiful, and $\tau\epsilon\chi\nu\eta$, art) – Fine Arts.

Under Park's four main provinces came these departments, shown on the opposite page:

PSYCHONOMY (LAWS OF THE MIND)

Department:
- I.   Glossology (Languages)
- II.   Psychology (Mental Sciences)
- III.   Nomology (Law and Government)
- IV.   Theology

ETHNOLOGY (STUDY OF NATIONS, GEOGRAPHICALLY AND HISTORICALLY)

- V.   Geography
- VI.   Chronography (Civil History and Antiquities)
- VII.   Biography
- VIII.   Callography (Poetry, Drama, Essays, etc.)

PHYSICONOMY (LAWS OF NATURE)

- IX.   Mathematics
- X.   Acrophysics (Natural Phenomena)
- XI.   Idiophysics (Natural History)
- XII.   Androphysics (Medical Sciences)

TECHNOLOGY (PHYSICAL ARTS)

- XIII.   Architechnics (Construction and Communication)
- XIV.   Chreotechnics (Useful Arts)
- XV.   Machetechnics (Arts of War)
- XVI.   Callotechnics (Fine Arts)

Each department contained at least four branches, designated as chapters.

To illustrate:

Idiophysics Chapter:	Chreotechnics Chapter:
I. Zoology	I. Agriculture
II. Botany	II. Horticulture
III. Mineralogy	III. Domiculture
IV. Geology	IV. Vestiture
	V. Furniture
	VI. Commerce

Carrying the division further, Park broke down each chapter. Geology, for example, contained the subdivisions Introductory, Systematic, Physical, and Descriptive. Commerce was subdivided into Principles, Sources, Cambistry, and Book-keeping.

An appendix contained A Select Catalogue of Books on all the Branches of Human Knowledge in systematic order.

A year after the publication of Park's Pantology, his classification was used in the Catalogue of the Library of Indiana State University. [7]

1850 S. Hastings Grant.

The life of a classification or cataloging system depends upon the whims of librarians. "New librarians, new systems" needs little more demonstration than Euclidean axioms. The classification Edward William Johnston applied in the Mercantile Library of New York in 1837[8] had a life span of seven years. Then came a new catalog[9] with its "classified" section arranged alphabetically from Africa to Voyages and Travels. Between them ranged man's knowledge in the order of the vagaries of the alphabet: Asia, Astronomy, Banking and Currency, Bibliography and Typography, Biography, etc. A few years later, however, a new librarian, S. Hastings Grant, restored system to the library by introducing a classification[10] based upon the work of Brunet.

Seth Hastings Grant was born on June 6, 1828, in Marshall, New York, the son of Dr. Asahel Grant. After the death of his young wife, Dr. Grant went to Persia as a medical missionary to the mountain Nestorians, leaving his two sons in the care of grandparents. He died at the age of thirty-six. When Seth was twelve years old he "hitchhiked," on foot, by canal boat, stage-coach, and steamboat, to the home of relatives in Illinois. He entered Princeton in the class of 1847 but left at the end of two years because of ill health. Grant went to New York City in 1846 to enter the publishing house of Wiley and Putnam. Three years later he became librarian of the New York Mercantile Library and held the position until 1866, when he left to engage in a real estate and brokerage business. He served as superintendent of the New York Produce Exchange, as secretary to Mayor Franklin Edson of New York, and as Comptroller of the City.

Grant was associated with Charles B. Norton and Daniel Coit Gilman, later president of Johns Hopkins University, on Norton's Literary Gazette and Publishers' Circular from 1850 to 1855, and was associate editor of the American Literary Gazette and Publishers' Circular from 1863 to 1871. Grant also played a prominent part in the Librarians' Convention of 1853, which he served as secretary. He died on May 9, 1910, in Elizabeth City, New Jersey.

The classification which Grant applied in the library in 1850 later became associated with the name of Frederic B. Perkins, who made several revisions of the original work. Grant's synopsis comprises the following main divisions and subdivisions:

THEOLOGY

Sacred Books and Commentaries   Systematic and Polemic Theology
Early Church History   Natural Theology and Evidences
Devotional Works and Sermons   Religious Philosophy

MENTAL AND MORAL SCIENCE

Moral Philosophy and Ethics   General Literature, Periodicals, &c
Logic, Rhetoric and Metaphysics   Poetry, Music and the Fine Arts
Language   Fiction
Education   Games, Sports and Amusements

POLITICAL SCIENCE

Law and Government   Political Economy; Commerce
                                            and Trade

HISTORY AND GEOGRAPHY

Universal Hist., Geography and Travels   Modern History
Physical Geography and Ethnography   Africa and Asia   Revolution
Ancient History   England   Spanish Amer.
                                                           & West Indies
Antiquities, Manners and Customs   Europe   North America
Mediaeval Hist., Heraldry & Crusades   South Seas &   United States
                                       Pacific
                     Biography and Correspondence

MATHEMATICS

Arithmetic, Algebra, Geometry   Trigonometry and Calculus

NATURAL SCIENCES

Natural Philosophy   Chemistry
Astronomy   Botany
Geology and Mineralogy   Zoology

MEDICAL SCIENCE

Anatomy and Physiology   Modes of Treatment; Homoeopathy
                                            Water Cure, &c.
Hygiene   Medical Jurisprudence
Phrenology and Mental Disorders   Animal Magnetism, Mesmerism, &c
Pathology of Special Diseases

TECHNOLOGY

Navigation, Mensuration, Surveying, &c.
Civil Engineering, Architecture, Carpentry, &c.
Steam Engine, Electric Telegraph, Hydraulic-Machines, Heating, Ventilating, &c.

Metallurgy, Dyeing, Photography
Agriculture, Horticulture, Mining
Weaving, Cooking, &c.

Tactics, Fortification, &c.

ENCYCLOPÆDIC

1853 Romain Merlin.

At the First Convention of Librarians held in New York City on September 15, 16, and 17, 1853, two papers on classification were read. One was in the form of a letter[11] from Romain Merlin, of Paris, describing the classification he had used in cataloging the library of the orientalist, Baron Antoine Isaac Silvestre de Sacy. The other was a paper by Librarian Lloyd P. Smith[12] describing the classification used in the catalog of the Library Company of Philadelphia.

Merlin's classification is significant because it reflects the influence of the emerging theory of evolution. His system, especially the division devoted to the Cosmological Sciences, is closer to today's theory of order than most schemes which were in current use. In developing his scheme, however, Merlin was limited by the field in which he worked. Silvestre de Sacy's library devoted to Orientalia naturally contained little material dealing with Western sciences and technologies. The three-volume catalog, compiled and edited by Merlin, was published in Paris in 1843-47.

Merlin thought that every bibliographical classification should be based upon a logical classification of the sciences. Its divisions should be taken from the nature of the objects to be classified, its order follow the laws of nature. Such a system, intelligible to all, would give great assistance to the memory. He described his system as follows:

> "In the universality of beings we see, as a first division, on one side the Creator, on the other the Creation. All the ideas that relate to God, to whatever opinion or religion they may belong, will form a principal group, that I shall designate by the title of THEOLOGICAL SCIENCES.

"The Sciences and Arts which treat of the whole or any portion of those myriads of created beings, shall be comprised under the common title of COSMOLOGICAL SCIENCES.

"Since cause is before effect, the science which treats of God should be before all other sciences, and it would be so in my classification, without the principles of analytical exposition by which my system is arranged, and according to which every science which embraces several objects ought to precede that which treats only of those objects. Now Theology has only God for its object, and there is another science which treats of God and the Creation, that is PHILOSOPHY; not Psychology, which only describes the human soul, not Moral Philosophy, which lays down rules for social life, but Philosophy, as known to the Ancients, treating of first causes, of the Essence of Being, of the Creator and created things; in a word, embracing everything in an encyclopedic manner; Philosophy will then precede Theology, and after it will come the Sciences which relate to created things."

From this order spring three great divisions,

I. PHILOSOPHY.
II. THEOLOGICAL SCIENCES.
III. COSMOLOGICAL SCIENCES.
    1. MATHEMATICAL SCIENCE.
    2. PHYSICAL   "
    3. ASTRONOMICAL   "
    4. GEOLOGICAL   "
    5. MINERALOGICAL "
    6. PHYTOLOGICAL   "
    7. ZOOLOGICAL   "
    8. ANTHROPOLOGICAL "

As to the sciences which relate to Man, their division and order are not less simple or less natural. I consider Man under two heads, Individual Man and Man in Society. Individual man presents me with two divisions, Physical Man and Moral Man. Society also furnishes me with two divisions, the Social or Political Sciences and the Historical Sciences.

This is, sir, the outline of my classification of the Sciences without the Bibliographical application. The application changes nothing of importance, it only adds numerous subdivisions and another class, POLYGRAPHY. 13

1853 Cambridge High School.

Another classification appeared in 1853 with the publication of a catalog of the Cambridge (Mass.) High School Library. In marked contrast to the plan of M. Merlin, this catalog reflected the "classical" arrangements of Bray, Elliott, and Brunet. It was the work of Ezra Abbot, pioneer American librarian and Biblical scholar.

Abbot was born in the hamlet of Jackson, Waldo County, Maine, on April 28, 1819. His mother, Phebe (Abbot) Abbot, who had taught herself Greek so that she could read the New Testament and teach her son, died while he was a child. After attending the local district school, Abbot went to Peterborough, New Hampshire, to study under his mother's brother, the Reverend Abiel Abbot.[14] He prepared for college at Phillips Exeter Academy, then went to Bowdoin, where he received his A. B. in 1840 and his A. M. in 1843. Abbot taught in Maine for a few years before he became a member of the faculty of Cambridge High School. An interest in bibliography led him to compile a catalog of the high school library. He then became an assistant in the Boston Athenaeum and, in 1856, assistant librarian of Harvard College. In 1872 Abbot was appointed Bussey Professor of New Testament Criticism and Interpretation in the Divinity School, a position he held until his death on March 21, 1884.

Abbot was a member of the American Oriental Society, the American Academy of Arts and Sciences, and the New Testament Committee for the Revision of the English Bible. His scholarship brought him many honorary degrees: A. M. from Harvard in 1861, L. L. D. from Yale in 1869, and from Bowdoin in 1878. Although a layman, Abbot received the S. T. D. from Harvard in 1872. The University of Edinburgh, on the occasion of its tercentenary, tendered him the degree of Doctor of Divinity, but Abbot died before he could receive it.

At the memorial services held for Abbot in the First Parish Church, Cambridge, Professor Joseph Henry Thayer praised Abbot's contribution to Biblical studies but added, "What an inestimable gain, if our friend could only have given himself to his life's work wholly and on the spot, instead of squandering his precious strength and mental powers for twenty-five years in teaching school and cataloguing books!"[15]

Abbot's interest in bibliography and cataloging, unfortunately, did not result in any treatise on these subjects. A good alphabetical catalog was satisfactory, he thought, for those who knew all the books which interested them and wanted only to learn if they were in the library. But for students he preferred a systematic arrangement because it would lead them to sources of information on particular subjects. In addition it would afford beginning

students "... a survey, as if from some eminence, of the territory that lies

before them, will enable them to understand better the relations of its differ-

ent parts to each other, will give them new conceptions of the varied objects

of interest which it presents, and animate them to press cheerfully through

the somewhat tangled and thorny paths by which it is to be entered. "[16]

His decision resulted in the compilation of A Classed Catalogue of the

Library of the Cambridge High School. Abbot used the following main divi-

sions in his catalog:

> Science of Mind, and of Man in His Higher Relations
> Mathematical Science
> Physical Science
> The Arts
> Language; With an Appendix
> Works of Imagination and Fancy, Wit and Humor
> History of Man, in his Higher Relations
> Encyclopaedias and Polygraphy

Abbot subdivided each of his main divisions according to its nature and

the needs of the library. Keenly aware of the dispersive effect of cross-di-

vision, he indicated the preferred location in "Notes" following the main di-

visions. Of the classification and method of description Abbot wrote:

> It is necessarily imperfect. The different branches of human know-
> ledge are so intimately connected, that no scheme of classification
> can be devised, in which the several classes will not run into each
> other; and in the practical application of any system it will be found
> that some books belong equally to two or more different divisions.
> When such is the case with respect to any work, its title has usually
> been recorded in full under only one of these divisions, and briefly
> noticed under the others, with a reference to the complete entry. The
> affinities between different classes have often been pointed out by
> notes, which will also, it is hoped, aid the student who wishes to find
> what the library contains on a particular subject.
>   The Alphabetical Index at the end of the volume will show
> at once whether a particular work belongs to the library. [17]

To illustrate Abbot's subdivisions and notes, the following is given:

SCIENCE OF MIND, AND OF MAN IN HIS HIGHER RELATIONS

Class

> I. MENTAL PHILOSOPHY; LOGIC; AESTHETICS
>   Note. For the History of Philosophy, see Class XXVIII.
>   For Aesthetics, compare Class XIV. Part V. and Class XVII.

II. THEOLOGY
    Part I. General Works; Natural Religion; Evidences of Revelation.
      II. The Sacred Scriptures.
      III. Other Works belonging to Christian Theology.
          Note. For Ecclesiastical and Sacred History, see
             Class XXVI.
      IV. Various Religions and Superstitions; Mythology.
          Note. Compare Class XVI. Part I. and Class XXVII.

III. MORAL PHILOSOPHY
    Note. For the History of Moral Philosophy, see Class XXVIII.;
    for the History of Morals and Manners, Class XXVII.

IV. POLITICAL AND SOCIAL PHILOSOPHY
    Note. For Political History, see Class XXV.; for Political
    Antiquities, Class XXVII.
    Part I. General Works on Government, Politics, and the Consti-
    tution of Society, with others, not included in Parts II. and
    III.; International and Constitutional Law.
      II. Political Economy, Trade, Finance.
          Note: For the Useful Arts, see Class XIV. For
             Statistics, see Class XXII.
      III. Law.
          Note. For International and Constitutional Law, see
             Part I.
V. EDUCATION
    Note. For the History of Education, see Class XXIX.

Abbot's continuing interest in providing a subject approach to books

led him, while at Harvard, to a consideration of subject headings. Aware that

the vagaries of titles dispersed closely-related material, he decided that

"subject entries" should be based upon the contents, not the titles of books.

His interest in classification obviously was responsible for his opposition to

specific entry and his adoption of the alphabetico-classed principle of subject

heading structure. He described his plan as follows:

> The arrangement of classes or subjects ... is alphabetical,
> not scientific; but the plan differs from the dictionary scheme in
> this, that a large part of these classes or subjects have numerous
> subdivisions, which, instead of being dispersed through the great
> alphabetical series, and thus widely separated from each other,
> are arranged in a secondary alphabetical series under the gener-
> al head.[18]

It is interesting to note that the catalog, which was on cards, two by five

inches in size, was divided into two parts, author and subject files. Charles

A. Cutter, who assisted Abbot in compiling the catalog, was influenced by the

older man into forsaking divinity for library work. He later wrote of Abbot's

theory:

The introduction of classes of literature, which none of the early dictionaries had, gave to Harvard College Library the first plan ever made for a complete alphabetical catalogue. It is sometimes termed the "mixed" or "half-way" system; a better, because more definitely descriptive name, is "alphabetico classed," inasmuch as its differentiae are class entry and alphabetic order, the differentiae of dictionary catalogues being specific entry and alphabetic order.[19]

1853 U. S. Military Academy.

The Military Academy at West Point, New York, founded by Act of Congress in 1802, had a collection of 15,500 volumes when it called upon "a private soldier," the assistant librarian, André Freis, to catalog its library. Two earlier catalogs had been printed, in 1822 and in 1830, but the growth of the collection had made them useless. The librarian, Henry Coppée, 1st Lieut. & Bt. Capt. 1st Art., remarked,

> The present catalogue, prepared with unremitting care by the Assistant Librarian, André Freis, it is believed will supply the deficiency in every respect. In an attempt to make a critical and minute division of classes, some works may have crept from their own into an analogous classification, but it is hoped that few errors even of this kind will be discovered. 20

The classification used in the Catalogue is an early "special library" attempt to organize all knowledge from the point of view of its specialty. It will be seen from the outline below that strictly military subjects head the classes, with related fields of the sciences following, while literature, theology, generalia, and miscellany stand at the very end.

1. Military Engineering, Fortifications, Attack, Defence, and Mines
2. Artillery and Pyrotechny
3. Strategy, Grand Tactics, and Military Miscellanies
4. Cavalry Tactics
5. Infantry and Infantry Tactics
6. Fencing and the use of the Sword
7. Equitation and Veterinary Art, &c.
8. Military Administration and Organization
9. Military Laws, Regulations, and Orders
10. General Military and Naval History
11. Battles, Sieges, and Campaigns
12. Military Biography and Memoirs
13. Military Antiquities
14. Military and Naval Periodicals
15. Military and Naval Dictionaries
16. Army and Navy Registers
17. Civil and Naval Architecture and Landscape Gardening
18. Machinery, Instruments, Applied Mechanics and Carpentry
19. Hydraulic Constructions, Canals, Bridges, &c.

20. Civil Engineering
21. Works on Materials
22. Works on Warming and Ventilating
23. Law of Nature and Nations, Treaties, &c.
24. Government and Politics
25. Political Economy, Metrology, Finance, Commerce, &c.
26. Laws, Law Treatises, Commentaries, and Reports
27. Mathematics in general
28. Arithmetic
29. Algebra
30. Geometry
31. Perspective and Descriptive Geometry
32. Trigonometry
33. Analytical Geometry
34. Method of Fluxions, Differential and Integral Calculus
35. Mensuration, Surveying, and Practical Geometry
36. Logarithms and Mathematical Tables
37. Mechanics, including Statics, Dynamics, Hydrostatic and Hydrodynamics
38. Natural and Experimental Philosophy in General
39. Optics
40. Navigation
41. Astronomy
42. Astronomical Observations
43. Astronomical Tables
44. General Works on Arts and Sciences
45. Chemistry
46. Electricity, Magnetism, Galvanism, and Meteorology
47. Natural History
48. Botany and Agriculture
49. Mineralogy
50. Geology
51. Medical and Surgical Works
52. Geography, Topography, and Statistics
53. Geography — Loose sheets of Maps
54. Voyages and Travels
55. Universal History and Chronology
56. Ancient History, Antiquities, and Mythology
57. Modern History of Continental Europe
58. English, Scotch, and Irish History
59. French History and Civil Memoirs
60. Asiatic and African History
61. American History
62. Biographical, Historical, and Classical Dictionaries
63. Biography and Personal Memoirs
64. Literary History
65. Metaphysical Philosophy
66. Logic and Intellectual Philosophy
67. Moral Philosophy
68. Poetry and Fictions
69. Grammar and Philology
70. Rhetoric and Criticism
71. Addresses
72. Journals and Treatises upon Education
73. Works on Painting, Sculpture, Music, and Illustrated Works of Engravings
74. Gymnastics and Swimming
75. Literary and Political Periodicals, Reports, and Registers
76. Bibliography

77. Dictionaries and Encyclopaedias
78. Theology and Ecclesiastical History
79. Miscellanies

Under each of the seventy-nine class groups the <u>Catalogue</u> lists the respective books alphabetically by author or title, the items being numbered consecutively in the left hand column. These numbers determined the shelving arrangement. The <u>Alphabetical</u> <u>Index</u> at the end of the volume then lists these same items alphabetically and cites the number for each, as shown in the following examples taken from the first two groups:

MILITARY ENGINEERING

231 Yule (Lieut. Henry).   Fortification . . . ;
                                         1 vol. 8vo. Edinburgh, 1851.
232 Zastrow (A. de). Historique de la Fortification . . .
         2me ed.
                         2 vols. 8vo. & Atlas 4to.   Paris, 1849.

ARTILLERY AND PYROTECHNY

233 Adye (Ralph Willett).   The Bombardier, and Pocket
         Gunner . . .
                         1 vol. 18 mo. (4 <u>copies.</u>) Boston, 1804.

234 Adye (Ralph Willett).   The Bombardier, and Pocket
         Gunner.   Eighth edition . . .
                         1 vol. 18 mo. (3 <u>copies.</u>) London, 1827.

ALPHABETICAL INDEX

Adye (R. W.). The Bombardier and Pocket Gunner, 233, 234.

Yule (H.). Fortification, 231.

Zastrow (A. de). Histoire de la Fortification permanente, 232.

Coppée, a military man by profession and, in his own words, a librarian <u>malgré</u> <u>lui</u>, nevertheless revealed his great appreciation of books and their use when he told the 1853 Librarians' Convention:

> The little service I had seen, and the partial fondness for certain kinds of reading, had given me no knowledge of the great progressive science of bibliography, a science nobler in its results than simple authorship, in that it classifies and makes available at one intelligent glance, masses of matter, rich specimens of mental ore, which otherwise would lie hidden and useless to the world. [21]

This is the first period in which Francis Bacon's classification does not enter in one or another of its varied forms. While Bacon's divisions are still being used in American libraries, Brunet's influence is increasing; his classification is being adapted, however, rather than adopted. Woodward's system, which foreshadowed the evolutionary order, appears for the last time, but the order is continued in Merlin's cosmological sciences. West Point presents an early special library classification. And at the end of the period the alphabetico-classed catalog appears on the American scene as the dictionary principle continues to drive classification from catalogs if not from shelves.

CHAPTER IX

The Old and the New

In philosophy as in art there is often as much of the creator in a work as there is of the realities interpreted and synthesized or portrayed. When a poet, a journalist, and a geologist enter the field of classification, the products of their efforts are bound to be diverse. Consciously, or unconsciously, each maker of schemes puts into his work a part of himself, his background, his interests, and his prejudices, as well as the knowledge of his age.

1855 Tennessee State Library.

The classification devised for the Encyclopaedia Metropolitana by Samuel Taylor Coleridge (1772-1834), English poet and philosopher, found what was perhaps its first, and only, library application in the 1855 Catalogue of the newly created Tennessee State Library. Return Jonathan Meigs III, who had been appointed commissioner to superintend the purchase of the library, reported to the General Assembly of Tennessee that, "The 'Classified Catalogue' has been prepared to show how imperfect the collection is, and to serve as a guide for its continuation." He added that Coleridge's classification had been used because, in spite of criticism, "nothing better perhaps has been offered as a substitute."

Return Jonathan Meigs, namesake of his grandfather, Colonel Meigs of Revolutionary fame, was born on April 14, 1801, near Winchester, in Clark County, Kentucky. After his father's death in 1808 he lived part of the time with an uncle, James Lamme, in Bourbon County, where he attended local schools. He studied law, was admitted to the bar in Frankfort in 1822, and subsequently practiced in Athens, Tennessee. Meigs later served as attorney general of Tennessee and as United States attorney for the Middle Tennessee District. In 1848-50 Meigs published a two-volume Digest of all the Decisions of the Former Superior Courts of Law and Equity, and of the Present Supreme

Court of Errors and Appeals in the State of Tennessee. With William F.

Cooper, he published the Code of Tennessee in 1858, the only code adopted by

the legislature until 1931. Meigs became state librarian in 1856.

In 1861, when his Northern sympathies placed him in danger of mob

violence, he resigned his position and went to New York. In 1863 he was ap-

pointed clerk of the Supreme Court of the District of Columbia, a position he

held until shortly before his death in 1891, on his ninetieth birthday.

Meigs had strong convictions concerning the value of libraries. In his

"Report," which prefaced the Catalogue, he told the Tennessee Assembly:

> An additional appropriation of ten thousand dollars, judiciously
> invested, would establish the library upon a solid foundation, and
> make it a truly desirable and useful resort for all the longing
> worshippers of wisdom, whose silent and often despised vigils
> have gradually delivered mankind from the misery and brutal
> degradation of the savage state, and led the race to the glorious
> liberty that belongs alone to the mind made free. [1]

Coleridge, whom Meigs chose to follow, turned his attention to classi-

fication in 1817 when he became interested in the production of a methodical

encyclopedia. Without method, he thought, there is only chaos. "From the

cottager's hearth or the workshop of the artisan, to the Palace or the Arsen-

al, the first merit, that which admits neither substitute nor equivalent, is,

that every thing is in its place."[2] Philosopher as well as poet, Coleridge

passed easily from one to the other; and perhaps the gap between the two is

not so great as commonly imagined. Leslie Stephen wrote:

> The loftiest poet and the loftiest philosopher deal with the same
> subject-matter, the great problems of the world and of human
> life, though one presents the symbolism and the other unravels
> the logical connection of the abstract conceptions. [3]

Coleridge's essay in classification, the "General Introduction ... or

A Preliminary Treatise on Method," was published in 1818 in the quarto edi-

tion of the Encyclopaedia Metropolitana. Later the author said that the work

had been so "bedeviled" by the editors that he was ashamed to own it. What

the original was perhaps never will be known.

Coleridge's concept of method was:

> The word Method ($\mu\acute{\epsilon}\theta o\delta o\varsigma$) being of Grecian origin, first

formed and applied by that acute, ingenious, and accurate People,
to the purposes of Scientific arrangement, it is in the Greek Language that we must seek for its primary and fundamental signi-
fication. Now, in Greek, it literally means a way, or path, of
transit. Hence the first idea of Method is a progressive transition from one step in any course to another; and where the word
Method is applied with reference to many such transitions in continuity, it necessarily implies a Principle of Unity with Progression. But that which unites, and makes many things one in the
Mind of Man, must be an act of the Mind itself, a manifestation of
intellect, and not a spontaneous and uncertain production of circumstances. This act of the Mind, then, this leading thought, this
"key note" of the harmony, this "subtile, cementing, subterran-
eous" power, borrowing a phrase from the nomenclature of legislation, we may not inaptly call the Initiative of all Method. It is
manifest, that the wider the sphere of transition is,the more comprehensive and commanding must be the initiative: and if we would
discover an universal Method, by which every step in our progress
through the whole circle of Art and Science should be directed, it
is absolutely necessary that we should seek it in the very interior
and central essence of the Human intellect. [4]

Coleridge based the first two main divisions of his classification upon
the relations of things, of which he found two principal kinds: (1) The relation that the Ideas or Laws of the Mind bear to each other, and (2) the relation that these Ideas or Laws bear to the external world. The first yields
the Pure Sciences; the second results in the Mixed and Applied Sciences. The
third division of Coleridge's classification dealt with the Biographical and
Historical, and the fourth division concerned the Miscellaneous and Lexico-
graphical. The scheme, or "Table of Contents" as it was called, was published
in the first edition of the Encyclopaedia Metropolitana.

FIRST DIVISION

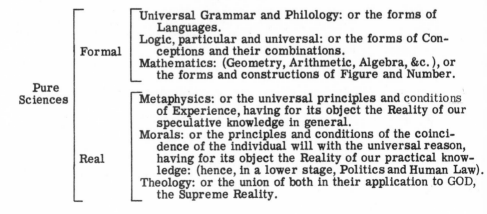

Pure Sciences

Formal

Universal Grammar and Philology: or the forms of
 Languages.
Logic, particular and universal: or the forms of Con-
 ceptions and their combinations.
Mathematics: (Geometry, Arithmetic, Algebra, &c.), or
 the forms and constructions of Figure and Number.

Real

Metaphysics: or the universal principles and conditions
 of Experience, having for its object the Reality of our
 speculative knowledge in general.
Morals: or the principles and conditions of the coinci-
 dence of the individual will with the universal reason,
 having for its object the Reality of our practical knowledge: (hence, in a lower stage, Politics and Human Law).
Theology: or the union of both in their application to GOD,
 the Supreme Reality.

SECOND DIVISION

Mixed and Applied Sciences

- Mixed
  - Mechanics
  - Hydrostatics
  - Pneumatics
  - Optics
  - Astronomy

- Applied
  - I — Experimental Philosophy
    - Magnetism
    - Electricity including Galvanism
    - Chemistry
    - Light
    - Heat
    - Colour
    - Meteorology
  - II — The Fine Arts
    - Poetry, introduced by Psychology
    - Painting
    - Music
    - Sculpture
    - Architecture
  - III — The Useful Arts
    - Agriculture, introduced by Political Economy
    - Commerce
    - Manufacture
  - IV — Natural History
    - Introduced by Physiology in its widest sense
    - Inanimate: — Chrystallography, Geology, Mineralogy
    - Insentient: — Phytonomy, Botany
    - Animate: — Zoology
  - V — Application of Natural History
    - Anatomy
    - Surgery
    - Materia Medica
    - Pharmacy
    - Medicine

THIRD DIVISION

Biographical and Historical — Biography Chronologically arranged, interspersed with introductory Chapters of National History, Political Geography and Chronology, and accompanied with correspondent Maps and Charts.

FOURTH DIVISION

Miscellaneous and Lexicographal — Alphabetical, Miscellaneous, and Supplementary:— containing a Gazetteer or complete Vocabulary of Geography: and a Philosophical and Etymological Lexicon of the English Language, or the History of English Words:— the citations arranged according to the Age of the Works from which they are selected, yet with every attention to the independent beauty or value of the sentences chosen which is consistent with the higher ends of a clear insight into the original and acquired meaning of every word.

Meigs followed Coleridge's general scheme, including his subject and geographic subdivisions, but he confined the fourth division to geography. He added polygraphy as a fifth division, in order to adapt a classification of knowledge to library needs. An alphabetical catalog preceded the classified catalog.

1858 St. Louis Mercantile Library.

The final battle in the conflict between Bacon and Brunet for dominance of American library classification was fought in the St. Louis Mercantile Library in 1857. When William P. Curtis compiled the first catalog[5] of the library in 1850 he took as a model the Harvard catalog of 1830 and adopted Brunet for the classified section. But Edward William Johnston, who prepared the next catalog, was a man of strong convictions and a Baconian of long standing. He rejected Brunet and installed the divisions of knowledge which Baron Verulam had developed over two and a quarter centuries before. His decision was influential in determining the course of American classification from 1870 to the present day.[6] For the origin of Johnston's classification it is necessary to turn to South Carolina of the 1830's.

In 1835 the trustees of the College of South Carolina (University of South Carolina) created a new position — secretary of the board of trustees and librarian — and appointed Johnston to fill it. Johnston remained at the college less than three years, but during his stay he developed a system of classification and compiled a catalog[7] of the library's books.

Johnston was born in 1799 at Cherry Grove, later Longwood, a mile east of Farmville in Prince Edward County, Virginia. His father was Lt. Peter Johnston who at sixteen had run away from Hampden-Sydney College to join the cavalry of Lt. Col. "Light Horse" Harry Lee. When the Revolution was over, Peter practiced law and served as a member of the Virginia legislature. In 1788 he married Mary Wood of Goochland, daughter of Col. Valentine and Lucy (Henry) Wood, a sister of Patrick Henry. Nine sons and a daughter were born to the couple, one of them the Confederate general, Joseph Eggleston Johnston.

Little is known of Johnston's early life. In 1811 his father was appointed a judge of the General Court of Virginia for the Prince Edward District, but exchanged circuits with Judge William Brockenbrough. The family moved to southwestern Virginia and settled at Panecillo, on the edge of the town of Abingdon. It is probable that Edward William was educated at home as was his brother Joseph, for "Mrs. Johnston inherited her mother's talents and attainments. She was so highly educated as to be competent to fit her sons for college not only in the elements of learning, but in the ancient classics as well."[8] He may later have attended Abingdon Academy.

After Johnston completed the catalog of the College of South Carolina, he went to New York City and compiled a classed catalog[9] for the Mercantile Library Association there, using the classification he had applied in South Carolina. He then turned to school teaching and established the Roanoke Female Institute at Botetourt Springs, Virginia, where his uncle, Charles Johnston, had built a summer resort about 1821. The school lasted only three sessions, from 1839 to 1842, but it was to cause Johnston to engage in a duel a decade later in 1852, when he and John M. Daniel, editor of the Richmond Examiner differed concerning the aesthetic value of Hiram Powers' statue, the "Greek Slave." Daniel had used a picture of the statue to parody the dress Johnston had prescribed for his students: "For Winter, Bottle-green Circassian or Merino, with Capes of the same. For those below 12 years, Pantalets like the dress."[10] The duel, fought at Bladensburg, Maryland, fortunately was bloodless.

Johnston had edited the Columbia Telescope for a time while working at the College of South Carolina, and after the failure of his female seminary he returned to journalism. In December 1841, with John H. Pleasants and John Woodson, he established the Independent in Washington, D. C., but the paper ceased publication about six months later. Johnston next was associated with Pleasant's Richmond Whig and then worked for the National Intelligencer in Washington for ten years — a long period for Johnston to remain settled in one place. During these years he contributed regularly to the Southern Literary Messenger and other periodicals, frequently using the nom de plume "Il Segretario." During his residence in Washington Johnston became involved in a number of bibliographic projects which apparently gained a considerable reputation for him. Fragmentary manuscript sources in the Library of Congress and in the National Archives reveal that Johnston devoted some time (probably employed by the Hamilton family) doing the "Indexes"[11] for the papers of Alexander Hamilton and arranging for their binding before they were turned over to the Department of State in January 1850. At the same time, he was acting as Secretary to the Board of Commissioners appointed to carry out certain stipulations of the Treaty of Guadalupe Hidalgo with Mexico.

By the winter of 1853-54, Johnston had moved to New Orleans where he was chief editor of the New Orleans Crescent; in 1855 he went to St. Louis, joining Mitchell on the Intelligencer there. In 1858 he became an associate editor of the St. Louis Leader along with Charles L. Hunt. After the failure of that paper the same year, he went to the St. Louis Mercantile Library Association, succeeding William P. Curtis as librarian of the institution in 1859.

When the Civil War broke out, Johnston opposed secession but later changed his mind and denounced the government in bitter terms. Refusing to take the oath of allegiance, he was forced to resign from the library on January 28, 1862. He devoted the rest of his life to free-lance journalism and teaching at the Christian Brothers' College in St. Louis. Johnston died on December 9, 1867, in his house on Dayton Street after a long illness; his second wife, Margaret, survived him but one day.

The New Orleans Crescent summarized his scholarship in an editorial: "If men could bequeath their knowledge, as they do their material property, to posterity the heir of Edward William Johnston would be possessed of a rich legacy indeed."[12] Johnston did bequeath part of his knowledge, but the nature of the bequest and its influence have long been unknown.

There was never any doubt in his mind about catalogs:

> For there is but one real method of arranging the contents
> of large libraries; and this is the systematic; the regular class-
> ing of books, each under the subject of which it treats, so as to
> bring together, for the student, in one body, all that the collection
> affords, as to each separate matter; while every matter, of course,
> finds its own due place, in a right intellectual arrangement of all
> human knowledge. To this, as a convenient key, a mere Index, an
> alphabetical list, should be, and is here, attached: but a mere al-
> phabetical method (if, indeed, it can be called such) can never, no
> matter how well executed, supply the place of a true one. There
> is nothing to recommend it, except its facility of execution. For
> to make its (so called) classified Index at all accomplish what it
> assumes to do, it would have to be as large and minute as a regu-
> lar systematic one, while totally destitute of its high advantage of
> rational arrangement. 13

In his 1836 South Carolina catalog, Johnston gave the following detailed
description of his classification:

> The arrangement adopted in the following Catalogue, is that
> of the Baconian system of knowledge: the Books, that is to say,
> are placed in three great Classes – of Memory, of Judgement, or
> of Imagination – according as, by their subject, they belong to the
> mere particulars and instrumental part of knowledge; or to Sci-
> ence proper, whether Speculative or Exact; or to the department
> of the Imagination.

> Of these three heads, History, taken in its larger sense,
> forms the first. It is divided into what may (in contradistinction
> to Natural History) be called <u>History Proper</u>; and <u>Natural History</u>.

> History proper has the following branches or subdivisions.

> I. Descriptive History, or Geography, comprising whatever
>   can give an exact idea of Countries at a definite period;
>   their Inhabitants, Institutions, Manners, Language, Liter-
>   ature, Commerce, Arts, &c., as well as the region itself.
>   This subdivision comprehends, therefore, Systems of
>   <u>Geography</u> and <u>Hydrography</u>; <u>Topography</u> and <u>Local His-</u>
>   <u>tories</u>; together with <u>Voyages</u> and <u>Travels</u>. These are
>   all placed in the order of the Antiquity, in Profane His-
>   tory, of the several Countries to which they relate.

> II. <u>Narrative History</u> follows; beginning with bodies or sys-
>   tems of History, and descending to that of particular
>   Countries or Races or Associations. In these, the his-
>   toric arrangement observed is the same with that al-
>   ready indicated. The Biographies of Sovereigns or
>   Statesmen, and Memoirs forming the materials for His-
>   tories, are placed in this class.

> III. Personal History, or <u>Biography</u>, comes next; and is chiefly
>   confined to the Lives of private persons and of Literary
>   men. In this subdivision, Bodies or Collections of Bio-
>   graphy are included, unless they are formed upon the de-
>   sign of illustrating the history of a particular country or

order, to which they are then referred; as Kippis's
"Biographia Britannica," Bower's "Lives of the Popes,"
or the like.

IV. Literary History and Bibliography, or the account of the
Literature of certain times or regions or dialects or
orders of men; and that of Books themselves, whether
written or printed, their material, form, &c., make the
next division.

V. Ecclesiastical History follows; comprising, besides the
history of the Christian faith and Church in general,
that of its Religious Orders, of its different Sects,
and the Lives of Ecclesiastics.

VI. Chronology and Antiquities – the Appendices to History
proper – close the first great division of History.

Its other great branch – Natural History – is distributed
as follows.

I. Systems, general Treatises, and Collections. Accounts
of the Natural History of particular regions are, of
course, placed among the latter.

II. The Animal Kingdom – Zoology.

III. The Vegetable Kingdom – Botany.

IV. The Mineral Kingdom – Geology and Mineralogy.

V. Chemistry – the history of the organic properties of Matter.

VI. Agriculture and Gardening: which, though more strictly
belonging to the Mechanical Arts, are placed here, as
dependencies upon Botany and Chemistry.

The second Capital Division of knowledge – that of subjects
belonging to the Judgment – Philosophy, or Speculative Knowledge
– is subdivided into, 1st, the several branches of what is usually
termed Moral Philosophy; 2d, the various departments of Theology,
Natural and Revealed; 3rd, Grammar; 4th, the Art of Government;
5th, the Mathematical Sciences; 6th, the Art of Healing. These,
again, in their several subdivisions, are distributed as follows.

Moral Philosophy embraces three branches:

I. Metaphysics: or what concerns the phenomena and principles of Thought:

II. Ethics: the rules according to which it is found that Individual Good must be pursued:

III. Education: or the Art of advantageously modifying, in the
young, Thought and the Affections.

Theology has the following main branches:

Natural Theology: the Science which ascertains, from

mere Reason, the existence of a God, and our duties towards him.

II. Revealed Theology: comprehending the several Texts and Versions of the Christian Scriptures: the various Apparatuses to the same: the works of Commentators: Systems of Divinity: Homilies and Miscellaneous Theology: Treatises on the Evidences of Christianity.

III. Heteredox Theology, with Mythology and other Superstitions.

Grammar includes,

I. Philology – the rules and vocabularies of particular Languages.

II. Universal Grammar and Logic.

III. Literary Criticism, embracing Reviews and other literary Ephimerides.

IV. Rhetoric: the art of communicating our ideas, by composition, agreeably or forcibly. It includes the several sorts of Eloquence, Literary composition in general, and Epistles.

V. Elocution – the art of expressive Gesture and Enunciation – closes the department of Grammar.

Whatever concerns the Art of Government is, in this arrangement, placed under the three heads of either Politics, Political Economy, or Jurisprudence.

I. Politics comprehends the Theory of Government and its Mechanism: the history of particular Politics; that of Public Negotiations: and State papers in general.

II. Political Economy includes Statistics, and whatever relates to the Industrial resources and the population of Countries.

III. Jurisprudence comprises Natural and National Law; the general Theory of Legislation; the Law of particular States; with Ecclesiastical and Martial Law. In this body, also, are placed the Publications of the English Public Records Commission – that munificent and appropriate gift of the noble nation, from which our own Institutions are so largely derived. A part of these (as the Foedera) belong more strictly to State papers: but it has seemed better not to separate them from the rest of the Collection.

The Mathematical Sciences are arranged in the following manner.

I. Mathematics, pure and Mixed.

II. Physics, or Natural Philosophy, in its several branches.

III. Encyclopaedias, and other Collections as to the Arts and
    Sciences, including Scientific Ephimerides.

Medicine — the closing division of Philosophy — embraces
Anatomy, Physiology, Materia Medica, Surgery, The Veterinary
Art, Recreations, Phrenology and Physiognomy.

Poetry — the third great division of knowledge — comprehends the Imaginative Arts in general: that is to say, Poetry proper,
whether Narrative, Didactic, or Dramatic; Treatises in the Fine
Arts; Facetiae; and Prose Fictions.

In Poetry proper, to distribute the books, not according to
their form of composition, but under the Language to which each
belongs, has seemed, for a Collection such as ours, the better
method of enumeration.

Thus far of the regular Classes. But a body of Writers
remains, reducible, from the variety of topics embraced in their
works, to no one division in particular. These are usually enumerated apart, as Polygraphs, or writers of Miscellanies. The
separate productions of such authors should, meantime, find
mention, at their proper places, in the general body of an Index
more regular and exact than the necessity of mere despatch in
drawing it up has suffered this present to be.

In his 1858 St. Louis catalog Johnston's explanation occupied but a

short paragraph:

The method here adopted is the Baconian, and has been stu-
diously made as simple and intelligible as may be. It places all
books, not mixing together various branches of knowledge, under
three great divisions: — those of History, (or the Memory,) — of
Philosophy, (or the Reason, the Judgment,) — and of Poetry, (or the
Imagination.)The authors who have mixed their subjects, or have
written separately on more than one, are assigned to the indeter-
minate class, of Polygraphs, or, writers on many things. 14

Despite Johnston's theory, this last essay in classification departed

widely from the Baconian divisions he had used earlier. Ironically, however,

his arrangement is closer to the spirit of Bacon, especially in Philosophy,

where the natural sciences and the useful arts are at last brought together.

The class as a whole, however, reflects Brunet's faculty divisions rather than

the God, Nature, Man sequence of Bacon. The following abstract shows Johns-

ton's main subdivisions. Brunet's main divisions are also given for the sake

of comparison.

Johnston	Brunet
HISTORY	
PHILOSOPHY	
Theology	THEOLOGY
Jurisprudence	JURISPRUDENCE
Political Science	SCIENCES AND ARTS
Political Economy	Philosophy
Sciences and Arts	Economics
Philosophy (Proper)	Political Science
Natural Sciences and	Natural Sciences
Useful Arts	Arts and Crafts
Education	Writing and Printing
Philology	Fine Arts
POETRY	Useful Arts
Literature	Recreative Arts
Fine Arts	LANGUAGE, AND
POLYGRAPHS	LITERATURE
	HISTORY

1860 U. S. Naval Academy.

"On the morning of Friday, Oct. 10, 1845, at eleven o'clock, a group of about 50 to 60 midshipmen of the United States Navy were assembled in a room in one of the buildings of old Fort Severn at Annapolis. Most of them were veterans of five years' service with the fleet and ranged up to twenty-seven years of age. Many had four years of service to their credit. Only about half a dozen were youngsters, thirteen to sixteen years old, with no sea experience.

"These were the first students of the new naval school founded by Secretary of the Navy George Bancroft — the first of more than 17,500 midshipmen who have passed through the United States Naval Academy in a hundred years. "[15]

A few hundred books which had belonged to the libraries of ships-of-war and navy yards were transferred to form the nucleus of the Academy library. The library had increased to 8,548 printed volumes and pamphlets, 25 manuscript volumes, 200 sheets of loose maps and charts, 12 photographs of lighthouses, and 8 sheets of loose engravings when a printed catalog became indispensable. Thomas G. Forde, the assistant librarian, was assigned the task of preparing it.

Forde's work, which was published in 1860 as the Catalogue of the

Library of the U. S. Naval Academy, comprised two parts: I. Alphabetical
Catalogue and II. Analytical Catalogue. A variant of the Brunet system formed
the basis for the arrangement of the analytical part. It ranged from Theology
and Philosophy through History, Biography, Geography, and the various sciences to Naval Science and Arts, followed by Manufactures, Law and Politics,
Literature, Polygraphy, and Bibliography.

SYNOPSIS OF THE ANALYTICAL CATALOGUE.

Theology.
1. Sacred Writings, Commentaries, Criticism.
2. Natural Theology, and the Evidences of Christianity.
3. Miscellaneous Theological Works.
4. Ecclesiastical History.

Mental and Moral Philosophy.
1. Mental Philosophy, and Logic.
2. Moral Philosophy, and Education

History.
1. General Treatises and Lectures on History, Universal History, Chronology, &c.
2. Ancient History, Antiquities, Mythology, Numismatics.
3. Continental Europe.
4. England, Ireland, Scotland.
5. Asia, Africa, Australia.
6. North and South America.
7. Naval and Military History.

Biography.
1. Collective Biography.
2. British Biography.
3. American Biography.
4. Miscellaneous Biography.
5. Naval and Military Biography.

Geography and Terrestrial Physics.
1. Universal, Descriptive, and Historical Geography, Ethnography, &c.
2. Physical Geography, and Meteorology.
3. Voyages, Travels, Geographical Explorations and Surveys.
4. Atlases Maps, &c.

Mathematical Science and Arts
1. Mathematics in General, including Collected Works, Histories, Dictionaries, Journals, &c.
2. Arithmetic, and Algebra.
3. Geometry. Trigonometry, Descriptive and Analytical Geometry, Geometry of Curves, &c.
4. Calculus of Differential, Integral and other functions.
5. Mathematical Tables and Instruments.
6. Mensuration, Surveying, Engineering, &c.
7. Miscellaneous Mathematical Works.

Astronomy and Geodesy.	1. Histories and Journals of Astronomy. 2. General, Physical and Practical Astronomy. 3. Observations, Observatories, and Instruments. 4. Ephemerides, Catalogues, Maps, and Tables. 5. Cometography. 6. Miscellaneous Astronomical Works. 7. Geodesy, and Geodetical Operations.
Physical Science and Arts.	1. Natural Philosophy in General. 2. Mechanics. 3. Optics, Acoustics. 4. Heat, Electricity, Magnetism. 5. Chemistry, and Chemical Arts. 6. Miscellaneous Works.
Natural History.	1. Natural History in General. 2. Zoology, Anatomy, Physiology, Botany. 3. Geology, Mineralogy.
Military Science and Arts.	1. Artillery, Small Arms, Pyrotechny. 2. Military Engineering and Tactics. 3. Military Organization, Laws, Courts, Statistics, &c. 4. Military Dictionaries, Journals and Miscellanies.
Naval Science and Arts.	1. Navigation, Nautical Astronomy, Tables and Instruments. 2. Maritime Geography. 3. Naval Archtecture, Docks and other Constructions. 4. Seamanship, Naval Tactics, Rigging, Stowage, Sail and Mast-Making, &c. 5. Steam Navigation. 6. Naval Ordnance and Gunnery. 7. Naval Signals. 8. Naval Organization, Laws, Courts, Statistics, &c. 9. Nautical Dictionaries, Journals and Miscellanies.
Arts and Manufactures.	1. General and Miscellaneous Works. 2. Steam Engine and other Machinery. 3. Civil Engineering. 4. Civil Architecture, Drawing and Painting.
Law and Politics.	1. National and International Law, Maritime and Military Law. 2. Political Economy. 3. Government Documents, Reports, &c. 4. Miscellaneous Works.
Literature.	1. Grammar, and Language. 2. Dictionaries of Languages. 3. Rhetoric, and Criticism. 4. Poetry, and the Drama. 5. Novels and Romances. 6. General Literature, Histories of Literature, &c.
Polygraphy.	1. Encyclopoedias, Dictionaries of the Arts and Sciences, Collected Works, &c. 2. Proceedings, Reports, &c., of Academies and Societies. 3. Scientific, Art, and Literary Journals and Magazines.
Bibliography.	1. American and Foreign Bibliography.

No numbering system is apparent, but the books were arranged "in sep
arate cases according to subjects ...." The two service academies thus differed not only in the structure of their catalogs but also in classific ation. In
contrast to the West Point catalog of 1852, which was arranged according to
a special library classification, the Naval Academy had followed Jefferson's
theory of expanding areas of specialty in a general scheme.

1862 J. Peter Lesley.

To J. Peter Lesley, geologist, clergyman, and librarian, a reasonable
arrangement of every collection in the hands of man was "a call of the soul,
to be obeyed." He thought that a "merely empirical adjustment of minerals
to the drawers which contain them, or of books to the shelves on which they
stand, fortuitously numbered as they are obtained, and indexed alphabetically
for the convenience of servants, justly embarrasses, depresses, and disgusts
the thinker."

Peter Lesley, Jr., was born in Philadelphia on September 17, 1819, the
son of a cabinet maker. In early manhood, disliking the name Peter, he adopted the signature J. P. Lesley, the "J." from "Junior" transferred to a more
prominent place. He entered the University of Pennsylvania at fifteen and
received his A. B. in 1838. On the advice of physicians he did not continue
his studies but found outdoor work with the state geological survey. Lesley
attended the Princeton Theological Seminary and was licensed to preach by
the Philadelphia Presbytery in 1844. He abandoned theology for geology in
1852 to return to the Pennsylvania geological survey.

His first book, A Manual of Coal and its Topography (1856), established
his reputation as a geologist. Lesley became professor of mining at the University of Pennsylvania in 1859. He remained at the university until his retirement in 1883, serving as dean of the Science Department of the Towne
Scientific School. In 1863 the Pennsylvania Railroad sent him to Europe to
study the Bessemer steel process and rail manufacture. From 1873 to 1887
Lesley, as state geologist, headed the second geological survey of Pennsylvania.

When the survey completed its field work in 1887, the results were published in 77 octavo volumes of text, 33 atlases, and a grand atlas. The final report was published in 3 volumes in 1892-95. Lesley was an original member of the National Academy of Sciences and served as president of the American Association for the Advancement of Science in 1884. He died in Milford, Massachusetts, on June 1, 1903.

When Lesley became secretary and librarian of the American Philosophical Society in 1858, the orderly mind of the geologist turned to the problem of book classification. The two-volume Catalogue of the American Philosophical Society Library, published in 1863-66, exhibited the result.

Lesley described his theory of classification in the Preface. [16] Four maxims governed the arrangement:

1. The general library therefore is a picture of a generous intellect, well stored, well ordered, and open to enlargement in all directions.

2. Its compartments represent the grand natural divisions of knowledge.

3. Its classification should be in an ascending and advancing series.

4. Its treasures, like those of memory, should be preserved in the natural order of time, and the natural order of space should be ancillary and complementary, wherever applicable.

Eight main classes progressing "from the universal to the special, from the abstract to the concrete, from the inorganic to the organic, and from matter to mind," provided for man's knowledge in books. Each class, with the exception of the first, General Science, advanced beyond the point where the preceding class had left it; theory is at the beginning and practice follows. Thus, in the Mathematical Sciences, Pure mathematics (2^1) was followed by Mathematics applied to Astronomy (2^2), Mathematics applied to Geodesy (2^3), and Mathematics applied to Mechanics and Physical questions (2^4). Another rule of arrangement was that certain subjects of transitional nature must be placed at the end of the class in order to carry over the train of development to the beginning of the next class. The outline of the system follows:

1. GENERAL SCIENCE.

1. Encyclopedias &c. 1^2. Learned Societies. 1^3. Catalogues of Libraries.

2. THE MATHEMATICAL SCIENCES.

2. Mathematics. 2^2. Astronomy &c. 2^3. Geodesy &c. 2^4. Physics.

3. THE INORGANIC SCIENCES.

3. Chemistry. 3^2. Mineralogy. 3^3. Mining. 3^4. Geology and Palaeontology.

4. THE ORGANIC SCIENCES.

4. Biology. 4^2. Botany &c. 4^3. Zoology &c. 4^4. Medicine &c.

5. THE HISTORICAL SCIENCES.

5. Chronology. 5^2. Ethnology. 5^3. Archaeology. 5^4 History.

6. THE SOCIAL SCIENCES.

6. Sociology. 6^2. Manufactures. 6^3. Commerce. 6^4. War 6^5. Law.

7. THE SPIRITUAL SCIENCES.

7. Language. 7^2. Belles-Lettres. 7^3. Fine Arts. 7^4. Logic &c.
7^5. Education 7^6. Religion.

8. PERSONAL SCIENCE.

8. Biography.

Under the principal analytical law of arrangement, the library observed two other rules: the law of space and the law of time. Wherever a geographical arrangement could be made, it was adopted. Such was the case with learned societies and their publications, library catalogs, observations of astronomical observatories, books of geography, voyages and travels, ethnology, local history, manufactures, laws, language, and belles-lettres, as well as whole ranges of books in the various physical sciences. The geographical sequence proceeded like that of history, from the east westward. In other sections a chronological arrangement was adopted for rapid reference, and the dates of the titles were arranged in a column on the right side of the page. For example:

m'. NETHERLANDS.

Paezi bassi. Descrizione di tutti i--. Guicciardini. Anvers.
                                               1 vol.   F   1567

United Provinces of the Netherlands. Observations on the--.
   Sir W. Temple. Lond. 2 vols. (See Stat. 6.)   8° 1705

Hollande. La richesse de la--. London. (See Hist. 5⁴.)
                                               2 vols. 8° 1778

Amsterdam. Description of the city house of--
   (with a description of its emblematic sculpture
   &c.) Amst. (M 227 6) pp. 98.   pam. 8° 1782

Amsterdam. Le guide de--, ou description de ce
   qu'il y a de plus d'entretenant. Amsterdam. 1 vol. 8° 1802

Subdivisions depending upon the subject were provided, such as:

II. The Mathematical Sciences
   IV. Physics
      a. Encyclopediana
      b. Principia et Miscellanea
      c. Attraction and Gravity
      d. Statics
      e. Hydrostatics
      f. Pneumatics
      g. Optics
      h. Thermotics
      i. Electricity
      k. Galvanism
      l. Magnetism
      m. Instrumenta

Lesley was a pioneer in the use of color in classification.

The eight classes of our books are thus collected into eight
suites of bookcases, as their titles on cards are arranged in eight
drawers. To facilitate the handling of the books, they are also
spotted on the back with paper patches of eight different colors,
corresponding to the eight suites of bookcases; and each different drawer of the card catalogue is filled with cards of a corresponding color. It is not easy therefore for either a card or a book
to get astray. The convenience might be extended to the printed
catalogue by tinting the pages devoted to each class division with
its appropriate color. In the choice of colors there was nothing
arbitrary. White being of course the color for the first class,
General Science, the colors of the other seven followed in the order of the solar spectrum:

   For Mathematics &c. . . . . red, ... II.
      Chemistry &c. . . . . orange, ... III.
      Natural History &c. . . . . yellow, ... IV.
      Chronology &c. . . . . .green, ... V.
      Sociology &c. . . . . blue, ... VI.
      Language &c. . . . . indigo, ...VII.
      Biography &c. . . . . violet, ...VIII. [17]

Book size was disregarded in shelving, except where a lower shelf or shelves were devoted to larger books. Lesley knew this practice might be a fatal defect to those who were more disposed to please the eye than assist the brain, but he believed that working scholars would soon be cured of undue aestheticism in externals.

The notation does not meet today's requirements (e. g. , II, III D. Maps. p''' GREAT BRITAIN), but the classification represents another ingenious American attempt, before Harris, Dewey, and Cutter, to solve a problem as old as man's records. Lesley's work is an excellent example of the adaptation of the evolutionary order to the classification of books. It is especially interesting to compare it with that of the botanist, Stephen Elliott, in the 1826 catalog of the Charleston Library Society[18] and with the system devised by Henry Evelyn Bliss in the twentieth century. [19]

With the classifications of the poet, the journalist, and the scientist, the long "prehistoric" era of American library classification ends. We have briefly surveyed many American essays in the subject. We have traced the philosophies of these pioneers back to the renaissance that took place in Ancient Greece following the decline of the Aegean civilization. The long story, although sketchily told, reveals a striking continuity in the development of library classification; the theory of independent origins has no place here. There was much ingenuity, but the patterns into which the sciences and disciplines of knowledge could be grouped were surprisingly few. There was progress, but it was discontinuous like the intellectual life it reflected. Now it is time to turn to the "historic period" — to those who built upon this unknown past.

BACKGROUND OF DECISION: "HISTORY"

CHAPTER X

Pioneers of the Seventies

The failure of the Librarians' Convention of 1853[1] to result in a permanent organization seriously retarded the progress of American librarianship. There were no professional channels for the interchange of ideas; each librarian worked more or less in isolation. Occasional letters, visits to libraries, and, above all, printed catalogs provided information about common problems and their solutions. As a result early American classification was presumed to be nonexistent, because unknown.

> The work of developing bibliographical classification schemes began later in the United States than in other countries, but once begun it was carried on with great zeal. Interest in classification first arose in the United States in the seventies. [2]

In these words Georg Schneider summarized the history of American library classification, expressing not only his own opinion but also the opinions of all who have written on the subject. Library school curricula reflect a similar conception. The preceding chapters have brought to light for the first time the widespread interest of pioneer American librarians in classification and some of their systems. Succeeding chapters will reveal the historic continuity of the systems of the "historic" period with those of the past.

1870 W. T. Harris.

William Torrey Harris, long considered the founder of American library classification, was born in North Killingly (Putnam), Connecticut, on September 10, 1835, the son of William and Zilpah (Torrey) Harris. He entered Yale in 1854 but left in his junior year convinced that the college had little more to teach him. With a classmate, Robert Seney Moore, of Hudson, New York, who shared his interest in shorthand, Harris went west to teach the new subject. In 1858 he was appointed a teacher in the Franklin Grammar School in St. Louis and remained with the St. Louis public school system as teacher, principal, assistant superintendent, and superintendent until 1880.

Harris' early interest was in the parapsychological studies – phrenology, mesmerism, hydropathy, and all the rest. Diverted from these pursuits
by a lecture given by A. Bronson Alcott, he turned to the works of Theodore
Parker and developed a lifelong interest in German literature and philosophy. In St. Louis Harris met a student of Hegel and Goethe, Henry Conrad
Brokmeyer, a man "of great brilliancy of mind, a bit erratic, master of many
trades and a self-made man who was at home in the woods or at the bar, yet
was able to meet the social élite."[3] It was Brokmeyer's influence that led
the "Yankee teacher" to the German philosopher, Hegel.

In 1866 Harris was one of the founders of the St. Louis School of Philosophy, and the following year he established the Journal of Speculative
Philosophy, which carried as a motto Alcott's "Philosophy can bake no bread,
but it can give us God, Freedom and Immortality." Among the contributors
to this journal were the American philosophers Howison, Peirce, Royce,
Dewey, and James.

Harris returned to the East in 1880 to join Alcott at the Concord School
of Philosophy. And there in the "Chapel," a box-shaped structure with Gothic trimmings which stood in Alcott's orchard, Harris expounded the myster-
ies of Hegel and his "Dialectic" to the "Hypatias in muslin and straw-hatted
Kants"[4] who for nine summers sought culture in the "American Weimar."

In 1889 President Harrison appointed Harris U.S. Commissioner of
Education, a post he held until June 1906. The bibliography of Harris' writings contains 479 titles, philosophical, educational, and miscellaneous. Among
them are his Introduction to the Study of Philosophy (1889), The Spiritual
Sense of Dante's Divina Commedia (3 vols., 1889), and The Psychologic Foundations of Education (1898). Harris died in Providence, Rhode Island, on November 5, 1909.

While working on a course of study for the St. Louis schools, Harris
became interested in library classification. He believed that libraries were

important in modern education and that good catalogs were necessary to make them truly efficient. A mere index of authors which enabled a reader to determine whether or not a book was in the library, and where it was placed if the library had it, was not enough: there must be an index of subjects to guide the reader to the books on any subject. He thought that the advantages "gained by presenting to the eye of the reader for constant use an exhaustive scheme of classifying 'Human Learning as preserved in books,'"[5] were obvious. And to Harris classification meant shelf as well as catalog arrangement.

It has long been believed and taught that the classification of Chancellor Bacon, by some strange incident of saltatory evolution, leaped through the centuries, was inverted by Harris,[6] and made into a completely new classification. Thus, by virtue of the discontinuity, Harris was acclaimed the "father of American classification," and Dewey, who followed him, his intellectual son, but the honor was given without factual basis.

Harris was led to attempt a classified catalog of the St. Louis Public School Library by "the eminent practical success" of the classification contained in the "Catalogue of that excellent collection, the St. Louis Mercantile Library." He adopted Johnston's general plan, inverted the order of the major divisions, and made changes in the subdivisions, notably in Philosophy. Harris' classification thus springs not directly from Bacon, but from a classification which had been developed and applied as early as 1836 in the College of South Carolina. But let Harris continue the story.

> The general unfitness of this [Bacon's] system*[7] for the classification of books is apparent; it was not intended for it. But its principle of division is of great value. To be applied to the use of a library, it is necessary to seize and not lose sight of its spirit, in the details which Bacon gives. It will be found that in minor divisions and sections the content exercises a predominating influence on the classification, while in the principal divisions the form is the guiding principle.
>   Inverting the order in which Bacon considers the system, Science should come first on account of its furnishing the method and principles for what follows.

I. SCIENCE gives the department of books in which conscious
   system prevails.
II. ART (Aesthetics) gives the department in which "organic
   unity" or unconscious system prevails.
III. HISTORY gives the department in which the system is determined by accidental relations, such as time and place. 8

With these guiding principles before us, our system develops
as follows:

SCIENCE unfolds into
   I. Philosophy, or the most general principles, the forms and
      archetypes of all the rest. It has the strictest, most sys-
      tematic method, and is the source of all system to the
      other sciences.
   II. Theology — the science of the Absolute, just as Philosophy
       is the science of Science.
   III. Social and Political Sciences, including the treatises upon
        the institutions which relate man to his fellow-men in
        society and the state. His essential life as a spiritual
        being is conditioned upon his ascent above his merely
        natural, individual condition, by means of combination in
        the social organism.
        These are —
        1. Jurisprudence (in which the social organism appears as
           a constraining necessity acting upon the individual
           from without).
        2. Politics (in which the individual reacts against this
           constraint, and exhibits himself as the free producer
           of the Universal, which is placed over him in the shape
           of Law).
        3. Political Economy.
        4. Education.

        { Social science. (Social science as
          Political Economy, exhibits the
          principles of combination, by means
          of division of labor, and how this re-
          sults in the conquest of nature and
          the dedication of it to the service
          of man. As Education, it exhibits
          the process of initiating the indi-
          vidual into the conventionalities of
          the social organism — man's appren-
          ticeship in acquiring the use of the
          tools of intelligence.)

        5. Philology. (Philology is placed in the division of the So-
           cial and Political Sciences, because, as Science of Lan-
           guage, it is the science of the instrument that lies at
           the basis of all combination or organization. Language
           (The Word) is the image of Reason, and is not a natural
           product, but the invention of self-conscious thought; it
           is not found but made — partly by the poetic phantasy,
           and partly by the reflective understanding. For the rea-
           son that Mind becomes, as it were, crystalized or fixed
           in Language, we place Philology as a connecting link
           between the Spiritual and Natural. The language of a
           people embalms all the achievements of that people act-
           ing as a social, political, or spiritual organization.)
           These latter four sciences treat of the means through
           which man arrives at a comprehension of the necessity

of the social organism, and through which the constraint becomes internal, and hence becomes freedom.

IV. Natural Sciences and Useful Arts: the former unfold the laws of Nature; the latter apply them to social uses. The transition is formed by Medicine, which is partly science, partly art.

1. Mathematics is the science of the pure forms of Nature — time and space.

2. Physics is Nature treated dynamically, and hence quantitatively or mathematically.

3. Natural History is Nature organically considered, hence qualitatively and descriptively. Chemistry forms the transition from quantitative to qualitative; it is the realm where quantity constitutes qualitative difference. Astronomy is a hybrid, belonging to Mathematics and Natural History.

In Natural History we commence with the Mineral or Earth-organism, and ascend through the Plant and Animal to Man as a merely natural being [Ethnology].

4. Medicine is closely allied to Natural History, and its subjects take up in a new form the same content.

5. The useful arts and trades start from Natural Science and proceed to unite with it a purely empirical element.

ART unfolds —

I. The Fine Arts.

II. Poetry.

III. Prose Fiction.

IV. Literary Miscellany, comprising rhetorical works (orations) and literary essays which have either an Art form more or less impure, or are so related to works of Art in their subject-matter as not to be separated from this class.

HISTORY —

I. Geography and Travels form the first or most external class under History.

II. Civil History is the Normal type of this division.

III. Biography and Correspondence. Heraldry and Genealogy also fall properly under this head.

An APPENDIX is subjoined for certain works, or collections of works, which treat of topics belonging to each of the three general divisions.

Minute Subdivisions.

Caution should be taken with regard to such works as do not fall readily into a special class under the general number of the section; they should be left without special letters, until, by the addition of similar works, they become too numerous, when a special sub-class may be made, giving it a letter.

Numbering.

Instead of the inconvenient method of marking the classification of books by indicating all the grades (e. g. Hygiene = Sci. X. 5. d), it is better to have the classes numbered from 1 to

100, so as to have only two figures for most classes, and to add
letters for subclasses as they arise. In this way the general
numbering need not change, although new subclasses may be made
frequently. The books on the shelves should be alphabetically arranged within the subclasses (e. g. those of Hygiene numbered
"57. d" should be alphabetically arranged) according to the name
of the chief author (i. e. the most distinguished name, when there
are several authors' or editors' names in the title). This name
and the subclass number should be written plainly on the book-
label, so that the dullest library-boy can put any book into its
exact place on the shelves, or find it instantly when he has obtained its classification from the catalogue. This system of numbering is one of the most practical and valuable features of the
system here described. [9]

A modification of Harris' scheme made by the Peoria Public Library in

1882 is sometimes confused with the original work.

However competent Harris was as a student of Hegel, he showed little

perception into Bacon's system. It cannot be repeated too often that Bacon's

divisions were fundamentally methodological: the collection of facts, natural

and civil, in History; their imaginative representation in Poetry; their trans-

mutation, through classification and interpretation into science, in Philosophy.

Harris' essay, as well as Johnston's, upon which it was founded, again empha-

size the fact that there never existed a classification which was even remote-

ly in the Baconian spirit. The fantastic division of the natural sciences in his-

tory and in philosophy proves that Bacon's "adapters" were little familiar

with his fundamental theory.

One wonders what the future of American library classification would

have been had Harris, the Hegelian, followed his master and not Johnston's

variant of Francis Bacon. Would the long dominance of Bacon and d'Alembert,

and later of Brunet, have been ended by an infusion of German idealism? As

it happened, German theory, which appeared for a time under Cogswell at Har-

vard in the 1820's only to be superseded by Brunet, was to have no influence

on American classification until the appearance of Otto Hartwig's Halle Schema

in 1888.

1876 Melvil Dewey.

Few names in any profession ever became as widely known as that of

Melvil Dewey, architect of the Decimal Classification. Pioneer and crusader, and, in his own words, a gadfly who prodded others into action, Dewey was "perhaps the most energetic and fertilizing personality in modern librarianship."[10]

Dewey was born in Adams Center, New York, on December 10, 1851, the youngest child of Joel and Eliza (Green) Dewey. After a haphazard education in Adams Center, he taught school at Toad Hollow and Bernhard's Bay and then entered Amherst College. Dewey graduated in 1874 but remained at the college as assistant librarian until the spring of 1876, when he moved to Boston. Within a few months Dewey founded, or assisted in founding, the Readers and Writers Economy Company (later the Library Bureau), the American Library Association, the American Metric Bureau, and the Spelling Reform Association, all of which he managed for several years. He also assisted in establishing the Library Journal and served as its editor during its early years.

From 1883 to 1888 Dewey was librarian of Columbia University, where he founded the first school of library science in 1887. When he became secretary of the board of regents of the University of the State of New York and state librarian in 1888, Dewey moved the library school to Albany, where it became the New York State Library School. In 1905 he resigned his positions as state librarian and director of the library school. The resignations marked his virtual retirement from the library profession. He died at the Lake Placid Club, Miami, Florida, December 26, 1931.

Dewey became interested in library classification in 1873 while working as a student assistant in the Amherst library. But for this interest he might have become a college professor or a missionary to Turkey – his earlier vocational interests. Dewey studied the literature of library science for several months and visited over fifty libraries for firsthand information on library arrangement. Although he was primarily interested in cataloging and indexing, Dewey was amazed at the fixed-location systems he found used in most of the libraries he visited and dreamed for months afterward of devising a better system which would solve the problem for thousands of libraries. One Sunday morning, in the Amherst chapel, during a long sermon by President Stearns, the answer came to him: use the simplest symbols, Arabic numerals, to number a classification of all knowledge.

On May 8, 1873, Dewey, aged twenty-two, presented his plan to the Amherst Library Committee. The committee approved the young student librarian's recommendation, and Dewey, assisted by his lifelong friend, Walter Stanley Biscoe, and members of the Amherst faculty, developed the Decimal Classification. Curiously, Dewey was more concerned with the extrinsic factor of notation than with classification itself. "As to the filosofical or rational divisions," he wrote, "my opinion is not valuable, the Amherst faculty being the authors of most of this part of our scheme."[11]

The system was tried out in the Amherst Library for three years before it was published in 1876 as A Classification and Subject Index for Cataloguing and Arranging the Books and Pamphlets of a Library. The pamphlet contained 12 pages of explanation, 12 pages of tables, and an index in 18 pages. A description of the scheme was also published the same year in a special report of the Bureau of Education.[12] Despite the emphasis later placed upon the D. C. as a method of shelving books systematically it was not originally developed for that purpose. "The system was devised for cataloguing and indexing purposes, but it was found on trial to be equally valuable for numbering and arranging books and pamphlets on the shelves."[13]

Following a custom of long standing when discussing decimal classification, it is necessary at this time to advert briefly to the systems of La Croix du Maine and Nathaniel B. Shurtleff. It has been customary to cite, not quote, the former and to misinterpret the latter. In 1583 La Croix du Maine presented a plan to Henry III of France "Pour dresser une bibliothèque parfaite & accomplie de tous points."[14] The library was to consist of 10,000 volumes arranged in 100 bookcases ("buffets") of 100 volumes each, these in turn arranged in 7 "orders":

    1-17   Religion
18-41   Arts and Sciences
42-62   Description of the Universe
63-72   Mankind
73-81   Nobility ("hommes illustres en guerre")
82-96   Works of God (Natural History)
97-107 Memoirs (Miscellanea)

And so the books ran from Almighty God in "buffet" 1 to the End of the World in "buffet" 107. The author had found 100 cases insufficient, the decimal system confining.

Shurtleff's plan, on the contrary, provided merely for the physical shelving of books, because he thought that the purposes of libraries were so different that a common classification was impossible. Born in Boston in 1810, Shurtleff received an A. B. degree from Harvard in 1831 and an M. D. in 1834. A Democrat, he was mayor of Boston for three terms, 1868-70, long enough for Boston to annex Dorchester and Roxbury. Shurtleff served as trustee of Harvard University and the Boston Public Library and as librarian of the American Academy of Arts and Sciences. He was an antiquary who wrote on subjects as far removed as a perpetual calendar, library classification, and the Bay Psalm Book. The decimal system that Shurtleff introduced[15] into the Boston Public Library in the summer of 1852 required the construction of alcoves, ranges, and compartments or shelves in multiples of ten. The alcoves were devoted to subjects, and the ranges to their subdivisions. Thus the location, or call number, $\frac{111}{3}$ indicated the third book on the 111th shelf.

Decimal notation was not uncommon in American libraries before Dewey's time — it was even used in the Amherst library to indicate the shelves and the subjects arranged on them. Dewey, however, used decimals to denote subjects and not shelves, transforming the arrangement of the Amherst library from a fixed to a movable or relative system. There was, as he said, nothing new in relative or movable location, for it had been used in many libraries.

Dewey divided knowledge into nine special libraries, called classes:
1. Philosophy 2. Religion 3. Sociology 4. Philology 5. Natural Science 6. Useful Arts 7. Fine Arts 8. Literature 9. History, and added a class 0

for works which dealt with no one subject. He based his classes upon the divisions William Torrey Harris had derived from the work of Edward William Johnston. The following chart illustrates the evolution of the D. C.

E. W. Johnston (1858)	W. T. Harris (1870)	Melvil Dewey (1876)
9 History	Science	0 General Works
Philosophy	1 Philosophy	1 Philosophy
2 Theology	2 Theology	2 Religion
3 [Social Sciences]	3 Social and Political Sciences	3 Sociology (Social Sciences)
Jurisprudence	Jurisprudence	
Political Science	Politics	
Political Economy	Political Economy Education	
1 Philosophy (Proper)	4 Philology	·4 Philology
5 Natural Sciences	5 Natural Sciences	5 Natural Sciences
6 and Useful Arts	6 and Useful Arts	6 Useful Arts
3 Education		
4 Philology		
Poetry	Art	
8 Literature	7 Fine Arts	7 Fine Arts
7 Fine Arts	8 Literature	8 Literature
	9 History	9 History
0 Polygraphs	0 Miscellany	

Note the separation of 4 Philology and 8 Literature in all three. This is the answer to Bliss's plaintive question as to why Dewey had separated them when no one else ever had.

Dewey's libraries, or classes, were subdivided into divisions, sections, etc. He described his scheme as follows:

> These special libraries or classes are then considered independently, and each one is separated again into nine special divisions of the main subject. These divisions are numbered from 1 to 9, as were the classes. Thus 59 is the ninth division (Zoology) of the fifth class, (Natural Science.) A final division is then made by separating each of these divisions into nine sections, which are numbered in the same way with the nine digits. Thus 513 is the third

section (Geometry) of the first division (Mathematics) of the fifth class, (Natural Science.) This number, giving class, division, and section, is called the classification or class number, and is applied to every book or pamphlet belonging to the library. All the geometries are thus numbered 513; all the mineralogies 549;and so throughout the library, all the books on any given subject bear the number of that subject in the scheme. Where a O occurs in a class number it has its normal zero power. Thus, a book numbered 510 is Class 5, Division 1, but no section. This signifies that the book treats of the Division 51 (Mathematics) in general, and is not limited to any one section, as is the geometry, marked 513. If marked 500, it would indicate a treatise on science in general, limited to no division. A zero occurring in the first place would in the same way show that the book is limited to no class. The classification is mainly made by subjects or content regardless of form; but it is found practically useful to make an additional distinction in these general treatises, according to the form of treatment adopted. Thus, in Science we have a large number of books treating of science in general, and so having a 0 for the division number. These books are then divided into sections, as are those of the other classes, according to the form they have taken on. We have (1) the philosophy and history of science, (2) scientific compends, (3) dictionaries, (4) essays, (5) periodicals, (6) societies; (7) education, and (8) travels — all having the common subject, Natural Science, but treating it in these varied forms. These form distinctions are introduced here because the number of general works is large, and the numerals allow of this division without extra labor, for the numbers from 501 to 509 would otherwise be unused. They apply only to the general treatises, which, without them, would have a class number ending with two zeros. A dictionary of mathematics is 510, not 503, for every book is assigned to the most specific head that will contain it, so that 503 is limited to dictionaries or cyclopedias of science in general. In the same way a general cyclopaedia or periodical treats of no one class, and so is assigned to the Class 0, divided into cyclopaedias, periodicals, etc. 16

For the geographical subdivision of subjects there was also provided a scheme based upon his historical divisions in the Class 900.

The first complete divisions of the system are found in the second edition. 17 They were:

000 General Works.	500 Natural Science.
010 Bibliography.	510 Mathematics.
020 Library Economy.	520 Astronomy.
030 General Cyclopedias.	530 Physics.
040 General Collections.	540 Chemistry.
050 General Periodicals.	550 Geology.
060 General Societies.	560 Paleontology.
070 Newspapers.	570 Biology.
080 Special Libraries. Polygraphy.	580 Botany.
090 Book Rarities.	590 Zoology.
100 Philosophy.	600 Useful Arts.
110 Metaphysics.	610 Medicine.
120 Special Metaphysical Topics.	620 Engineering.
130 Mind and Body.	630 Agriculture.

140 Philosophical Systems.	640 Domestic Economy.
150 Mental Faculties. Psychology.	650 Communication and Commerce.
160 Logic.	660 Chemical Technology.
170 Ethics.	670 Manufactures.
180 Ancient Philosophers.	680 Mechanic Trades.
190 Modern Philosophers.	690 Building.
200 Religion.	700 Fine Arts.
210 Natural Theology.	710 Landscape Gardening.
220 Bible.	720 Architecture.
230 Doctrinal Theol. Dogmatics.	730 Sculpture.
240 Devotional and Practical.	740 Drawing. Design. Decoration.
250 Homiletic. Pastoral. Parochial.	750 Painting.
260 Church. Institutions. Work.	760 Engraving.
270 Religious History.	770 Photography.
280 Christian Churches and Sects.	780 Music.
290 Non-Christian Religions.	790 Amusements.
300 Sociology.	800 Literature.
310 Statistics.	810 American.
320 Political Science.	820 English.
330 Political Economy.	830 German.
340 Law.	840 French.
350 Administration.	850 Italian.
360 Associations and Institutions.	860 Spanish.
370 Education.	870 Latin.
380 Commerce and Communication.	880 Greek.
390 Customs. Costumes. Folk-Lore.	890 Minor Languages.
400 Philology.	900 History.
410 Comparative.	910 Geography and Description.
420 English.	920 Biography.
430 German.	930 Ancient History.
440 French.	940 Europe.
450 Italian.	950 Asia.
460 Spanish.	960 Africa.
470 Latin.	970 North America.
480 Greek.	980 South America.
490 Minor Languages.	990 Oceanica and Polar Regions.

(940–980 bracketed as "Modern")

Dewey then divided each of the divisions into sections, as the following illustrates:

USEFUL ARTS.

600 Useful Arts.	650 Communication. Commerce.
601 Philosophy.	651 Writing. Cipher. Typewriters.
602 Compends.	652 Penmanship, Materials. Methods.
603 Dictionaries. Cyclopaedias.	653 Short hand. Abbreviations.
604 Essays. Lectures. Addresses.	654 Telegraphy. Cables. Signals.
605 Periodicals. Magazines. Reviews.	655 Printing. Type. Stereos. Publishing.
606 Societies. Fairs. Exhibitions.	656 Transportation. Railroading, etc.
607 Education. Schools of Technology.	657 Book-keeping. Accounts.
608 Patents.	658 Business manuals. Methods. Tables.
609 History of Useful Arts.	659 Advertising and other topics.
610 Medicine.	660 Chemical Technology.
611 Anatomy.	661 Chemicals; Salts, Paints, etc.

612 Physiology.

613 Hygiene. Gymnastics. Training.

614 Public health. See also 629, San. Eng.

615 Materia medica. Therapeutics.

616 Pathology. Diseases. Treatment.

617 Surgery. Dentistry. Anaesthetics.

618 Obstetrics. Sexual Science.

619 Veterinary medicine.

620 Engineering.

621 Mechanical.

622 Mining.

623 Military.

624 Bridge and Roof.

625 Road and Railroad.

626 Canal.

627 River and Harbor.

628 Sanitary. Water-works.

629 Other branches.

630 Agriculture.

631 Soil. Fertilizers, Drainage.

632 Pests. Hindrances. Blights. Insects.

633 Grains. Grasses. Fibres. Tea, etc.

634 Fruits. Orchards. Vineyards.

635 Kitchen Garden. See 716, Flowers.

636 Domestic animals.

637 Dairy. Milk. Butter. Cheese.

638 Bees. Silkworms.

639 Fishing. Trapping.

640 Domestic Economy.

641 Cookery. Gastronomy.

642 Confectionery. Ices.

643 Food. Dining. Carving.

644 Fuel. Lights. See also 697, 665, 621. 32

645 Furniture. Carpets. Upholstery.

646 Clothing. Toilet. Cosmetics.

647 Servants. Training. Duties. Wages.

648 Laundry.

649 Nursery. Children. Sick-room.

662 Pyrotechnics. Explosives.

663 Beverages; Wines, Liquors, Ales, etc.

664 Foods; Sugar, Starch, etc.

665 Lights; Gas, Oil, Candles, etc.

666 Ceramics, Glass, Clay, Cement, etc.

667 Bleaching. Dyeing. Inks.

668 Other organic chemical industries.

669 Metallurgy. Assaying.

670 Manufactures.

671 Articles made of Metals.

672 Of Iron and Steel; Stoves, Cutlery, etc.

673 Of Brass and Bronze; Bells, etc.

674 Lumber and articles made of wood.

675 Leather   "   "   "   " leather.

676 Paper   "   "   "   " paper.

677 Cotton, Wool, Silk, Linen, etc.

678 Rubber and articles made of rubber.

679 Celluloid and other.

680 Mechanic Trades.

681 Watch and Instrument-making.

682 Blacksmithing. Horseshoeing.

683 Lock and Gun-making.

684 Carriage and Cabinet-making.

685 Saddlery and Shoe-making. Trunks.

686 Book-binding.

687 Clothes-making. Hats.

688

689 Other trades.

690 Building.

691 Materials. Timber, Stone, etc. See 620. 1

692 Plans and Specifications.

693 Masonry. Plastering, etc.

694 Carpentry. Stair-building.

695 Slating and Tiling.

696 Plumbing. Gas and Steam-fitting.

697 Warming and Ventilation.

698 Painting, Glazing. Paper-hanging.

699 Car and Ship-building. See 623. 8.

Each of the sections was still further subdivided according to the requirements of the subject. The subdivisions 621 to 621. 69 for Mechanical Engineering serve as an example of this.

     621   Mechanical Engineering.
          May be subdivided like 620 and 620. 0.
     .1   Steam Engineering. See 536. 81.
     .11   Mechanism of Steam Engine.
     .12   Marine Engines and Ship Propulsion. See 699.

.13   Locomotive Engines.
.14   Traction Engines.
.15   Portable Engines.
.16   Stationary Engines.
.17
.18   Steam Generation. Boilers. Furnaces.
.19   Steam Heating. See 697.

.2   Water Engines or Motors.
.21   Water Wheels. See 532.84.
.22   Overshot and Breast Wheels.
.23   Undershot Wheels.
.24   Turbines.
.25   Water Pressure Engines. See 532.82.
.26   Hydraulic Presses. See 532.81.
.27   Hydraulic Ram. See 532.83.
.28
.29   Mill Dams. Sluices, etc. See 628.

.3   Electrical Machines.
.31   Dynamo Machines. See 537.83.
.32   Electric Lighting. See 537.83.
.33   Electric Railways.
.34   Transmission of Electric Force. See 537.84.
.35   Storage of Electric Force. See 537.84.

.4   Air and Gas Engines.
.41   Caloric Engines.
.42   Compressed Air Engines.
.43   Ignited Gas Engines. See 536.82.
.44   Binary Vapor Engines.
.45   Windmills.

.5   Air Compressors. Ice Machines.
.6   Blowing and Pumping Engines.
.61   Piston Blowers.
.62   Rotary Blowers. Fans.
.63   Centrifugal Blowers.
.64   Steam Pumps and Pumping Engines.
.65   Piston Pumps.
.66   Rotary Pumps.
.67   Centrifugal Pumps.
.68   Fire Engines. See 352.3, Fire Dep't.
.69

Following the schedules of the classification came the relative index,

which Dewey considered "the most important feature" of his system, describ-

ing its use as follows:

RELATIV INDEX. — The Alfabetical Subject Index is designed to guide, both in numbering and in finding the books. In
numbering, the most specific head that will contain the book having been determined, reference to that head in the Index will give
the class number to which it should be assigned. In finding books
on any given subject, reference to the Index will give the number
under which they ar to be sought on the shelves, in the Shelf Catalog,

of in the Subject Catalog. The Index gives after each subject the
number of the class to which it is assigned. Most names of countries, towns, animals, plants, minerals, diseases, etc., hav been
omitted, the aim being to furnish an Index of Subjects on which
books ar written, and not a Gazetteer or a Dictionary of all the
nouns in the language. Such subjects will be found as special
chapters or sections of books on the subjects given in the Index.
The names of individual subjects of biografies will be found in
the Class List of Biografy.

This index was to serve as a key to the contents of the classification and

guide users to books and pamphlets on the shelves and to entries in classed

catalogs. Its use would remove the greatest objection to classed catalogs —

"the impossibility of knowing just where to put a book in cataloging, and just

where to look for it when it is again wanted." Dewey's belief in the index led

him to state further that "A clerk, if he only knows the subject of his book,

by the use of the index can class just as the chief of the catalog department

would class, and usually the difficulty is not in deciding what a book is about,

but where to put it in the scheme." His naive faith in this feature of his sys-

tem was unjustified, however, in the light of the rapidly growing complexity

of knowledge.

In succeeding editions the D. C. was expanded to provide for new de-

velopments in knowledge. The original pamphlet of 42 pages was enlarged to

1927 pages in the 14th edition, later shrinking to 872 pages in the 15th revised

edition.

In 1895 the Institut Internationale de Bibliographie, now the Fédération

Internationale de Documentation (F. I. D.), adopted the D. C. as the basis of

its comprehensive index to published information. From it was developed the

Universal Decimal, or Brussels, Classification. Thus the divisions of know-

ledge devised by Francis Bacon, rearranged and expanded by American librar-

ians, returned to the Old World.

Ernest A. Savage, retired Chief Librarian of Edinburgh Public Librar-

ies, epitomized Dewey's contribution to classification and librarianship: "No

other book [Decimal Classification] has had a more powerful influence upon li-

brary administration than this invention of Melvil Dewey, a celebrated American

librarian. Puck-like, he put a girdle round the earth with his 'damned dots'
(as Lord Randolph Churchill bluntly described something he didn't understand) and with them American library methods were carried from Albany to
the Antipodes. "[18]

1879 Jacob Schwartz.

Few classification systems have exhibited more ingenuity than the one
Jacob Schwartz developed for the Apprentices' Library of New York.[19] Faced
with the problem of recommending an existing classification for adoption in
the library, Schwartz studied the various systems of "shelf-arrangement" in
use at the time but found none free of serious faults. Many libraries were
arranged in logical order, no two alike, ". . . and the only thing that the classifiers from Aristotle to Messrs. Cutter and Perkins are agreed upon is — to
disagree. "[20]

Schwartz was born in New York City on March 13, 1846. He was only
seventeen years old when he joined the staff of the Apprentices' Library, and
twenty-five when he succeeded William Van Norden as chief librarian in 1871.
For the next two decades Schwartz contributed his talents freely to the library
world. He was one of the original members of the American Library Association, a lecturer at the Columbia College School of Library Economy during
its opening year, 1887, and a frequent contributor to the Library Journal.
Most of his contributions dealt with cataloging and classification, but some
were in a lighter vein. such as the poem "Three Little Maids in the Library
School, " which he dedicated "by permission" to Melvil Dewey. Also of a
semihumorous character was "King Aquila's Library: a Sequel to 'King Leo's
Classification. '"[21] Schwartz left the Apprentices' Library in 1900; nothing
more is known of him.

Schwartz thought that all possible shelving arrangements could be reduced to three forms: the Numerical, the Alphabetical, and the Classified. It
occurred to him that a system embodying the best features of all three would
"approach nearer perfection than any other. " He began the development of

the Combined System in 1871, and in December applied it to new purchases.
In November 1873 he applied the classification to the whole library. "Every
volume was then taken down from the shelves, furnished with new paper covers, registered, classified, catalogued, renumbered, relettered and replaced
on the shelves. " The next catalog published by the library, that of 1874, contains a brief description of the system. The first detailed description is in
Schwartz's article "A Mnemonic System of Classification, "[22] but "A New
Classification and Notation, " published in 1882, gives an even more complete
development.

   Schwartz's system represented an attempt to translate the principles
of the alphabetico-classed catalog to the arrangement of books on the shelves.
The order was, therefore, alphabetical and the scheme mnemonic. Schwartz
divided human knowledge into three main classes – History, Literature, and
Science – and subdivided each of these into seven "departments. " There were
actually twenty-three: twenty devoted to octavos and the remaining three to
quartos and larger sizes – an interesting adjustment of classification to the
size of the books. A synopsis of Schwartz's alphabetical classes follows:

    I.   MNEMONIC CLASSIFICATION: HISTORY
        A.   American History and Travels
        B.   Biography
        E.   European History and Travels
        G.   Geography: General Works
        H.   History: General Works
        O.   Oriental History and Travels
        S.   Sociology
   II.   MNEMONIC CLASSIFICATION: LITERATURE
        F, Q, and X. Folios, Quartos, and Xtraordinary Sizes
        K.   Kallography or "literature"
        L.   Language
        N.   Novels
        P.   Periodicals
        R.   Reference and Rare Books
        W.   Works (Collected)
   III. MNEMONIC CLASSIFICATION: SCIENCE
        C.   Cosmology
        D.   Decorative and Fine Arts
        J.   Jurisprudence
        M.   Medical Science
        T.   Theology and Philosophy
        U.   Useful Arts
        Z.   Zoology

Each of the main classes was subdivided into subclasses and divisions according to the nature of the subject. His classification of Medical Science provided:

Class M. – Medical Science.

Sub-Classes.	Division A.	Division B.	Division C.	Division D.
0 General works	History	General works	Encyclopedias	Philosophy of medicine
1 Anatomy and physiology	General works	Bones	Muscles and nerves	Viscera and vessels
2 Disease and pathology	General works	Special diseases	Mental disorders	Special systems
3 Forensic medicine	General works	American	European	Oriental
4 Health and hygiene	General works	Dietics	Stimulants and narcotics	Alcohol and temperance
5 Institutions	General works	American	European	Oriental
6 Materia medica	Medical chemistry	Materia medica	Pharmacy	Toxicology
7 Public health	General works	American	European	Oriental
8 Surgery	General works	Vulnar surgery	Normal surgery	Topical surgery
9 Woman and sexual science	General works	Diseases of males	Diseases of females	Obstetrics

He also devised a somewhat intricate "Alphabetical Table of Author Numbers" to provide author numbers in each of the four divisions of his subclasses. The following is a sample of his arrangement:

IV. – ALPHABETICAL TABLE OF AUTHOR NUMBERS

Alphabet Combination.	Division A.	Division B.	Division C.	Division D.	Alphabet Combination.	Division A.	Division B.	Division C.	Division D.	Alphabet Combination.	Division A.	Division B.	Division C.	Division D.
Lou	54	263	563	863	Pin		313	613	913	Stu	87	363	663	963
Lu		264	564	864	Pl		314	614	914	Sua		364	664	964
Ly		265	565	865	Poa	71	315	615	915	Sun		365	665	965
Maa	55	266	566	866	Pon		316	616	916	Taa	88	366	666	966
McG		267	567	867	Pra		317	617	917	Tal		367	667	967
McO		268	568	868	Pro	72	318	618	918	Tar		368	668	968
Mad	56	269	569	869	Pu		319	619	919	Te	89	369	669	969
Mal		270	570	870	Q		320	620	920	Tha		370	670	970
Mar		271	571	871	Raa	73	321	621	921	Tho		371	671	971
Mas	57	272	572	872	Ral		322	622	922	Tia	90	372	672	972
Mat		273	573	873	Rar		323	623	923	Toa		373	673	973
Mau		274	574	874	Rea	74	324	624	924	Ton		374	674	974
Mea	58	275	575	875	Rel		325	625	925	Tr	91	375	675	975
Mem		276	576	876	Rer		326	626	926	Tu		376	676	976

The classifying of a work such as Mayo's <u>Elements</u> <u>of</u> <u>the</u> <u>Pathology</u> <u>of</u> <u>the</u> <u>Human</u> <u>Mind</u> involved the following steps:

Class M   Medicine
Subclass 2   Disease and pathology
Division C   Mental disorders

Then by reference to the "Author Table" for Mayo in Division C, the book number is found to be 574. The complete call number therefore is M.2574. Class number and book number are ingeniously fused together. "Title numbers," figures or lower case letters, were added to differentiate individual works.

Schwartz maintained that his pioneer effort of combining the three fundamental forms of shelf arrangement influenced directly, or indirectly, all succeeding systems. He was one of the three classification makers mentioned by Dewey in his "Aknowlejments." Dewey added, however, that although the system resembled his own in some respects, he had not seen the work until all essential features of the Decimal Classification were decided upon.

The Baconian divisions of knowledge with d'Alembert's modifications, which Jefferson had introduced into this country around 1770, were shorn of their "Chapters" and dressed in decimals a century after by Melvil Dewey. During the intervening hundred years had worked men, who, while adapting the system to changing knowledge, still continued the tradition — among them Zachariah Poulson, Thaddeus Mason Harris, Edward William Johnston, and William Torrey Harris. The process of American library classification was continuous, if not always progressive. It was a product, not of the seventies, but of a long history.

CHAPTER XI

Brunet Remodeled

The Brunet system lingered on in a few American libraries after it had
been generally displaced by the Baconian divisions of Johnston, Harris, and
Dewey. Of the four variants of Brunet described below three came to be identified with the names of the librarians who published them, although they had
been applied many years earlier by long-forgotten men. The first "inverts"
Brunet as Harris inverted Bacon.

1880 Newton Free Library.

Brunet's main classes have been arranged in various orders, but they
were never completely inverted like those of Francis Bacon until 1880. In the
Class Catalogue of the Newton Free Library of Newton, Massachusetts, published that year in accordance with a request from the City Council, the titles
were arranged in the sequence History, Belles Lettres, Arts and Sciences, and
Theology. The outlines below show the Newton classification in comparison
with Brunet and the four-year-old Decimal Classification.

BRUNET	NEWTON	DECIMAL
		0 General Works
5 History	1 History 2 Biography 3 Travels and Description	9 History

4 Belles Lettres	4 Language and Liter-
	    ature [Including
	    Bibliography]
		4 Philology
		8 Literature

3 Arts and Sciences	5 Fine Arts 6 Useful Arts 7 Natural Science	7 Fine Arts 6 Useful Arts 5 Natural Sciences
2 Jurisprudence	8 Social Science	3 Sociology
	9 Philosophy	1 Philosophy
1 Theology	10 Theology	2 Theology

The following subdivisions illustrate the detail of the system:

LANGUAGE AND LITERATURE – Class 4

Language, History of
Literature, History of
English Language: –
 Dictionaries
 General Works
English Literature: –
 Dictionaries and Histories
 Poetry, Collections of
 Poetry
 Drama and Dramatic Literature
 Essays, Letters, Lectures, etc.
 Occasional Addresses
 Folk-Lore and Miscellany
 Rhetoric
 Elocution
 Selections for Reading and Speaking
French Language: –
 Dictionaries, etc.
French Literature: –
 History of
 Works in French
 Translations
German Language: –
 Dictionaries
German Literature: –
 History of
 Works in German
 Translations
Italian and Spanish Language: –
 Dictionaries
Italian and Spanish Literature: –
 History of
 Works in Italian and Spanish
 Italian, Spanish, and Portuguese Translations
Norwegian, Swedish, and Russian Literature
Asiatic Literature
Greek and Latin Language: –
 Dictionaries, etc.
Greek and Latin Literature: –
 History of
 Works in Latin
 Translations
Ancient Classics for English Readers

BIBLIOGRAPHY
 General Cyclopaedias
 Libraries: –
  History, Economy, etc.
  Catalogues
 General Periodicals: –
  History, etc.
  General Periodicals, List of

FICTION

NATURAL SCIENCE — Class 7

Natural Science
Mathematics
Astronomy
Physics
Chemistry and Microscopy
Physical Geography and Meteorology
Geology and Mineralogy
Biology, Evolution, Ethnology, and Heredity
Physiology, Anatomy, Medicine, and Hygiene
Zoology
Taxidermy
Botany
Annuals, Reports, etc.

SOCIAL SCIENCE — Class 8

General Works
Statistics
Political Science: —
    Government, Politics, etc.
    Slavery
    United States Government Reports
Political Economy
    Labor and Wages
    Money and Business
    Taxation and Finance
    Commerce
    Weights and Measures
Law, etc.
Associations: —
    Charitable Institutions and Reforms
    Secret Societies
Insurance and Fire Department
Education
    Schools and Colleges
Woman

An index of subjects followed the classified arrangement. On the shelves the books were arranged by subject but in fixed location. The librarian in charge was Miss Hannah P. James (1835-1903), a prominent librarian of the period, who served as a vice-president of the A. L. A. in 1896-97 and was a contributor to the Library Journal.

1881 Frederic B. Perkins.

More than a century after his great-great-grandfather, Thomas Clap, had pioneered in book classification at Yale, Frederic Beecher Perkins published in San Francisco A Rational Classification of Literature for Shelving and Cataloguing Books in a Library (1881).

Perkins' work in classification came near the end of a diversified and restless literary career, one closely paralleling that of Edward William Johnston. He was born on September 27, 1828, in Hartford, Connecticut, the son of Thomas Clap Perkins and Mary Foote (Beecher) Perkins. Henry Ward Beecher was an uncle and Edward Everett Hale a brother-in-law. Perkins entered Yale with the class of 1850 but left in 1848 to study law in his father's office. In 1860 Yale conferred on him the honorary degree of Master of Arts. Although he was admitted to the bar in 1851, he preferred editorial and library work. Perkins was at various times connected with the New York Tribune, his uncle's Christian Union, and his brother-in-law's Old and New.

His introduction into library work came in 1857 with his appointment as librarian of the Connecticut Historical Society. Perkins later was a bibliographer, secretary, and special cataloger at the Boston Public Library. He was a member of the first cooperation committee of the American Library Association and served for years as the editor of the A. L. A. Catalog. From 1877 to 1880 he was an associate editor of the Library Journal. In 1880 Perkins became librarian of the San Francisco Free Public Library, a position he held until November 1887, when he resigned to resume editorial work. In 1894 he returned to the East and died in Morristown, New Jersey, in 1899, after a five-year illness.

Charles Dudley Warner wrote of Perkins' career:

> He had talents of a very high order — a touch of that which is called genius — and it is safe to say that if he had confined his effort to any one pursuit he would have attained great distinction. But beginning as a lawyer, he was then a teacher, a compiler, a librarian; with an erudition that made his services of great value, he spent a good part of his life in work that was unacknowledged, and gave himself little leisure for the creative work which was his business in life.... If he had possessed a certain stability of temperament and given his genius full play in a congenial direction, and had not been so much at the demand of other people for perfunctory literary work, he might have had, as we say, a high position in American letters. [1]

When Perkins became librarian of the San Francisco library in the summer of 1880, he found "Mr. Dui's plan" in use there. "The more I use that plan," he said, "the less I like it — which, of course, means nothing for those

who do like it. " The wastage of shelves by the grouping of books of different
sizes, the injury to books by moving them to insert others, and loss in speed
of service "by preventing the local memory of the book's place on the shelf, "
made fixed location, in Perkins' opinion, a sound principle of shelf arrangement. Thus Perkins recapitulated the objections of the librarians who opposed
the "new" idea of movable or relative location.

The Perkins Classification originated in the one "drawn up" by S. Hastings Grant, long librarian of the New York Mercantile Library, under whom
Perkins had worked. Perkins revised Grant's work for successive issues of
the catalog of that library in 1866, 1869, and 1872, and each time enlarged the
number of topics or "ultimate sections. " He rationalized the system in the
following words:

1. Religion. God, his dealings with man, man's duties to him.

2. Philosophy. Man's nature and natural duties to other men.

3. Society. Man's social activities in organization.

4. History (with geography and travels). The record of these social
   activities in time, having, for convenience' sake, along with it
   the account of the region in which they are exercised.

5. Biography. A similar record, but of individuals.

6. Science. The truth as to the materials of the universe within
   which man lives, about himself as a material part of it, and
   about his investigations of it.

7. Art. Man's dealings with the material universe: 1. for subsistence; 2. for enjoyment.

8. Literature. Man's mechanism for recording all these things,
   and the record of his use of that mechanism for pleasure. [2]

The eight "classes" had the following main subdivisions, or "chapters:"

CLASS A – RELIGION

Chap. I. Bible, biblical study
      II. History of religion
     III. Systematic theology
      IV. Christian polity
       V. Devotional
      VI. Practical
     VII. Collective works

CLASS B – PHILOSOPHY

      I. Mental philosophy:
         history and systems
     II. Mental philosophy:
         departments
    III. Mind and body
     IV. Moral philosophy

CLASS C – SOCIETY

   I. Government and law
   II. Public administration
   III. Social organization
   IV. Political economy
   V. Education: methods and departments
   VI. Education: institutions and reports
   VII. Business

CLASS D – HISTORY

   I. General geography and travels
   II. Universal history
   III. Historical collaterals
   IV. Ancient history
   V. Mediaeval history
   VI. Modern and European history
   VII. Asia
   VIII. Africa
   IX. South seas, Australasia, single islands
   X. America, except United States
   XI. United States

CLASS E – BIOGRAPHY

Chap. I. Collective: generally and by nations
   II. By classes
   III. Genealogy and names

CLASS F – SCIENCE

   I. General treatises
   II. Mathematics
   III. Natural philosophy
   IV. Astronomy
   V. Cosmology

   VI. Geology
   VII. Chemistry
   VIII. General natural history and zoology
   IX. Botany
   X. General medicine
   XI. Hygiene
   XII. Medical practice
   XIII. Surgical practice

CLASS G – ARTS

   I. General treatises
   II. Engineering
   III. Architecture, building
   IV. Military arts
   V. Naval arts
   VI. Mechanic arts and trades
   VII. Agriculture
   VIII. Domestic arts
   IX. Fine arts
   X. Music
   XI. Recreations

CLASS H – LITERATURE

   I. History of literature
   II. Philology
   III. Linguistics
   IV. Critical science
   V. Poetry
   VI. Drama
   VII. Fiction
   VIII. Oratory
   IX. Collections
   X. Periodicals
   XI. Encyclopaedias
   XII. Bibliography
   XIII. Libraries

As a sample of the complete expansion, a few of the seventy-four sections of the chapter Public Administration in the class Society are given, as well as the cross references.

   II. Public Administration.

       Church polity, A774.
       Church and state, A777.
       Sunday laws, A780.
       Morals of politics, B264.
       Biographies of statesmen, E89-90.

C. 91 Government generally; history of institutions.
 "   92 Republicanism.
 "   93 Elective franchise.
 "   94 Woman suffrage; for.
 "   95   against.
 "   96 Legislation and administration generally.
 "   97 Public documents of the U. S. ;
              Congressional debates.
 "   98   President's annual messages and documents,
              by sessions of Congress.
 "   99   Executive documents, by sessions of Congress.

Since the Arabic numbers extended through all the subdivisions of a

class, the Roman numbers were not used in practice. At the very end of his

"Explanations" Perkins reluctantly, or perhaps as an afterthought, gave a few

directions for arranging a "library on shelves." No author numbers were

used; the books were numbered serially under each class as received, e. g.,

C94.1, C94.2, etc., for works on Woman Suffrage.

1882 John Edmands.

The Mercantile Library of Philadelphia appointed John Edmands librar-

ian in 1856. During his fifty-nine years of association with the library, the

last fifteen as librarian emeritus, Edmands acquired wide recognition as a

bibliographer and book expert. He modified and expanded the existing classi-

fication[3] and devised a system of book numbers which was later adopted, with

some modifications, by the Minneapolis Public Library.

Edmands was born on February 1, 1820, in Framingham, Massachusetts,

the son of Jonathan and Lucy (Nourse) Edmands. He spent the first sixteen

years of his life on a farm, attending the district school for a few months each

year. Then, after five years of service as a carpenter's apprentice he began,

at the age of twenty-one, to prepare for college at Phillips Academy, Andover,

Massachusetts. In 1847, after graduating from Yale, he taught school for one

year in Rocky Mount, North Carolina. Edmands then returned to Yale to study

in the Divinity School. Although he did not graduate until 1851, he was licensed

to preach in 1850.

Edmands' library career began in 1845 when he was appointed librarian

of the Yale College Society of the Brothers in Unity. While occupying this

position he published a pamphlet Subjects for Debate with References to Authorities, which later was to develop into Poole's Index to Periodical Literature. Following several years' service as an assistant in the Yale College
Library, Edmands moved to Philadelphia in 1856 to take charge of the Mercantile Library. He was an original member of the American Library Association and served for a time as its vice-president. He was also president of
the Pennsylvania Library Association. Edmands remained in Philadelphia,
active in literary, civic, and religious circles until his death in 1915 at the
age of ninety-five.

When Edmands died, the Board of Directors of the library drafted a
resolution containing this tribute:

> ... Not the least of Mr. Edmand's work was the origination and
> application of a comprehensive system of classification that is
> still in use in the Library. It has proved equal to all require-
> ments, though the list of books is steadily and rapidly growing
> in number and variety. [4]

Edmands rearranged the classification previously used in the Mercantile Library to make it "a more natural one" and "more useful for the purposes of study, and as an aid in the finding of books. " He abandoned the former practice of designating the classes by numerals and substituted letters –
capitals for the primary classes and small for the subordinate classes.

His classification, in which the influence of Brunet is obvious, provided
the following main divisions:

    A. Theology
    B Sociology and Law
    C General History
    D History of Asia and Africa
    E History of Europe
    F History of America
    G Voyages and Travels (General)
    H Travels in Asia and Africa
    J Travels in Europe
    K Travels in America
    L Biography
    M Philosophy and Education
    N Mathematics and Physics
    O Natural Science
    P Medical Science
    R Useful Arts
    S Fine Arts

T Language and Literature
V Poetry and Drama
W Bibliography
X General and Miscellaneous Works
Y Foreign Literature
   Prose Fiction [in alphabetical order]

Each class was subdivided as in the following:

SOCIOLOGY AND LAW – B

B   Theory of Society and Government; Sphere of Woman; Woman's
    Rights.
Bb Political Economy.
Bc Labor; Production; Capital; Co-operation; Strikes; Wages;
    Communism; Socialism.
Bd Protection; Free Trade; Tariff.
Bf Finance; Banking; Currency; Revenue; Taxation; National
    debt; Credit.
Bg General treatises; Periodicals.
Bh Law of Nature and of Nations; Civil and Canon law; Maritime law.
Bj Constitutional and Statute Law; Equity; Commercial Law; Law
    of Real Property; Patent and Copyright Law; Law of Insurance;
    Medical Jurisprudence; Rules of Order.
Bl Trials; Proceedings and Reports; Courts; Evidence; Oaths;
    Practice.
Bm Slavery and the Slave-trade; Colonization; Emigration.
Bo Crime; Punishment; Prisons and Prison Discipline.
Bp Pauperism and Poor Relief; Charity Organization.
Bs Associations; Free Masonry; Odd Fellowship; Friendly Societies.

Edmands then devised a scheme of book numbers[5] to provide for the

shelving of books in alphabetical order in each division. He first constructed

a table which included all possible combinations of letters, based upon a com-

parison of the names found in several large catalogs. The names were then

distributed over a range of ten thousand numbers (0 to 9999) in each of the

subordinate classes. For example:

Aa   1-20 Abe
Abf 21-40 Acz
Ada 41-60 Aer
Aes 61-80 Aim
Ain 81-100 Albe

Thus Adams' Political Economy would be classed in Bb Political Economy

and assigned an author number between Ada 41-60. Edmands' system pro-

vided that books by the same author, wherever classed, would be assigned the

same author number. The numbers were treated as decimals, hence were in-

definitely expandable.

1882 <u>Lloyd</u> <u>Smith</u>.

George Campbell's classification[6] of the Library Company of Philadelphia had been limited to the catalog; on the shelves the books were arranged
by size in four groups – folios, quartos, octavos, and duodecimos – which gave
them "a neat and uniform appearance." The books were kept under lock and
key, the titles on their backs visible through the wires which protected them,
so that it was easy to tell whether a volume was "in" or not. This method of
shelving persisted until 1878, when the Loganian Library and most of the
Company's books were moved to the Ridgway Branch. Lloyd Smith, the librarian, then abandoned the fixed location by size and applied the classification to
the books on the shelves.

Lloyd Pearsall Smith was twenty-seven years old, a graduate of Haver-
ford College, and a successful young publisher when he became assistant librarian of the Library Company of Philadelphia in 1849. Two years later he
succeeded his father, John Jay Smith, as librarian.

During his thirty-five years in this position, until his death in 1886,
Smith achieved note as an editor and brilliant after-dinner speaker. He also
had a brief military career in 1863 when he left the library for three months
to aid in the defense of Gettysburg with the Germantown Company, a volunteer
unit. He was the first editor of <u>Lippincott's</u> <u>Magazine</u> when it began in January 1868, and was an associate editor of the <u>Library</u> <u>Journal</u> at its birth in
September 1876.

One of the first problems faced by the new librarian in 1851 was that of
the catalog – or catalogs – for there were now four: the "great Catalogue" compiled by George Campbell in 1835, two supplements listing the library's books
through 1849, and a manuscript record of subsequent additions. Smith decided
that a consolidated catalog, however desirable, was out of the question because
of the great expense, some $5,000 the project would cost. He therefore decided
to consolidate only the supplements and to compile an "alphabetical Index to the
whole" which would answer the needs of the library. He described his plan:[7]

I. To examine whether the author's name (if any) is already indexed, if not, to index it on a slip of paper, adding a short title of the book and the page of the Catalogue on which it is to be found.

II. To index the translators' and annotators' names.

III. To take the most important word or words of the title, and index it by them, as well as, in some cases, by some other word more likely to be referred to as the subject.

It will sometimes happen, therefore, that, on this plan, a book will be indexed five or six times, or even more: e.g., "6,411,0. The Spy Unmasked; or, Memoirs of Enoch Crosby, alias Harvey Birch, comprising many interesting anecdotes never before published. By H. L. Barnum. New York, 1828."

This work (like all biography, poetry, and sermons) is not at present indexed at all. By the plan proposed it will be found under either of the following references:

	Page
Barnum, H. L. Spy Unmasked	924
Spy, Unmasked	924
Crosby, E., Memoirs of	924
Birch, H., Memoirs of	924

He added, "I flatter myself that when this plan is carried out, the Library Company of Philadelphia will possess a Catalogue unsurpassed for facility of reference by any in the world."

In 1878 when Smith abandoned fixed location by size, the classification he applied as the basis of shelving books was essentially that used by George Campbell in 1835. He moved Bibliography from the beginning, where Campbell had put it, to the end, which was more in accord with Brunet, and over a period of some four years he made other additions and changes to make the system conform to the knowledge and books of the period. Smith's "Synopsis"[8] was:

Class A.	RELIGION.
E.	JURISPRUDENCE.
I.	SCIENCES AND ARTS.
O.	BELLES LETTRES.
U.	HISTORY.
Y.	BIBLIOGRAPHY AND THE HISTORY OF LITERATURE.

Subclasses.	a, b, c, d, e, etc.
Divisions.	1, 2, 3, 4, etc.
Subdivisions.	+, △, ☐, IV, V, VI, etc.

The notation Smith devised is frequently cited by teachers of library science as a horrible example of what to avoid. The following section of Class

E Jurisprudence illustrates his method of subdivision and the notation as well.

Class E. JURISPRUDENCE.

a General treatises on laws: legal miscellanies, periodicals, and
     history; professional ethics; the law of evidence;oaths;courts.
   1. Law dictionaries.
b Law of nature and of nations. Sea laws. Diplomatic and consu-
     lar manuals.
c Treaties.
d Ancient, civil, feudal, and ecclesiastical law.
e Common law and Equity.
   1. Law of real property. Conveyancing.
   2. Commercial law.
   3. Law relating to women, marriage, and divorce. (See I g 2.)
f Constitutional and municipal law and commentaries.
   1. The United States.
   2. Particular States, alphabetically.
   3. Great Britain.
       . Constitutional history.
       . Colonial.
   4. Continental Europe.
   5. Asia.
   6. Other countires.
g Parliamentary law and practice. Rules of order.
h Criminal and penal law. Police and prison discipline. Houses of
     refuge and correction. Detectives. Crime.
   1. Capital punishment.
i Medical jurisprudence.
k Trials.
   1. Criminal and State trials.
   2. Reports. Trials in civil cases.
       . English.
       . American, alphabetically by states.
   3. Individual and particular cases.
   4. Ecclesiastical trials.
m Patent law; Copyright.
n Military law; treatises on courts martial. Army regulations.
     Militia laws.
   1. Trials by court-martial.

The index to the 1882 classification contained not only Smith's class

numbers but those of his friend, "Mr. Melvil Dui, " to whom he was indebted

for the use he made of Dewey's Index.

Brunet's direct influence upon American library classification came to

an end with these systems. His indirect influence, however, continues in the

Decimal Classification, heritage of the work of E. W. Johnston, who fused Ba-

con and Brunet in the system he applied in the 1858 catalog of the St. Louis

Mercantile Library.

CHAPTER XII

The End of the Story

Only three more systems remain to be described before we return to
the Library of Congress and the problem of its classification. Two are American: one from Massachusetts, the other from California. The third is the
product of a German university.

1888 Halle Schema.

At this point it is necessary to depart briefly from the American scene
to describe the system Otto Hartwig developed for the library of the University of Halle. [1] Despite the important contributions of the Germans to the organization of knowledge, this was the first German system to have any real
influence on American classification. It must be added that its effect was
slight, and that was chiefly upon the new Library of Congress Classification
to be developed in the twentieth century.

Hartwig was born on November 16, 1830, at Wichmannsḥausen in Hesse.
He studied theology and philosophy at the universities of Marburg, Halle, and
Göttingen. After receiving his doctorate in philosophy from Marburg he entered library service in that institution. Hartwig remained in the library at
Marburg from 1857 until 1860, when he became minister of the German church
at Messina, Sicily. He abandoned the ministry, however, because each time he
had to preach a strange stage fright overcame him, and he could neither mem-
orize nor read his sermons. Hartwig returned to Germany in 1866, served as
an instructor at the gymnasium in Rinteln, Hesse, and in 1876 succeeded the
famous philologist, Gottfried Bernhardy, as librarian of the University of Halle
where he remained for twenty-two years.

Hartwig was one of the founders, and for over twenty years editor, of the
well-known Centralblatt für Bibliothekswesen. The decline of the Neuer An-
zeiger für Bibliographie und Bibliothekwissenschaft after Julius Petzholdt's

retirement as editor created a need for a new organ for the interchange of
ideas on library science; to fill this need the Centralblatt was established
under the editorship of Hartwig and Karl Schulz, librarian of the Supreme
Court of Germany. Schulz left the journal after three years, but Hartwig continued as editor until his death in December 1903.

As was the case in many other libraries, it was the erection of a new
building that brought the question of classification into prominence. The new
library building at Halle was opened in the fall of 1880, and the books were
moved to the new quarters in twenty-one days. Hartwig then began the task
of recataloging and reclassifying the entire library.

Hartwig based his classification upon the division of knowledge, traditional in German thought, into Geistes- und Naturwissenschaften. To serve
as the transitional discipline he drew Geography from its usual position as
an appendix to History and placed it between the grand divisions. The main
classes of his scheme and, to illustrate his method of subdivision, the principal subdivisions of medicine are given below, in English equivalents.

A	Bibliography and General Works
B	Linguistics, General and Oriental
C	Classical Philology
D	Modern Philology
E	Fine Arts
F	Philosophy
G	Education
H	History of Civilization and Comparative Religion
I	Theology
K	Law
L	Political and Social Sciences
M	Auxiliary Sciences of History
N	History
O	Geography
P	Natural and Mathematical Sciences, General
Q	Physics and Meteorology
R	Chemistry
S	Natural Sciences
	(Mineralogy, Geology, and Paleontology, Botany, and Zoology)
T	Agriculture. Forestry. Technology
U	Medicine
Ua	General Works
Ub	Anatomy
Uc	Physiology
Ud	General Pathology
Ue	General Therapeutics

Uf   Pharmacology. Toxicology
Ug   Medical Practice
       Internal Medicine
Uh   Infectious and Constitutional Diseases
Ui   Systemic and Organic Diseases
Uk   Surgery
Ul   Ophthalmology. Otology. Dentistry
Um   Gynecology. Obstetrics. Pediatrics
Un   State Medicine. Medical Jurisprudence
Uo   Veterinary Medicine

Hartwig (or "der 1. Amanuensis Dr. W. von Brünneck, " who developed

the schedule) frequently abandoned logical subdivision in K Law and resorted

to an "alphabetisch geordnet" arrangement like the following:

Kd

Monographien zum Römischen Recht, mit Ausschluss des
Erbrechts, alphabetisch geordnet.

A - K

A.

Acceptatio (Annahme) s. Vertrag sub Ke.
Acceptilatio.
Accessio (Eigenthumserwerb durch Verbindung).
   1.   Im Allgemeinen.
   2.   Einzelne Arten des Eigenthumserwerbs durch accessio.
        a.   Adplumbatio und ferruminatio
        b.   Commixtio und confusio.
        c.   Inaedificatio.
        d.   Alluvio.
             α.   Ueberhaupt.
             β.   Alveus derelictus.
             γ.   Insula nata.
Accessio possessionis s. Ersitzung.
Accord s. Erlass.
Act, actus legitimi s. Handlung.
Actio, Anspruch,
   1.   Ueberhaupt.
   2.   Concursus actionum. [2]

Hartwig was assisted by several members of the faculty at Halle, but

the planning and final integration of their work was his.

1892-93 C. A. Cutter.

Charles Ammi Cutter, one of the great figures in American library his-

tory, was born on March 14, 1837, in his father's house on Copp's Hill, Boston.

Frail and nearsighted, Charles was selected as the future clergyman of the family, perhaps by the maiden aunts with whom he lived from early childhood. Having prepared for college at the Hopkins Classical School, Cutter entered Harvard at the age of fourteen. He graduated in 1855, third in a class which numbered Charles W. Eliot, later president of Harvard, and Justin Winsor, well-known historian and librarian. After a year as tutor, Cutter entered the Harvard Divinity School. He graduated in 1859, receiving the coveted Bowdoin Prize for his essay "Persecutions for Religion's Sake during the Colonial Period in New England." Cutter preached a few sermons but was never regularly ordained.

He turned to library work instead, becoming an assistant to Ezra Abbot in the Harvard Library. For the next eight years he worked closely with Abbot, whose influence led him to devote his life to the new profession of librarianship. In 1868 Cutter succeeded William Frederick Poole as librarian of the Boston Athenaeum.

While at the Athenaeum, Cutter developed his Rules for a Dictionary Catalogue, first published as Part II of Public Libraries in the United States. [3] Cutter also contributed to this Report an essay[4] on cataloging which is as useful today as when it was published. H. B. Wheatley wrote of Cutter's Rules:

> All those who prepared the British Museum rules are gone from us; but happily cataloguers can still boast of Mr. Cutter of Boston, one of the foremost of our craft. Mr. Cutter has prepared a most remarkable code of rules, and has not only laid down the law, but has also fearlessly given the reasons for his faith, and these reasons form a body of sound opinion. May he long live to do honour to Bibliography, a cause which knows no nationality. [5]

Cutter was an original member of the American Library Association and its president in 1888 and 1889. He represented the association at the International Library Conferences in London in 1877 and 1897 and at the latter read a paper describing his classification.

In 1893 Cutter, feeling the need for more freedom, left the Athenaeum after twenty-five years' service to become librarian of the new Forbes Library in Northampton, Massachusetts. In the new position "he could finish the classification, apply his rules without criticism, and above all, develop his ideas as to how a library should serve the public." Cutter reported to the library, "On October fourth I began work with a janitor and three assistants ... not having either a chair or a table, nothing in fact within its walls but unpacked boxes of books."[6] He remained at the Forbes Library until his death on September 6, 1903, in Walpole, New Hampshire, near the mountains he loved.

Cutter began his work in classification in 1873 when he prepared outlines for history and library economy. It is probable that his work on the Rules interrupted the development of his classification. Shortly after the first A. L. A. conference in 1876, when a new room with a capacity of 50,000 volumes was made available at the Athenaeum to relieve the congestion of shelves carrying double, and even triple, rows of books, he returned to the problem. Cutter foresaw the continuing growth of the library and knew that each move entailed the changing of "shelf marks," a long and expensive process. He decided, therefore, to abandon fixed location "and to adopt a method which will allow the books to be moved hereafter, whenever necessary, without any change of the marks on the catalogues."[7]

At first Cutter was attracted to the "Amherst decimal plan"[8] because it was simple and symmetrical. But he soon found that the system with its decimal notation would not afford the close classification he considered necessary. Cutter objected not to the ten main classes but to the selection and arrangement of the subdivisions. He then began to devise "something better," selecting the letters of the alphabet as the basis of his notation. At Dewey's suggestion, Cutter combined both figures and letters and developed a classification which comprised thirty-six main divisions. Before applying the system in the Athenaeum, Cutter tried it out in the town library in Winchester, Massachusetts, where he was then living. Published in 1879 as the Winchester Town Library Class- and Author-Lists, Cutter's synopsis discloses the theory of organization which was to appear later in his Expansive Classification:

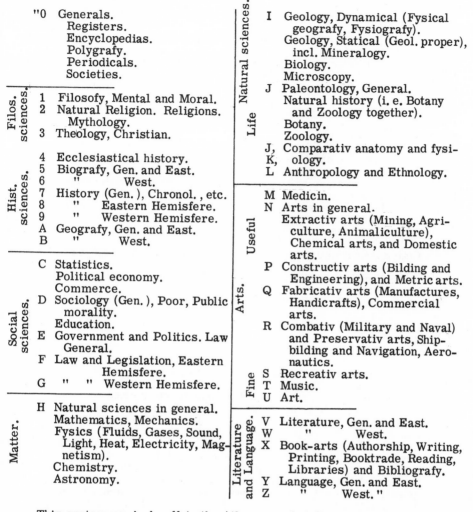

"0 Generals.
    Registers.
    Encyclopedias.
    Polygrafy.
    Periodicals.
    Societies.

Filos. sciences.
1 Filosofy, Mental and Moral.
2 Natural Religion. Religions.
   Mythology.
3 Theology, Christian.

Hist. sciences.
4 Ecclesiastical history.
5 Biografy, Gen. and East.
6 "   West.
7 History (Gen.), Chronol., etc.
8 "   Eastern Hemisfere.
9 "   Western Hemisfere.
A Geografy, Gen. and East.
B "   West.

Social sciences.
C Statistics.
   Political economy.
   Commerce.
D Sociology (Gen.), Poor, Public
   morality.
   Education.
E Government and Politics. Law
   General.
F Law and Legislation, Eastern
   Hemisfere.
G "   "   Western Hemisfere.

Matter.
H Natural sciences in general.
   Mathematics, Mechanics.
   Fysics (Fluids, Gases, Sound,
   Light, Heat, Electricity, Mag-
   netism).
   Chemistry.
   Astronomy.

Natural sciences.
Life
I Geology, Dynamical (Fysical
   geografy, Fysiografy).
   Geology, Statical (Geol. proper),
   incl. Mineralogy.
   Biology.
   Microscopy.
J Paleontology, General.
   Natural history (i. e. Botany
   and Zoology together).
   Botany.
   Zoology.
J, Comparativ anatomy and fysi-
K, ology.
L Anthropology and Ethnology.

Arts.
Useful
M Medicin.
N Arts in general.
   Extractiv arts (Mining, Agri-
   culture, Animaliculture),
   Chemical arts, and Domestic
   arts.
P Constructiv arts (Bilding and
   Engineering), and Metric arts.
Q Fabricativ arts (Manufactures,
   Handicrafts), Commercial
   arts.
R Combativ (Military and Naval)
   and Preservativ arts, Ship-
   bilding and Navigation, Aero-
   nautics.

Fine
S Recreativ arts.
T Music.
U Art.

Literature and Language.
V Literature, Gen. and East.
W "   West.
X Book-arts (Authorship, Writing,
   Printing, Booktrade, Reading,
   Libraries) and Bibliografy.
Y Language, Gen. and East.
Z "   West."

This system worked well in the Athenaeum, but Cutter was not wholly satisfied. The many requests he had received to adapt the Athenaeum system to the needs of small libraries led him to attempt to devise a more nearly perfect system. The **Expansive System** which he then developed was first tried out in the Cary Memorial Library in Lexington, Massachusetts. Cutter called his new system "Expansive" because it was designed in seven schedules of increasing fullness which could be applied to collections ranging in size from a village library to a national library of a million volumes. The first six expansions were published between 1891 and 1893.[9] In both the Introduction and the schedules themselves the author described his system in clear and simple terms. Cutter worked on the seventh expansion, but its development was interrupted by his death in 1903. After his death several parts of the seventh expansion were published, but they were inferior to the work Cutter had created or revised.

> The incompleteness of the seventh expansion is twofold. The technology was never finished. It was given up after having been delayed, first, by an attempt to complete it with the help of a committee from the various engineering societies, which attempt failed because one member of this committee was determined to organize a great financial organization to handle it; and, secondly, by the World War.[10]

Cutter sought to devise, not a classification of knowledge, but a logical and practical method for the arrangement of books. The two were not far apart, however, and he thought that a work of permanent value could be achieved only by a classifier who based his work upon a classification of knowledge. Cutter described his system:

> The expansive classification follows the evolutionary idea throughout, in natural history putting the parts of each subject in the order which that theory assigns to their appearance in creation. Its science proceeds from the molecular to the molar, from number and space, through matter and force, to matter and life; its botany going up from cryptogams to phanerogams; its zoology from the protozoa to the primates, ending with anthropology. The book arts follow the history of the book from its production (by authorship, writing, printing, and binding), through its distribution (by publishing and bookselling), to its storage and use in libraries public and private, ending with its description, that is, bibliography, suitably divided into general, national, subject, and selective. Economics, too, have a natural order — population, production, distribution of the things produced, distribution of the returns, property, consumption. Fine arts are grouped into the arts of solid — the landscape gardening, architecture, sculpture, casting; and the arts of the plane — painting, engraving, etc. ; and the mixed arts, being the smaller decorative and semi-industrial arts.
> Similar examples of logical, or, if you please, natural arrangement, are: Putting Bible between Judaism — to which the first part, the Old Testament, belongs — and Christianity, whose sacred book forms the second part; putting Church history between Christian theology and history; putting statistics between geography and economics, since it might have gone in either; putting music between the recreative arts and the fine arts. There are many such transitions, part of them, at least, novel in classification. They are not merely ingenuities pleasing only to their contriver; they have a certain practical value, since they bring books together which one may wish to use at the same time.[11]

Cutter's "First Classification" provided the following classes:

A   Works of reference and generalia
B   Philosophy and Religion
E   Historical sciences
H   Social sciences
L   Sciences and Arts, both Useful and Fine
X   Language
Y   Literature
YF   Fiction

The development of Class L Sciences and Arts, both Useful and Fine,

through the second and third expansions, illustrates Cutter's method.

Second (Expansion)	Third (Expansion)
L Physical sciences	L Science in general, and Physical sciences
M Natural history	M Natural history in general, Microscopy, Geology, Biology
	N Botany
	O Zoology
Q Medicine	Q Medicine
R Useful arts	R Useful arts in general
	S Engineering and Building
	T Manufactures and Handicrafts
	U Defensive and Preservative arts
V Recreative arts, Sports and games, Theatre, Music	V Recreative arts: Sports, Theatre, Music
W Fine arts	W Fine arts

The increasing specificity of each expansion may be readily seen in the

classification of Steamships:

1. L   Sciences and Arts, both Useful and Fine
2. R   Useful arts
3. U   Defensive and Preservative arts
4. UN   Nautical arts
5. UU   Ships, Shipbuilding, etc.
6. UUS   Steamships

Cutter's index recorded the progression:

Statute law (comparative) . . . . H, ^{3}K, ^{5}KL, ^{6}KM
Steam engines . . . . L, ^{2}R, ^{3}T, ^{5}TA, ^{6}TC
Steamships . . . . L, ^{2}R, ^{3}U, ^{4}UN, ^{5}UU, ^{6}UUS
Steel . . . . L, ^{2}R, ^{3}T, ^{5}TG, ^{6}TK
Stellar system . . . . L, ^{4}LR, ^{6}LS
Stereopticon . . . . L, ^{4}LH, ^{5}LK, ^{6}LKS
Stereoscope . . . . L, ^{4}LH, ^{5}LK, ^{6}LKS

The Expansive Classification used letters as the notation for subjects

and figures for form and geographical subdivisions. The form subdivisions

were:

1 Theory of the subject
2 Bibliography of the subject
3 Biography of the subject, i. e. , lives of persons connected with it
4 History of the subject
5 Dictionaries of the subject
6 Hand-books, etc. , of the subject
7 Periodicals limited to the subject
8 Societies devoted to the subject
9 Collections of works on the subject by several authors

Cutter provided a Local List of geographic subdivisions, which he

described:

> The order here adopted, after taking up the World and its
> great divisions, first those running east and west (the zones),
> then those running north and south (the lunes, – which bring in
> first the Pacific Ocean with Polynesia and then the Atlantic),
> passing through the Mediterranean Sea and the Levant, and what
> is almost its synonym, the Turkish Empire, enters Europe from
> the south, takes up successively Greco-Roman, Celtic, Teutonic,
> Scandinavian, Turanian, and Slavic Europe, goes over to Asia
> through the Balkan Peninsula, crosses that continent by the north
> and returning by the south leaps from India across the Arabian
> Sea to Africa, which it circuits, going south on the east side and
> coming back to the north on the west coast, then taking leave of
> Africa at the western islands, passes to America, which it tra-
> verses from north to south.

He synopsized the order:

```
The World . . . . . . . . . . . . . . .  11
Zones (running East and West) . . . . .  13, 14
Lunes (running North and South) . . . .  15-29
Continents . . . . . . . . . . . . . . .  30-99
Europe . . . . . . . . . . . . . . . . .  30
Asia . . . . . . . . . . . . . . . . . .  60
Africa . . . . . . . . . . . . . . . . .  70
America . . . . . . . . . . . . . . . .  80
```

Subdivisions like the following were provided by the List:

82   Canada, Dominion of

> All the provinces, towns, etc. , may be arranged
> alphabetically under 82, or the following order
> may be adopted:

821   British Columbia
822   Northwest Territory
8225   Athabasca
823   Alberta
8235   Saskatchewan
824   Assiniboine
8245   Keewayden
825   Hudson Bay and Northeast Territory
8255   Manitoba
826   Ontario, Upper Canada
827   Quebec, Lower Canada

```
828    New Brunswick
829    Nova Scotia
8295   Prince Edward Island
8297   Cape Breton Island
8298   St. Lawrence River

8299   The Great Lakes
                Better in 90

83     United States
```

> All the states, towns, etc., may be arranged al-
> phabetically under 83, or the following order
> may be adopted:

Subdivisions 84-949 then list the separate states and parts of the United

States.

An interesting feature of Cutter's classification was its reversibility,

which made it possible to provide either, or both, a subject and an area ar-

rangement. Thus under the Natural Sciences the sequence might be:

Natural Sciences - Germany

```
N47    Botany - Germany
O47    Zoology - Germany
PB47   Fishes - Germany
PE47   Birds - Germany
```

or

Germany - Natural Sciences

```
47N    Germany - Botany
47O    Germany - Zoology
47PB   Germany - Fishes
47PE   Germany - Birds
```

The following summary from the Catalog of "A. L. A." Library, of 1893,

reflects the structure and divisions of Cutter's system as it neared completion:

OUTLINE OF THE EXPANSIVE CLASSIFICATION

A	General Works.	MQ		Paleontology.
AD	Dictionaries.	MV		Biology.
AE	Encyclopaedias.	N		Botany.
AI	Indexes.	O		Zoölogy.
AM	Museums.	P		Vertebrates.
AP	Periodicals.	PW	Anthropology and Ethnology.	
AQ	Quotations.	Q	Medicine.	
AR	Reference Books.	R	Useful Arts, Technology.	
AS	Societies.	RC		Metric Arts.
B	Philosophy.	RCZ	Extractive and Productive Arts.	
BG	Metaphysics.	RD		Mining.
BH	Logic.	RF		Metallurgy.

BI	Psychology.	RG	Agriculture.
BM	Moral Philosophy.	RJ	Animaliculture.
BR	Religion.	RQ	Chemical Technology.
BS	Natural Theology	RT	Electric Arts.
BT	Religions.	RY	Domestic Economy.
C	Christianity and Judaism.		Constructive Arts.
CA	Judaism.	S	Engineering.
CB	Bible.	SG	Building.
CC	Christianity.	SJ	Sanitary Engineering.
CE	Apologetical Theology.	SL	Hydraulic Engineering.
CF	Doctrinal Theology.	ST	Arts of Transportation.
CK	Ethical Theology.	T	Fabricative Arts.
CP	Ecclesiastical Polity.	U	Art of War.
CR	Ritual Theology.	UN	Nautical Arts.
CX	Pastoral Theology.	V	Athletic and Recreative Arts.
D	Ecclesiastical History.		Fine Arts.
E	Biography.	VV	Music.
F	History (with local list).	W	Art, Fine Arts.
FF	Antiquities	WD	Plastic Arts.
FN	Numismatics.	WE	Landscape Gardening.
FS	Chivalry.	WF	Architecture.
FV	Heraldry.	WJ	Sculpture.
G	Geography and Travels (with local list).	WL	Arts of Design.
		WM	Drawing.
H	Social Sciences.	WP	Painting.
HB	Statistics.	WQ	Engraving.
HC	Economics, Political Economy.	WR	Photography.
		WS	Decorative Arts.
I	Demotics, Sociology.		Arts of Communication by Language.
IK	Education.		
J	Civics, Political Science.	X	English Language.
K	Legislation.	X11	Language in General.
KW	Woman.	XX	Oratory.
KX	Societies.	Y	English and American Literature.
L	Sciences and Arts.		
LA	Sciences (Natural).	YD	Drama.
LB	Mathematics.	YF	Fiction.
LH	Physics, Natural Philosophy.	YJ	Juvenile Literature.
		YP	Poetry.
LO	Chemistry.	Y11	Literature in General.
LR	Astronomy.	Z	Book Arts.
M	Natural History.	ZN	Private Libraries.
MB	Microscopy.	ZP	Public Libraries.
MC	Geology.	ZT	Bibliography.
MD	Mineralogy.	ZY	Literary History.
MG	Physiography.		

The problem of "internal" notation or book marks then attracted Cutter's attention. Prevailing practice was to arrange books within the classes serially, chronologically, or alphabetically. To preserve the alphabetical order wherever used and to provide a means for shelving and locating books Cutter devised a system of book marks universally known today as Cutter numbers.

Books on the shelves are kept alphabeted by authors by marking them with the initial of the author's family name followed by one or more decimal figures assigned according to a table so constructed that the names whose initials are followed by some of the <u>first</u> letters of the alphabet have the <u>first</u> numbers, and those in which the initials are followed by <u>later</u> letters have <u>later</u> numbers.

E. g., Gardiner, G16.   Gore, G66.
      Gerry, G36.   Graham, G76.
      Gilman, G42.   Grote, G89.
      Glover, G51.   Guizot, G94.

If the books are arranged in the order of these numbers, of course they will be in alphabetical order.[12]

Cutter's original author table provided only two numbers as above. Kate E. Sanborn later developed the Cutter-Sanborn 3-figure Alphabetic Table.

It is interesting that Cutter, unlike Dewey, did not favor a classed catalog. In "Common Sense" he stated: "It does not strike me as a very sensible proceeding to classify books on the shelves systematically, and then to classify them in the catalog on the same system, making the catalog only a glorified shelf-list, when one might get another kind of information by arranging the catalog differently, in alphabetical subject order, for instance."[13]

Writers on library classification have become so fond of the term "inverted Baconian," first applied to the system of W. T. Harris, that they have applied it to Cutter's scheme. It would be difficult, however, to find a classification less Baconian in character, either in the original spirit of the originator, or in the work of his adapters. Cutter's work is far closer to "Brunet," as found in Stephen Elliott and Ezra Abbot, modified by the author's concept of evolution.

Cutter produced the best classification of the nineteenth century. While his system was less "scientific" than that of J. P. Lesley, its other features — notation, specificity, and versatility — make it deserving of the praise it has received. Henry Evelyn Bliss, critic and classification maker, although highly critical of Cutter's system and its notation, wrote:

Yet, here lies the library classification that has brought into service some of the most valid principles and in the historical situation has best served as a stepping-stone to the

future. Those principles, tho imperfectly embodied, have been
in a sense prophetic, and they have aided to redeem the problem from the "subject-index illusion." High respect and grati-
tude are due from those who have followed. [14]

1894 J. C. Rowell.

The University of California Library at Berkeley was established in

1868. Seven years later, in 1875, its collection of 13,600 volumes was put in

charge of a youthful librarian, Joseph Cummings Rowell, who had graduated

from the university the year before. He remained with the library for sixty-

five years and played a major part in transforming it from a small college

library into one of the great university collections of the country.

Rowell was born in Panama on June 29, 1853, of New England parents

and received his early education in the public schools of San Francisco. He

graduated from the University of California in 1874, a member of its second

four-year class, but he did not receive his M. A. until twenty-nine years la-

ter. In 1935 his alma mater honored him with an L. L. D. degree. Rowell was

vice-president of the A. L. A. in 1891 and first president of the California Li-

brary Association (1895-97). He also was prominent in California civic and

educational associations. In 1920 he retired from the librarianship but con-

tinued to work daily as librarian emeritus and university archivist, a position

he held until his death on November 13, 1938.

Rowell's bibliographical works covered a wide field ranging from Cal-

ifornia maps to American sonnets; but his most valuable contributions were

the Contents-index he prepared in 1890 for the University of California Li-

brary and his Classification of Books in the Library. [15]

Rowell's classification, like that used by T. Clap of Yale, was based upon

the university curriculum: "... in its collocation of subjects [it] is believed

to more nearly conform to courses of instruction at present pursued in the

University than do other schemes now in print." [16] Rowell's scheme com-

prised the following main groups: Generalia (including Bibliography); Philoso-

phy and Religion; Geography and History; Social Sciences; Science and Tech-

nology; Fine Arts, Language and Literature. His notation, like that used by

Cutter in his 1882 essay, employed letters and numerals. Unlike Cutter, Rowell used the letters A, B, and C for his "generalia" classes, and figures 1-999, in arithmetical sequence, for the systematic divisions:

A Bibliography in General. Anonyms, Pseudonyms.
    Bibliographies of special subjects are arranged under such subjects, adding lower case a to class mark.

B Encyclopedias; Dictionaries of general knowledge.
    Encyclopedias on special subjects are arranged under such subjects, adding lower case b to class mark.

C Periodicals: General, Literary, Unclassified.
    Periodicals, including society publications, on special subjects are arranged under such subjects, adding lower case c to class mark.

1–14	Philosophy
1a	Bibliography
1b	Dictionaries
1c	Periodicals
16-51	Religion
52	Biography: Collective
53	Biography: Individual
54-60	Geography
61-255	History
256-287	Politics, Government, Administration, Droit public
289-299	Law
300-314	Social Science, Customs, Social Institutions
315-332	Political Economy
333-336	Science (Physical). History, General works.
337-355	Mathematics
357-371	Astronomy
372-400	Physics
401-423	Civil Engineering
425-428	Natural Science, Natural History
429-430	Meteorology
431-439	Geology, Descriptive and general
440-441	Paleontology
442-448	Botany
459-460	Biology of Plants and Animals (treated together)
461-478	Zoology
480-505	Medicine
506	Industrial Arts, in general and unclassified
507-521	Agriculture
523-551	Chemistry (including Chemical Technology)
554-575	Mining (including Metallurgy and Manufactures from Metals)
580-588	Manufactures
590-598	Building Arts
600-605	Architecture
610-611	Domestic Economy
613-616	Recreation. Sports. Games.
617-621	Business.
623-630	Art of War
632-679	Aesthetics. Fine Arts
682-999	Language and Literature

For additions, lower-case letters were assigned to these figures, e. g.

```
10      Psychology; Mental Science
  10p     Phrenology
  10y     Physiognomy
```

An interesting feature of Rowell's system is his attempt to collocate theory and practice, science and technology. Electrical Engineering 387-390 follows Electricity 382-386. Following Communication in 619 are

```
620 Transportation, Navigation, Express
621 Seamanship, Nautical Astronomy
```

Curiously, Business 617-621 is followed by the Art of War 623-630. Paralleling the schedule in the right hand margin are references to related topics, e. g

```
554      Mining. General treatises, Exploitation [ Ore deposits 436
   554e    Mining Accidents                            [ Surveying 402
```

Another interesting feature is the special classification provided for California under United States: Local History and Travel. The States are arranged alphabetically, each with a single number; then comes California, with the following arrangement to provide for local needs.

```
230 California:  Travel
231      "       History
232      "       Single Counties:  Alpine to Napa
233      "         "         "     Nevada to Yuba
234  San Francisco
236  Alameda County; Oakland
237  Berkeley
```

Hartwig, Cutter, and Rowell bring to a close the story of the background of decision. Briefly described was a period of two and a half millennia: from Ionia of the seventh century before Christ to California in the closing years of the nineteenth century. Three main streams of thought were discernible: (1) the educational and philosophic system, which, originating in Greece, followed the development of Western thought and culminated in the French System of Jacques-Charles Brunet; (2) the seventeenth-century divisions of Francis Bacon which, modified and adapted by d'Alembert and Jefferson, were transmitted to Melvil Dewey by Johnston and W. T. Harris; (3) the evolutionary order, in the nineteenth century, of Merlin and Lesley, which Cutter transmuted into his Expansive Classification. It is now time to return to the Library of Congress and its problem: what classification for the future?

THE "NEW" L. C. CLASSIFICATION

CHAPTER XIII

Quest – Experiment – Decision

John Russell Young's question concerning the future classification of the Library of Congress was raised after the Library had occupied its new building. For, like political revolutions, library reclassifications occur, not when conditions are hopeless, but when they begin to improve. The provision of additional shelf space serves as an incentive for the creation of new systems of book arrangement.

The new building was completed in February of 1897, but the extra session of the Congress called by President McKinley to revise the tariff had delayed the move from the Capitol until summer. The work of transferring the Library from the crowded quarters it had occupied for nearly a century was not begun until August 2. Favored by the weather, the carefully planned project was completed in ten weeks. "As an engineering feat this would merit high praise," wrote Young.

On the new shelves the order of the 750,000 volumes and 200,000 pamphlets revealed serious deficiencies in classification which the crowded conditions in the Capitol had concealed. Martel made a survey of the "subjective system," examining its theoretical structure, the adequacy of its subdivisions, and its potential expansibility — or receptiveness to new developments in knowledge. Late in December, he submitted a preliminary report to Librarian Young advising against any revamping of the old system. In the same month the Librarian issued an order which postponed immediate consideration of the classification problem. He directed that a thirty-year accumulation of uncataloged and unbound material stored in the basements of the Capitol be fully cataloged and on the shelves by the following March. In "The Library of Congress and Its New Catalogue: Some Unwritten History" Hanson has left us an account of the predicament in which he and Martel found themselves.

It was an impossible task, but remonstrance was futile,
and there was no choice but to go ahead. Attempts were first
made to utilize ... political appointees, especially one who
claimed to have some knowledge of foreign languages. It was
soon found that this knowledge did not suffice to decipher titles,
and the writer and his chief assistant, the present head of the
Division [Martel], were accordingly obliged to devote the hours
from 7:00 P.M. until one or two in the morning, Sundays and
holidays included, to the sorting. By March, the collection was
arranged on shelves by countries, departments, and sets, and
though little actual cataloguing had been accomplished, some
extremely valuable books had been unearthed, and the collection was ready for further and more detailed treatment. [1]

When Martel and Hanson completed their "shelf cataloging," they re-

turned to the classification problem. Experiments were made in several

chapters which had been subdivided, among them Chapters 24 Politics and

25 Mathematics, as well as in some, like Poetry, in which a simple alphabeti-

cal arrangement seemed satisfactory. Book numbers were assigned, and,

for the first time in the history of the Library, a shelflist was developed. [2]

These tests, however, confirmed the findings of the preliminary survey:

that any attempt to revamp the old system by adding book numbers, rearrang-

ing the divisions, or providing additional divisions would not only be as labor-

ious and time-consuming as a complete reclassification, but the final product

would still be unsatisfactory. A scheme devised for a library of less than

10,000 volumes from a classification of knowledge now nearly three centur-

ies old had become entirely inadequate. The remedy was systematic reclas-

sification according to a modern system. The principal object should be: "To

facilitate the use of the library by the orderly arrangement of the books, in

divisions corresponding to the literature existing upon various subjects,

classed within each department of science according to their relation as

established in bibliographical systems of classification based upon scientific

authority. "[3]

For one who was not a librarian, Young had definite opinions concern-

ing the nature and purpose of a classification for the Library. No system of

classification would be devised or adopted which would disintegrate the gen-

eral collection. Each department would maintain its representative character, but the main purpose of classification would be the consolidation of the general library. What might be taken from the shelves to strengthen the medical collections or to develop a law library, what might be contemplated in the way of a Congressional library of reference, could and should be replaced; "... there must be no invasion of the general library's domain as one of universal reference."

Two courses were open: to choose from the classification schemes already existing in printed form the one best suited to the needs of the Library; or, to build up an "eclectic" system which would profit by the experience of other large reference libraries and utilize the best features of all existing classifications.

In considering the first course the desirability and importance of uniformity in classification as well as in other bibliographical work were kept in mind. The possibility that the Library of Congress, in its position as national library might, through its choice, influence other libraries was also a consideration. Another important factor was the potential effect the decision might have on future national cooperation in the library field, and on the Library's own position to benefit from, as well as to share in, both national and international bibliographic projects. It was recognized that the needs of the Library should not be the sole controlling factor in the choice.

Three systems available in printed form merited careful consideration: Dewey's Decimal Classification, Cutter's Expansive Classification, and Hartwig's Halle Schema. The Decimal Classification, which had been adopted by many American libraries and had served as the basis of several bibliographical projects both in this country and abroad, deserved special study. Martel summarized the relative advantages and disadvantages of the system for Young in 1898.

A. – Its advantages

1. It exists in printed form, elaborately worked out and must therefore save a great amount of time and money to any library adopting it.

2. Its extensive use and the later editions having profited by actual tests of the classification in various libraries.

3. A library adopting it may derive benefits from cooperative work undertaken on the basis of the Decimal classification and its active participation in such cooperative work may be much facilitated.

4. Advantages of a figure notation over letter. Figures being written quicker, with less danger of mistake than letter combinations, which are difficult to catch with the eye and to remember.

5. Relative location and possibility of indefinite intercalation of books and subdivisions.

[6] Mnemonic features.

B. – Its disadvantages

1. The system is bound up in and made to fit the notation, not the notation to fit the classification.

2. A rigidity of notation, which renders intercalation of new sections difficult and prevents a proportionate adjustment of the notation, according to the needs and circumstances of the individual library. Long and complicated marks cannot, therefore, be avoided, and that in classes, where they are specially undesirable.

   Example of lack of proportion in the allotment of figures is philosophy with 1 figure, history being allotted the same.

   In this Library, history, which would include also descriptive works, covers fully two decks, and in addition, the alcoves and first floor of the galleries in north half of Reading Room; philosophy, on the other hand, occupies of 84 ranges on deck 8, only 6, ranges 45-50. That is, the Library would with the Decimal Classification have over 36 times as many books in the 900ds as in the 100ds.

3. The divisions are fixed and any library adopting the classification, stands committed to its defects of arrangement.

4. Divisions and classes will arise for which the Decimal has not provided. Its division into 10, and again 10, does not readily allow of intercalation of new divisions, except as subsections. In the edition of 1885 there was no provision for Bacteriology. In edition of 1894 this large class was assigned a place under Tallophyta. In political science and administration, in history, there are incessant changes. The rigidity of the Decimal system makes it particularly difficult to deal with them.

5. Mnemonic features are of no consequence to the reader. It does not pay in a large library to sacrifice simplicity of notation to mnemonic elements. If the latter are to be considered the Expansive system is distinctly superior.

6. Uniformity in classification is impossible even if same

notation and classification is adopted in different libraries.
In Zoology and Physiology, Richet at Paris, Carus at Leipzig, and Field at Zürich have all used the decimals without
attaining uniformity in the disposition of the same books or
articles.

7. It has been found unsuitable to the needs of reference librar-
    ies by many of the librarians and bibliographers best quali-
    fied to judge. Some of these that may be mentioned are: Bil-
    lings, Harvard, Delisle, Deniker, Dziatzko, Hartwig, Fumagalli,
    Van der Haeghen.

8. Of 127 libraries of 25,000 volumes and over, reporting on
    classification in 1893, 42 reported using Decimal, but almost
    all of these with more or less modification.

9. The author claims right of preventing reprinting of the clas-
    sification, or any part of it with variations, unless such varia-
    tions are distinctly noted by using letters or other marks for
    the new heads, the decimal numbers not to be printed with
    changed meanings without clear indication of the fact. [4]

Of the other two systems, Martel thought that much assistance could

be derived from Hartwig's Halle Schema but that its adoption, even in modi-

fied form, could not be seriously considered except in a university library.

The most recent system, Cutter's Expansive, had much in its favor but was

hampered by an unsatisfactory notation and was incomplete in some of the

most important classes.

No final decision on what classification or classifications were to form

the basis for the new system was made at this time, but the Catalogue Divi-

sion "was authorized to proceed with the reclassification of Bibliography ac-

cording to an eclectic system, [to be] prepared and submitted for the consid-

eration of the Librarian and Chief Assistant Librarian."

For practical reasons the bibliographical collection, Chapter 38, was

the first to receive attention. Extensive additions to all departments of the

Library, which had long been in abeyance for want of space in the old Library

in the Capitol, were to be made as rapidly as possible. It was therefore de-

sirable to put the bibliographical apparatus into better condition for use in

the new cataloging program. Furthermore, since Bibliography would consti-

tute a basic reference collection separate from the general collections, the

new classification devised for it would not preclude the choice of an existing

system for the rest of the Library. Class Z <u>Bibliography</u> <u>and</u> <u>Library</u> <u>Science</u>
was completed in 1898,[5] and 6,372 volumes were recorded in the new Z
shelflist. This shelflist, on cards, was also a classed catalog; the entries
were fuller than the usual shelflist entries, and an author and subject index
were provided. It was designed to serve as the basis of a bibliographical
handbook of the Library.

The order of the main divisions, and Library Science in detail, follow
Cutter's plan. He had "kindly furnished" the Library an advance outline of
his <u>Seventh</u> <u>Expansion</u> <u>of</u> <u>the</u> <u>Book</u> <u>Arts</u>. For the other divisions, especially
National and Subject Bibliography, original schedules were devised. For na-
tional bibliography proper (i.e., the country as a subject), there were provisions for form, period, and subject subdivisions, present and prospective.
The arrangement of Subject Bibliography alphabetically by subject and the
subjects by period, form, topics, and countries recalls Schwartz's attempt to
fuse classification and subject headings. It is this feature — alphabetic-classed
instead of systematic arrangement — and not the collocation of bibliography
which has made Z the most unsatisfactory of the Library of Congress schedules.

The following synopses illustrate both Cutter's influence and the independent elements in the classification:

CUTTER		L. C.	
Z BOOK ARTS		Z BIBLIOGRAPHY AND LIBRARY SCIENCE	
<u>Production</u> ZA-ZK		4- 8	History of books and bookmaking
Authorship ZA-ZC		40-115	Writing
Writing ZD-ZG			41-42 Autographs
Printing ZH-ZJ			43-48 Calligraphy. Penmanship
Binding ZK			49-51 Typewriting
			53-100 Shorthand
<u>Distribution</u> ZL-ZM			103-104 Cryptography
Publishing and Bookselling ZL			105-115 Paleography
Book buying ZM		116-550	Book industries and trade
			116-265 Printing
<u>Storage</u> <u>and</u> <u>use</u> ZN-ZS			266-275 Binding
Libraries			278-550 Publishing and bookselling
(Private ZN. Public		551-661	Copyright. Intellectual property
ZP-ZS.)			657-659 Liberty of the press
<u>Description</u> <u>and</u> <u>use</u> ZT-ZZ		665-997	Libraries and library science
Bibliography ZT-ZX			687-718 The books
(General ZT-ZV. Subject			Acquisition, cataloging,

ZW. National ZX.)
Literary history ZY
Selection of reading ZZ

classification, reference
use, etc.
719-880 Library history. Reports.
Statistics
881-980 Library catalogs and
bulletins
987-997 Private libraries. Book
collecting.
998-1000 Book prices. Booksellers' catalogs
1001-8999 Bibliography
1041-1107 Anonyms and pseudonyms
1201-4941 National bibliography
5051-7999 Subject bibliography
8001-8999 Personal bibliography

In the Library of Congress scheme Authorship and Literary History were to

be classed in P Language and Literature, a far more logical place than their

inclusion in the mechanical aggregate of books about books.

After the completion of Class Z, Young decided that the work of reclas-

sification could not be continued, in view of the increasing acquisitions, with-

out additional staff. [6] Hanson insisted that delay would only aggravate the

problem, but Young overruled him. Hanson wrote later:

It was apparent that these representations had little effect,
due perhaps in part to the fact that the health of the librarian was
failing rapidly, and he had neither the time, strength, nor the keen
appreciation of the situation which would have enabled him to go
before Congress with a strong plea for additional help and funds. [7]

John Russell Young died suddenly on January 17, 1899. Herbert Put-

nam, librarian of the Boston Public Library, succeeded him as eighth Librar-

ian of Congress on April 5. Hanson lost little time in presenting his plans to

the new Librarian, who had shown his interest in classification at the 1896

Hearings on the "Condition of the Library." On April 21 he sent Putnam the

following memorandum, which included the first outline of the proposed sys-

tem.

I take the liberty to supplement our talk about the classification by the following brief explanations.
In planning the new notation I had partly in mind Dr. Poole's
scheme of a significant [mnemonic] letter for the class with consecutive numbers for the books, not the divisions within the class.
According to Poole, H stood for history, P for political science,
M for music, etc. He would allow some 30,000 numbers for history and these we were expected to block out sufficiently to cover
the number of subdivisions provided.
The result was, that, before we had classified and listed

5,000 books in history, the alphabetical order was broken in
many places, the numbers being exhausted. Mr. Martel and I
in talking it over decided to drop the plan of a significant letter
as of little value. To apply the consecutive number scheme to
divisions, not books; for individual books the Cutter tables should
serve.

We secured by this a class and subsection mark possessing no mnemonic features, but presenting a call number easily
remembered, written or followed in placing or finding books. As
to the book number the fact that it begins with a letter is in my
opinion a considerable advantage, as the assistants soon learn
to look for the initial of the author after finding the section. It
saves time both in finding and replacing books, and, I dare say,
there is less danger of misplacement under this system, than if
the class and section numbers were followed by decimals for the
book number.

As an example illustrating the elasticity of the system,
take the section Z 999 (antiquarian catalogues). A catalogue of
Harrassowitz is marked in full Z 999. H29. In the same division
under the letter H two figures could be made to accommodate
99 different books, three figures 999, four figures 9999, etc.

The twenty-six letters would give space for respectively,
2574 books with two figures, 25,974 with three, 259,974 with
four, etc.

Of course, in order to secure strict alphabetical and
chronological order of all the works of any one author happen-
ing to fall in the same division, we are often forced to use three
and even four figures after the author's initial even where there
may be at the outset a comparative small number of books in a
section.

I know, that at some of the best known libraries there is
a strong feeling against using the initial letter for the book number on the ground that it introduces a letter in the midst of figures, that the Harrassowitz catalogue noted above should be
marked Z 999. 387, if that number were not previously taken,
rather than Z 999. H29. But I so far have been unable to see,
that the former system offers advantages superior to the latter.

After adopting the notation used so far in the reclassification, I have been encouraged by seeing that other libraries
have followed practically the same lines in planning a new notation. I can refer particularly to Harvard University Library.

James D. Brown in his Adjustable classification, printed
in his recent Manual of library classification follows same lines,
and finally the Committee on the International scientific catalogue in their schedule presents almost the same form of notation for classes and subdivisions. I enclose also a tentative list
of classes, showing their assignment and sequence under the
present system of notation. There are, of course, many questions
still pending. The present list represents an attempt to bring together after the general works at the beginning of A, the classes,
which may be said to include the humanities, in a wide sense, followed by the arts and sciences. [8]

A	1-200	Polygraphy; Encyclopedias; General Periodicals; Societies &c.
A	201-3000	Philosophy.
A	3001-B9999	Religion; Theology; Church history.
C	1-9999	Biography; and studies auxiliary to history.
D	1-9999	General history; periods; and local (except

		America) with geography.
E- F		America; history and geography.
G		Geography; general; and allied studies (e. g. Anthropology and Ethnology).
H	1-2000	Political science.
H	2001-9999	Law.
I	1-8000	Sociology.
I	8001-9999	Women; Societies; clubs etc.
J	1-2000	Sports; amusements.
J	2001-9999	Music.
K		Fine arts.
L-M		Philology & Literature.
N		Science; Mathematics; Astronomy; Physics; Chemistry.
O		Natural history; general; Geology.
P		Zoology; Botany.
Q		Medicine.
R		Useful arts; Agriculture.
S		Manufactures.
T		Engineering.
U		Military, Naval science; light houses; life saving; fire extinction.
V-Y		Special collections.
Z		Bibliography (Book arts).

At the University of Wisconsin, which had adopted the Cutter System while Hanson was there, the irregular sequence of letters and the arbitrary use of preliminary numbers proved to be drawbacks. Hanson then began to experiment with a notation of one or two letters to indicate classes and Arabic numbers for divisions and subdivisions, using Cutter numbers for the individual books. The Wisconsin Library made no use of these experiments, but as several visiting librarians – particularly Miss Olive Jones, at that time librarian of the Ohio State University Library – had been impressed by the simplicity and elasticity of the notation, the draft was saved. This draft probably formed the basis of the preceding Outline.

Under Putnam, the new Librarian, the Library renewed its quest for a solution to the problem of classification. In Putnam's words,

> The present classification of the Library is but a slight expansion of that adopted by Thomas Jefferson in 1815 for his library of 6,700 volumes. It is meager, rigid, and inelastic, and unsuited to a library of a million volumes. The entire library must be reclassified.
>
> An indispensable record in a library is a list of the books composing each class as they stand on the shelves, and identifying them by their accession numbers. This is called the "shelf list." It is the basis of every inventory. There is no shelf list of the 700,000 books and 250,000 pamphlets in the Library of

Congress. One must be written. [9]

The duties of the "catalogue-shelf" department were:

1. To classify, locate, enter on shelf lists, number and catalogue the current accessions to the Library in the form of books and pamphlets. During the year beginning July 1, 1900, these are likely to exceed 40,000 volumes.

2. To reclassify, relocate, enter on shelf lists, and renumber the entire existing collection of books and pamphlets. [10]

In connection with the survey of possibilities for a new classification, Putnam, Martel, and William Parker Cutter (nephew of C. A. Cutter) made an extensive trip to visit libraries using either the Decimal or the Expansive Classification. They also called on the authors of these schemes and suggested to them certain changes in their classifications. "Mr. Cutter expressed himself as perfectly willing to make any changes which after careful consideration seemed necessary. Mr. Dewey absolutely refused to make any, basing his argument on the inconvenience which would result to the large number of libraries already using the Decimal Classification." [11]

An examination of the changes proposed by the Library makes clear the reason for Dewey's adamant attitude. Had he accepted them, the D. C. would no longer have been the D. C. The "Sketch of Programme" for conferences at the New York State Library, at Amherst, and at Northampton is given below to illustrate the conflicting theories of this period in regard to classification.

1. Examination of
   a) the classification of books on the shelves at Albany
   b) the classed catalogues
   c) records, correspondence etc. relating to use of system in other libraries; propositions for modifications etc. etc. (as far as they are open to inspection)

2. Cooperation in the 20th century edition of D. C. (if adopted by Library of Congress)
   Extent of modifications
   I. Broader basis (e. g. Alphabet for main classes; subdivided decimally (or otherwise) giving shorter marks and better distribution of "space"; as 1 letter for Philosophy, 3 for History and Geography, 3 for Social sciences, exclusive of Education etc. etc.)

II. Order of sequence of main divisions
    (e. g. Language and literature to be contiguous
    divisions i. e. 400 and 800 to be 700 and 800, exten-
    sively modified.
III. Modifications in arrangement of subdivisions
    a) General e. g.
      Order of "01 to 09" (general works at beginning of
      subjects)
      Application of alphabetical arrangement wherever
      there are many (coordinate) topical subdivisions
      Order of countries e. g.
        1. Change to geographical arrangement: countries
          under S. A. (981-989)
        2. Change to alphabetical arrangement: local sub-
          divisions as Counties, towns etc. under U. S.
          Provinces, departments etc. under France
          (Countries under Germany or at least 943.5
          with 943.1; 943.44 & 943.45 better before
          943.1 or after 943.58. 943.8 (general) with
          947.5 (Cf. 943.74) etc. etc.
    b) Special
      300 to be entirely rearranged e. g.
        330-339 Economics arrange 332, 336, and
          change 332.4 Coins and coinage. Mints
            to 332. Money
          change 332.1 Banks and banking
            to   332.4
          change 326   Slavery
            to   331   Labor (except Slavery in U. S. which
                    is 973.711 E441.)
        370-379 Education to be separate class
        380-389 Commerce (Transfer to 330-339: Economics)
        390-399 Custums. Costume. Popular life
          (Transfer to various main divisions:
              Anthropology
              Antiquities (with History. Auxiliary
                studies)
              Fine Art
              Folk literature etc. etc.
    400 Prepare entirely new scheme of classification of
        language (400-499, Cf. II above)
          Consult Cutter, Hartwig, Gröber, Paul, & Geiger,
          Bühler, etc. etc.
    500 Science (Consult Royal Society)
        510 Mathematics (consult Société mathématique)
        520 Astronomy (consult Houzeau and Lancaster)
        530 Physics (especially 537 Electricity Cf. Crerar
          Library)
        540-547 Chemistry (consult Crerar Library)
        548-569 Geology. Paleontology (Consult Royal
          Society, Margery, etc. etc.
        570 Provide general division Natural history etc. etc.
    600
        610 Medicine (transfer to 500's i. e. not with but
          before Useful arts, Technology etc. and after
          Natural sciences)
        620 Engineering (especially 621.3 Electrical engi-
          neering has at present six divisions)
        630 Agriculture (consult W. P. Cutter; Cf. also Wyer,

                          Vermorel etc. etc.)
        650 Commerce (Transfer to 300's)
             652 Typewriting ⎤   transfer to
             653 Shorthand   ⎬   Z Writing. Printing.
             655 Printing   ⎦   Book Arts.
        780 Music (Make separate class)
        800 Literature
             (Cf. 400 Language. Prepare entirely new scheme.
             Consult Cutter, Harvard, Hartwig etc. etc.)
        900 Geography and History
             (Cf. III, a) above. Change arbitrary arrangement
             of countries, and of local subdivisions to geo-
             graphical and alphabetical, respectively. Pro-
             vide general division America. Correct errors
             in period divisions (consult for example W. D.
             Johnston: History of England; Bibliothèque na-
             tionale: History of France; etc. etc. [12]

The Montreal Conference of the A. L. A. in 1900 afforded another op-

portunity for the exchange of opinions on classification. Both Hanson and

Martel attended, and their reports record the comments of many prominent

librarians. Among those interviewed were Clement W. Andrews, John Crerar

Library; John S. Billings, New York Public Library; Walter S. Biscoe, New

York State Library; William I. Fletcher, Amherst College; William C. Lane,

Harvard University; George T. Little, Bowdoin College; Ernest Cushing Rich-

ardson, Princeton University; J. C. Rowell, University of California; and W. H.

Tillinghast, Harvard University. On his return to Washington, Martel reported

to the Librarian that the Decimal Classification had been adopted in only a

few large reference libraries, and that in these it had been extensively modi-

fied. The chief defects of the system were found to be:

1. The disproportionate allotment of space.

2. Unscientific arrangement of many classes and divisions.

3. Arbitrary division and subdivision of classes and subjects by tens.

4. Disinclination on the part of its makers to change these defects,
    and revise the scheme, or permit this to be done by others
    except under onerous restrictions; "in order to protect other
    users of the system from confusion."

Martel continued:

        As the system grows older without change these faults be-
    come more serious and aggravating and fewer libraries will be in-
    clined to take them into the bargain. With respect to all of them
    Cutter's E. C. is superior, while offering the same advantages as

far as such may be derived from employing a ready made scheme.
On the basis of a large collection of books, such as that of
the L. of C., and from the E. C., D. C., the Halle scheme and other
sources a classification better suited to the library can be made,
and the certainty that it too will not be faultless in the end can
hardly be urged in favor of adopting an inadequate system and
starting in with its many superannuated defects.

Herbert Putnam, Librarian of Congress, made the final decision late
in 1900, not long after the expressions of opinion from the librarians at the
Montreal Conference reached him in October. And, in the closing days of
the year, the Library of Congress began to develop its new classification.
Few decisions in library history have been so carefully made. Two Librarians of Congress and their skilled assistants, with the aid of the best professional advice available, had weighed the problem for three years. At the 1905
Conference of the American Library Association in Portland, Oregon, Putnam
summarized the problem and its solution:

How excellent a service if the national library could adopt
a classification which would become universally current! We have
had visions of such a one. They have passed. We long considered
existing systems, in the hope that one of these might be adopted by
us, if that could be seen to have a clear prospect of general adoption. We considered long, but felt obliged to conclude that no existing system likely to be generally current would serve our purpose
without modifications which would defeat the very purpose of uniformity – that is, identical call numbers. We have proceeded to
construct a system of our own, and have thus added one more crime
to the calendar, and further confusion.

CHAPTER XIV

Development

The few records which remain of the development of the new Library
of Congress Classification are like Bacon's antiquities — "remnants of history which have casually escaped the shipwreck of time."[1] Abstracted reports of the Catalogue and Classification divisions in the annual reports of
the Librarian, brief prefaces or introductions to the schedules, and some
scattered memoranda exist. Little material is left from which to weave a
history of the Library's effort to organize systematically the records of
man's life and achievements, or to chronicle the growth of a chart of knowledge which today comprises eight thousand five hundred printed pages. Like
all pioneers, Hanson, Martel, and their assistants were more interested in
the work than in its recording.

Soon after Putnam had decided that the Library of Congress would develop a new classification, a provisional outline, obviously based upon the one
submitted to Young in 1898, was drawn up in February 1901.[2] This outline is
given below, with a corresponding outline of the final system, to illustrate the
structural evolution of the plan.

EARLY ORGANIZATION		FINAL ORGANIZATION	
A (in part)	Polygraphy. General Works	A	General Works. Polygraphy
A501-3000	Philosophy	B-BJ	Philosophy
A3001-B	Religion; & Theology	BL-BX	Religion. Theology
C	Biography Studies auxiliary to History	C	History. Auxiliary Sciences
		D	History. Universal and Old World
D	History (except America)	E-F	America

E-F	America. History and Geography	G	Geography. Anthropology. Folklore. Manners & Customs. Sports and Games
G	Geography; & allied studies: Anthropology; etc.	H	Social Sciences
		H-HA	General Works. Statistics
H-J-K	Social Science Economics Political science	HB-HJ	Economics
		HM-HX	Sociology
L	Law	J	Political Science
M	Education Sports. Amusements	K	Law
N	Architecture Graphic Arts	L	Education
		M	Music
P	Music	N	Fine Arts
Q	Philology and Literature	P	Language and Literature
R	Science. General Mathematics Astronomy Physics Chemistry	Q	Science General Mathematics Astronomy Physics
S	Natural history. General Geology. Mineralogy		Chemistry Geology Natural History
T	Botany Zoology		Botany Zoology
U	Medicine	R	Medicine
V	Useful Arts Agriculture Manufactures	S	Agriculture
		T	Technology
W	Engineering Military and Naval science	U	Military Science
		V	Naval Science
Z	Bibliography	Z	Bibliography and Library Science

The fluidity of the early organization of the classification was pointed out in the first Outline published, in 1903. "They are subject to revision and probably to some transposition and change of class mark before final arrangement is completed." The order of the main classes and their notation, however, had been, on the whole, definitely fixed by 1904; the changes by which the exceptions were transferred to the places they occupy today are shown in the following comparison of the early plan with the 1903 and 1904 editions of

the Outline Scheme of Classes:

EARLY ORGANIZATION	OUTLINE (1903)	OUTLINE (1904)
Philosophy A 501-3000 Religion A 3001-B	B Philosophy—Religion	B Philosophy—Religion
Social Science H-J-K		H-HA Social Sciences.General Statistics
Economics	H Statistics. Economics	HB-HJ Economics
Political science	J Sociology	HM Sociology J Political Science
Law L	K Law	K Law
Education M Sports. Amusements	L Education Sports. Amuse- ments	L Education GV Sports and games (sub- class of G)
Music P	M Music (subclasses M, ML, MT)	M Music (subclasses M, ML, MT)
Philology and Q Literature	P Philology (Language and literature)	P Philology (Language and literature)
Science. Gen- R eral Mathematics Astronomy Physics Chemistry	Q Science QA QB QC QD	Q Science QA QB QC QD
Natural history. General S Geology. Mineralogy	QH QE	QH QE
Botany Zoology T	QK QL	QK QL
Medicine U	R Medicine	R Medicine (subclasses R-RZ)
Useful Arts V	T Technology (subclasses T-TQ, TR-TX)	T Technology (subclasses T-TP, TR-TX)
Agriculture	S Agriculture. Plant and animal industry (subclasses S-SK)	S Agriculture. Plant and animal industry (subclasses S-SK)
Manufactures	TS	TS
Engineering W Military and Naval science	TA, TB, TC, etc. U Military Science V Naval Science	TA, TB, TC, etc. U Military Science (subclasses U-UH) V Naval Science (subclasses V-VM)

Comparison of the 1904 Outline with current editions of the various schedules reveals that very little transposition has been found necessary during the intervening half century. Six classes (M, Q, R, S, U, and V) comprised the same subclasses in 1904 as they do now. In classes B, J, L, N, and P, however, all the subclasses have been developed since 1904, while the earliest published schedules (E-F in 1901 and Z in 1902) have had no radical changes through their respective later editions in 1913 and 1958 and in 1910, 1927 and 1959. The only major changes in subclasses that have taken place since 1904 are charted below:

Class	Outline (1904)	Later Editions
A		AZ added
C	C and (CA) CF	C and (CA) deleted CJ CN, CR, CS, CT added
D		DX added
G	GD	GD deleted
H		HN, HQ, HS, HT, HV, HX added
T	TB TG TH TJ TK TU	TG TJ-TL TK TN TF TH

Most of the schedules were drafted, at least in outline, during the first decade of the twentieth century. American history was the first area classified. Martel developed the schedules, which were published in January 1901 with the modest title, America, History and Geography. Preliminary and Provisional Scheme of Classification. The last number in Class E was "751 McKinley, 2 [2d term] 1901-."

H – Social Sciences.

One of the few classes concerning which richer sources remain than mere "Tanquam tabula naufragii" is Class H Social Sciences. This is not to

say that its development is fully documented; but from the existing records
a more detailed story of its origin can be made than is possible with the other classes. The following account, though of necessity brief, can be considered as a type study of the development of the Library's classification as a
whole. Similar problems confronted the classifiers in other areas of knowledge; they differed only in the nature of the subject being organized.

As early as 1899 Hanson and Martel had worked out this synopsis:

```
H     1-2000  Political Science
      2001-9999  Law
I     1-8000  Sociology
      8001-9999  Woman; Societies, Clubs, etc.
```

On July 17, 1901, the Librarian received a report on the classification of the
Social Sciences from Dr. Roland P. Falkner, who had left the Wharton School
of the University of Pennsylvania to become the head of the new Division of
Documents in the Library. Among the documents included in Falkner's report was a draft outline for the classification of Political Science, Economics,
and Sociology. Falkner based his draft upon the Decimal Classification, Cutter's Expansive, and the Harvard Classification for economics and sociology.
The sequence of the subjects and the amount of space to be assigned them
were the chief objects of his analysis. He found Cutter's arrangement better
than the others, but he thought it should be reorganized to make it consistent
with the methods of subject presentation currently used by writers and edu-
cators in the field.

At the outset Falkner criticized the terminology which had been employed to indicate the larger divisions of the subject. He used the term "Social Sciences" in protest against the caption "Sociology" for the designation
of the entire group. Falkner maintained that the caption "Sociology" had its
origin in the fertile brain of Dewey, and, although widely used by librarians,
it had no scientific standing whatever among experts in these subjects. "We
may not be agreed upon what to call the general group of subjects but we are
certainly agreed not to call it sociology, as we have reserved this term for
the description of a special science treating of the structure and organization

of society, apart from its economic and political organization."

Falkner's draft provided the following sequence:

> POLITICAL SCIENCE AND ADMINISTRATION
> ECONOMICS (Political Economy, Public Finance, Statistics)
> SOCIOLOGY

His main divisions and subdivisions were:

> POLITICAL SCIENCE
> The State in General
> Forms of Government
> Political Functions
> Government Structure, Constitutions, etc.
> Administration
>
> ECONOMICS
> Generalia, incl. Economic history
> Basic notions of Economics, PROPERTY, POPULATION
> Economic Processes. PRODUCTION AND DISTRIBUTION
> (including the marketing of products) EXCHANGE
> Subsidiary sciences, PUBLIC FINANCE, STATISTICS
>
> SOCIOLOGY
> Social Organization and Institutions
> Woman
> Providence and Thrift
> Temperance
> Charities and Benevolence
> Crime and Corrections

When Martel received Falkner's draft he began the great task of developing Class H, which ever after remained his favorite. Terminology and the order of the social sciences bothered Martel, as they had Falkner. A recently-discovered manuscript, "H-J-K Social Sciences," dated 1901, gives Martel's reasoning and solution of the twin problem.

> Terminology. Three or four distinct views are held by economists and sociologists as to the proper limits of Sociology as a science. Comte, who coined the word, Spencer, Ward and others conceived the province of Sociology as coextensive with the entire field of the special social sciences. In deference to Dr. Falkner's protest that this notion has no scientific standing whatever and in accordance with that one of the prevailing views which is accepted by him the group is designated as the Social Sciences and the term Sociology is reserved for the special field not occupied by the coördinate sciences: Economics, and Political Science.

> Sequence. Similar differences are exhibited in the order of the classes and subdivisions as arranged by writers and classifiers. Space forbids demonstration drawn from the arrangement of the matter in systematic treatises. The following summaries of schemes of classification illustrate the diversity of treatment:

Falkner
  Political sci.
  Economics
  Finance
  Statistics
  Sociology
  (Law not treated)

Cutter
  Statistics
  Economics
    (incl. Finance)
  Sociology
  Political sci.
  Law

Dewey
  Statistics
  Political sci.
  Economics
  Law
  Administration
  Sociology

Hartwig
  Law
  Political (i. e. Social) Sciences. General
    Economics (Theoretical)
      Production (Volkswirthschaft). Agriculture
        and Industry
      Finance
      Sociology
      Political Science (Politics)
      Statistics

Harvard
  Sociology
  Economics
  Statistics
  Insurance
  Political science

Richardson
  Sociology
  Economics
  Political science
  Law

Bonazzi
  Sociology
  Political science
  Economics
  Commerce
  Finance
  Statistics

The order Statistics, Economics, Sociology, Political Science, Law is here adopted. Statistics as an auxiliary to all of the special sciences composing the group precedes. The Law collection does not require much development of the classification at present; its position at the end of the group permits future expansion of the scheme without affecting the other main divisions. Provision is made in the scheme for classification of special law with the subject, e. g. Labor laws H963.

Assignment
of Space:

Form divisions wherever and however specified may be disregarded, they may be transposed and amplified, or others may be substituted. Minute subdivision of any subject by form or topic may be deferred until the accumulation of material demands it. "Special" should however be separated from "Comprehensive works" as a rule from the very beginning. The Harvard period divisions: literature before 1776, 1776-1876, 1876- may be applied wherever of advantage. "Local list" or single alphabet of countries is optional, depending on the nature of the literature to be divided; absolute uniformity of treatment is of doubtful expediency. The form division Miscellany. Pamphlets, may be placed at the end of each subject after "Special" instead of at the end of "General" and preceding "Special."

Following this preliminary discussion, Martel devoted some twenty-five finely penned pages to chart the structure of H Social Sciences. General works and Economics, including a Local List in two tables, predecessors of the elaborate H tables of today. The Martel manuscript contains many parenthetical

annotations, one of them an interesting comment on the decision to have Sociology follow Economics. Under the "General specials" subdivision of "Social Sciences. General works," Martel wrote, "Better under Sociology J. If
put here the whole group Sociology should precede Economics. Theoretically
this would be the better arrangement, Sociology being more inclusive and
covering a less strictly or well defined field." Sociology, however, retained
its position following Economics, and became the division HM in 1904, when
a second letter was added for subclasses.

During the following seven years Class H was tested, modified, expanded, and applied to 150,000 volumes. In developing the several subclasses Martel was assisted by William Dawson Johnston, Luis Perez, George M. Churchill, and Edwin Wiley. In 1907 Churchill assumed responsibility for the class
and prepared the schedules for the printer. The first edition (except subclass HT) was published in 1910, a year when over 2,000 pages of classification came from the press. Five years later appeared HT Social groups.
Classes. Races; in 1920 it was integrated into the second edition of Class H.

The remaining classes will be briefly treated in the order of the classification, with the main purpose of gathering in one place data which have hith-
erto been scattered or unrecorded.

A — General Works, Polygraphy.

An important adjustment of library classification to the physical nature
of books is the provision of a class for multitopical books. Class A General
Works, Polygraphy was designed to provide for this type of material. And,
since the logic of the classification, both as a whole and in its parts, progressed from general to special, this group of general and polygraphical material was placed at the beginning of the system. Since logical principles of
arrangement are impossible to find in such heterogeneous publications, the
order of the subclasses is alphabetical: AC Collections, AE Encyclopedias,
AM Museums, etc. Subclass AZ History of the Sciences in General. Scholarship. Learning is the sole exception. It represents an interesting "back-up"

in notation to provide for a type of literature unforeseen when the outline of
the class was charted in 1906 and AZ was destined for Directories. The complete A schedules were published in 1911.

B-BJ — Philosophy.

No area of knowledge is more difficult to chart and classify than philosophy and its peripheral subjects. Their pervasiveness and consequent sus-
ceptibility to cross-division furnished pitfalls for all classifiers. In developing the schedules for these subjects free use was made of other classifications, indexes, and systematic works. Among the most important sources
were the Cutter and Decimal Classifications, the latter in its expanded form
of the Manuel of the Institut International de Bibliographie (Bruxelles, 1904);
Otto Hartwig's Halle Schema; Schleiermacher's works; Benjamin Rand's
Bibliography of Philosophy, Psychology, and Cognate Subjects; the Psycho-
logical Index; and the index to the Zeitschrift für Psychologie und Physiolo-
gie der Sinnesorgane. Edwin C. Wiley (1872-1924), classifier in charge of
Philosophy and Political Science, was chiefly responsible for this class. He
was with the Library from 1906 to 1913 and later served for six years as librarian of the U. S. Naval War College. The schedules were published in 1910.

BL-BX — Religion.

Clarence Warner Perley (1867-1946), chief of the Classification Division from the time of its establishment in 1917 until his retirement in 1937,
developed the schedules for Religion. Perley had joined the staff of the Library in 1902, and his long service was interrupted only once, when he spent
the year 1904 at the John Crerar Library in Chicago. BL-BX was published
in 1927 after the schedules had been tested and revised in the classification
of 105,000 volumes.

C — Auxiliary Sciences of History.

The schedules for Class C were developed by several classifiers from
a preliminary draft prepared by Martel. They were Julian Leavitt and J. D.
Wolcott, CB History of Civilization and Culture; Perley, CC Archeology and

CT Biography; Alfred F. W. Schmidt, CD Diplomatics. Archives. Seals and

CE Chronology; J. D. Wolcott, CJ Numismatics and CR Heraldry; Martel and

Miss Malina Gilkey, CS Genealogy. Schmidt, who was chief assistant classi-

fier from 1913 to 1925, revised the entire class to eliminate inequalities of

treatment. Miss Mary W. MacNair assisted him in preparing the schedules

for publication in 1915. CN Epigraphy had to be deferred until the develop-

ment of PA Greek and Latin Languages and Literatures because of the close

relationship of these classes. Several years after the publication of PA in

1928, CN was developed by Perley, assisted by Miss L. Belle Voegelein, now

editor of classification schedules. This subclass was published in 1942; in

1948 it was integrated into a second edition of Class C.

D — Universal and Old World History.

After the publication of E-F American History in January 1901, work

was begun on Class D Universal and Old World History. Martel drafted the

schedules in 1901, and the work of development and application was carried

on by various classifiers. This was the first class, chronologically, in which

a second letter was used for the subclasses. The method was adopted not be-

cause of Cutter's influence but for reasons that were purely practical: to ef-

fect a better division of labor. It was much simpler to assign DA Great Bri-

tain to one classifier, DC France to another, and so on, than to attempt to de-

limit in advance the integers needed, D 1-999, Great Britain; D 2000-3000,

France, etc.

The first subclass completed, DA Great Britain, was the work of W.

Dawson Johnston (1871-1928), later librarian of Columbia University and or-

ganizer of the American Library in Paris. Schmidt developed nine of the

schedules: D General History. Europe (general), DB Austria Hungary, DC

France, DD Germany, DE Classical Antiquity, DF Greece, DG Italy, DJ Neth-

erlands, and DQ Switzerland. Alexis V. Babine (1866-1930) constructed DK

Russia and DR Balkan Peninsula. Cecil Knight Jones (1872-1945) was re-

sponsible for DP Spain and Portugal and for DT Africa. He later succeeded

Perley as chief of the Classification Division.

The work of developing the D schedules covered a period of fourteen years. Schmidt was in charge of the program until 1906, when he left the Library to teach at Howard University and George Washington University. During his absence the work was continued by Julian Leavitt, George M. Churchill, and Miss Nella J. Martin. Schmidt, who had returned to the Library in 1913, prepared the schedules for publication; Miss MacNair was responsible for the consistency of phraseology, typographical form, and also the index. Class D was published in 1916.

It is a truism that classification reflects the world we live in, or more precisely, the books which describe that world, its accomplishments and its failures. Within thirty-five years of the publication of Class D, two world wars occurred. Therefore it was unfortunately necessary to add supplements, D 501-659 and D 731-838, to provide for the voluminous war material. The preface to the subclass dealing with the first is quite revealing:

> Sketched in general outlines shortly after the publication of the earlier literature on the European War, the scheme as here presented exhibits expansions and modifications necessitated from time to time as new and unforeseen situations developed and the number of belligerent countries increased. The notation, quite generous as originally assigned, gradually proved inadequate to respond to the demands of logical arrangement, thus leading in several instances to the classification of special topics where considered on merit alone, they may appear to be misplaced.

E-F – America.

This class for American history, the first area classified, is described at the beginning of this chapter.

G – Geography, Anthropology, Sports and Games.

The schedules for Geography, Anthropology, Sports and Games were prepared in 1904 and 1905 by W. Dawson Johnston, C. K. Jones, and J. Christian Bay. S. C. Stuntz constructed subclass GV Sports and Games. Physical Training. The sections GR Folklore and GT Manners and Customs were deferred until the completion of the schedules relating to literature and the historical sciences. In April 1905 Perley assumed charge of the class and revised the

schedules for Geography and Anthropology. After Stuntz resigned in 1908 to
do government work in the field of botany, Perley also took over GV and prepared the schedules for the printer. The schedules, except those for GR and
GT, were published in 1910. GR and GT were published separately in 1915
but were incorporated into a second edition of the whole class which appeared
in 1928. This edition also contained a provisional scheme for atlases,
G 1001-3035.

H – Social Sciences.

The early history of Class H is treated at the beginning of this chapter as a type study of the development of the whole classification system.

J – Political Science.

Published in 1910 from copy prepared by Wiley, Class J represented
the work of three men. Johnston prepared the first drafts of subclasses JA
General Works, JC Political Science. Theory of State, and JK U. S. Constitutional History and Administration. Philip D. Phair, of the Division of Documents, drafted JX International Law and Relations, and Wiley developed the
other sections.

K – Law.

After years of delay, the development of schedules for the vast litera-
ure of Law is now under way. This is discussed in the final chapter, "The
Future."

L – Education.

Class L Education was published in 1911. Bay and Johnston had developed subclass L General Works and parts of LA History of Education, LB
Theory and Practice, LC Special Forms, Relations and Applications, and the
subclasses dealing with Universities and Colleges: LD United States, LE
Other American, and LF Europe. Schmidt later completed the schedules and
reclassified the collections, with the exception of LC, LJ College Fraternities
and Publications, and LT Textbooks. These subclasses were worked out in
detail by Schmidt's successor, Wolcott, who also assisted in the development
of other sections.

M – <u>Music</u>.

The Library's collections in the field of music were among the first to be organized in the new system. Oscar G. Sonneck (1873-1928), chief of the Music Division from 1902 to 1917, developed the schedules for Class M <u>Music</u> in 1902. Published in 1904, the class comprised M Music, ML Literature of Music, and MT Music Instruction. The nature of the Library's collections, especially in scores, led Sonneck to develop an arrangement which was closer to that found in the classed catalogs of publishers than the schemes developed by the leading American and European music libraries. A second, revised edition was published in 1917. Sonneck's prefatory comment is as timely today as when it was written a half century ago:

> ... book and scheme will clash at times, no matter how expanded or compressed the classification may be. In such cases, the conflict may often be settled by a judicious compromise. Where it cannot, the scheme will have to be amended, for the minds of authors will ever drift into channels unforeseen by the classifier, and the best scheme will soon become fossil unless adjusted to the uncontrollable current of literature.

N – <u>Fine</u> <u>Arts</u>.

The schedules for the fine arts were derived from various classifications and catalogs of special libraries. Among the most influential were the Decimal Classification, Cutter's Expansive, and the catalog of the library of the Kunstgewerbe-Museum of Berlin. The library of the Art Institute of Chicago offered many helpful suggestions from its experience in modifying the Decimal Classification to its needs. Class N was published in 1910.

P – <u>Language</u> <u>and</u> <u>Literature</u>.

The monumental Class P, which provides for the world's languages and literatures, past and present, took four decades to construct. It was begun in 1909 by Walther F. Koenig, who had come to the Library from a teaching position in the University of Pennsylvania. With the publication in 1948 of the last subclass, covering Russian literature, Class P today contains 2,350 pages of schedules and tables – over one-third of the pages in the entire Library of Congress Classification.

Although Koenig had begun the development of the class in 1909, the first schedules were not published until 1915. They were subclasses PN General Literary History and Collections, PR English Literature, PS American Literature, and PZ Fiction and Juvenile Literature, the work of Wiley.

Subclasses P Philology (General) and Linguistic, and PA Classical Philology and Literature, were published in 1928. They were the work of Koenig and, strangely enough, were the only sections of his great work that he saw through the press. He retired in 1930 and returned to Oldenburg, Germany. Subsequently, the schedule for Byzantine and Modern Greek literature and Medieval and Modern Latin literature was prepared by Mr. Perley. Although completed in 1933 it was not printed until 1942 as Subclass PA Supplement.

PB-PH Philology. Modern European Languages was sent to the printing office in 1930. It was expected that PJ-PM Languages and Literature of Asia, Africa, Oceania, America. Mixed Languages. Artificial Languages would soon follow, but this was not found practicable. During the following three years great difficulties were found in bringing PB-PH into consistency with the large number of books already classified. At the beginning of 1933 printing was resumed, but because of the long period during which the schedules had been in press, the printing of PJ-PM was deferred to a later time. PB-PH finally appeared in 1933, and PJ-PM in 1935. An Index to these languages and dialects, which also included P and PA, was prepared by Miss Voegelein and published in 1936.

PQ, Part 1, French Literature was developed and applied as early as 1913, but extensive purchases of French literature, especially old French, in addition to the normal annual increase of the Library's collections in that field, necessitated many changes. The schedules were not published until 1936.

PQ, Part 2, Italian, Spanish, and Portuguese Literature appeared the following year. These schedules were originally prepared by Koenig, but C. K. Jones provided many of the details and revised the Spanish and Portuguese names.

PT Teutonic Literatures, like PQ, was published in two parts. Part 1, German Literature, was prepared by Koenig and revised and prepared for printing by Perley in 1937. It was published the following year. Part 2, Dutch and Scandinavian Literatures, appeared in 1942. The Dutch, Flemish, and Afrikaans schemes were developed by Perley. Jules Dieserud had originally developed the section for Scandinavian Literature in 1915-16; it was edited by Perley to bring it into conformity with other parts of the classification before publication.

The last of these schedules to be published was the section of subclass PG devoted to Russian Literature. The Yudin Collection, which was the nucleus of the Library's Russian collections, had been classified in part according to a scheme devised by Babine. The scheme made no provision for translations and, moreover, its notation did not follow that of the other classes. In the 1930's Perley drafted schedules for the classification of translations, but the discontinuance of the Slavic Division and the decision to incorporate the Russian collections into the general collections made it necessary to develop a comprehensive scheme for Russian literature. Miss Voegelein developed the schedules, which were published in 1948.

Q – Science.

Class Q Science, published in 1905, was based upon many bibliographies of scientific literature and classification systems, the most important of which was the International Catalogue of Scientific Literature.

James David Thompson, in charge of Science at that time, was responsible for subclasses Q General Science, QA Mathematics, QB Astronomy, QC Physics, QD Chemistry, and QE Geology. He also prepared all the Q schedules for the press. The classification of geology, mineralogy, and petrology was planned in cooperation with F. B. Weeks, later librarian of the U. S. Geological Survey. QK Botany was prepared by Stuntz. Bay developed QH Biology, QL Zoology, QM Human Anatomy, QP Physiology, and QR Bacteriology. He left the Library's service in 1905 and later spent twenty years as librarian of the John Crerar Library in Chicago.

R – <u>Medicine</u>.

J. Christian Bay prepared the original schedules for Medicine in 1904. When he left the Library Perley assumed charge of the class. After extensive revisions had been made in applying the schedules to the collections, Perley prepared them for the printer. Class R was one of the ten classes published in 1910.

S – <u>Agriculture</u>.

S. C. Stuntz developed the schedules for Agriculture and related industries, on the basis of a plan outlined by Martel. As usual, other systems of classification and bibliographies were drawn upon, especially the systematic catalog of the library of the K. Sächsische Forstakademie, Tharandt (1900), upon which subclass SD Forestry was based. Churchill prepared the copy for the printer, and Class S was published in 1911.

T – <u>Technology</u>.

C. W. Perley developed the original schedules for T Technology (General) through TT Mechanic Trades in 1903 before he left to join the staff of the John Crerar Library. During his absence in 1904, Stuntz, who assumed charge of Technology, developed subclass TX Domestic Science, now Home Economics. In 1905 H. H. B. Meyer reorganized the scheme into four main groups.

<u>First draft</u> – 1903	<u>Reorganization</u> – 1905
T Technology. General	T Technology (General)
TA Engineering – General. Civil engineering	ENGINEERING AND BUILDING GROUP
TB Bridges and roofs	TA Engineering (General). Civil engineering
TC Hydraulic engineering (Rivers. Harbors. Canals)	TC Hydraulic engineering (harbors, rivers, canals)
TD Sanitary engineering	TD Sanitary and municipal engineering
TE Roads and pavements	TE Roads and pavements
TG Mechanical engineering	TF Railroad engineering and operation
TH Electrical engineering. Electrical industries	TG Bridges and roofs

TJ Mineral industries

TK Railroads

TL Motor vehicles. Cycles. Aeronautics

TP Chemical technology

TQ Electrochemistry. Electrometallurgy

TR Photography

TS Manufactures

TT Mechanic trades

TU Building

TX Domestic science

TH Building construction

MECHANICAL GROUP

TJ Mechanical engineering and machinery

TK Electrical engineering and industries

TL Motor vehicles. Cycles. Aeronautics

CHEMICAL GROUP

TN Mineral industries. Mining and Metallurgy

TP Chemical technology

TR Photography

COMPOSITE GROUP

TS Manufactures

TT Trades

TX Domestic science

Meyer also revised the schedules for TA Engineering (General). Civil Engineering to TN Mineral Industries. Mining and Metallurgy, with the exception of TH Building and Construction and TK Electrical Engineering and Industries. In 1907 A. Law Voge, formerly with the Concilium Bibliographicum of Zürich, developed subclasses TH and TK, and the sections of TA relating to structures and materials. In the same year Perley, the original classifier, resumed charge, revised the entire class and prepared it for the press. This class was another one of the ten published in 1910.

U – Military Science.

Perley prepared the schedules for Military Science in 1903 on the basis of the arrangement used in the Classification and Index published that year by the Military Information Division of the Adjutant-General's Office (U. S. War Department). Class U was among the schedules published in 1910.

V – Naval Science.

The schedules for Naval Science were developed in 1904 by Stuntz. The

arrangement of material relating to navies follows, in general, the classification of Military Science, which was based upon the Classification and Index
mentioned above. The general order of the publications of the British Hydro-
graphic Office was followed in the arrangement of sailing directions and similar lists in VK Navigation. Merchant Marine. Perley assumed charge of
this class in 1905 and made numerous changes. The schedules were published
in 1910.

Z — Bibliography and Library Science.

The construction of Class Z, which occurred before the final decision
was made on a classification for the Library of Congress, is described in
the preceding chapter.

CHAPTER XV

Description — Theory and Structure

The Library of Congress Classification, which has been applied to over 6,000,000 volumes during the past sixty years, contains 8,500 pages of schedules, tables, and indexes. So vast a system can of necessity be described here only in terms of high generality — of theory, structure, and principles — rather than of details and practice. And, since no two classes are identical in their divisions, illustration instead of description must serve as exposition.

The Classification was constructed, as we have seen earlier, to provide for the needs of the Library of Congress, with no thought to its possible adoption by other libraries. In fact, the Library has never recommended that other libraries adopt its system, although an increasing number of them are now using it. The functions of the Library, the composition of its collections and its expected acquisitions, and the ways the collections were to be used determined the organization and detail of the system. As the Library was established by the Congress for its own use, it was assumed that the branches of knowledge known collectively today as the Social Sciences — the basic reference materials of a lawmaking body — would be extensive and diverse. Today's statistics[1] prove the correctness of the assumption: the two classes H Social Sciences (General, Statistics, Economics, and Sociology) and J Political Science contain 1,500,000 volumes. The historical sciences, Classes C-F and Class L Education, add 1,083,000 more for a total of 2,583,000 volumes of the 6,128,000 in the classified collections of the Library. And Class K Law which remains unclassified, will increase the total by another million.

In addition to this tendency toward concentration in certain areas of knowledge, another factor had to be taken into consideration: the Library received and would continue to receive and to catalog considerable material which university and other scholarly libraries ordinarily would not acquire.

The Library not only purchased books but received them through national and international exchange, Smithsonian deposit, copyright deposit, and as gifts. Their miscellaneity made a comprehensive and minute classification necessary. To supplement the dispersive dictionary catalog it was decided to develop a classed catalog and to admit readers freely to the shelves.

It was recognized that the classification should, in brief,

1. be oriented primarily toward the requirements of the Congress and secondarily to those of other government departments and agencies, scholars, and all other users;

2. provide for large amounts of diverse material, both scholarly and popular, for which no existing classification was adequate; and

3. afford a systematic approach to the Library's resources through the classed catalog and the arrangement of the books on the shelves.

Upon these assumptions the general structure of the system was based:

I.   A General Works. Polygraphy

II.   B-P Humanistic Disciplines and the Social Sciences

III. Q-V Natural Sciences and Technology

IV.   Z Bibliography and Library Science

Groups II. and III. reflect the sharp dichotomy of Hartwig's division of knowledge[2] into Geistes and Naturwissenschaften. The primary purpose of the Library, that of legislative reference, determined their order. The Classification, therefore, although universal in scope, is in its organization a special library classification.

Within this general structure are the following classes and subclasses:

I.   A General Works. Polygraphy

II.   B-P Humanistic Disciplines and the Social Sciences
       B-BJ   Philosophy
       BL-BX   Religion
       C-F   History
       C   Auxiliary Sciences
       D   Universal and Old World
       E-F   America
       G   Geography. Anthropology. Folklore, etc.
       H-L   Social Sciences
       H   General

HA	Statistics
HB-HJ	Economics
HM-HX	Sociology
J	Political Science
K	Law
L	Education
M	Music
N	Fine Arts
P	Language and Literature

III.   Q-V   Natural Sciences and Technology

Q	General Science
QA	Mathematics
QB-QE	Physical Sciences
QB	Astronomy
QC	Physics
QD	Chemistry
QE	Geology
QH-QR	Biological Sciences
QH	Natural History. General Biology. Cytology
QK	Botany
QL	Zoology
QM	Human Anatomy
QP	Physiology
QR	Bacteriology. Microbiology
R	Medicine
S	Agriculture
T	Technology
U	Military Science
V	Naval Science

IV.   Z   Bibliography and Library Science

Martel later rationalized the structure of the system.

The concept underlying it may be stated as follows: (1. Class A) General works: Periodicals, Societies, Collections, Encyclopedic works etc. (2. Class B) Theory, or theories, of man concerning the universe: Philosophy and Religion. (3.-6. Classes C-F) History and auxiliary sciences. (7. Class G) Geography and Anthropology: G, Descriptive and physical geography — man's abode and source of his means of subsistence; GF, Anthropogeography — man as affected by and affecting his physical milieu; GN, Physical anthropology and ethnology and Primitive or Prehistoric man; GR, Folklore, Tradition — mind and soul of man in transition from primitive to advanced culture; GT, Manners and customs; and GV, Amusements, sports, etc., related to GR; as a class, G may be therefore regarded as supplementary to History and leading to groups (8.-9. Classes H-J) Economic and Social evolution of man, (10. Class K) Law, (11. Class L) Education, and (12. Class M), (13. Class N), and (14. Class P) Fine arts and Letters — the esthetic and intellectual development and state of man. Together, classes B-P form the group of the Philosophico-historical and philological sciences. The second group embraces the Mathematico-physical, Natural, and Applied Sciences: (15. Class Q) Science, (16. Class R) Medicine, (17. Class S) Agriculture, (18. Class T) Technology, (19. Class U) Military science, and (20. Class V) Naval science. Bibliography, which in many libraries is distributed through the different classes, is kept together in the Library of Congress and forms together with Library science (21. Class Z).[3]

In the classification of sciences like geography and anthropology,

which could not be considered wholly social or cultural, it was the human

element rather than the physical or organic that determined their position

in the system.

> The same reasons which determined the positions, in the
> system, of History and the Social Sciences also justified prefer-
> ence in favor of these classes in the collocation of subjects re-
> lated in some of their aspects to other classes. This is notably
> the case with the subjects grouped as subclasses in class C, His-
> tory — Auxiliary sciences, and G, Geography — Anthropology —
> Folk-lore — Manners and customs — Sports and games, amuse-
> ments. This latter group including on the one hand the material
> dealing with the earth as the abode of man and as the theater,
> the stage, of his history and his social activities, and on the oth-
> er with primitive man himself, his being in social infancy and in
> transition to civilized state, has been found a most satisfactory
> association of subjects difficult to allocate. Physical Geography
> (GB) and Oceanography (GC) might have been excepted and placed
> with Geology (QE). Much and important material on these sub-
> jects is found, however, in the periodicals and collections in Gen-
> eral Geography (class G) and certain aspects connect them with
> GF, Anthropogeography — their position in class G is not without
> its advantage. All subjects of this character which include as-
> pects relating them more or less closely to other subjects in
> other classes are represented in those classes by provision for
> an alternative classification indicating the actual classification
> preferred in the Library of Congress; or, typical works of spe-
> cial interest in two or more classes are represented in the card
> shelf list by duplicate entry in the classes concerned, where these
> entries serve at the same time as an effective reference connect-
> ing the related subjects. 4

Within the classes, and in condensed form in many of the divisions and

subdivisions, the same general principles of arrangement have been followed.

1. General form divisions: Periodicals, Societies, Collections, Dic-

tionaries, etc.

2. Theory. Philosophy

3. History

4. Treatises. General Works

5. Law. Regulation. State Relations.

6. Study and Teaching

7. Subjects and subdivisions of subjects progressing from general to

specific, as far as possible in logical order. When among a number of coordi-

nate subdivisions of a subject a logical principle of order was not discernible an alphabetical arrangement was employed.

1. Form Subdivisions. Throughout the classification form subdivisions
adapted to the requirements of the various subjects are incorporated in the
schedules or added in the form of tables. These subdivisions provide for
periodicals, societies, collections, encyclopedias, dictionaries, etc. They vary
in content and in order, as well as in extent, and represent arrangements tested in actual practice in the various divisions of the system. The following
excerpts illustrate these differing degrees of breakdown according to the
scope of the subject.

```
GV    Baseball.
862      Periodicals. Societies,
            Commissions, etc.
                ***
QR    Bacteriology.
1        Periodicals, societies, etc.
6        Collected works (nonserial).
9        Dictionaries. Encyclopedias.
                ***
HM    Sociology.
         Periodicals.
1           English.
3           French.
5           German.
7           Other.
9        Societies.
            Cf. H 10-19; HN 55, etc.
13       Congresses.
15       Collections.
17       Dictionaries.
                ***
```

ASTRONOMY

```
QB
1     Periodicals, societies, etc.
2     Exhibitions. Museums.
3     Collections (nonserial).
4     Observations.
         Alphabetically by place, except where the observatory
            has a well-known special name, e.g., Lick Observa-
            tory, not Mount Hamilton.
         Series of memoirs published by observatories are in-
            cluded here, but annual reports are classified in QB 82.
6     Star catalogs (including zone observations, etc.).
         Cf. QB 815, Photometric catalogs.
               821, Double stars.
               835, Variables.
               851, Clusters and nebulae.
               881, Classed catalogs.
      Ephemerides.
7        Early
         Modern.
```

QB	8	Nautical and air (or aeronautical) almanacs. By country, A-Z.
	9	Other yearbooks.

General tables.

11	Early.
12	Modern.
14	Dictionaries.

SOCIAL SCIENCES (GENERAL)

H

Periodicals.

All periodicals of a general, more or less mixed character, i.e., most of the serials called "Political," "Social," or "Economic" journals. Special periodicals are to be classified with the subject in HA, HB, etc. In case of doubt prefer H 1-8.

1	Polyglot. American and English.
	.A1-2, Polyglot; .A3-Z, American and English.
3	French.
5	German.
7	Italian.
8	Other.
9	Yearbooks.

Societies.

Cf. HA 1; HB 1-9; HM 9; HN 54-55; HS; HV, etc.; also JK 674, Civil service reform; JS 302-303, Civic reform associations.

10	International.
11	American and English.
13	French.
15	German.
17	Italian.
19	Other.

Congresses. Exhibitions.

Cf. HA 9-12; HB 21; etc.

21	International.
22	American and English.
23	French.
25	German.
27	Italian.
29	Other. By country, A-Z.

Collections.

31	Monographs by various authors.
33	Collected works of individual authors.
35	Essays, papers, etc.
39	Pamphlets.
41-49	Encyclopedias. Dictionaries.

Arranged like H 11-19. Cf. note at head of H 1-8.

The importance and volume of government publications (official documents) in the Library made it necessary to make special provisions for them in many classes. Two subclasses, J of Class J Political Science and L of Class L Education, are devoted almost entirely to documents, while the contents of HA Statistics are predominantly documentary in character. In other

parts of the schedules document subdivisions varying in extent with the subject are provided. In HJ Public Finance, where documents are many, the document numbers precede the usual form subdivisions:

```
HJ
 9-99   Serial documents.
 9-10      United States.
   11         By state.
12-99      Other countries.
101-109 Periodicals. Societies. Yearbooks.
  113   Congresses.
117-119 Collections (Monographs. Papers).
121-129 Dictionaries.
```

Under Waterways in HE there is the following arrangement for U. S. documents

```
HE  Waterways.
        By country – Continued.
          United States.
            Documents, laws, etc.
              Congressional documents.
393. A1           General collections.
                    Arranged by date of earliest document.
                  House of Representatives. Committee on
                    Rivers and Harbors.
    . A12            Collected set.
    . A13            By session. By date.
                  Senate.
    . A16            Collected set.
    . A17            By session. By date.
                  Other documents.
    . A19            Serials.
    . A2             Separate documents. By date.
    . A3     Collections of monographs, etc.
    . A4     Congresses.
    . A5-Z5 General works.
    . Z7     Minor works.
393. 5      By state, A-W.
394         River improvement. By name of river, A-Z.
              Under each:
              e. g.              Mississippi.
                                   Documents.
             (1) . M38               Collections.
             (2) . M39               Separate documents.
             (3) . M4A-Z   General works. By author.
             (4) . M5A-Z   Special. Minor.
                                 Cf. TC 425.
```

In other classes, where documents are less numerous, condensed subdivisions
like the following are provided.

```
SF  Animal culture.
        Documents.
          United States.
11            Federal.
13            States, A-W.
```

SF 15   Other countries, A-Z.
         e.g. .F7 France.
          .J3 Japan.

Special arrangements are also provided when geographical tables are used:

    HE Postal service. By country.
6651-7500 Other countries.
        Under each:
  10 nos.   5 nos.
   (1)   (1)   Serial documents.
                               Reports and statistics of Post
                                 Office Department.
                               Laws and decisions (when se-
                               rial), etc.
                               Regulations published at irregu-
                               lar intervals, E + By date.
                               Local documents, guides, etc.,
                               in subdivision (6) or .Z7.
                               Documents on special topics,
                               e. g. Classification, employees,
                               with topic in subdivision (9),
                               (5), or in HE 6100-6241.
   (2)   (2)   Special documents. Laws.
   .A1   Separate documents. By date.
                                 Laws.
   .A5   Official. By date.
   .A7-Z   Nonofficial. By author.
                    ***

    HV Social Pathology.
        By country.
  101-516   Other countries.
          Under each:
  10 nos.   5 nos.
                      Documents.
   (1)   (1)   General.
   (2)   State, <u>see</u> (9) or (4).
   (3)   City, <u>see</u> (10) or (5).
        [omission here]
   (9)   (4)   By state, A-Z.
                      Under each (using successive Cutter
                        numbers):
                          Documents.
                        (1)   Serial.
                        (2)   Special.
                        (3)   Societies. Associations.
                        (4)   General works. History,
                               policy, etc.
   (10)   (5)   By city, A-Z.

2. Theory. <u>Philosophy</u>. This subdivision is chiefly used in main and subclasses and less frequently in the smaller divisions of subjects. In Mathematics
one number, QA 9 Philosophy has been provided, while in PN General and Comparative Literature, where "Aesthetics" has been added to theory and philosophy, the numbers are many, ranging from PN 45 General works through the

"relations" classes like PN 48 Nature and PN 55 Relation to science and on
to PN 57 Individual characters in literature, A-Z, e. g. .F3 Faust; . T8 Tris-
tan and Isolde.

Under Sociology, a pervasive discipline, the following arrangement is
provided:

```
HM  Sociology.
24      Philosophy. Theory. Method.
25      Relation to social work.
            Cf. HN 29; HV 40.
26      Relation to philosophy.
            Cf. B 63, Relation of philosophy to sociology.
27      Relation to psychology.
            Cf. BF 57, Relation of psychology to sociology.
30      Relation to ethics.
            Cf. BJ 51, Relation of ethics to sociology.
(31)    Relation to religion, see BL 60.
(32)    Relation to education, see LC 189-191.
33      Relation to politics.
            Cf. JA 76, Relation of political science to sociology.
34      Relation to law.
35      Relation to economics.
            Cf. HM 211, Economic elements, forces, laws.
36      Relation to history and geography.
            Cf. HM 104, Historical sociology.
37      Relation to anthropology.
38      Relation to science.
39      Relation to art and literature.
            Cf. PN 51, Relation of literature to sociology.
```

Similarly:

```
BR   Christianity, Church history.
100      Philosophy of Christianity. Philosophy and Christianity.
            See BL 51 for Philosophy of Religion in general.
            Prefer BR 120 for Early works.
110      Psychology of religious experience, conversion, etc.
            Cf. BL 53 Religion and psychology.
112          Enthusiasm.
(113)        Ecstasy. Trance states. Stigmatization.
            See BV 5090-5091 Mystic phenomena.
            Prefer biography for individual cases.
114          Fanaticism.
115      Christianity in relation to special subjects.
            e. g. .C5  Civilization.
                  .E3  Economics. Labor.
                  .H4  Health and healing.
                  .P4  Peace.
                  .P7  Politics and government. Democracy, etc.
                  .W2  War.
                  .W4  Wealth.
```

3. History. Period divisions subdivide the history of each science and its
divisions and subdivisions whenever necessary. These divisions, like all the

others, are adapted to the requirements of the various subjects. In some

classes early works on the subject are classified under its history.

```
CN  Epigraphy.
55      History.
            ***

HM  Sociology.
        History.
19          General.
22          By country, A-Z.
            ***

RJ  Pediatrics.
        History.
36          General.
37          General special.
38          Ancient.
39          Medieval.
40          Modern.
42          By country, A-Z.
            ***

HJ  Public finance.
        History.
        Ancient.
211         Classic Orient.
213         Egypt.
214         Other oriental (not A-Z).
                e.g. India.
215         Greece and Rome.
            Greece.
217         General.
219         Athens.
221         Other (Sparta, etc.)
            Rome.
223         General.
225         Special. Minor.
227         Provinces.
228         Other.
230     Medieval and modern (General).
        Medieval.
231         General.
232         Byzantine.
233         Mohammedan.
234         Other.
        Modern.
235         General.
                Including 19th century.
236         20th century.
                Including World Wars.
240         Colonial finance.
                Cf. HJ 2025; JV.
241-1839  By country.
            History, statistics..., administration.
            ***

 G  Geography
        History of geography.
```

Cf. G 290-306, History of voyages of discovery.
Z 6001-6028, Bibliography of the literature of geography.

G 80	General.
81	General special.
82	Ancient and medieval.
	Including Chinese.
	Ancient.
	Cf. DE 23-31, Classical antiquity.
	DF 27-41, Ancient Greece.
	DG 27-59, Ancient Rome.
	Modern authors.
84	General works.
86	General special.
	Classical authors (Greek and Roman).
87. A1	Collections.
. A3	Selections, extracts, etc.
. A6-Z	Individual authors.
	Under each:
	(1) Texts.
	(2) Translations.
	(3) Commentaries. Criticism.
	Sources and ancient authors other than Greek and Roman.
87. 5	Modern works.
. 7	Texts with translations.
88	Voyages.
. 5	Special regions, A-Z.
	Works of geographical interest not provided for in D-F.
. 7	Other special, A-Z.
	Geographic names, see G 107-107. 5.
	Medieval to 1600/1650.
	Including works of medieval geographers.
	Modern writers.
89	General works.
. 5	General special.
90	Early writers (including Oriental) other than those
	in G 91-94.
91	Early Christian.
92	Viking age.
93	Arabic geographers.
94	Other later ("Scholastic") to 1420/1492.
95	15th-16th centuries (1420/1492 to 1600/1650).
	For discovery of seaway to India, see also G 280-286.
	Modern, 1600/1650 -
	Cf. D-F for special subjects.
96	General works.
	For treatises, see G 113-115.
97	17th-18th centuries.
98	19th century.
99	20th century.

4. Treatises. General Works. The subdivisions provided for comprehensive

works are adapted to the individual subjects and their literature. They range

from a single number to many, according to the "age" of the subjects and the

kinds of general works published in the several fields. The earlier literature

of a subject is separated in special subdivisions corresponding to the stages in the development of the subject as expressed in the printed books of successive periods.

```
GV  Recreation.
        Water sports.
            Yachting.
813             General works.
                    Including yacht sailing.
                    ***

SD  Forestry.
371     Comprehensive works.
373     General and popular works.  Elements.  Primers.
                    ***

TP  Chemical technology.
144     Early works (to 1800).
145     Treatises (1801-  ).
                    ***

HM  Sociology.
        General works.  Treatises.
51          English.
55          French.
57          German.
59          Italian.
61          Other languages.
66      Compends.  Elementary textbooks.
68          Syllabi, outlines.
                    ***

NE  Engraving.
        General works.  Treatises.
            Before 1851.
830             Technical.
835                 Minor.
840             Popular.
                1851-.
850             Technical.
855                 Minor.
860             Popular.
863             Miscellaneous.
                    e. g.  Suppressed plates.
865         Addresses, essays, lectures.
870         Miscellaneous minor works.
            Collectors' manuals.
880             Before 1851.
885             1851-.
                    Cf.  NE 85-215.
                    ***

Q  Science (General).
        Early works (to 1800).
151         Ancient.
153         Medieval.
155         15th-17th centuries.
157         18th century.
        General works, 1801-
```

Q 158   Comprehensive works.
                    e. g. Humboldt's Cosmos.
    159   Minor works. Compends, etc.
              Outlines, syllabi, see Q 181.
              Textbooks.
    160   Advanced.
    161   Elementary.
                    Including laboratory manuals.
    162   Popular works.
    163   Juvenile works.

                       ***

    BD Epistemology. Theory of knowledge.
              General works.
150-158   Early to 1800*
161-168   1801-*
    171   Popular works. Truth. Certitude, etc.

*TABLE
    (0) Early works (including Latin and Greek).
    (1) English.
    (2) French.
    (3) German.
    (4) Italian.
    (5) Spanish and Portuguese.
    (6)
    (7)
    (8) Other, A-Z.
                       ***

5. Law. Regulation. State Relations. Following the example of Melvil Dewey,
Martel decided that Law, whenever possible, should be classified by "subject"
throughout the classes B-J and L-Z. The plans of both systems, however,
called for the later development of detailed schedules, or Tables, for legal
materials. Although Martel's "point five" was not always followed in practice
it did bring about a scattering of legal material which no previous system
(except the D. C.) had ever achieved. The results of this dispersion of the
literature of one of the oldest of the social sciences have been unfortunate
both in theory and in practice. In 1949 "point five" was substantially modified and the centrifugal forces in the classification of Law arrested. Since
that time work has been started on the development of schedules for Class K,
a discussion of which will be found in Chapter XVIII. The Future.

6. Study and Teaching. Like Treatises and General Works, this subdivision
is adapted to the needs of the various subjects and their literatures. In Philosophy there is only one number, B 52, while in Technology, a sequence of

numbers, T 61-173, provides places for individual countries and schools as well as for general education in the subject. In HM Sociology the following arrangement is found:

```
    Study and teaching. Schools.
45      General works.
47      By country, A-Z.
            Under each:
                (1) General works.
                (2) Local, A-Z.
                        Including special schools.
```

In NA Architecture the numbers range from 2000 to 2320 – by country from 2101, America, to 2284, individual Pacific islands.

The divisions for study and teaching under individual subjects are preferred for all branches of knowledge above the elementary level. Provisions for primary and elementary teaching material are made in LB Theory and Practice of Education but even here there are exceptions, e. g.

```
(1589)  Mathematics, see QA 11, 135-137.
(1592)  Home Economics, see TX.
```

Likewise, although LB 1591 covers all the arts broadly, the study of fine arts is in N. There the breakdown is very detailed, as shown in the following illustration or in NC 390-670 Study of Graphic Arts where separate classes are provided even for "self-instruction" – NC 650 for popular and NC 655 for juvenile works.

```
    N                   FINE ARTS

        Study and teaching.
          Art study in the elementary school.
                Cf. NC 390-635, Study of drawing; also
                    LB 1187-1188, Art for the kindergarten.
350         General
353         In the United States.
354             States, A-Z.
355             Cities, A-Z.
357             Special systems.
                    Under each:
                        (1) Teachers' manuals; (2) Text-books.
                Special grades.
361                 Primary.
362                 Grammar.
363                 High school.
365             In foreign countries, A-Z.
370             Picture study in the school and the home.
                Lists of pictures for schools.
```

N 373   Select lists.
   375   Dealers' catalogs.
   377   Supplies, materials, etc.
   380   Study of the history of art.
                        Cf. N 5305, Outlines, syllabi.
   385   In the United States.
   390   In other countries, A-Z.

The most extensive provisions for education were made in Music, where

a subclass MT Musical Instruction and Study is devoted to the subject.

      1   Theory of musical instruction and study in general
    2-5   History and criticism
  6-950   Instruction and study
      6   General
   7-38   Rudiments, notations, etc.
  40-74   Composition
  78-85   Interpretation, conducting, etc.
     88   Liturgical instruction, etc.
 90-150   Analytical guides (Hermeneutics)
    155   Juvenile study of harmony, etc.
    165   Tuning
170-810   Instrumental technics
740-810   Juvenile
820-949   Singing and voice culture
890-949   Juvenile (school, etc.)
    950   Choreographical instruction

Each of the divisions is subdivided according to its requirements. A typical

example for instrumental study and teaching contains the following:

          Viola.
   280   General observations.
   282   Systems and methods.
              Studies and exercises.
   285   General.
   286   Orchestral studies.
   292   Two violas.
   293   Concert studies.
   294   Teaching pieces.
              Instructive editions.
   295   Several composers.
   297   Single composers.
   298   Self-instructors.

In sharp contrast to MT are the subdivisions under Zoology in QL:

   51   Study and teaching.
   52   Outlines, syllabi, etc.
   53   Laboratory manuals.
                Cf. QL 812, Anatomy laboratory manuals.
   55   Laboratory animals.
                Scientific works only. For breeding and raising as a
                   profession, see SF 77.
   57   Use of pictures, lantern slides, etc.
   58   Other special.
                e.g. Mathematical methods.

7. <u>Divisions</u> and <u>Subdivisions</u>. The divisions and subdivisions of the various sciences and disciplines were derived from the conventional divisions used in treatises and systematic works, in educational curricula, and in other classifications. The chief factor, however, especially in the detailed construction of the schedules, was the treatment of the subjects in books. The system therefore was based upon both deductive and inductive methods. The subjects, divisions, and subdivisions progress from general to specific as far as possible in logical order. When a logical principle of order was not discernible among a number of coordinate subdivisions of a subject, an alphabetical arrangement was followed.

How these principles were applied can be illustrated more effectively than described in words. The illustrations which follow are drawn from areas of knowledge that differ markedly from each other in content and divisions: H <u>Social Sciences</u>, N <u>Fine</u> <u>Arts</u>, and Q <u>Science</u>. The progression is from class synopsis to division outline to complete schedules. Asterisks indicate the classes and detailed subdivisions chosen as examples.

SYNOPSIS

Social Sciences

```
  H  General works
 HA  Statistics
```

Economics

```
 *HB  Economic theory
HC-HD  Economic history and conditions
  HC     National production and economic
              Conditions (By country)
  HD     Agriculture and industry
              Land
              Agriculture
              Corporations
              Labor
              Industries
  HE  Transportation and communication
  HF  Commerce, including tariff policy
  HG  Finance (General).  Private finance
              Money
              Banking
              Insurance
  HJ  Public finance
```

Sociology

HM General works. Theory
HN Social history and conditions. Social problems
    Social reform
HQ-HT Social groups
  HQ   Family. Marriage. Woman
  HS   Societies: Secret, benevolent, etc. Clubs
  HT   Communities. Classes. Races
HV Social pathology. Social and public welfare
    Criminology
HX Socialism. Communism. Anarchism

ECONOMIC THEORY

HB
1-9 Periodicals.
21 Congresses. Exhibitions.
31-55 Collections.
61 Encyclopedias.
71 Economics as a science.
72   Relation to philosophy, religion, ethics.
73   Relation to politics and law.
74   Relation to other special topics, A-Z.
*75-129 History (including biography).
151-179 Treatises. Compends.
195-199 General special.
201-205 Value.
221-236 Price.
251 Wealth.
301 Labor and wages (cf. HD 4801-8942, Laboring classes).
401 Rent and land (cf. HD 101-2206, Land and agriculture).
501 Capital. Saving.
531-549 Interest. Usury.
601 Profit. Income.
615 Risk and risk bearing.
701-751 Property. Ownership, etc.
771 Distribution.
*801-845 Consumption. Use of wealth. Luxury, etc.
849-875 Population.
881-3700 Demography. Vital statistics.
3711-3840 Crises. Business cycles.

HB
    Economic theory.
      Treatises, "systems," compends, textbooks.
        Medieval works with history in HB 79.
        Before Adam Smith (to 1776/89).
151   English and American.
153   French.
155   German.
157   Italian.
159   Other.
161-169   Classical period, 1776/89-1843/76.
        Subdivided like HB 151-159. Cf. HB 171-179.
      Recent, 1843/76-
        Cf. HB 161-169.
171   English and American.
.5   Textbooks.
        Including outlines, syllabi, etc.

HB 171.7   Minor popular.
   172   Pamphlets.
   173   French.
   175   German.
   177   Italian.
   179   Other.
        General special.
   195   Economics of war.
          Economics of distribution, see HB 771.
   199   Other.
            e.g. Profit motive, economy of abundance, economic
               equality.
       Value.
   201   Theory.
         History of theory.
   203   General.
   205   By country, A-Z.
      Price.
         Cf. HD 6977-7080, for works on cost of living.
   221   Theory of price.
   225   Index numbers.
           Cf. HG 223, Standard of value.
        History and collections of prices.
   231   General (including Modern).
   232   Early and Medieval.
   233   Special, by subject, A-Z.
           For broad fields only.
           e.g. .A3 Agricultural prices.
           Cf. HD 9000-9999, Special industries and trades.
   235   By country, A-Z.
   236   Regulation of prices. By country, A-Z.
          .A3 General works.
          Cf. HB 845, Sumptuary laws.
   251   Wealth.
   301   Labor and wages. Wage fund.
        Theory only; for Laboring classes, see HD 4801-8940.
   401   Rent and land.
        Cf. HD 101-1395, Land and agriculture.
   501   Capital. Saving.
        Including Capital and labor, but not Laboring classes.
        Cf. HB 301, Labor and wages.
        Biography of Karl Marx in HX 39.5.
       Interest and usury.
        Cf. HF 5681.I6, Commercial arithmetic.
            HG 1621-1639, Banking practice.
   531   History.
   535   Early works to Adam Smith, 1776.
   539   Later works.
        Individual countries.
   545   United States.
   547   Individual states, A-W.
   549   Other countries, A-Z.
   601   Profit. Income.
        Prefer HC.
   615   Risk and risk bearing.
       Property.
   701   General works. Ownership.
   711   Private property.
   715   Inheritance.
           Cf. HJ 5801-5819, Inheritance tax.

Personal, <u>see</u> K; cf. HF 1263, etc.
Public, <u>see</u> HD 3840-4730, State and municipal industries;
 HD 1266 and HJ 3803+, State domain, etc.; JK 1606-
 1686, etc.

	751	Other special.
HB	771	Distribution.
		Consumption.
	801	General works. Theoretical works.
	805	Historical and descriptive works.
		Special.
	821	Inequality of distribution of wealth.
	831	Use of wealth. Leisure classes, etc.
	835	Ethics of wealth. "Mammonism."
	838	Hoarding. Misers.
	841	Luxury.
		Cf. BJ 1535. L9, Luxury as a vice.
	845	Sumptuary laws.

***

SYNOPSIS

Fine Arts

N	Fine Arts (General)
NA	Architecture
NB	Sculpture
NC	Graphic arts in general. Drawing. Design
*ND	Painting
NE	Engraving
NK	Art applied to industry. Decoration and ornament

OUTLINE

Painting

ND

25-1257	General.
1259-3416	Special.
*1700-2399	Water-color painting.
2450-2490	Other methods of painting.
2550-2876	Mural painting.
2890-3416	Illumination. Miniatures.

ND	Water-color painting.
1700	Periodicals.
	Societies.
1711	United States.
1712	Other American.
1713	Great Britain.
1714	France. Belgium.
1715	Germany. Austria.
1716	Italy.
1717	Netherlands. Belgium.
1718	Scandinavia.
1719	Spain and Portugal.
1720	Switzerland.
1721	Other countries.
1725	Museums. Collections.
	Exhibitions.

ND	1730	International.
	1731	United States.
	1732	Other American.
	1733	Great Britain.
	1734	Other European.
	1735	Other countries.
		Collected writings.
	1740	Several authors.
	1742	Individual authors.
	1750	Collective biography.
		History.
	1760	General.
	1770	Ancient.
	1780	Medieval.
	1790	Modern.
	1795	17th-18th centuries.
	1797	19th century.
	1798	20th century. Recent.
1801-2094		Special countries. Table III-A.

Under 3-figure places:
    (1) General.
    (2) Local, A-Z.
    (3) Special artists, A-Z.
Under 4-figure places:
    (1) General.
    (2) Special divisions, A-Z.
    (3) Special cities, A-Z.
    (4) Special artists, A-Z.

		Study and teaching.
	2110	General.
	2113	Outlines, syllabi, etc.
	2115	Special topics.
		General works.
	2125	Early works to 1800.
	2130	General works since 1800.
	2133	Technical treatises.
	2135	Elements.
	2137	Juvenile.
	2140	General special.
	2145	Miscellaneous.
	2150	Addresses, essays, lectures.
		Reproductions of water-colors.
	2160	General.
		Special countries and special artists, in ND 1801-2094.
		Special subjects of water-color painting.
	2190	Human figures.
	2200	Portraits.
	2240	Landscapes.
	2241	Sketching.
	2270	Marines.
	2280	Animals. Birds.
	2290	Still life.
	2300	Flowers. Fruit.
	2310	Architectural subjects.
	2350	Genre.
	2360	Miscellaneous.
		Materials for water-color painting.
	2380	General.
	2395	Catalogs.

ND 2397   Outline design cards.
    2399   Painting-books for children.

***

SYNOPSIS

Science

Q   Science (General)
QA Mathematics
QB Astronomy
QC Physics
QD Chemistry
*QE Geology
QH Natural history
QK Botany
QL Zoology
QM Human anatomy
QP Physiology
QR Bacteriology

OUTLINE

Geology

QE
1-350   General.
351-399 Mineralogy.
420-499 Petrology.
*500-625 Dynamic and structural geology.
651-700 Stratigraphic geology.
701-990 Paleontology. Paleozoology. Paleobotany.

DYNAMIC AND STRUCTURAL GEOLOGY

Physical and tectonic

500 Periodicals, societies, etc. Collections.
501 General works. Geophysics.
           Including physical history of the earth.
505 Essays and miscellany.
506 Geological cosmogony.
507   Deluge, etc.
508 Age of the earth. Geologic time.
509 Interior of the earth.
           Temperature, internal structure, etc.
511 Earth's crust. Isostasy.
           Cf. QB 331.
515 Geochemistry.
     Volcanoes and earthquakes.
521   General works.
       Volcanoes.
  .5   Periodicals, societies, etc.
522   General works.
523   Individual, A-Z.
           e.g. .C7 Colima.
                 .E8 Etna.
                 .K5 Kilauea.
                 .L3 Lassen.

QE 523		.P3 Pelée.
		.P8 Popocatepetl.
		.V5 Vesuvius.
524		Western hemisphere.
		Including Hawaii.
527		Eastern hemisphere.
528		Geysers, hot springs, etc.
529		Miscellany.

Earthquakes. Seismology.
    Building construction in volcanic regions in TH 1095.

531	Periodicals, societies, etc.
	Serial publications limited to observations in QE 532.
532	Observations.
	Publications by observatories.
533	Early works (to 1800).
534	General works, 1801–
	Special.
535	Western hemisphere.
536	Eastern hemisphere – Europe.
537	Eastern hemisphere – Asia, etc.
539	Miscellaneous topics.
	e.g. Microseisms.
540	Observatories.
	.A2 General.
	.A5-Z Special.
	e.g. .K4 Kew Observatory.
541	Instruments. Seismometry.
	Including tables, calculations, etc.
545	Natural gases and vapors.
565	Coral islands and reefs. Atolls.
566	Special, A-Z.
571	Erosion and deposition.
	e.g. .G7 Great Barrier reef, Australia.
	Cf. GB, Physical geography.
	Glaciers and glacial action.
	Cf. QE 697, Glacial epoch.
575	Periodicals, societies, etc.
576	General works.
578	Moraines.
581	Aqueous erosion. Sedimentation and deposition.
	Cf. S 623, Agriculture.
597	Aerial erosion.
599	Landslides.
	Cf. GB 481-488, Earth movements, subsidences, etc.
	For descriptive works, disasters, etc., see DA-F.
	.A2 General works.
	.A5-Z By country.
	Structural geology.
601	General works.
602	Stratification.
605	Jointing and cleavage.
606	Faulting and folding.
608	Metamorphism.
611	Veins, dikes, necks, bosses, laccoliths, etc.
	Cf. TN 263, Ore deposits.
615	Miscellaneous.
	e.g. Colloids and geology.
621	Mountain building.
625	Effect of plants and animals in geology.

In the illustrations given thus far the order of the divisions and sub-divisions has been systematic — based on logical principles of division and classification. When such principles were not discernible or seemed impractical, a simple alphabetical sequence like the following was employed.

NK	Art applied to industry — Decoration and ornament
	Special subjects, alphabetically.
3600-3640	Alphabets, initials, etc.
3660	Book ornamentation
3700-4680	Ceramics
4700-4890	Costume
5000-5015	Enamel
	Furniture. See 2200-2740.
5100-5430	Glass
5500-6050	Glyptic arts
5505-5733	Gems
5720	Cameos
5730	Intaglios
5750	Jade
5800-5998	Ivory
6020	Horn and bone
6050	Netsukes
6200	Leather work
6300-6399	Medals, plaques, etc.
6400-8450	Metal-work
6600-6699	Arms and armor
7100-7695	Gold and silver — Plate — Jewelry
7800-7899	Brasses
7900-7999	Bronzes
8100	Copper work
8200-8299	Ironwork
8350	Lead work
8400-8419	Pewter
8500	Mosaic ornaments
8550	Musical instruments

A similar order, based on Cutter numbers, was used for minute or end topics in many classes:

BP	Mohammedanism.
175	Special topics, A-Z.
	e.g. .A6 Animism.
	.C4 Children.
	.D4 Dervishes.
	.M2 Mahdi.
	See also DT108.3 History.
	.M4 Mecca and its pilgrimages.
	.M9 Mysticism. Sufism.
	.P7 Predestination.
	.S2 Saints.
195	Special sects and modifications, A-Z.
	e.g. .A1 General and miscellaneous.
	.A5 Ahmadiya movement.
	.A8 Assassins (Sect).
	.C3 Carmathians.

BP 195   .D8   Druses.
             .I8   Isma'ilites.
             .M7   Murjites.
             .M8   Mutazilites.
             .S4   Senussites or Senousis.
             .S5   Shi'ites.
             .S8   Sunnites.
             .Y5   Yezidis.

                   ***

HG
        Corporation finance.
             Administration.
4028   Special, by subject, A-Z.
                  e.g.   Accounting, see HF 5687.C7.
                  .B2   Balance sheets.
                  .C6   Contributions to welfare services.
                  .D4   Depreciation policy.
                  .D5   Dividends. Stock dividends.
                  .R4   Refinancing.
                  .R5   Reserve funds.
                  .S5   Sinking funds.
                  .S8   Stock transfer.

                   ***

QL
        Coleoptera (Beetles).
596   Systematic divisions, A-Z.
                  e.g. .B7   Bruchidae.
                        .B8   Buprestidae.
                        .C62   Cleridae.
                        .C65   Coccinellidae.

                   ***

CHAPTER XVI

Description: Auxiliaries and Articulation

The schedules do not always contain the detailed subdivisions of subjects. In some areas of knowledge where common principles of division and
classification exist and also in the geographical treatment of subjects it was
possible to devise tables of subdivisions applicable to a number of subjects.
Subject Subdivision.

The most notable of the subject tables, and unfortunately "the most frequently departed from, " are those Dr. Koenig constructed for Class P Language and Literature. These tables are in several expansions adapted to the
varying approaches to the material on mankind's many languages, dialects,
and literatures. The most frequently used numbers and the unfortunate exceptions are in many instances, however, given within the schedules as well.
The following example illustrates the use of three of the tables for the French,
Finnish, and Manx languages.

    French: PC 2001-2701 (I)
    Finnish: PH 101-293 (III)
    Manx: PB 1801-1847 (V)

By the application of tables the common subdivisions are, in effect, integrated
into the schedules.

LANGUAGE TABLES OF SUBDIVISION [1]				APPLICATION OF TABLES		
	I (900)	III (200)	V (50)	I French PC 2001-2701	III Finnish PH 101-293	V Manx PB 1801-1847
Study and teaching:						
General	65	19	7	2065	119	1807
General special . . .	66			2066		
e. g. Educational value						
By period, see I 53-58, 75-87, etc.						
By country, A-Z	68			2068		
By school, A-Z	69	21		2069	121	

(Continued.)	I (900)	III (200)	V (50)	I French PC 2001-2701	III Finnish PH 101-293	V Manx PB 1801-1847
General works:						
Early to 1800	70	22		2070	122	
Treatises (Philology,						
General).	71	23	8	2071	123	1808
General special	73			2073		
Relation to other lan-						
guages	74	24		2074	124	
History of the language						
General works	75	25	9	2075	125	1809
Earliest, see I 53, etc	(76)			(2076)		
Middle ages	77			2077		
(15th-) 16th century	79			2079		
(16th-) 17th century	81			2081		
(17th-) 18th century	83			2083		
19th century	85			2085		
20th century	87			2087		
By region, see Dia-						
lects, I 700-840, etc						
Compends	91			2091		
Outlines	93	26		2093	126	
Popular. Minor	95	27	10	2095	127	1810
Script	97	28		2097	128	
Grammar—						
Comparative (two or						
more languages) .	99	29		2099	129	
Historical	101	31		2101	131	
Treatises		33	11		133	1811
To 1800	103			2103		
Later	105			2105		
General special (Ter-						
minology, etc.).	107	34	12	2107	134	1812
Text-books		35	13		135	1813
Early to 1870	109			2109		
Later, 1871-	111			2111		
Readers —						
Series	113	36		2113	136	
Primers. Primary						
grade readers	115			2115		
Intermediate and		37			137	
advanced	117			2117		
Outlines, Syllabi, Tab-						
les, etc.	118			2118		
Examination questions,						
etc.	119			2119		
Manuals for special						
classes of stu-						
dents, A-Z.......	120	38		2120	138	
e. g., Commercial,						
Cf. HF.						

[1] Tables II and IV are omitted for reasons of space limitation.

Tables similar to those above are used in other classes, such as the following from J Political Science and C History – Auxiliary Sciences. In Class J the subdivisions for classifying the constitutional history of the United States are given in full in the schedule, but for the individual states blocks of numbers assigned to each derive their content from a special table.

JK Constitutional history – United States.
State government.
Individual states and territories.
For subject subdivisions see the table following the list of states.

2701-	District of Columbia.
2801-	Maine.
2901-	New Hampshire.
3001-	Vermont.
3101-	Massachusetts.
3201-	Rhode Island.
3301-	Connecticut.
3401-	New York.
3501-	New Jersey.

JK CONSTITUTIONAL HISTORY – UNITED STATES JK
Table of subject subdivisions under states in JK 2700-9599— Continued.

	Administration – Continued.
45	Political abuses, corruption, etc.
	General works only. For impeachment cases, see no. (59); contested elections, no. (79-80); and JK 2246: Corrupt elections.
	The Executive.
	The Governor.
51	General.
52	General special. By date.
53	Special, by subject, A-Z.
	Pardons, see JK 2458.
55	Civil service.
56	Lists of officials. Registers, see subdivision 31.
57	Salaries and fees of state officials.
58	Appointments and removals.
59	Impeachment.
	Under each:
	.A5-Z3 General. By author.
	.Z5 Cases, by date.
60	Special, by subject, A-Z.
	e. g. Pensions.
	The Legislature.
(61)	Legislative manuals, see (31) and (71).
	History.
66	General.
67	By date.
68	Representation. Districts.
69	Powers, etc.
70	Special (by date).
71	Organization and procedure.

74	Bill drafting. Legislative reference bureaus.
76	Upper House.
	.A2 Rules.
78	Lower House.
	.A2 Rules.
	Contested elections.
79	General. By date of issue.
80	Individual cases. By date.
	The Judiciary.
81	General. History.

Application of numbers 51-53 of the table results in the following class numbers for Maine and New Hampshire:

The Executive.	Maine	New Hampshire
The Governor.		
General.	2851	2951
General special.	2852	2952
Special, by subject, A-Z.	2853	2953

Likewise, for many foreign countries not provided with special arrangements in the schedules there are tables in four expansions adapted to the importance and literature of the various countries.

	JQ Constitutional history and administration.
	Asia. Africa. Australia. Oceania.
3200-3299	Algeria (1).
3450-3469	Madagascar (2).
3480-3489	Réunion (3).
6301	Fiji (4).

JQ   CONSTITUTIONAL HISTORY   JQ
Tables of subdivisions under countries not provided with special schemes
in JL, JN, and JQ — Continued.

Tables.				
1	2	3	4	
100 nos.	20 nos.	10 nos.	1 no.	
				Government. Administration — Cont.
22				History.
24	8	5.A1	.A5	General.
26	9	.A5	.A55	By date.
29				Special topics, by subject, A-Z.
(30)	(10A3)	(.A6)	(.A57	Administrative law, codes, See K.
				(Added entry here.)
31	10	.A7-Z	.A58	Treaties, manuals, etc.
35	.5	.5	.A59	Maladministration.
40	11	6		The Executive.
41			.A61	The chief executive.
42			.A63	Ministry.
	12			The civil service.

Tables – (Continued.)				
1	2	3	4	
100 nos.	20 nos.	10 nos.	1 no.	The Civil service (continued.)
45			.A65	Documents. Subarrange: .A Report. .B Manuals, guides, etc. Registers, lists, etc., see subdivision 21, 7, 4, .A4 above. .C Examinations. .D Other.
47			.A67	Treatises.
49			.A69	Special topics, A-Z.
49.S2	12.Z2	6.Z2	.A691	Salaries and pensions. *
50	12.Z3-9	6.Z3-9	.A693-698	Special departments, e.c. Interior.

*Not limited to civil service proper. Works dealing with service under the state in all branches to be classified here. Cf. HD 4939, 8013, 8023; JK 767-795.

Application of Tables

		Algeria	Madagascar	Réunion	Fiji
The Executive	JQ	3240	3461	3486	
The chief executive		3241	. . . .		6301.A61
Ministry		3242	. . . .		.A63
The civil service		. . . .	3462		
Documents		3245	. . . .		.A65
Subarrange:					
.A Report.					
.B Manuals, guides, etc. Registers, lists, etc., see subdivision 21, 7, 4, .A4 above					
.C Examinations.					
.D Other.					
Treatises		3247	. . . .		.A67
Special topics, A-Z		3249	. . . .		.A69

In CJ Numismatics the subdivisions for all countries (CJ 1800-4649) are derived from two tables, the use of which is shown in this sample application to the United States and Canada:

CJ Numismatics.
        By country. *
          America.

1800-1817	General, including North America (II).
1819	Spanish America (General).
1820-1849	United States (I).
	Commemorative and souvenir coins.

```
    CJ 1839            General works.
       1840            Special, by name, A-Z.
                           e. g. .M2 McKinley souvenir dollar.
       1841            Colonial.
       1842            Early national to 1860.
       1844            1861-1900.
       1845            1901-
  1860-1879            Canada (II).
  1890-1909            Mexico (II).
```

* For subarrangement under countries, unless otherwise provided for,
see Tables I-II, p. 57.

TABLES OF SUBDIVISIONS FOR NUMISMATICS
(CJ1800-4649)

```
II   I
0    0    Periodicals. Societies.
     1    Yearbooks.
     2    Collected works.
          Museums. Collections.
2    4        Public.
3    5        Private.
4    6    Sales catalogs. Coin values.
5    9    Dictionaries. Directories.
6    10   General works.
7    12   General special. Special aspects, relations, etc.
              Includes minor works.
          Material.
8    14       Gold.
9    15       Silver.
10   16       Bronze and copper.
11   17       Other.
12   19   Iconography.
          By period.
14   21       Medieval.
15   22       Early modern to 1789/1815.
16   24       Early 19th century, 1789/1815-1870.
17   25       Later 19th and 20th centuries, 1871-
19        Local, A-Z.
     28       States, provinces, etc.
     29       Cities and towns.
     30   Colonies in general (when necessary).
```

Numbers from Table		Subdivisions	Application to	
II	I		Canada (II)	United States (I)
4	6	Sales catalogs. Coin values.	1864	1826
12	19	Iconography	1872	1839

It will be noted that, due to a large amount of material on special commemora-

tive coins, the extra number 1840 is included in the United States schedule;

also, American historical periods necessitated modifications in the chrono-

logical sequence CJ 1841-1845.

In other fields of knowledge the subdivisions provided under some subjects serve as tables for the subdivision of similar or related topics. "Divided" or "Subdivided like" notes in text or footnotes refer to the divisions which are to be used.

	NK Art applied to industry.
	Metal work.
7800-7899	Brasses.
	(Including works on brass, bronze, and copper.)
	Divided like NK 4700-4799.
7900-7999	Bronzes.
	Divided like NK 4700-4799.
8100	Copper-work.
8200-8299	Iron-work. (Serrurerie. Schmiedekunst.)
	Divided like NK 4700-4799.

That is, the subdivisions represented by NK 4700-4799 given below are to be applied to the metals above.

	NK Costume and its accessories.
	In general to be classified in GT, Manners and customs.
	Military uniforms, see UC 480-485.
	Ecclesiastical vestments, see NK 4850.
4700	Periodicals.
4701	Exhibitions (by place).
	(General. Special periods in NK 4707-.)
4702	Museums (by place).
	(General. Special periods in NK 4707-.)
4703	Collections.
4704	General works.
	(Including collected works and dictionaries.)
4705	Collected designs.
4706	History.
4707	Ancient.
4708	Medieval.
4709	Modern.
4710	Recent.
4711	North America.
4712	United States.
4713-4796	Other countries. Table I.
4797	Collective biography.
4798	Special artists.
4799	Dealers' catalogs.

Similar provisions are made for certain country subdivisions under Dress and costume in GT:

	GT Manners and customs (General).
	Dress. Costume.
	By country.
	Europe.
	Great Britain. England (General).
730	General works.
	By period.

GT	731	Ancient.
	732	Medieval.
	733	Modern.
	734	15th-16th centuries.
	735	17th century.
	736	18th century.
	737	19th century.
	738	20th century.
		England (Local).
	741	By county, region, A-Z.
	742	By city, A-Z.
	750-762	Scotland.
		Subdivided like GT 730-742.
		Tartans, see DA 880.H76.
	770-782	Ireland.
		Subdivided like GT 730-742.
	790-802	Wales.
		Subdivided like GT 730-742.
	805	Other local, A-Z.
		e.g. .J4 Jersey.
	1240-1252	Switzerland:[1]
	1260-1272	Turkey. [1]

The footnote indicated by "[1]/" reads "Subdivided like GT 730-742," substituting for a note under each of the many other European countries divided in this same manner. This type of note may also indicate how a specific language or literature is to be divided.

	PH.	Other Finnish languages and dialects.
		Mordvinian.
	751-779	Language.
		(Subdivided like PH 601-629.)
	781-785	Literature.
		(Subdivided like PH 731-735.)

The subdivisions for the Mordvinian language are supplied from those given under Estonian:

		Estonian.
	PH	Language (VI).
	601	Periodicals. Societies. Collections.
	605	Study and teaching.
	606	General works.
	607	History of language.
		Grammar.
	609	Historical. Comparative. Descriptive.
	610	Text-books. Exercises. Conversation.
	611	Readers. Chrestomathies.
	612	Phonology. Phonetics.
	613	Morphology. Inflection. Accidence.
	614	Parts of speech (Morphology and Syntax).
	615	Syntax.
	619	Prosody. Metrics. Rhythmics.
	621	Etymology.
		Lexicography.
		Dictionaries.

PH	623	Estonian only.
	625	Estonian and other languages.
	627	Linguistic geography. Dialects.
	628	Special dialects, A-Z.
	629	Slang. Argot.

while the Mordvinian literature subdivisions are patterned after Lappish in

PH 731-735:

	Lappish.
701-729	Language.
	(Subdivided like PH 601-629.)
	Literature.
731	Treatises.
733	Texts.
735	Translations.
	Prefer GR.

Geographical Subdivision.

The order and extent of geographical and other local subdivisions are
adapted to the subjects under which they apply. The subdivisions are incorporated in full in many parts of the schedules or are provided in tables usually appended to the class in which they are used.

The major geographical areas are generally arranged in the following
order:

```
America
  North America
    United States
    British North America. Canada
    Mexico
  Central America
  West Indies
  South America
Europe
  Great Britain
  Continental countries
Asia
Africa
Australia and New Zealand
Pacific islands
Arctic regions
Antarctic regions
```

Within each continent or region the arrangement of countries is usually alphabetical. Wherever necessary, each country is likewise subdivided alphabetically by region, state, province, city, etc.

The geographical subdivisions provided in the schedules are adapted to the
subjects under which they are used. These vary from a simple arrangement like

```
SB  Plant culture and horticulture.
        History and conditions.
            By country.
83              United States.
85              States, A-W.
87              Other countries, A-Z.
```

and the slightly more detailed

```
ND  Painting.
            Portraits.
                Special countries.
1311                United States.
1312                Other American.
1313                Europe.
1314                    Great Britain.
1315                    Austria.
1316                    France.
1317                    Germany.
1318                    Italy.
1319                    Netherlands.  Belgium.
1320                    Russia.
1321                    Scandinavia.
1322                    Spain and Portugal.
1323                    Switzerland.
1324                    Other European.
1325                Oriental.
1326                    China and Japan.
1327                Other countries, A-Z.
```

to the lengthy tables in Class H Social Sciences. The example from HJ Public Finance given below illustrates the extensive treatment accorded the major countries (the United States in particular) and the use of tables to subdivide minor countries.

```
    HJ  Revenue. Taxation.
2360-3193   By country.
                General works, history, etc.
                Law, legislation, administration in HJ 3231-3698.
                United States.
2360                Collections.
                        Serial documents preferably in HJ 10-11.
                    General works.  History.
                        Including practice.
2362                General.
2368                Early to 1789.
2369                1789-1815.
2370                1815-1860.
2371                1861-1865/70.
2372                    Confederate States.
                            Cf.  HJ 3255-3257, Tax law and legislation.
2373                1865/70-1900.
2375                    1898 (War revenue act).
2377                1901-
2379                    War revenue acts, 1914-1918.
                            Arranged like HJ 4652.
```

HJ 2380	Defense and war revenue acts, 1938-1946.
	Arranged like HJ 4652.
2383	Facetiae, satire, etc.
2385	States collectively.
	Regions.
	Under each:
	.A1 General works. History.
	.A3 Early.
	.A4 1830/40-1900.
	.A6-Z8 1901-
	.Z9 Special.
2386	New England and Atlantic States.
2387	South.
2388	Middle West.
2389	Pacific.
2391-2442	States individually.
	Under each:
	General works. History.
	.A2 General.
	Early to 1800.
	.A29 Documents.
	.A3 Other.
	1801-1860.
	.A39 Documents.
	.A4 Other.
	1861-1865/70.
	.A49 Documents.
	.A5 Other.
	1865/70-1900.
	.A59 Documents.
	.A6 Other.
	1901-
	Documents.
	.A65 Serial.
	Cf. note under HJ 2360.
	.A7 Nonserial. By date.
	.A8-Z2 Other.
	.Z3 + Special.
	Reports of Commissions, Legislative committees, etc., on the revision, etc., of tax laws are placed here. Cf. HJ 3260-3361, Tax law and legislation.
2391	Alabama.
2392	Alaska.
2393	Arizona.
	South America.
	Under each:
	General works. History.
	(1) General.
	(2) Early to 1810/20.
	(3) 1810/20-1900.
	(5) 1901-
	(7) Special.
	(9) Provinces, A-Z.
2491-2497	General.
2501-2509	Argentine Republic.
2511-2519	Bolivia.
2521-2529	Brazil.
2531-2539	Chile.
2541-2549	Colombia.

Applying the table given above for South American countries is equivalent to including the following at this point in the schedule:

HJ 2541-2549	Colombia.
	General works. History.
2541	General.
2542	Early to 1810/20.
2543	1810/20-1900.
2545	1901-
2547	Special.
2549	Provinces, A-Z.

For Europe the schedules include subdivisions adapted to the history and situation in each of the major countries, as illustrated by Great Britain and France:

	Great Britain.
2600	Collections.
	General works. History.
2601	General.
2603	Early to 1700/1800.
2605	Medieval to 1600.
2608	Modern (General).
	Including 19th century (General).
2610	17th and 18th centuries.
2612	17th century.
2613	18th century.
2614	1783-1815.
2615	1800-1850/60.
2617	1850/60-1900.
2619	1901-
2621	Special.
	Subarrangement under HJ 2627-2629
	General works. History.
	.A1A-Z General.
	.A3A-Z Early.
	.A5A-Z Later.
	.A7-Z4 1901-
	.Z5A-Z Special.
2627	Ireland.
2628	Scotland.
2629	Wales.
	France.
	General works. History.
2641	General.
2643	Ancien régime (General).
2644	General special. Fermiers généraux, etc.
2646	Medieval to 1600.
2648	17th century.
2650	18th century.
2652	Modern (General).
2653	Revolutionary period to 1815.
2655	1815-1870/71.
2657	1870/71-1900.
2659	1901-
2661	Special.
2669	Local (Departments, provinces), A-Z.

For other countries there are subarrangement tables of 5 or 10 numbers similar to the South American pattern but differing in chronological divisions due
to variations in historical periods.

The tables of geographical subdivisions are usually appended, like those
in H Social Sciences and N Fine Arts, at the end of the schedules. They list
the subdivisions and the number or numbers, if in several expansions, assigned
to them. In practice the use of these tables, like the subject tables described
above, constitutes incorporation of the subdivisions into the schedules at each
of the points where applied. The following illustrate the use of the four detailed tables at the end of Class N Fine Arts.

```
        NE  Etching.
      1980      History.
 2001-2096      Special countries. Table I.

        NC  Graphic arts in general. Drawing. Design.
                History of drawing.
   101-376      Special countries. Table III.
                Under each:
                    (1) General.
                    (2) Local.
                    (3) Special artists, A-Z.

        NC  Study and teaching.
       390      History.
   401-584      Special countries. Table II.
                Under each:
                    (1) General.
                    (2) Local.

        ND  Painting.
                Water-color painting.
                History.
 1801-2094          Special countries. Table III-A.
```

TABLES OF SUBDIVISIONS

I (100)		II (200)	III (300)	III-A (300)
48	Austria	95	143	143
49	France	97	146	147
50	Germany	90	149	151
51	Greece	101	152	155
52	Italy	103	155	159
53	Netherlands	105	158	163
54	Holland	107	161	167
55	Belgium.Flanders	109	164	171
56	Russia	111	167	175
57	Scandinavia	113	170	179

58	Denmark	115	173	183
59	Iceland	117	176	187
60	Norway	119	179	191
61	Sweden	121	182	195
62	Spain. Spain and Portugal . . .	123	185	199
63	Portugal	125	188	203

Tables I to III-A list the geographical divisions of the world from "01 America" to 96, 184, 276, and 294, respectively, for Pacific Islands. Applying the tables to France, Italy, Sweden, and Spain for each of the subjects above, the following class numbers are derived:

I (100)		II (200)	III (300)	III-A (300)
NE 2049	France . . . . NC 497-498	NC 246-248	ND 1947-1950
2052	Italy 503-504	255-257	1959-1962
2061	Sweden 521-522	282-284	1995-1998
2062	Spain 523-524	285-287	1999-2002

Because the integer "1" stands for America in every case, the _preceding_ number in each country group (2000, 100, 400, and 1800 in the classes used to illustrate) is added to the "table number" for a particular country to obtain its correct class number. Table I provides only one number to each country; under Tables II, III, and III-A, however, each country has 2, 3, and 4 numbers, the significance of which is explained by tables such as those in the illustrations from NC.

Table IV in Class N differs from the others in that it is a composite of geographical and subject subdivisions and is consequently extensive, ranging from "01 America" to "913 Pacific Islands."

NA Architecture.
701-1613   Architecture of special countries. Table IV.
        For "Special artists" read "Special architects."

ND Painting.
201-1113   Special countries. Table IV.

TABLE IV

Europe.
250   General.
251   Folios (used only for NA 951).
(252)   Ancient. (See Ancient art in general period divisions, N 5315-5899, etc.)
253   Medieval (used only for NA 5453).
        In other cases see the general period divisions.
254   Modern.

ND 255   Renaissance (used only for NA 5455).
                      In other cases see the general period divisions.
    256   17th-18th centuries.
    257   19th century.
    258   20th century.
                  Special countries.

                  France.
    341   General works.
    342   Ancient.
    343   Medieval. Gothic. Romanesque.
    344   Modern.
    345   14th-16th centuries. Renaissance.
    346   17th-18th centuries.
    347   19th century.
    348   20th century.
    349   Special divisions, A-Z.
    350   Paris.
    351   Other special cities, A-Z.
    352   Collective biography.
    353   Special artists, A-Z.

Upon application of Table IV in the NA and ND classes selected for illustra-

tion, the class numbers for French architecture and painting are found to be

NA 1041-1053 (700 plus 341-353) and ND 541-553 (200 plus 341-353) respec-

tively. The following titles would thus fall into these class numbers:

Dictionnaire raisonné de l'architecture
   française du XIe au XVIe siècle .... NA 1041

L'Architecture française à l'époque gothique .... NA 1043

L'Art architectural en France depuis François Ier ....
   jusqu'à Louis XVI .... NA 1044

Examples of Modern French architecture (1928) ...... NA 1048

En Provence, documents d'architecture .... NA 1049. P8

Le vieux Paris . . . [Medieval and Renaissance
   architecture] .... NA 1050

L'Architecture moderne à Paris [1900-?] .... NA 1050

La peinture française. Les origines . . . a nos
   jours (1937) .... ND 541

Contemporary French painting (1946) .... ND 548

Rosa Bonheur; sa vie, son oeuvre .... ND 553. B6

In Class H, ten tables of varying expansions provide similar geograph-

ical subdivisions which are used as follows:

```
      HB  Economic theory.
 881-3700     Demography.  Movement of population.  Vital statistics.
                 Domicile (geographical distribution).
      1951        General works.
 1961-2160        By country.  Table II.[1]
                  Urban.
      2161           General works.
                        Cf. HT 201, Urban sociology.
 2171-2370           By country.  Table II. [1]
                     Rural.
      2371           General works.
 2381-2580           By country.  Table II. [1]
```

---

[1] For Table II, see p. 527-532. Add country number in Table to 1330, 1540, 1750, 1960, 2170, 2380, 2590, 2800, or 3010, as the case requires.

Table II[1] provides geographical subdivisions ranging from "1 America" to "197 Antarctic regions" — in this context HB 1961-2160. Since the first number, 1961, is used for America, it is necessary, as the notes added to the third edition of Class H indicate, to subtract 1 before adding the desired country number. Failure to do so results in a geographical subdivision other than the one needed, e. g.

1961+40 = 2001, the number for Nicaragua, instead of

1960+40 = 2000, the correct number for Honduras.

In HG Finance under Life Insurance the numbers for countries other than the United States are derived from Table VI;[1] they are then subdivided according to a table provided in the schedules below HG 9010-9200.

```
      HG  Life insurance.
 8941-9200    By country.
                United States.
                  Documents, see HG 8501-8511, State insurance de-
                     partment annual reports, etc.; HG 8917, State
                     regulation.
      8941          Associations (Underwriters').
                        Cf. HG 8754, Life insurance societies, associations,
                           etc.
      8943          Annuals.
                        Cf. HG 8955, Statistics.
                     Directories.
      8945             General.
      8947             By state, A-W.
      8949             By city, A-Z.
      8951          General works.  History.
      8952          Biography.
      8955          Statistics.
                        e. g. Dawes, Unique manual.  Cf. HG 8853, 8881.
                     Policy, etc.
                        Cf. HG 8901+
```

HG	8957	To 1900.
	8958	1901-
	8961	By state, A-W.
		For documents, see HG 8511, 8918.
	8962	By city, A-Z.
	8963	By company, A-Z.
		Under each:
		(1) Reports (Serial).
		(2) History.
		(3) Miscellaneous.
		Special reports now in (3) may be arranged chronologically and miscellaneous printed matter, announcements, etc., made (4).
		Cases, see HG 8909.
9010-9200		Other countries. Table VI, [1] modified.
		Under each:

5 nos.	2 nos.	
(1)	(1).A1-4	Documents.
(2)	.A5	Societies. Associations.
(3)	.A6	Annuals. Directories.
(4)	.A7-Z7	General works. History, statistics.
.Z9	.Z9	Policy, etc. Pamphlets, etc.
(5)	(2)	Local, A-Z.
.Z9	.Z9	By company, A-Z.

Note. For divisions of British Africa and Pacific islands, see HG 8550, notes.

---

[1] For Table VI, see p. 527-532. Add country number in Table to 9000.

Inasmuch as the United States has been treated individually in the schedules proper, the divisions for "Other countries" in Table VI begin with Canada, 10. It is necessary, therefore, to add the numbers in the Tables to HG 9000. Some of the countries are assigned five numbers, others two; the explanation of these appears below HG 9010-9200. Applied to Brazil and Scotland, respectively, 28-32 and 62-63 in the Table become HG 9028-9032 and HG 9062-9063 at this point in the schedule; to these numbers in turn is applied a table which produces the following arrangement of material under each:

COUNTRY			TABLE	COUNTRY
5 nos.				2 nos.
Brazil	5 nos.	2 nos.		Scotland
HG 9028	(1)	(1).A1-4	Documents.	HG 9062.A1-4
9029	(2)	.A5	Societies. Associations.	9062.A5
9030	(3)	.A6	Annuals. Directories.	9062.A6
9031	(4)	.A7-Z7	General works. History, statistics.	9062.A7-Z7
9031.Z9		.Z9 .Z9	Policy, etc. Pamphlets, etc.	9062.Z9
9032	(5)	(2)	Local, A-Z.	9063
9032.Z9		.Z9 .Z9	By company, A-Z.	9063.Z9

[Sample Page from Class H Social Sciences]

TABLES OF GEOGRAPHICAL DIVISIONS

The first number in curves (100), (200), etc., below the Roman numeral at head of column indicates the total number of divisions comprised in that table; the second number in curves (1), (2), (5;10), etc., indicates the number of subdivisions assigned to any one country in a given table.
May be modified to meet the requirements of special subjects, where different order and different distribution of numbers is desired.

I	II	III	IV		V	VI	VII	VIII	IX	X
(100)	(200)	(300)	(400)		(130)	(200)	(830)	(840)	(420)	(1000)
(1)	(2)	(2)	(4)		(1; 4)	(2;5)	(5;10)	(10;20)	(5;10)	(5;10)
1	1	1	1	America	1	1				11
2	3	3	3	North America	2	2				21
3	5	5	5	United States	3-6	3				31
4	7	8	9	Northeastern (New England)						41
5	9	11	13	Atlantic						51
6	11	14	17	South (Gulf, etc.)						61
7	13	17	21	Central						71
8	15	20	25	Lake region (St. Lawrence Valley).						81
9	17	23	29	Mississippi Valley and West.						91
10	19	26	33	Southwest (south of Missouri and west of the Mississippi River.						101
11	21	29	37	Northwest, and Rocky Mountains.						111
12	23	32	41	Pacific coast Colonial possessions						121
13	25	35	45	States, A-W (see p. 537)		8				131
14	27	38	49	Cities, A-Z (see p. 539)		9				141
15	29	41	53	Canada, British N. A. Provinces, A-Z: Alberta. Assiniboia. Athabasca. British Columbia. Franklin. Keewatin. Labrador. Mackenzie. Manitoba. New Brunswick. Newfoundland. Northwest Territories. Nova Scotia. Ontario (Upper Canada). Prince Edward Island. Quebec (Lower Canada). Saskatchewan Ungava. Yukon.	7-10	10	11-20	1-10	1-10	151
16	31	44	57	Mexico States, A-Z	11	12	21	11	11	161
17 .A1-5	33	47	61	Central America	13 .A1-5	14	31	21	16	171
17 .A6-Z	35	48	65	British Honduras	13 .A6-Z		36	26	19	181
18	37	49	69	Costa Rica	14		41	31	21	191
19	39	52	73	Guatemala	15		61	41	26	201

I	II	III	IV		V	VI	VII	VIII	IX	X (cont.)
20	40	55	75	Honduras	16		61	51	31	211
21	41	57	77	Nicaragua	17		71	61	36	216
22	42	59	79	Panama	18		81	71	41	221
22.5	43.5	61	80	Panama Canal Zone	18.5		86	76	45.5	226
23	44	62	81	Salvador	19		91	81	46	231
24	45	65	85	West Indies	20	16	101	91	51	241
24.5	47	68	89	Bahamas	20.5		106	96	53	246
25	49	71	93	Cuba	21		111	101	56	251
26	51	74	97	Haiti	22		121	111	61	261
26.5	52	76	99	Santo Domingo	22.5		126	116	64	266
27	53	77	101	Jamaica	23		131	121	66	271
28	55	80	105	Puerto Rico	24		141	131	71	281
28.5	56.5	83	109	Virgin Islands of the United States (Danish West Indies).	24.5		150.5	141-3[1]	75.5	286
29	57	85	112	Other	25				75.7	
				British West Indies Barbadoes. Bermudas. Falkland Islands. Leeward Islands. Trinidad. Windward Islands.			151	144		291
				Dutch West Indies Curaçao.			157	147		297
				French West Indies and other island possessions.[2] Guadeloupe. Martinique. Miquelon. St. Pierre.			159	149		299
30	58	86	113	South America	26	18	161	151	76	301
31	59	89	117	Argentine Republic	27-30	20	171	161	81	311
32	61	92	121	Bolivia	31	25	181	171	86	321
33	63	95	125	Brazil	32-35	28	191	181	91	331
34	65	98	129	Chile	36	33	201	191	96	341
35	67	101	133	Colombia	37	38	211	201	101	351
36	69	104	137	Ecuador	38	40	221	211	106	361
37	71	107	141	Guiana British Dutch French	39	42	231	221	111	371
38	73	110	145	Paraguay	40	44	241	231	116	381
39	75	113	149	Peru	41	46	251	241	121	391
40	77	116	153	Uruguay	42	48	261	251	126	401
41	79	119	157	Venezuela	43	50	271	261	131	411
42	81	122	161	Europe	44	52	281	271	136	421
43	83	125	165	Great Britain[3]	45-48	54	291	281	141	431
44	85	128	169	England and Wales		60	301			441
45	87	131	173	Scotland		62	311			451

I	II	III	IV		V	VI	VII	VIII	IX	X (Cont.)
46	89	133	177	Ireland		64	321			461
				Colonial pos-						
				sessions in						
				general.						

---

[1]Cf. HG 2701-3540.

[2]May be used for all French possessions in America or combinations of several of them.

[3]May be used for British Empire, "Greater Britain, " etc.

The subdivisions in the Natural Sciences, however, where political geography is relatively unimportant, emphasize physiographic and topographical regions and divisions.

```
QK  Botany.
        Ecology
            Physiographic regions.
930             Water.
931                 Marine.
932                 Fresh water.
            Land.
936                 Tropics.
937                 Alpine flora.
938                 Other special, A- Z.
                        e. g.  .C3  Caves.
                               .D9  Dunes.
                               .M6  Moors.
                               .S4  Semiarid regions.
            Topographical divisions.
939             North America.
940             United States.
941                 By state, A- W.
942                 By city, A- Z.

QL  Zoology.
        Invertebrates.
            Porifera (Sponges).
371             General treatises.
372             Geographical distribution.
                    Not divided by country.
    .1                  North America.
    .2                  Mexico, Central America, and West Indies.
    .3                  South America.
    .4                  Europe.
    .5                  Asia.
    .6                  Africa.
    .7                  Australia and New Zealand.
    .8                  Pacific islands.
    .9                  Arctic and Antarctic.
373             Systematic divisions, A- Z.
                    e. g.  .C2   Calcarea.
                           .D45  Demospongiae.
```

National or Country Collocation.

The problem of "subject" versus "country" has long disturbed library classifiers. When the L. C. was being developed, conventional practice (Decimal Classification) called for classification by subject or topic and, when necessary, for the automatic application of geographical numbers. Both the Decimal Classification and the Expansive Classification were developed on this basis. But, whatever the value of this method of treatment in many subjects, chiefly in Science and Technology, its validity seemed questionable in some fields of the Social Sciences. The practice provided for the comparative approach but failed to take into consideration many users whose main interest was in the institutions of particular geographical areas. The decision was made, therefore, to deviate from the practice whenever it was thought to impede rather than to facilitate the approach to certain subjects.

Class J Political Science was one of the most important fields in which application was made of the new "principle of collocating by country" topics frequently studied together. Under Constitutional History and Administration the following divisions were provided:

    JF General. Comparative.
    JK United States.
    JL British America. Latin America.
    JN Europe.
    JQ Asia, Africa, Australia, etc.

The divisions and subdivisions provided for comparative works in JF are repeated, in schedules or tables, under each country in JK-JQ. When needed, class numbers are provided also for institutions peculiar to individual countries. It is possible, in this way, to bring together under each country all material on its constitutional history and administration. Probably the need for "collocating by country" was first felt in connection with material on American political institutions; the arbitrary dispersion which "conventional practice" provided would have performed a grave disservice to the Library's chief clients, the Congress and the Executive departments.

Similar provisions are found in other classes, notably in Class H. In subclass HE Transportation and Communication the provisions for the Unit-

ed States postal service bring together the most important components of

the system — components previously schedulized for general comparative

works and subdivision by country. Where theory and practice are not immed-

iately obvious, notes and references like the following guide the classifier.

HE 6151   Free delivery.
                      For special arrangement for United States, <u>see</u>
                      HE 6451-56.

                Parcel post.
6173   By country, A-Z.
                    Except United States, HE 6471-6473.

In HG Finance the important topics under money are brought together

by country, with more exhaustive division for the United States.

```
HG   Finance.
          United States.
               Coinage.
551            Gold.
               Silver.
555               History.
556               Controversial literature.
               Bimetallism.
561               History.
562               Controversial literature.
566            Small coins.
          Paper money.
               Bureau of Engraving and Printing.
571               Annual reports.
573               Other works. Minor. Pamphlets.
581            National Currency Bureau.
               General.
583               Bank note paper.
584               Engraving of bank notes.
587               Laws.
591               History.
                     Including descriptions and catalogs.
593               Controversial literature.
               Special.
                  Treasury notes.
601                  History.
602                  Controversial literature, etc.
                  Greenbacks.
604                  History.
605                  Controversial literature, etc.
                  National bank notes.
                        Cf. HG 1866-1867, 2545-2565.
607                  History.
608                  Controversial literature, etc.
609                  Redemption agencies.
610            Federal reserve notes.
```

(611)	Emergency currency.
	Discussion in HG 538.
	National Currency Association act, May 30, 1908, in HG 483.
613	Miscellaneous.
	Nationalization of legal-tender money, Redemption of bank notes, Hygienic aspects of money, etc.
	Local paper money.
621	Bank note reporters.
622	History.
623	Controversial literature, etc.
627	By place, A-Z.
629	Tokens.
(630)	Credit instruments as money, see HG 357-358.
631	Miscellaneous plans.
	Counterfeit detectors.
641	General works.
	.A3 Periodicals.
643	Coin.
645	Paper.

Writing of this "deviation," a recent critic said, "The Library of Congress classifiers are the first to recognize the necessity of variations of treatment as between the different classes, and it is this feature of the scheme which has found so much favour in academic libraries. "[2]

Integration.

The organization of knowledge into a system of classes, subclasses, divisions, etc., upon some theory of the order of the sciences is but part of the process of developing a system of classification. It has frequently been asserted that the Library of Congress Classification is composed of a series of special classifications. There is an element of truth in the statement, for all realistic classifications must accept the divisions of knowledge currently used in the various disciplines. The statement, however, is based upon a logical absurdity – that the divisions of knowledge are mutually exclusive. As we have seen in Chapter I, knowledge, although unitary, is divided for purposes of study into sciences and disciplines which are modes of approach to the universe of knowledge and not segments of that universe. The use of varying principles or characteristics of division and classification in the several special classifications would produce a chaotic mechanical structure in which cross division would disperse the same subjects in many divisions. It is obvious, therefore, that the mechanical assembling of

special classifications would produce an encyclopedic classification devoid
of organic unity – the very antithesis of system.

In developing detailed schedules it was necessary at each step in the
process to define, explicitly or implicitly, the contents of each division and
its relationship, vertical or horizontal, to others. This process of integration and articulation was especially difficult in a system as vast and minute
as the L. C., and not all problems were satisfactorily settled even in the
minds of those who made the decisions. Some decisions were found to be
impractical, like the following, and were reversed.

ANATOMY AND HISTOLOGY

The subdivisions in curves have been
discontinued. See QK 641-663,
Morphology, anatomy, and embryology.

QK	
671	General works.
673	Laboratory manuals, techniques, microscopy, photomicrography.
	Cf. QH 201-251, Microscopy.
(683)	Individual groups, A-Z.
	Individual parts.
(684)	Root.
(685)	Shoot.
(686)	Stem.
(687)	Wood.
(688)	Bark.
(689)	Leaf.
(690)	Types of branching.
(691)	Inflorescence.
(692)	Flower.
(693)	Receptacle.

Other decisions had to be tentative because of the imperfect knowledge of the
subject. This was particularly true in the case of lesser-known languages,
as illustrated below:

P   PHILOLOGY. LINGUISTIC   P

Extinct (Ancient or Medieval) Asiatic
and European Languages of Disputed Relationship.

901	General.
	Languages of Central Asia, East Turkestan. Indo-Scythian
	(Scytho-Indian).
911	General.
	Here are temporarily classified treatises on the
	extinct languages discovered early in the 20th
	century.

P   911   General. (Continued)
                         Of the languages assigned by some authorities to the
                            Indo-European group, one has been variously termed
                            "Language I,:'' Tokhari ("Tocharisch") "Kasgarisch,"
                            "Shûle," "Turfanisch," "Koutchéen," "Kuchean."
                         It still flourished as a spoken language in the middle
                            of the 7th century C. E.
                         Another, belonging to the Iranian branch, and flourish-
                            ing as a spoken language as late as the 8th century
                            C. E. , has been named "Language II," North-Aryan,
                            Saka, Khotani, Khotanese. Upon agreement among
                            scholars as to nomenclature, special numbers may
                            be assigned to each of these languages.
                         The whole group — or part of it — may later be trans-
                            ferred to PK 7501.

                      Languages of Western Asia.
                         This and the following group (P 1001-1039) may be
                            transferred to PJ 2901+ , after more definite know-
                            ledge has been obtained by scholars.
                         Cf. J. Friedrich, "Altkleinasiatische sprachen" in
                            Reallexikon der vorgeschichte, hrsg. v. Max Ebert,
                            Berlin, 1924-
      941   General.
      943   Elamite.

      961   Other, A- Z.
                      Languages of Asia Minor and Southeastern Europe.
     1001   General.
                         Special, A- Z.
     1003   Cappadocian.
     1004   Carian.
                            Cf. P 1024.
     1005   Cilician.
     1006   Isaurian.
     1007   Lycaonian.
     1008   Lycian.
     1009   Lydian.
     1010   Mysian.
     1011   Pisidian.
     1021   Languages of Greece (previous to Greek immigration).
     1023   Pelasgian.
     1024   Lelegian.
                            Cf. P 1004.
     1031   Inscription of Lemnos.
                            Cf. PA 2400-2409 (Etruscan).
     1035   Minoan inscriptions. Disk of Phaestos.
     1039   Eteocretan.
                            Cf. A. J. Evans, Scripta Minoa, Oxford, 1909-

        The following notes as to scope and content and references to related
or preferred classes, etc. , illustrate some of the decisions made and the
ways in which they were recorded.

SCOPE NOTES AND RELATED CLASSES

GA   Cartography

Map making, and works about maps (General).
The construction, use, and reading of maps in a special field
are to be classified in B-Z, e. g. QC 878, construction of
weather maps; UG 470, Military mapping; etc.
Maps themselves are classified in G 3200-9980.
Cf. GA 109, Aerial cartography.
    GA 359-397, Marine cartography.
    GN 476.5, Primitive cartography.
    Z 692.M3, Care, repair, and preservation of maps in
    libraries.

101   Periodicals. Societies. Collections.

***

JX   International Law
                        Foreign Relations.

International questions treated as sources of or contributions to the theory of international law. All histories of
events, diplomatic history of wars, etc., go in History.
In case of doubt favor D-F (History).

***

PD   Germanic philology and languages.
2900-2999   New Norwegian (Landsmaal).
                For works exclusively or prevailingly devoted to
                the "Landsmaal" (i. e. the normalization and
                fusion of old and modern Norwegian dialects in-
                to one language, first systematically attempted
                by I. Aasen (1833-1896) in his Norsk grammatik,
                Christiana, 1864).

***

TA   Engineering - General.
497   Wind pressure in relation to engineering.
                Cf. TG 303, Bridges.
                    TH 891, Buildings.
                    TJ 825, Windmills.
                    TL 570-575, Aerodynamics.

***

N   FINE ARTS

                          History
5300   General.
5310   Prehistoric art. Origins of art.
            Cf. NK 1177, Ornament.
5315   Ancient and medieval art.
         Ancient art. Artistic archeology.
            Methods and aims of archeology, CC.
            Inscriptions, CN.

Historical studies, D.
Architecture, NA.
Sculpture, NB.
Prehistoric archeology, GN.
American archeology, E, F.
Antiquities (Local), D, E, and F.
Critics and historians (e. g. Winckelmann), N 8370-8375.

***

NK   ART APPLIED TO INDUSTRY

Other Arts and Art Industries

Alphabets. Initials.
          Cf. NE 2710   Engraving.
              ND 3335   Illumination.
              T 371   Mechanical drawing — Lettering.
              NA 2725   Architectural drawing — Lettering.
              TT 300   Sign-painting, show-cards, etc.
              Z 250-251 Type and type-founding.
3600   General (all periods).
3650   Beadwork.
3660   Book ornamentation.
          Cf. Book arts (General), Z 276; Illustrated books, Z 1023.
              Cover design, NC 973.
              Binding, Z 266.
              Illumination, ND 2890-3395.
              Alphabets and initials, NK 3600-3640.
              Book plates, Z 993-995.

***

PREFERRED CLASSES

(Material collocated elsewhere)

LB Theory and practice of education.
        Secondary education. High schools.
          Curriculum.
          Individual branches.
              Prefer subdivision "Study and teaching" under subjects
                in Classes B-J, M-Z.
(1630)   Language, see P-PM.
(1647)   Science, see Q 181-183.
(1655)   Geology, see QE 40-45.
(1676)   Home economics, see TX.

***

N Fine arts.
        Special subjects of art.
8215   Literary subjects. Scenes from the works of great authors.
              Illustrations by several artists, accompanying the text, are
                to be classified preferably in PA-PT, with added entry
                here. Added entries may also be made for the artists in
                NC, NE, or ND.
              Illustrations after the drawings or paintings of special ar-
                tists are to be classified under the artist in NC, NE, or

ND, as the case may be, with added entry here and in PA-PT under the author illustrated. In the case of authors such as Shakespeare, Dante, and Goethe classification in Literature is to be preferred.

***

PJ   Assyriology.
        Cuneiform writing.
            Treatises.
3191   To 1870.
3193   Later, 1871-
3197   History (of the decipherment).
3211   Origin and development.
            Special kinds.
(3215)   Sumerian, see PJ 4010.   Prefer
(3216)   Babylonian (New Babylonian).   PJ 3191-3211.
(3217)   Assyrian (New Assyrian).
(3221.1)   Hittite, see P 945.

***

CN   EPIGRAPHY

        Cf. Cuneiform writing, PJ 3191-3225.
            Hieroglyphics, P 211, PJ 1091-1097.
            Petroglyphs, GN 799.P4.
            Picture writing of the American Indians, E 98.P6.

        Ancient inscriptions.
130   Ancient Oriental, Asiatic, and African.
                Special languages, prefer PJ-PL.
135   Classic Orient (General).
(140)   Chinese, see PL 2995.
(165)   Hittite inscriptions, see P 945.
(170)   Old Persian, Achaemenian, etc., see PK 6128.
(190)   Semitic, see PJ 3081-3095.

***

QL   ZOOLOGY
                   Animal Culture in SF.

1   Periodicals, societies, etc.

                   EMBRYOLOGY

Works on the development of special types of organisms are to be classed in QL 958 or 959. Works on the development of special embryonic parts (e. g. germinal layers, primitive streak, notochord, etc.) and works on the later development of embryos are to be classed in QL 971. In the case of special organs preference is to be given to comparative anatomy, QL 821-950, with added entry in QL 958 or 959.
        Cf. QM 601-611, Human embryology.

951   Periodicals, societies, etc. Collections.

***

RC   Internal medicine. Practice of medicine.
49   Psychosomatic medicine.
            Cf. RC 435-576, Psychiatry.
            For psychosomatic aspects of individual diseases or
                diseases of an organ, region, or system, see the classi-
                fication of the disease.

                                    ***

SB   Plant culture and horticulture.
        Flowers and flower culture. Ornamental plants.
450   Floral picture books.
            Cf. QK 98, Pictorial works (Botany).
        Language of flowers, see QK 84.

                                    ***

U   Military science (General).
        History of military science.
            For military history, see D- F.
27   General.

                                    ***

JC   Political theory.
        Purpose, functions, and relations of the state.
(521)   The state and education, see LC 71-245.
(526)   The state and public hygiene, see RA.
(538)   The state and production, see HD 71-76; 3611-4730.

                                    ***

TH   BUILDING

            Buildings – Construction with Reference to Use
                    (Including specifications)

(4021) Public buildings, see NA 4170-4510.
(4161)   Monuments, Memorial arches, etc. , see NA 9320-9425.
(4171)   Mausoleums, etc. , see NA 6120-6199.
(4221)   Churches, see NA 4800-6113.
(4311) Mercantile and industrial buildings, see NA 6210-6581.
(4411) Transportation and storage buildings, see NA 6300-6370.
(4421)   Railway stations, see TF 300, NA 6310.
(4431)   Dock buildings, see TC 355.
(4441)   Ferry-houses, see NA 6330.
(4451)   Warehouses, see NA 6340.

                                    ***

Classes for Added Entries.

        Although all class numbers can be used for cross-references in the

Card Shelflist, there are some which were provided for this purpose alone.

These numbers are generally enclosed in parentheses.

BC Logic.
40-48   Special systems and theories.
                    Classed at present in B, General philosophic systems,
                    but to be represented here in card shelflist by ref-
                    erence entries.

***

JX International law.
            Collections. Documents. Cases.
191   Separate treaties.
                    Reference entry is to be made in card shelflist in
                    JX 200-1200, subdivision (7) under each country
                    which is party to the treaty ...

***

N Fine arts.
            Art and the state. Public art.
(8900-9084)   Special countries and cities. Table II.
                    For added entries for art commissions, etc.,
                    e. g. 8925.D6, District of Columbia;
                            8927.B7, Boston.
                    Books to be shelved N 6501-7413.

***

NC Graphic arts.
            Technique.
                Perspective.
(753)   Studies of perspective in the works of special artists.
                    (To be classified with biography, ND 237-1113,
                    NA, NC, etc., with added entry here.)

***

PA Greek philology and language.
            Grammar.
(389)   Grammatical usage of particular groups of writers,
                see PA (3517)-3564.
                    Make reference here.
(391)   Grammatical usage of particular authors.
                    Prefer classification under author, PA 3818-4500.
                    Make general reference to author here.

***

            Style. Composition. Rhetoric.
(408)   Particular groups of writers (A-Z, by groups),
                see PA (3517)-3564.
                    Make reference here.
(409)   Particular authors.
                    Prefer classification under author, PA 3818-4500.
                    Make general reference to author here.

***

PA Greek literature.
            Aesopus.

PA 3852   Translations and paraphrases.
               Latin.
                    Romulus. "Aesopus latinus. "
(3853)   Medieval derivations. [5]

---

[5]Cf. PA ... (Medieval Latin). The medieval fable literature forms a class
by itself with which the student of classical literature is little concerned.
Hence classification in PA ..., or in PQ-PT, of all the medieval collections
and their translations seems to be advisable. References, for the sake of
collecting all the Aesopus material, may be made here.

***

A separate class for bibliography (Z) having been developed in 1898

before plans were definitely settled for the new L. C. Classification, the need

for relating bibliography to the various subject fields was apparently felt,

and development of some classes included provisions like the following in

Class P:

P Philology. Linguistic.
29   Encyclopedias. Dictionaries.
(30)   Bibliography. Bio-bibliography, see Z 7001-7005.
       Make reference here.

***

501-769   Indo-European (Indo-Germanic) philology.
518   Encyclopedias. Dictionaries.
(519)   Bibliography, Bio-bibliography, see Z 7001-7005.
               Make general reference here.

***

PA Classical philology.
(29)   Bibliography. Bio-bibliography, see Z 7016-7026.
       Make reference here.

Alternative Classification.

Because the Library developed its classification solely for its own use,

little thought was originally given to alternative classes. Later, as more and

more libraries adopted the system, some consideration was given to the prob-

lem, chiefly in correspondence, unfortunately not in published statements. It

must be admitted, however, that the alternatives are not numerous.

Major changes could be effected by the transfer of subclasses, or di-

visions, from one class to another, e. g. , GB Physical Geography and GC

Oceanography to new subclasses QEA and QEB under Geology. Such transfers,

however, result in the addition rather than the integration of subject matter.
Dr. Koenig suggested that many subjects of interest to the student of Classical Philology could be brought within the orbit of PA by affixing a small
location label (PA), rather than by reclassification. The "sections" he enumerated illustrate the relativity of classification to purposes and interest:[3]

B	165-708	Greek and Roman philosophy.
BL	700-820	Greek and Roman mythology and religion.
CD	5201-5241, 5369. 5375-5377	Greek and Roman seals.
CE	42, 46	Greek and Roman chronology.
CJ	5581-5690	Greek and Roman medals.
CJ	4861-4865	Greek and Roman tokens.
CN		Greek and Roman epigraphy.
DE	1-5, 46-71	Classical antiquities.

cf. GT 175, 545-555, 2670, 3170; GV 17-35, 213, 573; HC 37-39;
HF 373-378; HG 237, 1555; HJ 215-228; HQ 510-511, 1134, 1136;
HT 863; JC 71-89; JV 93-98; JX 2011-2035; LA 71-81; LB
85-91; QC 84; U 33-35; V 37-39.

DF	10-16, 76-129	Greek antiquities.
DG	11-16, 75-143	Roman antiquities.
DE	1-12	Greek and Roman history.
DF	1-16, 207-289	Greek history.
DG	1-16, 201-365	Roman history.
DE	23-31	Greek and Roman geography.

cf. G 84-87; GA 213.

DF	27-41, 221, 251-289	Greek geography.
DG	27-59	Roman geography.
G	82-87	Ancient geography.
K		Greek and Roman Law.
ML	167-169	Greek and Roman music.
N	5605-5896	Greek and Roman art.
R	126-127	Greek and Roman medicine.
S	429-431	Greek and Roman agriculture.
T	16; TA 16	Greek and Roman technology and engineering.
Z	114	Greek and Roman paleography.

Less drastic, but more numerous and feasible, are the possibilities
afforded where "Cf." and "Prefer" notes are found. Libraries using the L. C.
Classification might find the alternatives better suited to their needs. Following are a few examples where a choice is possible, depending upon the
library's special field:

HB Economic theory.
71   Economics as a science.
72   Relation to philosophy, religion, ethics.

or one of the following:

B Philosophy (General).
53   Theory. Method. Scope. Relations.
63   Relation to economics and sociology.

BJ Ethics.
53   Relation to economics.

BR Christianity. Church history.
115   Christianity in relation to special subjects, A-Z.
             e.g. .E3 Economics. Labor.

***

LB Theory and practice of education.
         Primary education.
            Branches of study.
               Arithmetic, see QA 135-139.
(1534)   General works.
(1535)   By country, A-Z.

or

QA Mathematics.
         Arithmetic.
135   Study and teaching.
137   Teaching fractions.
139   Examinations, etc.

Other alternatives are described in the following chapter under Biography, Language and Literature, and Philosophy — subjects which the Library of Congress arranged in an unorthodox way.

The provision of alternative classes such as have been here described can accomplish a twofold purpose: (1) develop the classification to meet the needs of libraries in fields where the emphasis on subject collocation differs from Library of Congress practice, and (2) develop a classed catalog representing the various relationships of a subject with other fields.

CHAPTER XVII

Description: Conclusion

The description of the L. C. Classification thus far has dealt with theory and structure, with enumerative and non-enumerative subdivisions, and
with their integration into a systematic whole. In this chapter are treated
the extrinsic auxiliaries, notation and index, and the records in which the
contents of the classes are listed. A brief description of three areas in which
the Library of Congress departed from current norms or canons will conclude this exposition of the L. C. Classification.

Notation.

The correlation of the physical order of books and entries with the abstract order of the classification is effected by notation. As described in
Chapter I, two systems of symbols are needed: external notation for the classes and divisions, and internal for the arrangement of their contents.

External Notation

The main classes are designated by capital letters, the subclasses, with
the exception of the early classes Z and E- F, by two letters, and divisions and
subdivisions by integral numbers in ordinary sequence. Decimal numbers
are also used for expansion and for individual topics and geographic subdivisions. For topics in which no logical principle of classification is discernible, for biographees, and for the simple arrangement of countries, regions,
cities, etc. , in one alphabet, Cutter numbers are employed.

Q	SCIENCE
Q	Science (General).
QA	Mathematics.
QB	Astronomy.
QC	Physics.
81-119	Weights and Measures.
122-168	Experimental Mechanics.
811-849	Terrestrial Magnetism.
851-999	Meteorology.

885-896   Atmospheric pressure.
     889   Distribution, isobars, etc.

QE   Geology.
389   Special groups of minerals.
  .1   Native elements.
  .2   Sulphides, [etc.]
  .3   Sulpho salts.
  .4   Haloids.
391   Descriptions of special minerals, A- Z.
               e. g. .A5   Amber.
                     .B35 Barite.
                     .C2   Calcite.

           Volcanoes.
523   Individual, A- Z.
               e. g. .C7 Colima.
                     .E8 Etna.
                     .K5 Kilauea.

New subclasses, divisions, and topics can be added to the system in
several ways, by using

1. Letters I, O, (W)[1], X, and Y, which have not yet been used.

2. A third letter, e. g. Harvard's NAB Landscape Architecture and

    NAC City Planning. It is possible, by using the device of a third

    or even a fourth letter, to substitute completely new schedules.

3. Intervening numbers, as yet unused.

4. Decimal numbers.

5. Cutter numbers.

Internal Notation

The arrangement of the material within each class is generally alphabetical, by author and title. The "internal" notation used to designate the individual books is based upon a simplification of the book numbers devised
by Charles A. Cutter. The specificity of the L. C. Classification keeps the
number of books in each class at a minimum so that the long numbers in the
Cutter tables are unnecessary. The following tables form the basic pattern
of the scheme:

1. Where initial consonants (except the letter S) are followed by
        vowels or r,
     for second letter: a e i o r u
        use number: 3 4 5 6 7 8

2. Where initial vowels are followed by consonants,
   for second letter: b d l m n p r s t
   use number : 2 3 4   5 6 7 8

3. Where the initial letter S is followed by consonants or vowels,
   for second letter: a ch e h i m o p   u
   use number: 2 3 4 5   6   7-8 9

Since the numbers are used decimally they are indefinitely expansible:

1. Names beginning with consonants:

Carter	.C3	Cox	.C65
Cecil	.C4	Crocket	.C7
Cinelli	.C5	Croft	.C73
Corbett	.C6	Cullen	.C8

2. Names beginning with vowels:

Abernathy	.A2	Appleby	.A6
Adams	.A3	Archer	.A7
Aldrich	.A4	Arundel	.A78
Allen	.A45	Atwater	.A87
Ames	.A5	Austin	.A9

3. Names beginning with the letter S:

Sabine	.S15	Shank	.S45
Saint	.S2	Shipley	.S5
Schaefer	.S3	Smith	.S6
Schwedel	.S35	Steel	.S7
Scott	.S37	Storch	.S75
Seaton	.S4	Sturges	.S8
Sewell	.S43	Sullivan	.S9

The same plan is used to determine the notation for subjects, topics,

biographees, countries, etc.,which are arranged alphabetically under a single

number.

```
QL  Zoology
          Vertebrates.
              Aves (Birds).
696               Systematic divisions (Orders), A-Z.
                      e. g.  .A5  Anseriformes (Geese, ducks, etc. )
                             .G8  Gruiformes (Cranes, rails, etc. )
                             .P2  Passeriformes (Perching birds)

UH  Medical and sanitary service.
          Biography.
              Including nurses.
347           Individual, A-Z.
                  e. g.  . N6  Nightingale, Florence.

HG  Banking.
          Practice.
1656          Reserves.  By country, A-Z.
                  .A3  General works.
                  .G3  Germany.
                  .S9  Switzerland.
                  .U5  United States.
```

A further adaptation of the Cutter number for book arrangement appears in the so-called "official Cutter" (.A1, .A2, etc., as needed). This is used extensively for publications of government organizations, societies, and other corporate bodies and also, at times, for personal authors, when they constitute the subject represented by the class or subdivision. Used in such classes the Cutter number is a device by which all works for which the particular organization or personal author is responsible are kept together on the shelf ahead of descriptive or critical works by other authors. This type of Cutter number may appear in table form if applicable to a number of subjects. The following illustrate this practice.[2]

```
HA  Statistics.
        United States.
730         Cities, A-Z.
                Under each:
                    .A1-5  Official.
                    .A6-Z  Nonofficial.

HD  Economic history.
        Right of eminent domain. Expropriation.
        United States.
1262        Federal.
                .A1-5  Documents.
1263        States, A-W.
                .A1-3  Documents.
1265        Other countries, A-Z.
                Under each:
                    (1)  .A1-29  Collections.
                         .A3     Separate documents. By date.
                         .A5     Laws. By date.[3]
                         .A6-Z   General works.
                    (2)          Local, A-Z.

 Q  Science (General).
181     Study and teaching.
            Universities, colleges, etc.
                Under each:
                    .A1-7  Official publications.
                    .A1-4     Serials.
                    .A5-7     Nonserials.
                    .A8-Z  Monographs, by author.

PR  English literature.
        Anglo-Saxon literature.
            Individual authors and works.
            Aelfric.
                Separate works.
                    Under each:
                                Texts.
                    .A1         By date.
```

```
                      .A21-39  Translations.
                      .A4-49      French.
                      .A6-69      Other languages.  By language.
                      .A7-Z    Criticism.
          1525          Homilies.
```

Table 4 at the end of subclass B Philosophy (General) illustrates the provision of "official Cutter" numbers applicable to each philosopher assigned one integral number; these numbers place collected and separate works before critical works.

The ".A1 plus" numbers are also used where it is desired to place, at the beginning of a class, form or common subject subdivisions for which integral numbers are not available or to subdivide a minor topic.

```
      HC  Economic history and conditions.
            20th century.
          57      Reconstruction, 1919-1939.
                    .A15A-Z  Periodicals and societies.
                              Documents.
                    .A2          League of Nations.
                    .A3A-Z       Individual countries.
                    .A4          International offices.
                    .A5          Conferences.

      HB  Economic theory.
            History of economics.
        101-129     By country.
                      Under each:
                    .A2      History.
                    .A3      Collective biography.
                    .A5-Z  Individual biography.
```

In all cases these book or topic numbers are assigned at the shelflist and are recorded there as well as in the books and on the cards. The resultant call number _ class plus book number – links book and records and makes it a simple matter to find and replace the volume used.

Index.

At the present time, and until a combined index has been developed, it is more precise to use the plural indexes, rather than index. The entries in the indexes published thus far refer, with only a few exceptions, to the schedules of the classes and subclasses with which they are printed. Of varying fullness, the indexes are relative; specific topics are listed and their relations as well. The following extracts from dissimilar subjects illustrate the indexes.

BL-BX RELIGION

N

Nahum: BS 1621-5.
National council of the evangeli-
cal free churches: BX 6.N3.
National federation of religious
liberals: BX 6.N4.
Natural history
Bible: BS 661-7.
Religion: BL 262-3.
Natural theology: BL 175-290.
Nature-worship: BL 435-57.
Naval services: BV 199.N3.
Nehemiah: BS 1361-5.
Neonomianism: BT 813.
Nestorian church: BX 150-9.
Nestorianism: BT 1440.
New Church: BX 8701-49.

Novatian: BR 1720.N8.
Novenas (general): BX 2170.N7.
Numbers, Book of: BS 1261-5.
Nuncios: BX 1908.
Nuns and nunneries: BX 4210-6.
Nymphs: BL 325.F4.

O

Oaths.
Church laws: BV 763.O2.
Moral theology: BV 4780.O2.
Quakers: BX 7748.O2.
Obadiah: BS 1591-5.
Object lessons: BV 1535.
Oblates: BX 3820.
Women: BV 4410.O2.
Occidental mythology: BL 690-980.
Odin: BL 870.O3.

H SOCIAL SCIENCES

Industrial surveys: HC 28.
Industrial villages, Model:
HD 7526-7630.
Industrial Workers of the World
(I. W. W.): HD 8055.
Industries, Municipal, see Munici-
pal industries: HD 4421-4730.
Industries, State, see State indus-
tries: HD 3840-4420.
Industries and railways: HE 1044.
Industry, see Economic history:
HC-HD.
Industry, Control of: HD 45.
Industry, Decentralization of:
HD 2353.

Instalment buying: HF 5568.
Instalment plan: HF 5568.
Insurance: HG 9251-62.
Instinct in social psychology: HM 255.
Institutional care of the poor: HV 59-61.
Instruments, Taxes on: HJ 5801-19.
Insurable interest: HG 8517.
Insurance: HG 8011-9970.
Accounting: HG 8077.
Advertising: HF 6161.I6.
Agents: HG 8091-8102.
Annuals: HG 8019.
Associations: HG 8016.
Business: HG 8075-8102.

N FINE ARTS

Monograms: NK 3640.
Engraving: NE 2710.
Monumental sculpture: NB 1330 -
1880.
Reliefs: NB 1290-1.
Monuments, Municipal: NA 9335-55.
Monuments, Preservation of
Artistic monuments: N 8850.
Historic monuments: CC 135.
Monuments, Religious: NB 1750.
Monuments, Sepulchral: NB 1800-80.
Moorish art: N 6260-71.
Architecture: NA 380-88.
Decoration and ornament: NK 1275.
Industrial arts: NK 725.
Interior decoration: NK 1820.

O

Obelisks: DT 62.5.
Office buildings: NA 6230-3.
Old masters (Books of reproductions)
Drawings: NC 1020-1055.
Paintings: ND 1200.
Opera houses: NA 6820-40.
Orders of architecture: NA 2810-17.
Oriental art: N 7260-7379.
Ancient: N 5343-5.
Ceramics: NK 3805.
Decoration and ornament: NK 1185.
Furniture: NK 2285.
Industrial arts: NK 620.

R MEDICINE

Prosthetic dentistry: RK 641-666. | Psychoneurotic disorders: RC 530-552.
Prostigmine: RM 666.P86. | Psychopathic personality: RC 555.
Protectives, Skin: RM 307. | Psychopathology, see Psychiatry.
Protein therapy: RM 280. | Psychoses: RC 512-528.
Proteinotherapy: RM 280. | Psychosomatic disorders
Protozoan diseases: | Cause of skin diseases: RL 701-751.
  RC 118, 118.7, 120-216. | Psychosomatic medicine: RC 49.
Protracted pregnancy: RG 650. | Psychosurgery: RD 594.
Pruritus: RL 721. | Psychotherapy: RC 321-344, 475-489.
Psittacosis: RC 182.P8. | Hypnosis: RC 490-499.
Psoriasis: RL 321. | Mental healing: RZ 400-406.
Psychiatrists | Psychotic art: N 71.5.
  Biography: R 134, 153-684. | Ptomaine poisoning: RC 143.
  Directories: RC 335. | Public baths: RA 605-606.

Shelflist and Classed Catalog.

In the Library of Congress the shelflist and classed catalog have been inextricably interwoven since 1898 when the combined shelflist and classed catalog were developed for Class Z Bibliography and Library Science. The twin problem of classification and catalog then came to the fore: should the catalog be alphabetico-classed after the fashion of Spofford's 1869 Catalogue, classed in the order of the new classification, or should it follow the dictionary pattern which was being widely adopted? The dictionary pattern was selected because of the Library's desire to cooperate with other American libraries.[4] The Library, however, could not accept without reservations the principle of specific entry in the subject component of the dictionary catalog. Its "peculiar constituency" and administrative economy necessitated the introduction of synthetic devices to prevent complete dispersion: inverted headings, combined subjects, and the subordination of some subjects or aspects to others.[5]

The decision concerning subject vs. place, i.e. the subordination of place to subject or subject to place, was sometimes based upon a desire to correlate the dictionary catalog with the classification. Hanson, Chief of the Catalogue Division at the time, believed that strict adherence to the principle of specific entry would prove "well-nigh impossible in the catalog of a large and rapidly growing library." He and his assistant, Martel, unlike Cutter, thought that a classed catalog was essential to a scholarly library to supplement.

the dictionary catalog. Years later Martel stated his philosophy:

> Coming now to changes in the state of opinion with respect
> to the best form of the subject catalog there appears to be little
> if any abatement of the sharpness of disagreement, at least among
> librarians ministering mainly to professional and research work-
> ers. For general reference use in the public library the diction-
> ary catalog may be said to have proved its superiority — I make
> the reservation that in libraries mainly or exclusively devoted to
> reference service a classified catalog is needed, not to say indis-
> pensable, in addition. The shelflist fitted with guides and refer-
> ence entries answers the purpose very well. [6]

Two "shelflists" were therefore developed: the memorandum shelflist,

consisting of folio sheets in which brief entries were entered, and the Card

Shelflist of printed cards. [7] The Card Shelflist, despite its name, was a classed

catalog (of main entries, analytics, and references [added entries]) until 1940

when the Sheet Shelflist was discontinued. This first step toward a single

shelflist on cards was to make brief entries in the Sheet Shelflist in order

to guard against discrepancies in the call numbers of new material listed be-

fore the Card Shelflist sequence could be verified. In 1946-47 a special pro-

ject for supplying the Card Shelflist with brief entries for old material as

yet represented only in the Sheet Shelflist finally transferred call-number

control to the Card Shelflist and eliminated the need for making "skeleton"

entries on the sheets. The final step of conversion still awaits the transfer

to cards of the full information on all Sheet Shelflist entries antedating 1940.

With these changes and the discontinuance of added entries in 1942 the Card

Shelflist has lost most of the "classed catalog"[8] features it once had.

The advantageous use of the references Martel suggested is described

by Dr. Koenig in the "Prefatory Note" to Class P-PA:

> Shelf-list references. — Treatises dealing with several sub-
> jects are classified where they are of main interest; the other
> subjects are represented by means of shelf-list references under
> the various groups of classification to which they belong — for
> example, English literature and the classics ... [Lectures.]
> Collected by G. S. Gordon (Oxford, Clarendon press, 1912), contains:
> Tragedy, by C. Murray; Platonism, by J. A. Stewart; Theophrastus,
> by G. S. Gordon; Greek romances, by J. S. Philimore; Ciceronianism,
> by A. C. Clark; Vergil, by H. W. Garrod; Ovid, by G. S. Owen; Satura,
> by R. J. E. Tiddy; Senecan tragedy, by A. D. Godley. Each of these
> lectures may appear under its own proper classification number
> (indicated in red ink on the left hand upper corner) in the card

shelf list, the classification number at the foot of the printed
card showing the actual location of the collection; (main classification: PN 883 [Classical antiquity and literature in relation to modern literature];[9] references: PA 3134 [Single lectures on Greek drama], 4335 [History of Platonism], 4450 [In-
terpretation and criticism of Theophrastus], etc.)

Likewise, special subdivisions or aspects of certain subjects closely related to (and sometimes combined with) subdivisions and aspects of other subjects belonging to different
classes may by means of shelf-list references be represented
where they are of main interest – e. g. , Warren, Sir Thomas
Herbert, Virgil in relation to the place of Rome in the history
of civilization, Oxford, 1921: PA 6825 [Criticism and interpretation of Virgil since 1800]; references: PA 6019 [Relations of
Latin literature to history, civilization, etc.]; DG 78 [Roman
antiquities]; Ferguson, Wm. Duncan, The legal terms common
to the Macedonian inscriptions and the New Testament, Chicago,
1913 (Historical and linguistic studies in literature related to
the New Testament, 2d ser. vol. II, pt. 3): PA 875 [Semantics
of New Testament Greek]; references: CN (Inscriptions); K (Law).

Finally, shelf-list references may take the place of actual
specific classification wherever the alphabetical arrangement
under author is preferred and a classified list of subjects is
desired. The schedules for authors such as Homer, Plato, and
Virgil and the subdivisions under history of Greek or Roman
literature are illustrations in point.

In many cases topics are represented as shelf-list references to avoid too intricate a system of shelf arrangement. Libraries preferring specific classification will disregard the
curves. If need be, additional decimal numbers may be assigned
to subtopics now left without specific notation (cf. PA 3150; 3219
and 3138; 3984; 4040-54, etc.).

General shelf-list references. – In order to avoid duplica-
tion of entries, a single reference to the actual classification
may suffice. For instance, under PA (391) "Grammatical usage
of particular authors, " a single reference may be made to the
treatises on the language of a given author classified with that
author (e. g. , PA (391).H7: For treatises on the language of Homer, see PA 4175-4209. Cf. also P (30); P (519); PA (2072), etc. ,
and note 17 on p. 123.)

Experience has proved that by means of shelf-list references consistently and conscientiously made a detailed systematic bibliography may be compiled, useful alike to reference librarians and investigators and supplementing in many ways the
dictionary catalogue.

These are the elements which transform a shelflist into a classed catalog.

The added entries, in addition to the regular entries for the main subject of

a book or collection, introduce "depth analysis" by representing (1) a part

of a series classified collectively, (2) special subdivisions, aspects, or rela-

tions of a subject, (3) related subjects, and (4) alternative classes to serve

special interests.

Biography. Language and Literature. Philosophy.

The classification of Biography, Language and Literature, and Philosophy deserves attention since the arrangement of these subjects differs markedly from the canons of classification which prevailed when the schedules were developed.

Biography

It is possible to classify biography in several ways: by form in a biography class, regardless of subject; by form subarranged by subject; and by subject. These alternatives can be schematized as follows.

```
1. Form class:          Biography
      Biographees:          Bach, Johann S.
                            Bache, Franklin
                            Bacon, Francis

2. Form class:          Biography
      Subject:              Philosophy
        Biographee:           Bacon
      Subject:              Music
        Biographee:           Bach
      Subject:              Science
                              Chemistry
      Biographee:             Bache

3. Subject:             Philosophy
      Biographee:           Bacon
   Subject:             Music
      Biographee:           Bach
   Subject:             Science
                           Chemistry
      Biographee:           Bache
```

The policy of the Library of Congress is succinctly stated in a note at the beginning of subclass CT Biography, "General works: Collections and Individual biography not regarded as illustrative of any one special class or subject represented in the schedules of other classes. Cf. Bio-bibliography in Class Z. "

The following examples from various classes illustrate the provisions made for this subject.

```
GV  Recreation.
         Theatrical dancing.
1785        Biography.
         .A1     Collective.
```

```
GV 1785          .A2-Z  Individual.
                    e. g.  .D8  Duncan, Isadora.
                           .P3  Pavlova, Anna.

      GN  Anthropology.
              Biography.
      20          Collective.
      21          Individual, A-Z.
                    e. g.  .H7  Hrdlička, Aleš.

      QK  Botany.
              Biography.
      26          Collective.
      31          Individual, A-Z.
                    e. g.  .G8  Gray, Asa.

      ND  Painting.
              Biography.
                  Cf.  N 40, Fine arts (General).
              Collective.
      34          Early works to 1800.
      35          General works, 1801-.
      36          Popular works.
      38          Women painters.
                  Cf.  N 43, Fine arts (General).
              Individual, see ND 201-1113.
```

ND 201-1113, to which reference is made in the last illustration, stands for

"History of painting in special countries" and calls for application of Table

IV. [10] From this the number derived for biography of the French woman ar-

tist, Bonheur, for example, is ND 553. B6.

```
      HB  Economic theory.
              History of economics.
  101-129        By country.
                    Under each:
                    .A2      History.
                    .A3      Collective biography.
                    .A5-Z Individual biography.
      107        Germany.
```

According to the subarrangement table for countries the number derived for

Werner Sombart, the German economist, is HB 107.S75.

   The subdivisions for rulers, statesmen, philosophers, and noted literary

men are more extensive.

```
      DA  England.
              Victorian era, 1837-1901.
                  Victoria.
      552          Journal, letters, etc.
      553          Memoirs by contemporaries.
      554          Biography.
```

```
555          Personal special.
556          Compends.
557          Juvenile.
558          Minor.  Pamphlets, etc.
  .5            Jubilee pamphlets.
559        Other royal biography, A-Z.
             e. g.  .A1 Albert, prince consort.

JA   Political Science.
         Biography of publicists.
             For statesmen, prefer D-F.
             Cf.  JX, International law.
92         Collective.
93         American.
94         English.
95         French.
96         German.
97         Italian.
98         Other.
```

By far the most detailed biography subdivisions are found in subclasses PR
and PS English and American Literatures. These tables range from one integer or a Cutter number to 48 or 98 numbers, as shown below. Special provisions are also made within the schedules for the more voluminous authors,
e. g. Shakespeare, Byron, etc.

SUBDIVISIONS UNDER INDIVIDUAL AUTHORS [11]

I (98 nos.)	II (48 nos.)		Authors with forty-eight or ninety-eight numbers.
			Biography, Criticism, etc.
(50)	(28)	(78)	Bibliography, see Z 8001-9000.
51	29	79	Periodicals, Societies, Collections.
52	30	80	Dictionaries, Indexes, etc.
			General encyclopedic dictionaries only.
			Special dictionaries with subject.
			e. g. Characters, see 78 (Table I); 39, 89 (Table II).
			Concordances and dictionaries, see 91-92 (Table I); 45, 95 (Table II).
			General works.
53	31.A2	81.A2	Autobiography.
54	.A3	.A3	Journals; Letters; Memoirs.
55	.A5-Z	.A5-Z	General works.
56			Early life. Education.
57	32	82	Love and marriage. Relation to women.
58			Later life.
59	33	83	Relations to contemporaries. Times, etc.
			Cf. 73 (Table I); 36, 86 (Table II).

I (98 nos.)	II (48 nos.)		Authors with forty-eight or ninety-eight numbers. (Continued.)
60	34	84	Homes and haunts. Local associations. Landmarks. Cf. DA.
61			Anniversaries. Celebrations.
62			Memorial addresses. Treatment in literature.
63			Poetry.
64	35	85	Fiction.
65			Iconography. Portraits.
66			Monuments.
67			Relics.
68	36	86	Authorship.
69			Manuscripts. Authorship. For textual criticism, see 89 (Table I); 43, 93 (Table II).
70			Forgeries, etc. Cf. 42, 43, 45 (Table I); 23-4, 73-4 (Table II).
71			Sources.
72			Forerunners.
73			Associates. Followers. Circle. School. Cf. 59 (Table I); 33, 83 (Table II).
74			Allusions.
75	37	87	Chronology of works.
			Criticism and interpretation.
76	38	88	General works. Genius, etc. Prefer 55 (Table I); 31, 81 (Table II).
77			Philosophy. Prefer 76 or 82 (Table I), and corresponding numbers of Table II.
			Characters.
78	39	89	General.
			Special.
79			Groups, Classes. e. g. Women.
80	40	90	Individual.
81	41	91	Plots, Scenes, Time, etc.
	42.A-Z	92.A-Z	Treatment and knowledge of special subjects.
82			Philosophy. Religion. Ethics.
83			Law, Politics, etc.
84			History.
85			Art.
86			Nature.
87			Science.
88			Other, A-Z.
89	43	93	Textual criticism, commentaries, etc. To include discussion of manuscripts of classical or medieval authors and works.
90	44	94	Language, Style, etc. Prefer 76 (Table I); 38, 88 (Table II).
91	45	95	Dictionaries. Concordances.
92			Dictionaries.

SUBDIVISIONS UNDER INDIVIDUAL AUTHORS   (Continued.)

I (98 nos.)	II (48 nos.)		Authors with forty-eight or ninety- eight numbers
93	46	96	Concordances. Grammar. General. Special.
94			Use of words.
95			Syntax.
96	47	97	Versification, meter, rhythm, etc.
97	48	98	Dialect, etc.

The content of the biography class CT, thus restricted by the many

provisions under special subjects, comprises only the following divisions.

BIOGRAPHY

CT

21- 85	Biography as an art, etc.
93- 205	General collections.
210-3090	National.
3150	Individuals not identified with any country.
3200-9998	By subject.
3200-3830	Women.

National biography under countries is subarranged according to the two tables

below.

TABLES OF SUBDIVISIONS
(CT 210-3150)

I

0	Serials. Yearbooks.
1	Collections.
2	Early works to 1800.
3	Dictionaries, 1801-
4	General works, 1801-
5	General special. Special aspects.
6	Miscellaneous and minor.
7	Juvenile.
	By period.
(8)	Ancient, see D.
(9)	Medieval, see D.
	Modern.
10	15th-16th centuries.
11	17th-18th centuries.
12	19th-20th centuries.
13	20th century.
14	Colonies (General).
	Prefer CT 278-3090.
15	Local divisions, A-Z.
(16)	Cities, see D.
(17)	Rulers, see D-F.
18	Individual biography, A-Z.
	Including correspondence.
.Z9	Persons not known by name.

II

0	Serials. Yearbooks.
1	Collections.
3	General and miscellaneous works.
4	Minor works.
	By period.
	Ancient, see D.
	Medieval, see D.
	Modern.
5	To 1800.
6	1801-
7	Local divisions, A-Z.
	Cities, see D-F.
	Rulers, see D-F.
8	Individual biography, A-Z.
	Including correspondence.
.Z9	Persons not known by name.

Following National biography is

BIOGRAPHY BY SUBJECT
Based on general Library of Congress classification.
Numbers in parentheses are for added entries in card shelflist only.

Here it will be seen that, except for general biography of women, encyclope-

dists, scholars, and some miscellaneous groups, all biography is grouped by

special subject fields with CT class numbers in parentheses indicating that

the subject classes are to be preferred. Thus, although physically dispersed

on the shelves as subject-biography, the added entries under these numbers

provide for the collocation of the material in the classed catalog by biography-

subject, e. g.

```
CT
(9400)  Scientists.
(9410)     Mathematicians.
(9420)     Astronomers.
(9430)     Physicists.
(9440)     Chemists.
(9450)     Geologists.
(9460)     Naturalists.  Biologists.
(9470)        Botanists.
(9480)        Zoologists.
(9490)        Anatomists.
(9500)        Physiologists.
(9510)        Bacteriologists.
(9550)  Medicine.  Physicians.
(9600)  Agriculturists.  Horticulturists.
(9620)     Fishermen.
(9630)     Hunters.
(9650)  Technology.  Inventors.
(9670)     Engineers.
(9680)     Electricians.
```

The method thus affords a dual approach to biography:

I SHELVES AND SHELFLIST	II CLASSED CATALOG
Q Scientists 141 Collective 143 Individual, A-Z.	CT (9400) .A2 .A3-Z
QA Mathematicians 28 Collective 29 Individual, A-Z	CT (9410) .A2 .A3-Z
QB Astronomers 35 Collective 36 Individual, A-Z	CT (9420) .A2 .A3-Z

Language and Literature.

The development of schedules for the vast and voluminous area of the world's languages and literatures presented many problems. The advantages of uniform treatment throughout were carefully considered, but the final decision, like those in other subjects, was influenced by conditions peculiar to the Library, its collections (embracing copyright deposit), and the ways they would be used. It was thought that the treatment decided upon represented a good practical arrangement which at the same time preserved the essentials of the scientific order. The minor European literatures (Celtic, Romansch, Hungarian, Finnish, etc.), the dialect literatures, and the Slavic and Oriental literatures follow their language divisions in PB-PM. General and comparative literature, however, and the principal modern literatures, English, French, German, Italian, Spanish, etc., are collocated in PN-PT, apart from their language classes PC-PF. In PZ are classed fiction in English (including translations into English) and juvenile literature in English and other languages. The following synopsis reflects the arrangement.

PHILOLOGY. LINGUISTIC

    P   Comparative Philology. Linguistic.
            Indo-European Comparative Philology.
            Extinct Languages of Doubtful Relationship.
    PA   Classical Philology and Literature.
    PB   Modern Languages. General. Celtic.
    PC   Romanic.
PD-PF   Germanic.
    PD   General. Gothic. Scandinavian.
    PE   English.
    PF   Dutch. Friesian. German.
    PG   Slavic. Balto-Slavic. Albanian.
    PH   Finnish. Hungarian. Basque.
PJ-PL   Oriental.
    PJ   General. Hamitic. Semitic.
    PK   Indo-Iranian. Indo-Aryan. Armenian. Caucasian.
    PL   Altaic. Eastern Asia. Oceanica. Africa.
    PM   Hyperborean. Indian. Artificial Languages.

LITERARY HISTORY. LITERATURE

    PN   General.
    PQ   Romanic.
    PR   English.
    PS   American.
    PT   German. Dutch. Scandinavian.

Alternative arrangements are of course possible. Should it be preferred, French, Italian, Spanish, Portuguese, English, German, Dutch, and the Scandinavian literatures could immediately follow the languages. This would require an adjustment of the notation involving the use of three-letter combinations for some of the sections, e. g.

Italian language	PCD 1-1977
" literature	PCD 2001-
French language	PCF 1-1761
" literature	PCF 2001-4645
English language	PE 1-3729
" literature	PE 4001-9999
or better	PEL 1-5000
etc.	

Conversely, without changing the schemes, it would be practicable, if desired, to place the minor literatures in PV, PX, and PY by merely assigning to these literatures under the letters PV-PY blocks of numbers corresponding to those allotted to them in PB-PM – either as the scheme stands or by adapting several of the literature tables. The following literatures might thus be developed as

PV Slavic. Balto-Slavic. Albanian.

PX Finno-Ugrian and Basque.

PY Oriental.

but retain the corresponding subdivisions of PG-PL, for example:

PX 300-(498)	or 100-(298)[12]	Finnish literature.
		History.
300	100	Periodicals. Societies. Collections.
301	101	General works. Compends.
[etc.		etc.]
		Collections.
341	141	General.
342	142	Minor. Anthologies, etc.
[etc.		etc.]
		Individual authors. [12]
353	153	To 1600.
354	154	17th-18th centuries.
355	155	19th century.
356	156	20th century.
361-385	161-185	Local.
391-405	191-205	Translations.
(451-498)	(251-298)	Finnish literature. By subject (XXII).

In some of the less widely known languages divisions are provided in
their literatures for the classification by subject of material which seems
more useful kept together by language than dispersed throughout the classified collections. In other cases where general classification seems desirable
there are provisions for added entry, by subject, under the languages:

>   PH
> (451-498)   Finnish literature. By subject (XXII).
>   (Subjects other than literary history and literature
>   proper; for reference only; the material itself
>   is classified in Classes A-N, Q-Z.)

The divisions for subjects in Tables XX-XXII, XXVII, and XXVIII follow the
order of the main classification.

At the time when the foundations were being laid for the construction
of Class P, "conventional" practice called for the form classification of individual authors under Poetry, Drama, Essays, etc. Whatever value this arrangement provided for popular libraries, it did not seem suitable for a research library. Martel commented:

> In some classifications individual authors in literature
> have been classified by form under Poetry, Drama, Fiction, Es-
> says, etc. In the L. C. classification only collections are thus
> classified. A glance at the classification of individual American
> authors under Poetry, Drama, Fiction, etc., in the Dewey Decimal
> classification, for example, will quickly demonstrate the futility
> of such arrangement for the purpose of serious study: 811.3
> American poetry 1830-61 is represented by eight poets, including
> Poe (not found under Fiction) and Lowell, and not including Emer-
> son (classified with Essays) nor Holmes (with Humor); 811.4
> Poetry 1861-1900 boasts of six poets. Compare this, and the Eng-
> lish poets under 821, with any anthology, as for example Ward,
> and the absurdly vain attempt becomes manifest. On the other
> hand the student of poetry or drama, or any other form of liter-
> ature, will find all the authors of a given period and the works
> about them grouped in the L. C. scheme, and will not be at a loss
> to find his poets whether they are distinguished in other fields of
> literature or not. [13]

The following synopsis of French Literature illustrates the plan of the L. C.
system.

SYNOPSIS

FRENCH LITERATURE

>   PQ
>   History and criticism
> 1- 150   General

151- 221	Medieval
226- 307	Modern
400- 491	Poetry
500- 591	Drama
601- 771	Prose and prose fiction
781- 841	Folk literature (including texts)
	Collections
1101-1141	General
1161-1193	Poetry
1211-1241	Drama
1243-1297	Prose
	Old French Literature (to ca. 1500/50)
1300-1391	Collections
	Individual authors and works
1411-1545	To 1350/1400
1551-1595	(14th-) 15th century (to ca. 1525)
	Modern Literature
	Individual authors
1600-1709	16th century
1710-1935	17th century
1947-2147	18th century
2149-2551	19th century
2600-2651	20th century
3801-3999	Provincial, local, colonial, etc.

With the exception of the English renaissance (1500-1640), where individual authors are subarranged under the two groups Prose and poetry and The Drama, the _form_ of literature is specified only under the subdivisions History and criticism and Collections, [14] e. g.

	PQ	French literature.
		Old French literature.
		Collections.
		Poetry.
1308		Translations.
		Epic and narrative.
1309		General.
		Special.
1310		National. Chansons de geste.

Throughout all the literatures the arrangement under individual authors follows the general pattern

    Collected works
    Translations
    Individual works
    Translations
    Biography and criticism

which is contracted or expanded in accordance with the creativity of the author and his critics.

Philosophy

It is probable that Philosophy, because of its scope and abstractness, is the most difficult branch of knowledge to classify. Copleston wrote "That, practically speaking, any given thinker is limited as to the direction his thought will take, limited by the immediately preceding and the contemporary systems (limited also, we might add, by his personal temperament, his education, the historical and social situation, etc.) is doubtless true; ..."[15] To these difficulties must be added the problems of language, of publication, and of schools and theories. A rigid classification by subject seemed not only impossible but undesirable. Frequently the only existing editions of the individual works of many philosophers formed part of collections, collected works, or combinations of two or more works. It was decided therefore to collocate the resources of the Library on individual philosophers and to make added entries in the Card Shelflist under Logic, Metaphysics, Psychology, Ethics, and more specific subjects. The resultant arrangement is similar in many ways to the scheme for Literature. It provides:

OUTLINE

Philosophy (General)

```
B
  1-8     Periodicals.
 11-18    Societies.
   20     Congresses.
20.6-29   Collections.
   31     Yearbooks.
 41-48    Dictionaries.
 49-50    Terminology. Nomenclature.
   51     Encyclopedic works.
   52     Study and teaching.
 53-67    Theory. Method. Scope. Relations.
   56        Relation to theology and religion.
   61        Relation to history.
   63        Relation to economics and sociology.
   65        Relation to law and political science.
   66        Relation to literature.
   67        Relation to science.
   68     Curiosa. Miscellaneous writings. Satire, etc.
69-4695   History and systems.
 69-105     General works.
108-118     Ancient.
121-161     Orient.
125-128       China and Japan.
```

723-726	Special aspects.
723	Influence of Arabic philosophy.
725	Influence of Aristotle.
726	Influence of Northern Europe.
728-738	Special topics.
	Conceptualism see Nominalism and realism.
728	Mysticism.
731	Nominalism and realism.
732	Platonism.
734	Scholasticism.
737	Summism.
741-753	Arabian and Moorish philosophers.
755-759	Jewish philosophers.
765	European philosophers.
770-785	Renaissance philosophy.
775	General works.
778-780	Special topics.
778	Humanism.
779	Scepticism.
781-785	Individual philosophers.
790-4695	Modern philosophy.
791-798	General works.
801-804	By period.
801	17th century.
802	18th century.
803	19th century.
804	20th century.
808-843	Special topics.
808	Agnosticism.
809.A5	Animism.
812	Dualism.
814	Eclecticism.
816	Empiricism (Associationalism).
839	Scholasticism.
840	Semantics.
841	Spiritualism. The spiritual.
843	Utilitarianism.
851-945	United States.
851-855	General works.
858	Compends, outlines, etc.
861	Special topics, A-Z.
865-945	By period.
865-876	Colonial to 1750.
878-890	Revolutionary period to 1800.
893-945	19th and 20th centuries.
901-931	Early 19th century to 1860.
903-906	Special topics.
903	Scotch philosophy (Influence).
905	Transcendentalism. Brook farm. Concord school of philosophy.
908-931	Individual philosophers.
934-945	Later 19th and 20th centuries.
938-944	Special topics.
938	Evolution.
941	Idealism.
943	Monism.
945	Individual philosophers.
[981-4695	Other countries]

In expanded or abridged form the arrangement under individual philosophers is as follows:

    Collected works.
        Original texts. By date.
            Partial editions, selections, etc. By editor.
        Translations. By language, A-Z.
    Separate works.
        Subarranged:
            (1) Original texts. By date.
            (2) Translations.
                        Subarranged either by language, A-Z
                            or by the following scheme:
                            .1 Greek
                            .2 Latin.
                            .3 English.
                            .4 French.
                            .5 German.
                            .6 Italian.
                            .7 Spanish and Portuguese.
                            .8 Dutch.
                            .9 Other, A-Z.
            (3) Criticism and interpretation.
    General works.
        Biography, criticism, etc.

Then come the divisions of the subject:

    BC Logic
    BD Speculative Philosophy
            General Works
            Metaphysics
            Epistemology
            Methodology
            Ontology
            Cosmology
    BF Psychology. Parapsychology
    BH Aesthetics
    BJ Ethics

Philosophy concludes this description of the Library of Congress Classification – an exposition of the theory and structure of the system which has long been needed. Whether the treatment given in these three chapters – from theory to gross structure, through synopses and outlines to full schedules and auxiliaries – forms a satisfactory description only the future can decide.

Martin A. Roberts, when Chief Assistant Librarian, epitomized the Library's Classification in the following words:

> Its virtues are: (1) Comprehensiveness (every phase of human activity is accounted for; there is no "miscellaneous" residue), (2) particularity (topics are logical subdivisions of general subjects; not lumped within them), (3) expansiveness (new subjects find their

places by logical coordination within the existing scheme), (4) flexibility (the natural and economical arrangement of wholly different classes of material, and of material in small and large quantities is provided for), (5) practicality (the system is not based solely upon a philosophical classification of knowledge and does not force the material into arbitrary forms for the sake of logic), (6) articulation (cognate classes are at once related and differentiated by position and by necessary notes and cross references in the schedules), (7) simplicity (the notation is expressive and uncomplicated), (8) individuality (the scheme is that of the Library of Congress with its responsibility primarily to the Congress, and consequently arranges the material from that point of view), and (9) adaptability (in spite of its individuality the scheme is easily adapted to the use of other large or special libraries, American or foreign).

. . . .

In addition to enabling direct recourse to material on the shelves, by subject, the classification offers two advantages. (1) The shelf-list (the inventorial catalog which records the books in the exact order in which they are classified) becomes a class-catalog or catalogue raisonnée of the classified collections. There is now being developed a classed catalog on cards supplemental to the shelf-list. (2) The classification, as a logical development of related subjects, uses a terminology somewhat different from that employed by the catalog, where each subject stands by itself in merely alphabetic order. The varying viewpoints taken in the two processes furnish approaches to the material supplementary to each other. 16

Only ten years after the vast project had been undertaken, Martel, the

chief architect, summarized the Library's ambition and the problems en-

countered in its realization. As apt today as when written over forty five

years ago, his words form a fitting conclusion to this history and description

of the Library of Congress Classification.

It has been the endeavor from the beginning to incorporate in the classification scheme the results of the experience gained both in the first application of the schedules in reclassification and in later continued use in classifying new books. A certain ideal was kept in view but it was a practical one. The ambition was to make the best of an unrivaled opportunity and to produce a classification in which the theory and history of the subjects as represented in a great collection of books should constitute the principal basis for the construction of the scheme, compared and combined of course with their presentation as derived from other classifications and treatises. It was recognized beforehand and confirmed over and over again in the course of the undertaking that no amount of preliminary study, consultation and taking pains in the preparation of the provisional draft could produce other than a largely theoretical scheme, more or less inadequate and unsatisfactory until modified in application. A clearer and wider view of many a problem provisionally disposed of would often present itself as class after class was conscientiously worked over, discovering new aspects and relations of certain

subjects or the same relations in a different light and making
it desirable and sometimes necessary to revise an earlier decision and adopt a better solution. It may be admitted that with
all the effort spent in improving the schemes in the light of further experience an approach to the ideal in mind has been realized if at all only in a slight and imperfect degree. On the other
hand that degree might have been advanced materially if printing could have been postponed until all the schedules were completed. Many omissions, imperfections and inconsistencies might
have been eliminated if there had been more time. The responsibility for some of these may be laid in part at least upon the
hindrances incidental to the conditions under which the work had
to be carried on in order that the other services of the Library
might not be unduly interfered with. Whether the principle adopted and the manner and extent of its application were in the line
of progress remains perhaps for the future to demonstrate. [17]

CHAPTER XVIII

The Future

If, as Leibniz said, "Le présent est gros de l'avenir: le futur se pourrait lire dans le passé: l'eloigné est exprimé par le prochain," what is the future of library classification ? Many questions arise, most of them unanswerable. But first let us consider the immediate future of the L. C. Classification.

Law.

The last branch of knowledge to be brought into the Library of Congress Classification is Law. The nature of the subject, its pervasiveness, the vastness of its literature, and conflicting theories of classification make the task of developing schedules a difficult one. Unlike other disciplines, such as science and technology, which above the primitive stage are universal, legal systems are highly individual, products of various periods and cultures.

Historically, Law has received cavalier treatment at the hands of recent American classifiers. The chief responsibility for this rests upon the shoulders of Melvil Dewey, who was the first to atomize the ancient discipline, and of Charles Martel, who followed him. Both men, however, planned to develop detailed schedules for Law in their systems. In all previous classifications, Law, whatever its relative position in the hierarchy of the systems, remained an independent branch of knowledge. Brunet, who epitomized the oldest tradition, recognized the subject as one of the higher faculties and included it in his grand divisions. Bacon treated Law as a branch of Civil Philosophy; d'Alembert, a division of Morality; and Jefferson, a subdivision of Moral Philosophy. It remained for Dewey and Martel to disperse Law by "subject." Another of the higher faculties, Medicine, fortunately escaped a similar fate. The pathology and treatment of the diseases of special organs and systems were retained in Medicine, and not classed by "subject" as aspects of Anatomy and Physiology.

Accustomed to the dispersion of law, American "general" librarians took it for granted that the division was both logical and practical. As antithesis to thesis, law librarians, a small minority, became as imperialistic in their claims as the general librarians. There resulted another incident in the oft-recurring conflict between the special and general librarian regarding the structure, content, and specificity of a classification for a special discipline. The law librarians asserted their rights over many subjects which, although obviously useful to lawyers and students of the law, were integral parts of other branches of knowledge. For a time it seemed that even the traditional tenure of the Bible in Theology was insecure because the Book was used in the courts. Both parties to the conflict ignored, or forgot, that library classification follows as closely as possible the subject content and accepted divisions of the various branches of knowledge. Both sides failed to realize that a classed catalog would solve the problem regardless of the physical location of the books involved.

In the Library of Congress the Law Library remained a "special problem," as Martel described it over forty years ago, until 1948. Throughout the years there had been some talk and even a promise that Class K would be developed. But the fait accompli of dispersion and the conviction of successive Law Librarians that no detailed classification was needed for the management of the law collections barred the way to a solution of the problem. A constantly increasing demand for reference services in foreign law, to which classification has provided the most effective subject approach, and the development of administrative law encouraged a reconsideration of Class K. In order to stimulate interest in this field of classification the Library, in October 1948, published a scheme con structed by Miss Elizabeth Benyon for use in the Law Library of the University of Chicago. After a study of the criticism and suggestions relating to Miss Benyon's work, the Library of

Congress then took definite steps to develop a classification of Law adequate to its own needs and in conformity with its existing system of classification.

In the spring of 1949 a Library of Congress Committee on a Classification for Law was appointed. On the committee were representatives of the Law Library, the General Reference and Bibliography Division, and classifiers from the Subject Cataloging Division whose task it would be to develop the schedules. The first meetings were discouraging as the extremists stated and defended their views. Gradually, however, each side began to modify its position and points of agreement were reached. Through this committee's work a long step forward was finally made in the thinking of the Library of Congress in regard to the status of Law within its classification system.

There remained, however, the broader task of submitting the proposed plan to law librarians outside the Library, to ascertain the results of their experience, to reconcile differences, and to secure, if possible, unanimity of agreement. On May 16 and 17, 1949, a joint meeting of the Library Committee and the Committee on Cooperation with the Library of Congress of the American Association of Law Libraries was held in the Library. Discussion at first followed the pattern of that of the Library Committee in its initial stages – complete disagreement. Gradually, however, a spirit of reasonable compromise appeared, and on June 10 a unanimous joint report was submitted to the Librarian. Copies of the report also were sent to members of the A. A. L. L. for their information. On June 28, on the occasion of the annual meeting of the A. A. L. L. in Detroit, a panel discussion of the Library's tentative outline was held.

The outcome of these various meetings was the decision to develop Class K on the basis of the following statement of content and general structure:

1. The projected schedule K shall include

   a) Legal source materials;

   b) Books dealing with subjects in terms of legal principles involved;

      c) Materials which should be grouped with law materials be-
         cause of their relevance to the practice of the legal pro-
         fession and by generally accepted canons of classification.

2.   The following materials are not to be included in Class K:

      a) Books dealing with technical or managerial problems involved
         in operating under statutes or administrative rules or regu-
         lations; these are to be classified with the activity concerned;

      b) Non-legal materials, although they may be of interest to a law
         library, except for the materials listed under 1 (c).

3.   The structure and principles of arrangement suggested by the Li-
     brary Committee, except for some modifications in Anglo-Amer-
     ican Law, were found to be generally acceptable.

In order to apply the foregoing principles, a large number of legal topics which at present are dispersed through various classes of the Library of
Congress Classification will have to be incorporated in Class K. Inasmuch
as public international law forms a homogeneous unit in Class JX, it is intended to develop and apply the section of JX devoted to public international
law as a part of the law classification, its present notation being retained. For
libraries which may wish to use a K notation for international law, a place in
the notation (tentatively, KX) will be provided for the purpose. Private international law (Conflict of laws) will be developed in Class K.

<u>Tentative</u> <u>Outline</u> <u>of</u> <u>Class</u> K[1]

K   GENERAL WORKS. SOCIETIES. COLLECTIONS. EN-
            CYCLOPEDIAS. BIBLIOGRAPHY. LEGAL EDUCATION.
            THE PROFESSION OF LAW.

KA   PHILOSOPHY OF LAW. JURISPRUDENCE.

KB   I. HISTORY OF LAW IN GENERAL. COMPARATIVE JURIS-
           PRUDENCE.
      II. ETHNOLOGICAL JURISPRUDENCE (PRIMITIVE LAW).
    III. ANCIENT LAW (EXCLUSIVE OF ROMAN LAW).
           GENERAL.
           EGYPTIAN.
           GREEK.
           HELLENISTIC.
    IV. ORIENTAL LEGAL SYSTEMS.
         1. SEMITIC LAW.
           BABYLONIAN AND ASSYRIAN.
           JEWISH.
           SYRIAN.
           MOHAMMEDAN.
         2. HINDU (Cf. KS, India).
         3. BURMESE BUDDHIST.

KC   ROMAN LAW (ANCIENT).

KD   ROMAN LAW (MEDIEVAL).
          GERMANIC LAWS.

KE   CANON LAW.

KF   COMPARATIVE MODERN LAW.

KG   ANGLO-AMERICAN LAW (GENERAL AND COMPARATIVE).

KH   UNITED STATES: FEDERAL LAW AND STATE LAWS COL-
              LECTIVELY.
              KHA-KHZ: STATES, A-M, INCLUDING ALASKA AND HA-
              WAII.
              KIA-KIZ: STATES, M-W, INCLUDING PUERTO RICO AND
              VIRGIN ISLANDS.

KJ   GREAT BRITAIN.
          KJA   ENGLAND.
          KJB   WALES.
          KJC   SCOTLAND.
          KJD   IRELAND INCLUDING NORTHERN IRELAND.
          KJE   EIRE.
          KJF   CHANNEL ISLANDS. ISLE OF MAN.

KK   BRITISH AMERICA.
          CANADA.
              PROVINCES.
          BRITISH POSSESSIONS ON THE AMERICAN CONTINENT.
          AUSTRALIA. NEW ZEALAND.
          UNION OF SOUTH AFRICA.

KL   LATIN AMERICA: GENERAL AND REGIONAL (CENTRAL
              AMERICA. SOUTH AMERICA).
          KLA-KLZ, INDIVIDUAL COUNTRIES, A-Z.

     EUROPEAN COUNTRIES (Comparative European law, see KF).

KM   FRANCE.

KN   GERMANY.   The possibility of
              KNA-KNZ, STATES.   dividing Europe by
                                          regional groups of
                                          countries will be
KO   ITALY.   considered in the
                                          process of develop-
KP   RUSSIA.   ing the classifica-
                                          tion.
KQ   OTHER EUROPEAN COUNTRIES, A-Z.

KR   ASIA, GENERAL AND COUNTRIES, A-Z, EXCEPT INDIA
              AND RUSSIA.

KS   INDIA.

KT   AFRICA, GENERAL AND COUNTRIES, A-Z.

KU   PACIFIC ISLANDS.

(KX)   INTERNATIONAL LAW, see JX.

The workload of the Subject Cataloging Division made it impossible to begin the actual development of the schedules for the next two years. Then, early in 1952, Dr. Werner B. Ellinger of the Division was assigned the task of developing the classification with the assistance of the Library's Advisory Committee on Law Classification. The jurisdiction selected for beginning the development was German Law because of the influence of the system underlying it. As each section of the classification is completed it is being issued as a working paper and sent to librarians and scholars in the legal field. The Library hopes to receive at all stages of development the most expert opinion available so that Class K may embody the best subject and library knowledge. Thus far nine working papers have been prepared: (1) Modern German Law, (2) Roman Law, (3) History of German Law, (4) Canon Law, (5) Chinese Law, (6) English Law, (7) Law of Japan, (8) Classification of American Law (A survey), and (9) Law of the United States.

Index. One of the most frequent, non-theoretical criticisms of the L. C. Classification is that it has no general, or combined, Index. A start toward the compilation of one was made in 1947, when all existing indexes were cut and mounted on cards. Although lack of funds prevented the cutting of sub-entries, the mounted cards fill 60 trays. Excluding Law index entries, which will not be available for some time, a combined index would constitute a volume of approximately 1, 000 pages containing 100,000 entries. In view of the present workload no date of publication can be given.

Manual. Another criticism of the L. C. Classification is that, as Miss Mann observes, "There are no directions for its use." A Manual has long been talked about; one was even begun after the A. L. A. had made a survey of libraries for suggestions concerning its scope and contents. [2]

Abridgment. For several years there has been some interest in an abridgment of the L. C. Classification for use in smaller libraries. At least one attempt was made and abandoned. Unlike the D. C. which, originating in a small library, expanded over the years, and the E. C., which was "expansive" ab initio, the L.C. was constructed for use in a large library. Both from the point of view of theory and structure, as well as of notation, it is far simpler to expand than contract. With some changes in structure and notation, however, it is possible to abridge the L.C. — but to what degree is difficult to determine. And — the question is not purely rhetorical — would it still be the L.C. Classification?

Oscar G. Sonneck, who constructed Class M Music, pointed out that,

> A classifier of fair talent and skill could without much difficulty "telescope" our scheme into a suitable instrument for any collection of any size, by canceling unnecessary subdivisions, by substituting subdivisions needed for his special purposes, and by rearranging at his convenience the sequence of certain entries. He might then adopt the notation, i.e., the class numbers, etc., in our scheme bodily, regardless of the gaps that would result in the class numbers from cancellation of subdivisions, or he might (that would be easy) devise a scheme of notation of his own, naturally more condensed than ours, but, of course, still elastic enough for expansion and insertion. [3]

His suggestions have been followed in the Condensation of the Library of Congress M Classification, prepared by Mrs. Betsey Rovelstad for the Classification Committee of the Music Library Association. [4] This plan made provisions "For Small Libraries" and "For Very Small Libraries":

For Small Libraries		For Very Small Libraries
	COLLECTIONS	
1	Miscellaneous collections	1
2	Monuments, sources, facsimile reproductions, historical publications	2
3	Collected works of individual composers 3.3 Use 3 or with the class	3
4	Incomplete collections of miscellaneous mediums	Use 1
	INSTRUMENTAL MUSIC	
5	Collections of miscellaneous instrumental music	Use 1
6	Organ Miscellaneous collections Original compositions	6

```
              Original compositions (cont.)
    7             Collections
                     8-10 Use 11
   11             Separate works
                     12 Use 13
   13             Arrangements
                     14-14.3 Use 13
```

In another subject, classical literature, Walther F. Koenig advised the use of Synopses III and IV by smaller libraries instead of the complete schedules.

> The minute classification devised for some parts of the scheme may create the impression that it is intended for the use of large university libraries only; but an examination of the scheme will prove that any college library or any library desirous of owning a representative collection of classical literature may make use of this scheme by ignoring the minor subdivisions — in other words, by using the condensed schedules as represented in Synopsis III and IV.[5]

Similarly in other parts of the classification it is possible to abridge by using briefer tables in areas in which a library has little material or little interest.

Revision. The problem of revision and expansion is ever present, accentuated manifold by the bewildering developments which are taking place in this mid-twentieth century. Two of the earliest classes developed, the experimental Z Bibliography and Library Science and E-F American History, need extensive revision and perhaps even replacement by new schedules which will more adequately reflect today's thinking and the experience gained in a half century of classifying and classification making.

This is particularly true of Z, which was developed and applied in 1898. Serious consideration should be given to the dispersion of subject bibliography. If it still seems desirable to continue the collocation of subject bibliographies in Z, Cutter's order should be abandoned in favor of an arrangement that would parallel the L.C. sequence of subjects, e.g. from ZA-ZZ, providing classes such as

```
ZH     Social Sciences
ZHB    Economic Theory
ZJK    U.S. Constitutional History
ZQR    Bacteriology
```

Also, in view of its importance in arranging the tools of our trade, the section devoted to Library Science should be radically revised, or better still, a completely new schedule should be developed.

The history of the Americas, highly important in this Library as in all American libraries, is now compressed in many sections in E-F. These classes could be reorganized and expanded according to some pattern like the following.

AMERICA

United States (General)

Present		Revision
E 11-143	General	E
E 151-837	United States	EA
F 1-15	New England	EB
F 16-30	Maine	EBA
F 31-45	New Hampshire, etc.	EBB
F 106	Atlantic Coast. Middle Atlantic States	EC
F 116-130	New York	ECA
	etc.	
	Other	
F 1001-1170	British North America. Canada	F
F 1201-1391	Mexico	FB
F 1401-1418	Latin America	FA
F 1421-1440	Central America	FC
F 2201-3899	South America	FG

The tables of subdivisions now in use would be modernized and expanded.

Since library classification reflects man's activities and records, it is, like them, everchanging. Adjustments, revisions, and additions must constantly be made. These modifications, not nearly so drastic or radical as some critics assert, provide for the incorporation of new knowledge. Products of the application of the system to the daily flow of books, they are published in the quarterly L. C. Classification – Additions and Changes and are incorporated in revised editions of the schedules. Reprints now include a supplement containing additions and changes made since the original printing of the edition. Additions and changes adopted while a schedule is in press are published in the first quarterly prepared after publication of a reprint or new edition.

Future revisions of certain classes will combine or recombine some

subclasses or sections previously published separately or in a different se-
quence. The most important will be the publications of Class D and its two
World War supplements in one volume and the incorporation of subclasses
PN, PR, PS, and PZ in volumes reflecting the order of the Classification.
Format and typography of the publications will be improved and made more
uniform whenever possible.

Turning from the immediate future of the Library of Congress Classification to the future of the process of classification itself, prediction becomes more difficult. A renewed interest in the systemization of knowledge
has brought about considerable criticism of classification and of the "historic systems." The oldest non-theoretical objection to classification is
that it is too "space-consuming." "Space is the librarian's capital enemy,
and the more cruel as it turns his own weapons against himself. The more
ample the catalogue, the more liberal the expenditure, the more comprehensive the classification, the greater, sooner or later, are the difficulties from
lack of space."[6] The statement is obviously true: if the storage of books
rather than facility of access to them is the object, size, not subject, is the
most economical basis of arrangement. Constantly increasing land and
building costs and the ever-multiplying number of books produced each year
are conditions which must be faced. Selection, weeding, and partial storage,
as well as classification, are involved in the solution of the problem of "Büch-
erraum." "All writings pass through three stages, which may be called the
new, the old and the antique. In the first stage they have a value growing out
of their connection with present interests. In the second stage, they are at
their lowest worth. In the third stage they have acquired a value as records
of the past."[7] The most pessimistic view of the problem is found in the bibliographic Malthusianism which Saverio Bettinelli, Italian Jesuit and man of
letters, expressed in 1758. Prophesying that the birthrate of books would exceed man's ability to house them, he proposed: "Let us build a new city whose
streets, squares, and houses shall contain only books. Let him who would

study go there and live for as long as he needs; otherwise printed matter will soon leave no room for the goods, food, and inhabitants of our cities."[8] Nearly a century and a quarter later Spofford, in one of his pleas to the Congress for a new building, pointed out that "large portions of the Library might be colonized or stored in other buildings, while those found to be most constantly used might be retained in the Library."[9] He opposed colonization as a solution, however, because he thought it impossible to select books which would not be needed "for an immediate emergency." In 1902 at the Boston-Magnolia Conference of the A. L. A. Charles William Eliot, president of Harvard University, proposed that libraries be divided into books in use and books not in use — the live and the dead — and that different storage metnods be used. For the dead books he advocated size as the basis of arrangement. [10]

It is impossible to generalize on the subject; each library faced with a space problem (what library is not?) must solve the problem in the light of its collections and the needs of its readers. The separation of live books from dead books may be achieved on a vertical basis of subject, on a horizontal basis of chronology, or on both. The principles of division must be adapted to the disciplines: a recent publication in nuclear physics may supersede (except for historical purposes) many preceding works, while contemporary imprints in the humanities in the form of text, history, or criticism may prove of far less value than older works. Whatever the principles used to divide the quick from the dead (or dying), the less-used books can be declassified[11] and arranged by size in individual "colonies" or in cooperative storage libraries. It seems improbable, however, that classification will ever be completely abandoned for reasons of space. Whatever the solution to the problem, libraries that have classed catalogs, or at least good shelflists, will continue to have a satisfactory subject control of their collections. The new storage locations can be noted on the shelflist entries and added entries made for new acquisitions, the shelflist becoming a union shelflist or partial classed catalog of a library's holdings.

It is frequently asserted that the composite nature and physical form of books and the linearity of their shelving make classification an unsatisfactory method for exhibiting the subject resources of libraries! Much has been written which only elucidates the obvious: as applied to books on the shelves, classification cannot, nor has any competent librarian ever asserted that it oould, provide an exhaustive approach to the subject resources of libraries. This is truer today than when first stated many years ago, for an increasing amount of library materials — microfilms, music scores, films, recordings, etc. — are not physically suited for relative classification. Among the historic classifications criticized for failure in this regard is the D.C. Ironically it was not Dewey but his over-zealous followers who exaggerated the importance of physical shelving, which becomes chiefly a housekeeping device in large libraries, and laid classification wide open to this type of criticism. Actually, Dewey, as well aware as other early American librarians of the limitations of shelf arrangement, was primarily an advocate of the classed catalog and originally developed his classification for this purpose, not for shelving. "No one questions the immense superiority of a satisfactory classed catalogue," he wrote. Dewey recommended that multitopical books be classified in the most useful places and that other aspects and subjects treated be represented by cross-reference entries in their respective locations in the classed catalog — an old device recently rediscovered and named "depth analysis." The L.C. Classification was constructed to provide both for the arrangement of books and for a classed catalog.

One of the most efficient classifications ever devised for physical things is that used in conjunction with the "open-shelf system" in self-service markets. But, as in philosophy, science, library science, and all the other disciplines, there is always a classifier who can, or thinks he can, improve existing modes of organization. In a grocery store there appeared not long ago a new manager imbued with the evangelical zeal which is so often an

attribute of new administrators. After a desultory study of the classification in use he decided that the time had come for the installation of a·more
logical and efficient system. The manager, with his unwilling assistants, "re-
actionaries" interested only in the preservation of the status quo, devoted
many hours to a reorganization of the commodities – substituting an alphabetic order for the old classified arrangement. And then came the housewives. One looking for chicken soup on the shelf where the item had stood
with other soups found that she had a can of salmon; another who wanted corn
learned to her dismay that vinegar had replaced the canned vegetables. The
new manager somewhat impatiently explained the new system to the few cus-
tomers who, after their marketing, had the fortitude to listen. The arrangement, he said, was alphabetical like that found in dictionaries. There were
some necessary deviations from the alphabetical order, he added: cream of
tomato soup was shelved in the "T" and not the "C" section, and canned
corned beef was with the canned goods, not in the meat department. The
problem of catchup, or ketchup, along with succotash, had been referred to a
committee for study. To the left as one entered the store was section "A, "
and to the right, "Z. " Along the walls the merchandise was arranged from
animal crackers to zwieback. Some idea of the order may be gleaned from
the experience of one harassed shopper. She found aluminum foil, ammonia,
catsup, chicken, chicken soup, cherries, corned beef, dog food, herring, honey,
salmon, salt, tapioca, tea, tomato soup, toilet paper, vegetable soup, and waxed
paper in that order. Despite the "failure" of the original classification, it
was restored by a new manager two weeks later, and the housewives and the
clerks were happy ever after.

    In its main outlines this is a true story. It might well give pause to
some critics who assert that library classification even on the physical level
has failed. Substitute for the housewives the library's public and for the
clerks the deck attendants and there is a close parallel in finding wanted material. In a library the problem of finding and collecting matter is accentuated

by the fact that, unlike groceries, books must be returned to the shelves to be found, refound, collected, and returned, over and over again.

But the physical collocation of books on related subjects by classification, however efficient it may be, does not at the present, if it ever did, provide an adequate approach to their contents. Specialization and a constantly accelerating publishing activity make the "subject control" of man's knowledge one of the most pressing problems of the present time. It is "information" or "units of thought" rather than the containers (books, maps, films, recordings, etc.) that is important. As in the past there are two modes of approach — the one verbal, the other systematic — which are used in catalogs, bibliographies, and indexes. A newcomer, "mechanical bibliography," whether based upon alphabetical headings, classification, or other coding devices, should prove of great assistance in controlling the records of knowledge. But whatever the modes of control, the answer to the problem would seem to lie in a cooperative production and coordination of all these tools.

The revived interest in the contents of books has brought about a renewed interest in classification and classed catalogs. The effectiveness of the dictionary catalog with its subject component of subject headings is being questioned. The dictionary catalog can of course be improved but, as Jacob Schwartz[12] said, not on dictionary principles. Although ease and directness of approach are said to be characteristics of the dictionary catalog, the words have a Victorian ring: they certainly cannot honestly be applied to the catalogs of the large libraries of the present time. For these catalogs, as Hanson foresaw, are breaking down from specificity and massiveness. Whatever ease and simplicity of approach the dictionary catalog affords is achieved through a complicated system of references and alphabetico-classed elements. It is logically and linguistically impossible to express in brief, specific headings many past and current concepts. Division into separate author and subject catalogs, which has been proposed as a solution, evades the fundamental problem. The value of subject approach through subject headings should be reexamined, with the needs of the specialist and scholar in mind as well as the needs of the average man for whom this type of tool was originally developed.

Criticisms of the theory and structure of the "historic classifications" — the D. C. and the L. C. — have not been wanting. But as Kane said,

> There is not a system of classification in existence, even our most comprehensive and elaborate, that can stand undamaged before purely speculative criticism. Every library classification is a compromise, a balancing arrangement between the known past and the unknown future, between the physical rigidity of the existing stock of books and the flexibility of expansion to care for books that may come, even between a philosophy based upon enduring principles and a sheer, expedient eclecticism; and that kind of compromise must, in this imperfect world, forever keep changing, as the stock of books changes, and as the compromisers change their mental attitudes. [13]

Of the many theoretical critics only two, Bliss[14] and Ranganathan, [15] have made positive contributions to classification. The others have been content to assert that existing classifications have failed, that "newer" theories (innumerable) should form the basis of "new" systems. There is, however, some confusion among them concerning the material of classification. If, as was stated in the first chapter, the material of library classification is the divisions which specialists have developed in their subjects, many of these theories will never bear fruit. Until, however, the critics proceed from theory to blueprints — if not to full schedules — it is of course impossible to evaluate their contributions.

With the first library came the need for classification. Each system used has to some degree succeeded in introducing order into the amorphous mass of material received. Like all other human instruments, the value of any classification must be measured in terms of its relative success or value in achieving the ends for which it was devised. Between the poles of absolute failure and an unachievable absolute success there are many degrees; few human products, mental or material, either fail or succeed absolutely. But classification has made it possible for libraries to exhibit their contents and to service their readers at far less cost than would have been possible if their collections had remained unclassified; or, it may be added, than if librarians had waited for the construction of a perfect system. A rude shed provides better protection from the elements than the blueprints of a mansion.

The last, the most important and most unanswerable question concerning the future is: What raw material will the coming years provide for the classifier ? What will the books of the second half of the twentieth century be written about ? What new philosophies, therapeutics, religions, scientific discoveries, and technologies will man's fertile mind invent, discover, or stumble upon ? Will mankind at last learn the secret of a peaceful world or will war continue to be, as it has been in the past, the most fruitful source of material for the expansion of library classification ?

CHAPTER I

[1]Ernest A. Savage, "Introduction" to John L. Thornton's The Chronology of Librarianship (London: Grafton & Co., 1941), p. x.

[2]John Venn, The Principles of Empirical or Inductive Logic (London and New York: Macmillan and Co., 1889), p. 322.

[3] Συναγωγή—"Εἰς μίαν τε ἰδέαν συνορῶντα αγειν τὰ πολλαχῇ διεσπαρμένα, ἵν' ἑκαστον ὁριζόμενος δῆλον ποιῇ, περὶ οὗ ἂν ἀεὶ διδασκειν ἐθέλῃ"
and Διαίρεσις—"Τὸ πάλιν κατ' εἴδη δύνασθαι τέμνειν, κατ' ἄρθρα, ᾗ πέφυκε, καὶ μὴ ἐπιχειρεῖν καταγνύναι μέρος μηδέν, κακοῦ μαγείρου τρόπῳ χρώμενον·"

Plato Phaedrus 265. D, E in Plato, With an English Translation ("The Loeb Classical Library" [London: William Heinemann; New York: G. P. Putnam's Sons]), Vol. I (1933), trans. Harold North Fowler, pp. 532-33, 534-35.

Note: ἰδέα is sometimes translated as "form" because of Plato's theory. Although most translators, including Jowett, prefer the more literary "carver" for μαγείρος, "butcher" is closer to Plato's metaphor of disjointing. Originally "cook," μαγείρος, acquired the meaning of "butcher" because the trades were combined in early days.

[4]Peter Coffey, The Science of Logic (New York: Peter Smith, 1938 [reprinted from 1st ed., 1912]), I, 123.

[5]Morris R. Cohen, A Preface to Logic (New York: Henry Holt and Co., 1944), p. 77.

[6]Robert W. Hegner and Karl A. Stiles, College Zoology (6th ed.; New York: The Macmillan Company, 1951), p. 11.

[7] Federal Classification Act of 1949.

[8]General Schedule; there is also a C. P. C. (Crafts, Protective and Custodial) Schedule.

[9]William C. Berwick Sayers, An Introduction to Library Classification (8th ed.; London: Grafton & Co., 1950), p. 2.

[10]Ernest C. Richardson, Classification: Theoretical and Practical ("Montogue Publications" [3d ed; New York: The H. W. Wilson Co., 1930]), p. 26.

[11]Clement W. Andrews, The John Crerar Library ... 1895-1905 (Chicago, 1905), p. 13.

[12]Appendix B contains sample pages of American catalogs which illustrate cataloging methods, classifications, and shelving arrangements.

[13]Charles A. Cutter, Boston Athenaeum: How to Get Books, with an Explanation of the New Way of Marking Books (Boston: Press of Rockwell and Churchill, 1882), p. 7.

[14]Institut International d'Agriculture, Système de classification des sciences agricoles... Classification Scheme of Agricultural Science... Stoffeinteilung der Landwirtschaftswissenschaft (2d ed.; Rome: Villa Umberto I, 1942), p. 27.

[15]Walter Shepherd, A New Survey of Science (Rev. and enl. ed.; London [etc.]: George G. Harrap and Co. Ltd., 1949), p. 275.

[16]2d ed.; New York: The H. W. Wilson Co., 1939.

[17]2d ed.; London: Grafton & Co., 1944.

[18]William Stanley Jevons, The Principles of Science: A Treatise on Logic and Scientific Method (2d ed.; London: Macmillan and Co., 1883).

[19]Charles Woodruff Shields, Philosophia Ultima, or, Science of the Sciences (3 vols.; New York: C. Scribner's Sons, 1888-1905).

[20]Robert Flint, Philosophy as Scientia Scientiarum and A History of Classification of the Sciences (Edinburgh and London: William Blackwood and Sons, 1904).

[21]James Duff Brown, Subject Classification (London: The Library Supply Co., 1906), pp. 57-78.

[22]Shiyali R. Ranganathan, Philosophy of Library Classification ("Library Research Monographs," Vol. II [Copenhagen: Ejnar Munksgaard, 1951]), Chapter 2.

[23]See Chapter XI, 1882, Lloyd Smith.

[24]Margaret Mann, Introduction to Cataloging and the Classification of

Books (2d ed. ; Chicago: American Library Association, 1943), Chapter 6.

25David J. Haykin, Subject Headings: A Practical Guide (Washington: U. S. Government Printing Office, 1951), p. 70.

26Organization of Knowledge in Libraries ... , p. 306.

CHAPTER II

1Monticello, June 10, 1815. Jefferson Papers in the Library of Congress, 204: 36303.

2"A Bill for Amending the Constitution of the College of William and Mary, and Substituting More Certain Revenues for Its Support, " Julian P. Boyd (ed.), The Papers of Thomas Jefferson, Volume 2, 1777 to 18 June, 1779 (Princeton: Princeton University Press, 1950), pp. 535-43.

3"Report of the Commissioners Appointed to Fix the Site of the University of Virginia, &c. , " Roy J. Honeywell, The Educational Work of Thomas Jefferson ("Harvard Studies in Education, " Vol. XVI [Cambridge: Harvard University Press, 1931]), Appendix J, pp. 248-60. This report was signed and certified on August 4, 1818. It is usually referred to as the Rockfish Report because the commissioners met "in Rockfish Gap, on the Blue Ridge. "

4Letter to Judge Augustus B. Woodward, Monticello, March 24, 1824. Jefferson Papers, 226: 40383.

5Robert Flint, Philosophy as Scientia Scientiarum and A History of Classifications of the Sciences (Edinburgh and London: William Blackwood and Sons, 1904), pp. 104-05.

6Boyd, II, 541-42.

7Honeywell, The Educational Work of Thomas Jefferson, Appendix H, pp. 233-43.

8Letter to Watterston, May 7, 1815. Jefferson Papers, 204: 36275.

9Letter to Skipwith, Aug. 3, 1771. Boyd, I, 78-81.

10Letter to Dr. Benjamin Rush, Jan. 16, 1811. Jefferson Papers, 192: 34176.

[11] The sales Catalogue of Jefferson's library (1829) lists a 1621 Paris edition of Charron's work, as well as an 1820 edition by Amaury Duval (Paris: Chasseriau). His earlier library (1815) contained two English translations of the work, "Charron on Wisdom, Eng. by Lennard, p 4to" and "Charron of Wisdom, 2d and 3d books, Eng. by Stanhope, 8vo. " The first edition of De la Sagesse was published in 1601, predating Bacon's Advancement of Learning by four years.

[12] Letter to Judge Augustus B. Woodward, Mar. 24, 1824. Jefferson Papers, 226: 40383.

[13] Letter to Dr. John Manners, Feb. 22, 1814. Jefferson Papers, 200: 35676.

[14] Walter Shepherd, A New Survey of Science (London: George G. Harrap & Co. Ltd. , 1949), p. 274.

[15] A Catalogue of Books Forming the Body of a Library for the University of Virginia, to be Afterwards Enlarged by Annual Additions – An Explanation of the Views on which this Catalogue has been Prepared in F. W. Page, "Our Library, " The Alumni Bulletin of the University of Virginia, II (November 1895), 79. This printing of the "manuscript volume" is believed by Page to be its first.

[16] Ibid. , pp. 79-80.

[17] Jan. 31, 1806. Jefferson Papers, 156: 27351.

[18] Bacon's classification is described in Chapter IV.

[19] Jean L. d'Alembert, Discours préliminaire de l'Encyclopédie, publié intégralement d'après l'édition de 1763 ... (Paris: Armand Colin et Cie. , 1894).

[20] See Chapter VI, 1816 A. E. B. Woodward.

[21] Augustus E. B. Woodward, A System of Universal Science (Philadelphia: Edward Earle, Harrison Hall, and Moses Thomas, 1816), pp. 215-222.

CHAPTER III

[1]A sample page of this catalog appears in Appendix B.

[2]"Outlines of Professor Mitchill's Lectures on Natural History, in the College at New-York, delivered in 1809-10, previous to his departure for Albany, to take his seat in the Legislature of the State, " The Medical Repository (New-York), Third hexade, Vol. I [Vol. XIII of the whole work] (1810), pp. 257-67.

[3]Letter to Watterston, Monticello, May 7, 1815. Jefferson Papers, 204: 36275-36276.

[4]Jefferson Papers, 206: 36723.

[5]U. S. Congress, Joint Committee on the Library, Report, January 26, 1816 (14th Congress, 1st Session, Senate Report 26, Washington, 1816), p. 6.

[6]York Colonial Advocate, reprinted in Washington City Chronicle, November 7, 1829 [p. 2].

[7]Alphabetical Catalogue of the Library of Congress.

[8]Figures of the Past (Boston: Little, Brown and Company, 1926), p. 179.

[9]Ainsworth R. Spofford, A Book for All Readers (New York and London: G. P. Putnam's Sons, 1900), p. 363.

[10]In Subject Cataloging Division, Library of Congress.

[11]U. S. Congress, Joint Committee on the Library, Condition of the Library of Congress (54th Congress, 2d Session, Senate Report No. 1573, March 3, 1897), p. 222.

[12]Ibid., p. 48.

[13]James C. M. Hanson, "The Library of Congress and Its New Catalogue," in Essays Offered to Herbert Putnam, eds. William Warner Bishop and Andrew Keogh (New Haven: Yale University Press, 1929), p. 181.

[14]Ibid., p. 179.

CHAPTER IV

[1]Protagoras 313. C.

[2]Metaphysica 1078. b. 28-30.

[3]Phaedo 118.

[4]Cicero, De senectute, V. 13.

[5]Metaphysica 993. b. 20.

[6]"Τὰ (βιβλία) μετὰ τὰ φυσικά"

[7]Edward A. Parsons, The Alexandrian Library, Glory of the Hellenic World (London: Cleaver-Hume Press Ltd., 1952), p. 217.

[8]See Friedrich Schmidt, Die Pinakes des Kallimachos ("Klassisch-Philologische Studien," Heft 1 [Berlin: Verlag von Emil Ebering, 1922]).

[9]Arthur F. Leach, Educational Charters and Documents, 598 to 1909 (Cambridge [England]: University Press, 1911), p. 12.

[10]Charles H. Haskins, "A List of Text-Books from the Close of the Twelfth Century," Harvard Studies in Classical Philology, XX (1909), 75-94.

[11]Dominicus Gundissalinus, "De divisione philosophiae," ed. Ludwig Baur, in Beiträge zur Geschichte der Philosophie des Mittelalters (Münster), Band IV, Heft 2-3 (1903).

[12]A History of Cataloguing and Cataloguing Methods, 1100-1850: With an Introductory Survey of Ancient Times (London: Grafton & Co., 1939).

[13]Bibliotheca universalis (4 vols.; Tiguri: C. Froschouerum, 1545-55). Liber 20, "De re medica," was never published. Thus Liber 21, "De theologia christiana," was titled Liber 20 when it was printed.

[14]Encyclopaedia septem tomis distincta (Herborn [Nassau], 1630).

[15]Adapted from the Encyclopaedia Britannica, 11th edition (1910).

[16]See Morris R. Cohen, "The Myth about Bacon and the Inductive Method," The Scientific Monthly, XXIII (1926), 504-508.

[17]An outline of Bacon's divisions of knowledge in comparison with d'Alembert's and Jefferson's classifications is given at the end of Chapter II.

[18]Here is the source of Dewey's separation of 400 Language from 800 Literature.

[19]James Spedding, Robert L. Ellis, and Douglas D. Heath (eds.), The Works of Francis Bacon (London: Longman & Co. [etc.]), IV (1858), 336.

CHAPTER V

[1] Said to be the first book catalog printed in the British colonies of America. It is described in Samuel A. Green's Remarks on an Early Book-Catalogue Printed in Boston [Boston, 1896]

[2] Cotton Mather, Magnalia Christi Americana: or, The Ecclesiastical History of New-England, from its First Planting in the Year 1620 unto the Year of Our Lord, 1698 (London: printed for Thomas Parkhurst, 1702), III, 223.

[3] Austin B. Keep, History of the New York Society Library (New York: DeVinne Press, 1908), p. 12.

[4] Bibliothecae Americanae Quadripartitae viz: I. Generales, Sive Bibliotheca Regia Annapolitana; II. Provinciales; III. Decanales; IV. Parochiales, or Catalogues of the Libraries sent into the Severall Provinces of America, described by B. C. Steiner, "Rev. Thomas Bray and his American Libraries," in The American Historical Review, II (October 1896-July 1897), 64. MS of the Bibliothecae is in the library of Sion College, London. The New York Public Library has a transcript.

[5] Alfred C. Potter and Charles K. Bolton, "The Librarians of Harvard College, 1667-1877," in Bibliographical Contributions (Cambridge: Library of Harvard University), IV, No. 52 (1897), Appendix I.

[6] Copies of the catalog are located in the Harvard College Library, the American Antiquarian Society, the Massachusetts Historical Society, and the Bodleian Library.

[7] Conyers Middleton, Bibliothecae Cantabrigiensis ordinandae methodus quaedam; quam domino procancellario senatuique academico considerandam & perficiendam officii et pietatis ergo proponit (Cantabrigiae: Typis academicis, MDCCXXIII).

[8] Virginia Gazette, December 19, 1777. A copy of "A Catalogue of the Books in the Library at Westover belonging to William Byrd Esqr.," appears in John S. Bassett (ed.), The Writings of "Colonel William Byrd of Westover in Virginia Esqr." (New York: Doubleday, Page & Co., 1901), Appendix A,

pp. 413-443. The original manuscript catalog is in the possession of the Library Company of Philadelphia.

[9]At least six of these books, containing Byrd's bookplate, eventually came into Jefferson's possession and are now in the Library of Congress.

[10]Also spelled Proctor.

[11]"Letters of the Byrd Family," Virginia Magazine of History and Biography, XXXVII (April 1929), 108.

[12]"An Introduction to the Study of Philosophy, exhibiting a General View of all the Arts and Sciences," in The Present State of the Republick of Letters (London: Printed for William Innys, at the West End of St. Paul's), VII (1731), art. xxxvii, 376-92.

[13]This Catalogue is described in the following section, 1743 Yale College.

[14][Samuel Johnson] Noetica: Or the First Principles of Human Knowledge. Being a Logick, Including both Metaphysics and Dialectic, Or the Art of Reasoning. With a brief Pathology, and an Account of the gradual Progress of the Human Mind, from the first Dawnings of Sense to the highest Perfection, both Intellectual and Moral, of which it is capable. To which is prefixed, A Short Introduction to the Study of the Sciences (Philadelphia, 1752).

[15][Samuel Johnson] Elementa Philosophica: Containing chiefly, Noetica, or Things relating to the Mind or Understanding: and Ethica, Or Things relating to the Moral Behaviour (Philadelphia: Printed by B. Franklin and D. Hall, at the New-Printing-Office, near the Market, 1752).

[16]An English and Hebrew Grammar ... To Which is Added a Synopsis of All the Parts of Learning (London: Printed for W. Faden, 1767).

[17]Arthur A. Luce and T. E. Jessop (eds.), The Works of George Berkeley, Bishop of Cloyne (London, Edinburgh, Paris, Melbourne, Toronto and New York: Thomas Nelson and Sons, Ltd.), IV (1951), 52.

[18]Augustus E. B. Woodward, A System of Universal Science (Philadelphia: Edward Earle, Harrison Hall, and Moses Thomas, 1816), pp. 168-171.

[19]A Catalogue of the Library of Yale=College in New= Haven (NLondon:

Printed by L. Groen [sic], 1743). Clap compiled two other catalogs (a shelf-list and an alphabetical list) which still exist in manuscript form. Anna Marie Monrad, "Historical Notes on the Catalogues and Classifications of the Yale University Library," in Papers in Honor of Andrew Keogh (New Haven, 1938), p. 252.

[20] The Introduction was Samuel Johnson's, described in the preceding section, 1731 Samuel Johnson.

CHAPTER VI

[1] George Champlin Mason, Annals of the Redwood Library and Athenaeum, Newport, R. I. (Philadelphia: The Evans Printing House, 1891), p. 2.

[2] Ibid., p. 31.

[3] Ibid., Appendix C, p. 492.

[4] A Catalogue of the Books Belonging to the Library Company of Philadelphia; to which is prefixed, A Short Account of the Institution, with the Charter, Laws and Regulations (Philadelphia: Printed by Zachariah Poulson, Junior, in Fourth-Street, between Market-Street and Arch-Street, 1789), [p. xxxviii]

[5] A Selected Catalogue of Some of the Most Esteemed Publications in the English Language Proper to Form a Social Library, with an Introduction upon the Choice of Books (Boston: I. Thomas & E. T. Andrews, 1793); copies held by the American Antiquarian Society, the Massachusetts Historical Society, and Yale University. Reprinted in Earl L. Bradsher, "A Model American Library in 1793," Sewanee Review, XXIV (1916), 458-75.

[6] "The Ghost of Doctor Harris. From an original MS. of Nathaniel Hawthorne," The Living Age, CCXXIV (February 10, 1900), 345-49.

[7] Augustus E. B. Woodward, A System of Universal Science (Philadelphia: Edward Earle, Harrison Hall, and Moses Thomas, 1816).

[8] Ibid., p. 10.

[9] Letter to H. Hall, Washington, November 19, 1816. Original mounted

in L. C. copy of A System of Universal Science.

[10]The National Union Catalog lists but nine copies, including that of the Library of Congress.

[11]Woodward, A System of Universal Science, Table No. II at end of volume.

[12]Charles Woodruff Shields, Philosophia Ultima, or, Science of the Sciences (3 vols.; New York: C. Scribner's Sons, 1888-1905).

[13]Jefferson Papers, 226: 40383, March 24, 1824.

[14]Tallahassee, April 21, 1826. Jefferson Papers, 231: 41403.

[15]Anna Eliot Ticknor, Life of Joseph Green Cogswell as Sketched in His Letters (Cambridge: Riverside Press, 1874), p. 67.

[16]Ibid., pp. 133-34. Letter from Ticknor to S. A. Eliot, October 29, 1822.

[17]Karl Julius Hartmann (ed.), Vier Dokumente zur Geschichte der Universitäts-Bibliothek Göttingen (Chr. G. Heyne 1768. 1810. Jakob Grimm 1829. 1833) ("Hainbergschriften; Arbeiten Göttinger Bibliothekare," 4. Heft [Göttingen: Verlag von Dr. Ludwig Häntzschel & Co. g.m.b.h., 1937])

[18]Alfred Hessel, Geschichte der Bibliotheken (Göttingen: Dr. H. Th. Pellens & Co., A.-G., 1925), p. 99. "The Göttingen system now swept triumphantly through Germany," as translated by Reuben Peiss in Alfred Hessel's A History of Libraries (Washington, D. C.: Scarecrow Press, 1950), p. 79.

[19]In Nützliche Samlungen, June 23-July 7, 1755, bound with Hannoversche Anzeigen von allerhand Sachen, 1755 (Hannover, 1756), columns 785-864. This classification has escaped the notice of Petzhold and the other historians of classification.

[20]From a photostat of "Mr. Cogswell's notice of classes in Library." Courtesy of Harvard College Library.

[21]Benjamin Franklin, A Proposal for Promoting Useful Knowledge among the British Plantations in America [Philadelphia: Printed by B. Franklin, 1743]

[22]Catalogue of the Library of the American Philosophical Society, Held at Philadelphia for Promoting Useful Knowledge [Philadelphia: Printed by

Joseph R. A. Skerrett, 1824], p. xi.

CHAPTER VII

[1]Described in the following section.

[2]A Bibliographical, Antiquarian, and Picturesque Tour in France and Germany (2d ed.; London: Robert Jennings and John Major, 1829), II, 232-33.

[3]Systema . . . (Parisiis, ex. S. Mabre-Cramoisy, 1678). Reprinted in Io. David. Koelerus [Johann David Koehler], Sylloge aliquot scriptorum de bene ordinanda et ornanda bibliotheca (Francofurti, 1728), p. 1-112.

[4]"Quelques-uns prétendent qu'il n'a fait que prester son nom à l'Auteur veritable de ce Systeme.": Adrien Baillet, Jugemens des scavans sur les principaux ouvrages des auteurs . . . (Paris: A. Dezallier, 1685-1686), T. II, 1. ptie. (1685), p. 275.

[5]Divisio generalis bibliothecae totius in quatuor principales partes.

[6]For a detailed treatment of Garnier and his work see William T. Kane, S. J., "Jean Garnier, Librarian," Mid-America, XXII ([new series XI] 1940), 75-95, 191-222.

[7]Catalogue of Books Belonging to the Saint Louis Mercantile Library Association, January 1850 (St. Louis, 1850).

CHAPTER VIII

[1]A Catalogue of the Books Belonging to the Library Company of Philadelphia (Philadelphia: C. Sherman & Co., 1835).

[2][John Jay Smith] "Notes for a History of the Library Company of Philadelphia," in Waldie's Port Folio and Companion to the Select Circulating Library (Philadelphia, [1835]), p. 8.

[3]See Chapter XI, 1882 Lloyd Smith.

[4]Alphabetical and Analytical Catalogue of the New-York Society Library (New-York: Printed by James Van Norden, 1838).

[5]Pantology, or, A Systematic Survey of Human Knowledge (Philadelphia:

Hogan and Thompson, 1841).

[6]This essay was printed, with additions and amendments, in <u>Scientific</u> <u>Tracts, for the Diffusion of Useful Knowledge</u> (Boston: Light and Stearns, 1836)

[7]<u>Catalogue</u> ... (Bloomington: Printed by M. L. Deal, 1842).

[8]See Chapter IX, 1858 <u>St. Louis Mercantile Library</u>.

[9]<u>Catalogue of the Mercantile Library in New York</u> (New York: Printed by Edward O. Jenkins, 1844).

[10]<u>Catalogue of the Mercantile Library in New-York</u> (New-York: Printed by Baker, Godwin & Company, 1850).

[11]Dated August 29, 1853, to Charles B. Norton, of <u>Norton's Literary Gazette</u>, one of those responsible for calling the convention.

[12]See Chapter XI, 1882 <u>Lloyd Smith</u>.

[13]<u>Proceedings of the Librarians' Convention</u> ... <u>1853</u>. Reprinted for William H. Murray ([Cedar Rapids, Iowa: The Torch Press], 1915), pp. 48-49.

[14]Abiel Abbot was influential in founding the first public library in the United States in Peterborough in 1833.

[15]<u>Ezra Abbot</u> (Cambridge: Published for the Alumni of the Harvard Divinity School, 1884), p. 55.

[16]<u>A Classed Catalogue</u> ... <u>Cambridge High School</u> (Cambridge: John Bartlett, 1853), p. vi. The National Union Catalog lists only nine copies of this catalog.

[17]Ibid.

[18]Charles A. Cutter, "Library Catalogues," in <u>Public Libraries in the United States of America</u> (Washington: Government Printing Office, 1876), Part I, 540.

[19]Ibid.

[20]<u>Catalogue of the Library of the U. S. Military Academy, West Point, N. Y.</u>, <u>Exhibiting Its Condition at the Close of the Year 1852</u> (New-York: John F. Trow, Printer, 1853), p. [iii].

[21]<u>Proceedings</u> ... , p. 16.

CHAPTER IX

[1]Catalogue of the Tennessee State Library (Nashville: Southern Methodist Publishing House, 1855), pp. v-vi.

[2]Alice D. Snyder (ed.), S. T. Coleridge's Treatise on Method as published in the Encyclopaedia Metropolitana (London: Constable and Co. Ltd.,
1934), p. 12.

[3]Hours in a Library (New ed., with additions; New York: G. P. Putnam's
Sons, [etc.] 1894), III, 361.

[4]Snyder, S. T. Coleridge's Treatise on Method ... pp. 2-3.

[5]Catalogue of Books Belonging to the Saint Louis Mercantile Library
Association, January, 1850 (St. Louis, 1850).

[6]See Chapter X, 1870 W. T. Harris.

[7]Catalogue of the Library of the South Carolina College. The Books
Placed under an Analytical Arrangement, and their Titles Abridged (Columbia, S. C.: Telescope Print, 1836).

[8]Robert M. Hughes, General Johnston ("Great Commanders" [New
York: D. Appleton and Co., 1893]), p. 9.

[9]Systematic Catalogue of Books in the Collection of the Mercantile Library Association of the City of New-York (New-York: Harper & Brothers,
1837).

[10]Robert M. Hughes and Joseph A. Turner, "Roanoke Female Seminary,
Valley Union Seminary, Hollins Institute, and Hollins College," William and
Mary College Quarterly, IX (2d series, October 1929), 326.

[11]"I shall ... be able to finish the Indexes more at large and to have the
papers all bound, before they leave the house. This last is a point of great so-
licitude to the family and of no little importance to the Government. For, otherwise these important MSS will [be] exposed to neglect, injury, mutilation
and abstraction by every body handling them, as all may do." Letter from Edward Wm. Johnston to John M. Clayton [Secretary of State at the time] L. C.
Division of Manuscripts, John M. Clayton Papers, Nov. 19, 1849.

[12]December 11, 1867, p. 2.

[13]Catalogue Systematic and Analytical of the Books of the Saint Louis Mercantile Library Association (St. Louis, 1858), p. [x]

[14]Ibid.

[15]John Crane and Lieut. James F. Kieley, U. S. N. R. , United States Naval Academy: The First Hundred Years (New York and London: McGraw-Hill Book Co. , Inc. [1945]), p. 37.

The germ of the Academy was an earlier school organized in 1839 at the Naval Asylum, a home for aged seamen near Philadelphia.

[16]Also published as "On the Classification of Books, " in Smithsonian Institution, Annual Report (Washington: Government Printing Office, 1863), pp. 416-425. Lesley's influence as early as 1864 is shown by the preface to the Catalogue of Books in the Library of the Literary and Historical Society of Quebec: "For the suggestion on which I have acted in this classification of our books I am indebted to Mr. Leslie, the Secretary of the American Philosophical Society...."

[17]Catalogue of the American Philosophical Society Library, pp. 14-15.

[18]See Chapter VII, 1826 Charleston Library Society.

[19]A Bibliographic Classification, Extended by Systematic Auxiliary Schedules for Composite Specification and Notation (4 vols. ; New York: H. W. Wilson Co. , 1940-53.

CHAPTER X

[1]Charles Coffin Jewett, president of the convention, stated its object: "We meet to provide for the diffusion of a knowledge of good books, and for enlarging the means of public access to them. Our wishes are for the public, not for ourselves. " (Proceedings ... 1853. Reprinted 1915, p. 14). The topics discussed have a familiar ring even a hundred years later: new processes (the Smithsonian "stereotyped" catalog), classification systems, indexes to publications, a central national library, public libraries, public document

distribution, and international exchanges (including 51 participating institutions in six foreign countries).

For an excellent discussion of this convention see George B. Utley, The Librarians' Conference of 1853; A Chapter in American Library History, ed. Gilbert H. Doane (Chicago: American Library Association, 1951).

[2] Ralph Robert Shaw (trans.), Georg Schneider's Theory and History of Bibliography ("Columbia University Studies in Library Service," No. I [New York: Columbia University Press, 1934]), p. 210.

[3] Kurt F. Leidecker, Yankee Teacher: The Life of William Torrey Harris (New York: The Philosophical Library, 1946), p. 316.

[4] Van Wyck Brooks, New England: Indian Summer, 1865-1915 ([New York]: E. P. Dutton & Co., Inc., 1940), p. 333.

[5] Catalogue, Classified and Alphabetical, of the Books of the St. Louis Public School Library (St. Louis: Missouri Democrat Book and Job Printing House, 1870), p. x.

[6] "While most systems were essentially alphabetical and chronological at the time, Harris divided the 'empire of human knowledge' into classes." Leidecker, Yankee Teacher, p. 339.

[7] Footnote acknowledging the influence of "Edward Wm. Johnston, Esq."

[8] Catalogue ... St. Louis Public School Library, p. xiii.

[9] Ibid., pp. xv-xvi.

[10] William C. Berwick Sayers, A Manual of Classification for Librarians and Bibliographers (2d ed., revised; London: Grafton & Co., 1944), p. 112.

[11] "Mr. Perkins's Classification," Library Journal, VII (1882), 60.

[12] [Melvil Dewey] "A Decimal Classification and Subject Index," Public Libraries in the United States of America. Their History, Condition, and Management ... (Washington: Government Printing Office, 1876), Pt. I, pp. 623-648.

[13] A Classification ... for Cataloguing ... (Amherst, Mass., 1876), [p. iii]

[14]Les bibliothéques francoises de La Croix du Maine et de Du Verdier
... Par M. Rigoley de Juvigny (Nouvelle édition; Paris: Saillant & Nyon), II
(1772), xxv ff.

[15]Nathaniel B. Shurtleff, A Decimal System for the Arrangement and Administration of Libraries (Boston, 1856).

[16]"A Decimal Classification and Subject Index, " Public Libraries in the
United States of America ..., Pt. I, p. 624.

[17]Melvil Dewey, Decimal Classification and Relativ Index for Arranging,
Cataloging and Indexing Public and Private Libraries and for Pamflets, Clippings, Notes, Scrap Books, Index Rerums, etc. (2d ed. ; Boston: Library Bureau,
1885).

[18]Ernest A. Savage, Manual of Book Classification and Display for Public Libraries ("Library Association Series of Library Manuals, " [8] ed. William E. Doubleday [London: George Allen & Unwin Ltd. and the Library Association, 1946]), p. 67.

[19]Founded in 1820, this library was an outgrowth of the General Society
of Mechanics and Tradesmen of the City of New York, organized in 1785.

[20]Jacob Schwartz, "A New Classification and Notation, " Library Journal,
VII (1882), 149.

[21]Library Journal, XI (1886), 232-244.

[22]Library Journal, IV (1879), 1-7.

CHAPTER XI

[1]The Hartford Daily Courant, January 30, 1899, p. 8.

[2]Frederic B. Perkins, A Rational Classification of Literature for Shelving and Cataloguing Books in a Library (Revised ed. ; San Francisco: Francis,
Valentine and Co., 1882), p. v.

[3]John Edmands, "Explanation of the New System of Classification, "
Bulletin of the Mercantile Library of Philadelphia, I, No. 1 (Oct. 1, 1882),
22-28.

[4]Historical Sketch of the Mercantile Library, Philadelphia, and the

Ninety-third Annual Report for the Year 1915 [p. 17]

[5]"Numbering Scheme, " Bulletin of the Mercantile Library of Philadelphia, I, No. 3 (April 1, 1883), 68-70.

[6]See Chapter VIII, 1835 Library Company of Philadelphia.

[7]Proceedings of the Librarians' Convention ... 1853. Reprinted for William H. Murray ([Cedar Rapids, Iowa: The Torch Press], 1915), pp. 51-52.

The consolidated supplements and the general index were published in 1856.

[8]Lloyd P. Smith, On the Classification of Books, A Paper Read Before the American Library Association, May, 1882 (Boston: Library Bureau, 1882), [p. 10]

CHAPTER XII

[1]Schema des Realkatalogs der Königlichen Universitätsbibliothek zu Halle a. S. ("Beihefte zum Centralblatt für Bibliothekswesen, " III [Leipzig: Otto Harrassowitz, 1888]).

[2]Ibid. , p. 247.

[3]Public Libraries in the United States of America. Their History, Condition, and Management. Special Report, Department of the Interior, Bureau of Education (Washington: Government Printing Office, 1876), Pt. II, pp. [1]-85.

[4]"Library Catalogues, " Public Libraries ..., Pt. I, pp. 526-622.

[5]Henry B. Wheatley, How to Catalogue a Library (London: Elliot Stock, 1889), p. viii.

[6]Joseph L. Harrison, Forbes Library, the Half Century, 1894-1944 (Northampton: The Print Shop, 1945), p. 10.

[7]Charles A. Cutter, Boston Athenaeum; How to Get Books, With an Explanation of the New Way of Marking Books (Boston: Rockwell and Churchill, 1882), p. 6.

[8]See Chapter X, 1876 Melvil Dewey.

[9]Expansive Classification, Part I: The First Six Classifications (Boston: C:A. Cutter, 1891-1893).

[10]William Parker Cutter, Charles Ammi Cutter ("American Library Pioneers," ed. Arthur E. Bostwick, Vol. III [Chicago: American Library Association, 1931]), p. 44.

[11]Transactions and Proceedings of the Second International Library Conference Held in London July 13-16, 1897 (London, 1898), pp. 86-87.

[12]Expansive Classification ..., p. 140.

[13]"Common Sense in Libraries. Address of the President ...," Library Journal, XIV (1889), 153.

[14]The Organization of Knowledge in Libraries (New York: The H. W. Wilson Company, 1933), p. 241.

[15]Classification of Books ... ("University of California Library Bulletin," No. 12 [Berkeley, Calif., 1894]).

[16]Ibid., [p. 3].

CHAPTER XIII

[1]William W. Bishop and Andrew Keogh (eds.), Essays Offered to Herbert Putnam (New Haven: Yale University Press, 1929), p. 183.

[2]Parts of this experimental shelflist are still in existence.

[3][Charles Martel] "Classification in the Library of Congress" (Typescript in the Library of Congress, Subject Cataloging Division, dated February 1901), p. 3.

[4]Typed memorandum, Library of Congress, Subject Cataloging Division.

[5]Class Z was not published until 1902.

[6]Young's successor, Putnam, apparently agreed with him.

[7]Bishop and Keogh, Essays Offered to Herbert Putnam, p. 188.

[8]Letter dated April 21, 1899, in L C. Subject Cataloging Division.

[9]Report of the Librarian of Congress (Washington: Government Printing Office, 1899), p. 29.

[10]Ibid.

[11]William Parker Cutter, Charles Ammi Cutter (Chicago: American Library Association, 1931), p. 45.

[12]Typescript in Library of Congress, Subject Cataloging Division.

CHAPTER XIV

[1]"Tanquam tabula naufragii."

[2][Charles Martel] "Classification in the Library of Congress" (Typescript in the Library of Congress, Subject Cataloging Division), p. 7.

CHAPTER XV

[1]March, 1949.

[2]See Chapter XII, 1888 Halle Schema.

[3]Typescript [1918] in the Library of Congress, Subject Cataloging Division.

[4]Charles Martel, "The Library of Congress Classification; Some Considerations Regarding the Relation of Book or Library Classification to the 'Order of the Sciences,'" in Essays Offered to Herbert Putnam, eds. William Warner Bishop and Andrew Keogh (New Haven: Yale University Press, 1929), pp. 329-30.

CHAPTER XVI

[1]For sample pages see pp. 293-295.

[2]William C. Berwick Sayers, A Manual of Classification for Librarians and Bibliographers (2d ed.; London: Grafton & Co., 1944), p. 156.

[3]Class P: P-PA Philology. Linguistics. Classical Philology. Classical Literature (Washington: Government Printing Office, 1928), p. 417.

CHAPTER XVII

[1]W was used for medicine by the Armed Forces Medical Library, now the

National Library of Medicine.

[2]Other illustrations may be found in the preceding chapter, pp.

[3]Now in Class K Law.

[4]See James C.M. Hanson, "The Subject Catalogs of the Library of Congress," American Library Association, Papers and Proceedings of the Thirty-first Annual Meeting ... June 26-July 3, 1909 ("Bulletin," Vol. III, No. 5, September, 1909 [Chicago; American Library Association, 1909]), pp. 385-397.

[5]Later the subject of considerable adverse criticism.

[6]Charles Martel, "Cataloging: 1876-1926," American Library Association, Papers and Proceedings of the Forty-eighth Annual Meeting [Fiftieth Anniversary Conference] ... October 4-9, 1926 ("Bulletin," Vol. XX, No. 10, October, 1926 [Chicago: American Library Association, 1926]), p. 495.

[7]Classes Z and M and parts of P never had a Sheet Shelflist.

[8] Subclass M Music (Scores) was made a classed catalog in 1944.

[9] Bracketed material indicates the subject covered by the preceding class number.

[10]See p.

[11]In Class PN, PR, PS, PZ Literature – General, English, American; Fiction and Juvenile Literature (1915), pp. 220-22.

[12]300-(498) are the numbers used in PH for Finnish literature, but others, such as the suggested alternative 100-(298), could be used if desired. The period subdivisions can be modified, also, as has been done here by adapting the sequence in Table XXII.

[13]Typescript [1918] in the Library of Congress, Subject Cataloging Division.

[14]This is shown also in the SYNOPSIS reproduced above.

[15]Frederick Copleston, S. J., A History of Philosophy ("The Bellarmine Series," Vol. IX [London: Burns Oates & Washbourne Ltd.]), I (Rev. ed., reprinted 1951), 5.

[16]The Library of Congress in Relation to Research ([Washington] :

United States Government Printing Office, 1939), pp. 34-35. [Reprinted from Relation of the Federal Government to Research, National Resources Committee, 1938.]

[17]"Classification (From the Report of the Chief Classifier, Mr. Martel)" in Report of the Librarian of Congress ... For the Fiscal Year Ending June 30, 1911 (Washington: Government Printing Office, 1911), pp. 61-62.

CHAPTER XVIII

[1]The structure and notation are, of course, subject to change in the process of developing the complete schedules.

[2]By the late Cecil K. Jones, Chief of the Classification Division (1937-40), and the author.

[3]Library of Congress, Classification, Music and Books on Music. M: Music; ML: Literature of Music; MT: Musical Instruction and Study (Rev. ed.; Washington: U.S. Government Printing Office, 1917), Prefatory Note, p. 6.

[4]Mimeographed in 1953.

[5]Library of Congress, Classification, Class P, P-PA. Philology. Linguistic. Classical Philology. Classical Literature (Washington: U.S. Government Printing Office, 1928), Prefatory Note, p. i.

[6]Richard Garnett, Late Keeper of Printed Books, British Museum, Essays in Librarianship and Bibliography ("The Library Series," Vol. V [London: George Allen, 1899]), p. 61.

[7]Samuel C. Bradford, "The Science Library," Zentralblatt für Bibliothekswesen, Jahrgang 54, Heft 3 (März 1937), p. 122.

[8]Saverio Bettinelli, Lettere Virgiliane e inglesi e altri scritti critici, ed. Vittorio Enzo Alfieri (Bari: Gius. Laterza & Figli, 1930), p. 62. [Translation provided by author]

[9]Annual Report of the Librarian of Congress for the Year 1875 (Washington: Government Printing Office, 1876), p. 8.

[10]In 1725 Thomas Hollis (the first) of London, an early benefactor of

the Harvard Library, had advised a predecessor of Eliot "... if you want roome for modern books, it is easy to remove the less usefull into a more remote place ..." (Alfred Claghorn Potter, The Library of Harvard University; Descriptive and Historical Notes [4th ed.; Cambridge: Harvard University Press, 1934], p. 14.)

[11]The classified arrangement could well be retained in the less expensive space of storage libraries.

[12]"A Dozen Desultory Denunciations of the Dictionary Catalogue, with a Theory of Cataloguing," Library Journal, XI (1886), 470-4.

[13]William T. Kane, S.J., "Jean Garnier, Librarian," Mid-America, XXII ([new series XI] 1940), 216.

[14]Henry E. Bliss, A Bibliographic Classification, Extended by Systematic Auxiliary Schedules for Composite Specification and Notation (4 vols.; New York: H.W. Wilson Co., 1940-53).

[15]Shiyali R. Ranganathan, Colon Classification (Madras Library Association "Publication series," Vol. XVI [3d ed.; Madras: Madras Library Association, 1950]).

APPENDICES

APPENDIX A

Bibliography

Specific information about each bibliographic entry is contained in the notes section of this book, beginning on page 351. Numbers in brackets at the end of each bibliographic entry refer to the chapter and footnote where this information can be found.

Alembert, Jean L. d'. Discours préliminaire de l'Encyclopédie, publié intégralement d'après l'édition de 1763 . . . Paris: Colin, 1894. [II, 19]

Alsted, Johann H. Encyclopaedia septem tomis distincta. Herborn [Nassau], 1630. [IV, 14]

American Library Association. "Papers and Proceedings of the Thirty-first Annual Meeting . . .," Bulletin of the American Library Association, III (September, 1909), 385-397. [XVII, 4]

_____. "Papers and Proceedings of the Forty-eighth Annual Meeting . . .," Bulletin of the American Library Association, XX (October, 1926), 495. [XVII, 6]

American Philosophical Society. Catalogue of the American Philosophical Society Library . . . Philadelphia: American Philosophical Society, 1863-84. [IX, 17]

_____. Catalogue of the Library of the American Philosophical Society, Held at Philadelphia, for Promoting Useful Knowledge. Philadelphia: American Philosophical Society; Joseph R. A. Skerrett, 1824. [VI, 22]

Andrews, Clement W. The John Crerar Library . . . 1895-1905. Chicago, 1905. [I, 11]

Bacon, Francis. Works . . . Collected and edited by James Spedding, Robert L. Ellis, and Douglas D. Heath. London: Longman, 1858. [IV, 19]

Baillet, Adrien. Jugemens des sçavans sur les principaux ouvrages des auteurs . . . Paris: Dezallier, 1685-1686. [VII, 4]

Berkeley, George. The Works of George Berkeley, Bishop of Cloyne. Edited by A. A. Luce and T. E. Jessop. London: Nelson, 1951. [V, 17]

Bettinelli, Saverio. Lettere Virgiliane e inglesi e altri scritti critici. Edited by Vittorio Enzo Alfieri. Bari: Laterza and Figli, 1930. [XVIII, 8]

Bishop, William Warner, and Andrew Keogh, editors. Essays Offered to Herbert Putnam by his Colleagues and Friends on his Thirtieth Anniversary as Librarian of Congress, 5 April 1929. New Haven: Yale University Press, 1929. [III, 13, 14; XIII, 1, 7; XV, 4]

Bliss, Henry E. A Bibliographic Classification, Extended by Systematic Auxiliary Schedules for Composite Specification and Notation. New York: Wilson, 1940-53. [IX, 19; XVIII, 14]

Bliss, Henry E. The Organization of Knowledge in Libraries. New York: Wilson, 1933. [XII, 14]

———. The Organization of Knowledge in Libraries and the Subject-Approach to Books. New York: Wilson, 1939. [I, 16, 26]

Bradford, Samuel C. "The Science Library," Zentralblatt für Bibliothekwesen, LIV (March, 1937), 122. [XVIII, 7]

Bradsher, Earl L. "A Model ᴀᴍᴇᴀican Library in 1793," Sewanee Review, XXIV (1916), 458-475. [VI, 5]

Brooks, Van Wyck. New England: Indian Summer, 1865-1915. New York: Dutton, 1940. [X, 4]

Brown, James D. Subject Classification. London: The Library Supply Co., 1906. [I, 21]

Byrd, William. The Writings of "Colonel William Byrd, of Westover in Virginia, esqr". Edited by John Bassett. New York: Doubleday, Page & Co., 1901. [V, 8]

Byrd family letters. Virginia Magazine of History and Biography, XXXVII (April, 1929), 108. [V, 11]

Cambridge, Mass., High School Library. A Classed Catalogue of the Library . . . Cambridge: John Bartlett, 1853. [VIII, 16, 17]

Charleston Library Society. A Catalogue of the Books Belonging to the Charleston Library Society. Charleston: A. E. Miller, 1826. [IX, 18]

Cicero. De senectute. V. 13. [IV, 4]

Clayton, John M. Papers. Nov. 19, 1849. Library of Congress. Division of Manuscripts. [IX, 11]

Coffey, Peter. The Science of Logic. New York: Peter Smith, 1938. [I, 4]

Cogswell, Joseph Green. Letter to George Ticknor, in Anna Eliot Ticknor, Life of Joseph Green Cogswell as Sketched in His Letters. Cambridge: Riverside Press, 1874. [VI, 15]

———. Notice of Classes in Library. Photostat in Harvard College Library. [VI, 20]

Cohen, Morris R. "The Myth about Bacon and the Inductive Method," The Scientific Monthly, XXIII (1926), 504-508. [IV, 16]

———. A Preface to Logic. New York: Henry Holt, 1944. [I, 5]

Copleston, Frederick, S.J. A History of Philosophy. London: Burns Oates & Washbourne Ltd., 1951. [XVII, 15]

Crane, John de Murinelly Cirne, and Kieley, Lieut. James F., U.S.N.R. United States Naval Academy: The First Hundred Years. New York: McGraw-Hill, 1945. [IX, 15]

Cutter, Charles A. Boston Athenaeum: How to Get Books, With an Explanation of the New Way of Marking Books. Boston: Rockwell and Churchill, 1882. [I, 13; XII, 7]

_____. "Common Sense in Libraries. Address to the President . . . ," Library Journal, XIV (1889), 153. [XII, 13]

_____. Expansive Classification. Boston: C. A. Cutter, 1891-1893. [XII, 9, 12]

_____. "Library Catalogues," Public Libraries in the United States of America. Their History, Condition, and Management. Special Report, Department of the Interior, Bureau of Education. Washington: Government Printing Office, 1876. [VIII, 18, 19; XII, 4]

_____. "Rules for a Dictionary Catalogue," Public Libraries in the United States of America. Their History, Condition, and Management. Special Report, Department of the Interior, Bureau of Education. Washington: Government Printing Office, 1876. [XII, 3]

Cutter, William Parker. "Charles Ammi Cutter," American Library Pioneers. Edited by Arthur E. Bostwick. Chicago: American Library Association, 1931. [XII, 9; XIII, 11]

Dewey, Melvil. A Classification and Subject Index for Cataloguing and Arranging the Books and Pamphlets of a Library. Amherst, Mass., 1876. [X, 13]

_____. Decimal Classification and Relativ Index for Arranging, Cataloging and Indexing Public and Private Libraries and for Pamflets, Clippings, Notes, Scrap Books, Index Rerums, etc. Boston: Library Bureau, 1885. [X, 17]

_____. "A Decimal Classification and Subject Index," Public Libraries in the United States of America. Their History, Condition, and Management. Special Report, Department of the Interior, Bureau of Education. Washington: Government Printing Office, 1876. [X, 12, 16]

_____. "Mr. Perkin's Classification," Library Journal, VII (1882), 60. [X, 11]

Dibdin, Thomas Frognall. A Bibliographical, Antiquarian, and Picturesque Tour in France and Germany. London: Robert Jennings and John Major, 1829. [VII, 2]

Dui, Melvil, see Dewey, Melvil

Edmands, John. "Explanation of the New System of Classification," Bulletin of the Mercantile Library of Philadelphia, I (October 1, 1882), 22-28. [XI, 3]

_____. "Numbering Scheme," Bulletin of the Mercantile Library of Philadelphia, I (April 1, 1883), 68-70. [XI, 5]

Encyclopaedia Britannica. Eleventh edition. Cambridge, England: University Press, 1910-11. [IV, 15]

Ezra Abbot. Cambridge: Published for the Alumni of the Harvard Divinity School, 1884. [VIII, 15]

Flint, Robert. Philosophy as Scientia Scientiarum and A History of Classifi-
    cations of the Sciences. Edinburgh and London: William Blackwood and
    Sons, 1904. [I, 20; II, 5]

Franklin, Benjamin. A Proposal for Promoting Useful Knowledge among the
    British Plantations in America. Philadelphia: Printed by B. Franklin,
    1743. [VI, 21]

Garnett, Richard. Essays in Librarianship and Bibliography. London: George
    Allen, 1899. [XVIII, 6]

Garnier, Jean. Systema bibliothecae collegii parisiensis Societatis Jesu. Paris:
    S. Mabre-Cramoisy, 1678. [VII, 3, 5]

Gesner, Konrad. Bibliotheca universalis. Tiguri: C. Froschouerum, 1545-55.
    [IV, 13]

Green, Samuel A. Remarks on an Early Book-Catalogue Printed in Boston . . .
    Boston, 1896. [V, 1]

Gundissalinus, Dominicus. "De divisione philosophiae," edited by Ludwig Baur,
    Beiträge zur Geschichte der Philosophie des Mittelalters, IV, 2-3 (1903).
    [IV, 11]

Halle. Universität. Bibliothek. "Schema des Realkatalogs der Königlichen
    Universitäts-bibliothek zu Halle a. S.," Beihefte zum Centralblatt für
    Bibliothekswesen, III. [Leipzig: Otto Harrassowitz, 1888]. [XII, 1, 2]

Hanson, James C. M. "The Library of Congress and Its New Catalogue," in
    William Warner Bishop and Andrew Keogh, editors. Essays Offered to
    Herbert Putnam. New Haven: Yale University Press, 1929. [III, 13, 14]

_____. Outline of proposed classification system in letter to Librarian Her-
    bert Putnam, dated April 21, 1899. Library of Congress. Subject Catalog-
    ing Division. [XIII, 8]

_____. "The Subject Catalogs of the Library of Congress," Bulletin of the
    American Library Association, III (September, 1909), 385-397. [XVII, 4]

Harris, Thaddeus M. A Selected Catalogue of Some of the Most Esteemed
    Publications in the English Language Proper to Form a Social Library,
    with an Introduction upon the Choice of Books. Boston: I. Thomas & E. T.
    Andrews, 1793. [VI, 5]

Harrison, Joseph L. Forbes Library, the Half Century, 1894-1944. Northamp-
    ton [Mass.] : The Print Shop, 1945. [XII, 6]

Hartmann, Karl Julius, editor. Vier Dokumente zur Geschichte der Universi-
    täts-Bibliothek Göttingen. Göttingen: Verlag von Dr. Ludwig Häntzschel
    & Co., 1937. [VI, 17]

Haskins, Charles H. "A List of Text-Books from the Close of the Twelfth
    Century," Harvard Studies in Classical Philology, XX (1909), 75-94.
    [IV, 10]

Hawthorne, Nathaniel. "The Ghost of Doctor Harris," The Living Age, CCXXIV (February 10, 1900), 345-49. [VI, 6]

Haykin, David J. Subject Headings: A Practical Guide. Washington: U.S. Government Printing Office, 1951. [I, 25]

Hegner, Robert W., and Karl A. Stiles. College Zoology. New York: The Macmillan Company, 1951. [I, 6]

Hessel, Alfred. Geschichte der Bibliotheken . . . Göttingen: Dr. H. Th. Pellens & Co., A.-G.; Hochschulverlag, 1925. [VI, 18]

_____. A History of Libraries. Translated with supplementary material by Reuben Peiss. Washington: Scarecrow Press, 1950. [VI, 18]

Honeywell, Roy J. The Educational Work of Thomas Jefferson. Cambridge: Harvard University Press, 1931. [II, 3, 7]

Hughes, Robert M. General Johnston. New York: Appleton, 1893. [IX, 8]

_____ and Joseph A. Turner. "Roanoke Female Seminary, Valley Union Seminary, Hollins Institute, and Hollins College," William and Mary College Quarterly, IX (October, 1929), 326. [IX, 10]

Indiana University. Catalogue of the Library of Indiana State University . . . Bloomington: Indiana University; M. L. Deal, 1842. [VIII, 7]

International Institute of Agriculture. Système de classification des sciences agricoles . . . Classification Scheme of Agricultural Science . . . Stoffeinteilung der Landwirtschaftswissenschaft. Rome: International Institute of Agriculture, 1942. [I, 14]

International Library Conference. Transactions and Proceedings of the Second International Library Conference Held in London July 13-16, 1897. London: Printed for members of the conference, 1898. [XII, 11]

Jefferson, Thomas. "A Bill for Amending the Constitution of the College of William and Mary, and Substituting More Certain Revenues for Its Support," The Papers of Thomas Jefferson. Edited by Julian P. Boyd. Princeton: Princeton University Press, 1950. [II, 2]

_____. "A Bill for Establishing a System of Public Education," in Roy J. Honeywell, The Educational Work of Thomas Jefferson. Cambridge: Harvard University Press, 1931. [II, 7]

_____. Catalogue. President Jefferson's Library. A Catalogue of the Extensive and Valuable Library of the Late President Jefferson, (copied from the original ms., in his handwriting, as arranged by himself,) to be sold at auction, at the Long room, Pennsylvania Avenue, Washington city, by Nathaniel P. Poor, on the [27th] February, 1829 . . . Washington: Printed by Gales and Seaton, 1829. [II, 11]

_____. A Catalogue of Books Forming the Body of a Library for the University of Virginia, to be Afterwards Enlarged by Annual Additions — An Explanation of the Views on which this Catalogue has been Prepared, in F. W. Page, "Our Library," The Alumni Bulletin of the University of Virginia, II (November, 1895), 79-80. [II, 15, 16]

Jefferson, Thomas. Letters (204:36303 [II, 1]; 200:35676 [II, 13]; 156:27351 [II, 17]; 192:34176 [II, 10]; 204:36275-36276 [II, 8; III, 3]; 206:36723 [III, 4]; 226:40383 [II, 4, 12; VI, 13]; 231:41403 [VI, 14]). Library of Congress. Manuscript Division.

_____. The Papers of Thomas Jefferson. Edited by Julian P. Boyd. Princeton: Princeton University Press, 1950. [II, 2, 6, 9]

Jefferson Papers. Library of Congress. Manuscript Division.

Jevons, William S. The Principles of Science: A Treatise on Logic and Scientific Method. London: Macmillan, 1883. [I, 18]

Johnson, Samuel. Elementa Philosophica: Containing chiefly, Noetica, or Things relating to the Mind or Understanding: and Ethica, or Things relating to the Moral Behaviour. Philadelphia: Printed by B. Franklin and D. Hall, 1752. [V, 15]

_____. An English and Hebrew Grammar . . . To Which is Added A Synopsis of All the Parts of Learning. London: Printed for W. Faden, 1767. [V, 5]

_____. "An Introduction to the Study of Philosophy, exhibiting a General View of all the Arts and Sciences," The Present State of the Republick of Letters, VII (1731), 376-92. [V, 12]

_____. Noetica: Or the First Principles of Human Knowledge. Being a Logick, Including both Metaphysics and Dialectic, Or the Art of Reasoning. With a brief Pathology, and an Account of the gradual Progress of the Human Mind, from the first Dawnings of Sense to the highest Perfection, both Intellectual and Moral, of which it is capable. To which is prefixed, A Short Introduction to the Study of the Sciences. Philadelphia, 1752. [V, 14]

Kane, William T., S.J. "Jean Garnier, Librarian," Mid-America, XXII (1940), 75-95, 191-222. [VII, 6; XVIII, 13]

Keep, Austin B. History of the New York Society Library. New York: De Vinne Press, 1908. [V, 3]

La Croix du Maine, François G., sieur de. Les bibliothéques françoises de La Croix et de Du Verdier. Edited and revised by Rigoley de Juvigny. Paris: Saillant & Nyon, 1772-73. [X, 14]

Leach, Arthur F. Educational Charters and Documents 598 to 1909. Cambridge, England: University Press, 1911. [IV, 9]

Lee, Samuel. The Library of the Late Reverend and Learned Mr. Samuel Lee. Containing a Choice Variety of Books upon all Subjects; particularly, Comentaries on the Bible; Bodies of Divinity. The Works as well of the Ancient, as of the Modern Divines; Treatises on the Mathematics, in all

Parts; History, Antiquities; Natural Philosophy Physick, and Chymistry; with Grammar and School-books. With many more Choice Books not Mentioned in this Catalogue. Exposed at the most easy rates, to sale, by Duncan Cambell; bookseller at the Dock-head over-against the Conduit. Boston Printed for Duncan Cambell book-seller at the Dock-head over-against the Conduit. 1693. [Facsim. ("Americana Series; photostat reproductions by the Massachusetts Historical Society," no. 36). Boston, 1921.] [V, 1]

Legipont, Oliver. Dissertationes philologico-bibliographicae, in quibus de adornandâ, & ornandâ bibliothecâ. Nürnberg: Impensis P. Lochneri & Mayeri, 1747.

Leibniz, Gottfried. De arte combinatoria. Leipzig, 1666.

_____. Historia et commendatis linguae charactericae universalis. Amsterdam and Leipzig, 1765.

_____. Idea bibliothecae publicae secundum classes scientiarum ordinandae. Leipzig, 1718.

Leidecker, Kurt F. Yankee Teacher: The Life of William Torrey Harris. New York: Philosophical Library, 1946. [X, 3, 6]

Lesley, J. Peter. "On the Classification of Books," in Smithsonian Institution. Annual Report. Washington: Government Printing Office, 1863. [IX, 16]

Letters. See Cogswell, Joseph Green; Jefferson, Thomas; Rush, Richard; Ticknor, George.

Librarians' Convention, New York, 1853. Proceedings of the Librarians' Convention held in New York City, Sept. 15, 16, and 17, 1853. [Cedar Rapids, Iowa: The Torch Press], 1915. [VIII, 13, 21; X, 1; XI, 7]

Literary and Historical Society of Quebec. Catalogue of Books in the Library . . . Quebec: Literary and Historical Society of Quebec; G. T. Cary, 1864. [IX, 16]

Mann, Margaret. Introduction to Cataloging and the Classification of Books. Chicago: American Library Association, 1943. [I, 24]

Martel, Charles. "Cataloging: 1876-1926," Bulletin of the American Library Association, XX (October, 1926). [XVII, 6]

_____. "Classification (From the Report of the Chief Classifier, Mr. Martel)," in Report of the Librarian of Congress . . . For the Fiscal Year Ending June 30, 1911. Washington: Government Printing Office, 1911. [XVII, 17]

_____. Classification in the Library of Congress. Typescript, February 1901. Library of Congress. Subject Cataloging Division. [XIII, 3; XIV, 2]

_____. "The Library of Congress Classification; Some Considerations Regarding the Relation of Book or Library Classification to the 'Order of the Sciences,'" in William Warner Bishop and Andrew Keogh, editors. Essays Offered to Herbert Putnam. New Haven: Yale University Press, 1929. [XV, 4]

Martel, Charles. Typescripts, 1901, 1918. Library of Congress. Subject
Cataloging Division.

Mason, George C. Annals of the Redwood Library and Athenaeum, Newport,
R.I. Philadelphia: Evans Printing House, 1891. [VI, 1, 2, 3]

Mather, Cotton. Magnalia Christi Americana: or, The Ecclesiastical History
of New England, from its first planting in the year 1620 unto the year of
Our Lord, 1698. London: Printed for Thomas Parkhurst, 1702. [V, 2]

Matthiä, Georg. "Project, wie eine offentliche Bibliothec in die bequemste
gemeinnützige Ordnung zu bringe," Nützliche Samlungen, June 23-July 7,
1755. [VI, 19]

Meigs, Jonathan. "Report," in Tennessee State Library. Catalogue. Nashville:
Southern Methodist Publishing House, 1855. [IX, 1]

Merlin, Romain. Paper describing classification in library of the Baron Antoine Isaac Silvestre de Sacy, in Proceedings of the Librarians' Convention. 1953. [VIII, 11]

Middleton, Conyers. Bibliothecae Cantabrigiensis ordinandae methodus
quaedam; quam domino procancellario senatuique academico considerandam & perficiendam officii et pietatis ergô proponit. Cantabrigiae: Typis
academicis, 1723. [V, 7]

Mitchill, Samuel L. "Outlines of Professor Mitchill's Lectures on Natural
History, in the College at New York, delivered in 1809-10, previous to
his departure for Albany, to take his seat in the Legislature of the State,"
The Medical Repository, XIII (1810), 257-67. [III, 2]

Monrad, Anna Marie. "Historical Notes on the Catalogues and Classifications
of the Yale University Library," in Papers in Honor of Andrew Keogh.
New Haven: Privately printed, 1938. [V, 19]

New Orleans Crescent, December 11, 1867, 2. [IX, 12]

New York Mercantile Library Association. Catalogue . . . New York: New
York Mercantile Library Association; Edward O. Jenkins, 1844. [VIII, 9]

_____. Catalogue . . . New York: New York Mercantile Library Association;
Baker, Godwin & Co., 1850. [VIII, 10]

_____. Systematic Catalogue of Books in the Collection of . . . New York:
New York Mercantile Library Association; Harper & Brothers, 1837.
[IX, 9]

New York Society Library. Alphabetical and Analytical Catalogue . . . New
York: New York Society Library; James Van Norden, 1838. [VIII, 4]

Norris, Dorothy. A History of Cataloguing and Cataloguing Methods, 1100-
1850: With an Introductory Survey of Ancient Times. London: Grafton &
Co., 1939. [IV, 12]

Page, F. W. "Our Library," The Alumni Bulletin of the University of Virginia, II (November, 1895), 79-80. [II, 15, 16]

Park, Roswell. "Outline of philosophy" in Scientific Tracts, for the Diffusion of Useful Knowledge . . . Boston: Light and Stearns, 1836. [VIII, 6]

_____. Pantology, or, A Systematic Survey of Human Knowledge. Philadelphia: Hogan and Thompson, 1841. [VIII, 5]

Parsons, Edward A. The Alexandrian Library, Glory of the Hellenic World. London: Cleaver-Hume, 1952. [IV, 7]

Perkins, Frederic B. A Rational Classification of Literature for Shelving and Cataloguing Books in a Library. San Francisco: Francis, Valentine and Co., 1882. [XI, 2]

Philadelphia Library Company. A Catalogue of the Books, . . . Philadelphia: Philadelphia Library Company; Zachariah Poulson, Jr., 1789. [VI, 4]

_____. A Catalogue . . . Philadelphia: Philadelphia Library Company; C. Sherman & Co., 1835. [VIII, 1]

Philadelphia Mercantile Library Company. Historical Sketch of the Mercantile Library, Philadelphia, and the Ninety-third Annual Report for the Year 1915. [XI, 4]

Plato. Phaedo. 118.

_____. "Phaedrus. 265. D, E," in Plato, With an English Translation. Translated by Harold North Fowler. London: Heinemann; New York: Putnam, 1933. [V, 3; I, 3]

_____. Protagoras. 313. C. [IV, 1]

Potter, Alfred C. and Charles K. Bolton. "The Librarians of Harvard College, 1667-1877," Bibliographical Contributions, IV (1897), Appendix I. [V, 5]

Potter, Alfred C. The Library of Harvard University; Descriptive and Historical Notes. Cambridge: Harvard University Press, 1934. [XVIII, 10]

Quincy, Josiah. Figures of the Past. Boston: Little, Brown, 1926. [III, 8]

Ranganathan, Shiyali R. Colon Classification. Madras: Madras Library Association, 1950. [XVIII, 15]

_____. Philosophy of Library Classification. Copenhagen: Ejnar Munksgaard, 1951. [I, 22]

Richardson, Ernest C. Classification: Theoretical and Practical. New York: Wilson, 1930. [I, 10]

Roberts, Martin A. The Library of Congress in Relation to Research. Washington: United States Government Printing Office, 1939. [XVII, 16]

Rowell, Joseph C. "Classification of Books . . . ," University of California Library Bulletin, No. 12 (1894). [XII, 15, 16]

Rush, Richard. Letter to H. Hall, Nov. 19, 1816, in Augustus E. B. Woodward. A System of Universal Science. (Library of Congress copy.) [VI, 9]

St. Louis Mercantile Library Association. Catalogue of Books . . . , January, 1850. St. Louis: Chambers & Knapp, 1850. [VII, 7; IX, 5]

_____. Catalogue Systematic and Analytical of the Books . . . St. Louis: Printed for the Association, 1858. [IX, 13, 14]

St. Louis Public School Library. Catalogue, Classified and Alphabetical, of the Books . . . . St. Louis: Missouri Democrat Book and Job Printing House, 1870. [X, 5, 8]

Savage, Ernest A. "Introduction" to John L. Thornton. The Chronology of Librarianship. London: Grafton & Co., 1941. [I, 1]

_____. Manual of Book Classification and Display for Public Libraries. London: George Allen & Unwin Ltd. and the Library Association, 1946. [X, 18]

Sayers, William C. Berwick. An Introduction to Library Classification. London: Grafton & Co., 1950. [I, 9]

_____. A Manual of Classification for Librarians and Bibliographers. London: Grafton & Co., 1944. [I, 17; XVI, 2]

_____. A Manual of Classification for Librarians and Bibliographers. Second edition, revised. London: Grafton & Co., 1944. [X, 10]

Schmidt, Friedrich. Die Pinakes des Kallimachos. Berlin: Verlag von Emil Ebering, 1922. [IV, 8]

Schneider, Georg. Theory and History of Bibliography. Translated by Ralph Robert Shaw. New York: Columbia University Press, 1934. [X, 2]

Schwartz, Jacob. "A Dozen Desultory Denunciations of the Dictionary Catalogue, with a Theory of Cataloguing," Library Journal, XI (1886), 470-4. [XVIII, 12]

_____. "King Aquila's Library: a Sequel to 'King Leo's Classification'," Library Journal, XI (1886), 232-244. [X, 21]

_____. "A Mnemonic System of Classification," Library Journal, IV (1879), 1-7. [X, 22]

_____. "A New Classification and Notation," Library Journal, VII (1882), 149. [X, 20]

Shepherd, Walter. A New Survey of Science. London: Harrap, 1949. [II, 14]

_____. A New Survey of Science. Revised and enlarged edition. London: Harrap, 1949. [I, 15]

Shields, Charles W. Philosophia Ultima, or, Science of the Sciences. New
    York: Scribner's, 1888-1905. [I, 19; VI, 12]

Shurtleff, Nathaniel B. A Decimal System for the Arrangement and Adminis-
    tration of Libraries. Boston: Privately printed, 1856. [X, 15]

Smith, John Jay. "Notes for a History of the Library Company of Philadelphia,"
    in Waldie's Port Folio and Companion to the Select Circulating Library.
    Philadelphia, 1835. [VIII, 2]

Smith, Lloyd P. On the Classification of Books, a Paper Read Before the
    American Library Association, May, 1882. Boston: Library Bureau,
    1882. [XI, 8]

Snyder, Alice D., editor. S. T. Coleridge's Treatise on Method as published
    in the Encyclopaedia Metropolitana. London: Constable, 1934. [IX, 2, 4]

South Carolina College. Catalogue of the Library of the South Carolina College.
    The Books Placed under an Analytical Arrangement, and their Titles
    Abridged. Columbia, S.C.: Telescope Print, 1836. [IX, 7]

Spofford, Ainsworth R. A Book for All Readers. New York: Putnam, 1900. [III, 9]

Steiner, B. C. "Rev. Thomas Bray and his American Libraries," The Ameri-
    can Historical Review, II (October 1896-July 1897), 64. [V, 4]

Stephen, Leslie. Hours in a Library. New York: Putnam, 1894. [IX, 3]

Tennessee State Library. Catalogue . . . Nashville: Southern Methodist Pub-
    lishing House, 1855. [IX, 1]

Thornton, John L. The Chronology of Librarianship. London: Grafton & Co.,
    1941. [I, 1]

Thou, Jacques A. de. Catalogus bibliothecae Thuanae . . . tum secundum
    scientias & artes à clariss. viro Ismaele Bullialdo digestus . . . Paris:
    impensis Directionis, 1679. [VII, 12]

Ticknor, Anna Eliot. Life of Joseph Green Cogswell as Sketched in His Let-
    ters. Cambridge: Riverside Press, 1874. [VI, 15, 16]

Ticknor, George. Letter to S. A. Eliot, Oct. 29, 1822, in Anna Eliot Ticknor,
    Life of Joseph Green Cogswell as Sketched in His Letters. Cambridge:
    Riverside Press, 1874, pp. 133-4.

United States Congress. Joint Committee on the Library. Condition of the Li-
    brary of Congress. March 3, 1897 . . . Washington: Government Printing
    Office, 1897. [III, 11, 12]

_____. Report . . . January 26th, 1816. Washington, 1816. [III, 5]

United States Library of Congress. Alphabetical Catalogue of the Library of
    Congress. Washington: Government Printing Office, 1864. [III, 7]

United States Library of Congress. Report of the Librarian of Congress, 1875, 1898, June 30, 1911. Washington: Government Printing Office, 1876, 1899, 1911. [XIII, 9, 10; XVIII, 9]

_____. Classification Division. . . . Classification. Class P: P-PA Philology. Linguistics. Classical Philology. Classical Literature. Washington: Government Printing Office, 1928. [XVI, 3; XVIII, 5]

United States Library of Congress. Music Division. Classification, Music and Books on Music. M: Music; ML: Literature of Music; MT: Musical Instruction and Study. Washington: Government Printing Office, 1917. [XVIII, 3]

United States Military Academy, West Point. Catalogue of the Library . . . , Exhibiting Its Condition at the Close of the Year 1852. New York: United States Military Academy; John F. Trow, 1853. [VIII, 20]

United States Naval Academy, Annapolis. Catalogue of the Library . . . June 30, 1860. Annapolis: United States Naval Academy; R. F. Bonsall, 1860.

Utley, George B. The Librarians' Conference of 1853; A Chapter in American Library History. Edited by Gilbert H. Doane. Chicago: American Library Association, 1951. [X, 1]

Venn, John. The Principles of Empirical or Inductive Logic. London: Macmillan, 1899. [I, 2]

Virginia. Commissioners to Fix the Site of the University of Virginia. "Report of the Commissioners . . . &c.," in Roy J. Honeywell. The Educational Work of Thomas Jefferson. Cambridge: Harvard University Press, 1931. [II, 3]

Virginia Gazette, December 19, 1777. [V, 8]

Virginia Magazine of History and Biography, XXXVII (April, 1929), 108. [V, 11]

Washington City Chronicle, November 7, 1829. [III, 6]

Wheatley, Henry B. How to Catalogue a Library. London: Elliot Stock, 1889. [XII, 5]

Wilkins, John, Bishop of Chester. An Essay towards a Real Character, and a Philosophical Language . . . London: Printed for S. Gellibrand, 1668.

Woodward, Augustus E. B. A System of Universal Science. Philadelphia: Edward Earle, Harrison Hall, and Moses Thomas, 1816. [II, 21; V, 18; VI, 7, 8, 12]

Yale College. A Catalogue of the Library of Yale College in New Haven. New London: Printed by L. Groen [sic], 1743. [V, 19]

Sample Pages of Early American Catalogs

8 MATHEMATICS.

3. Geometry.

Euclid's Elements, by Cunn, 9 4 5
              by Whiston, 9 4 6
              by Scarborough, 9 1 2
              by Gregory, 6 1 2
              by De Chales,
Des Cartes Geometria, 9 4 24 & 18 3 14

4. Trigonometry.

Briggs's Logarithms, ... 9 2 13
Harris's Trigonometry, ... 9 5 1

5. Optics.

Newtons Optics, 5 6 13 & 9 4 10 & 9 3 10
      Optical Lectures, 5 6 12 & 9 4 11
Bp. Barkley's Theory of Vision, ... 5 6 30
         Defence of it, 5 6 31
Wells's Optics, ... 5 6 18
Molineux's Dioptics, ... 9 3 2

6. Conic Sections.

Barrow's Archimedes, ... 6 5 28
Apollonai Conicorum, ... 9 1 12
Stone's Conic Sections, ... 9 3 8

7. Astronomy.

Whiston's Astronomical Lectures, 9 4 15
         Principles, ... 9 4 16
Watts's 9 7 19
Gregory's { Astronomy, 2 Vol. 9 4 17 18
Keil's { Latin & English, 9 4 19 20
Wells's 5 6 19
Derham s Astrotheology, 5 6 5

8. 4

NATURAL PHILOSOPHY. 9

8 A Mixture of all sorts of Mathematics.

Ward's Mathematics, 9 4 2
   Newtoni Arithmetica, Universalis, 9 4 12 13
               [& 5 6 11
—— Principia Mathematica, 9 3 11 in Eng 5 6 9 10
Wells's Mathematics, . . 5 6 18 to 20
Ozanam's Cursus Mathematicus, 5 Vol 5 6 21 to 25
              [& 9 5 15 to 19
      Fortification, ; ... 9 5 20
The Philosophical Transactions, 5 Vol. 5 4 10 to 14
              [& 9 2 3 to 7
Bion of Mathematical Instruments, Fol. 6 3 1 & 6 1 8
Wallis's Algebra, etc. 6 3 4
Hayes of Fluxions, ... 6 3 6
Taylor Methodus Incrementorum, 9 3 1
Cotesii Harmoniæ Mensurarum, 9 3 9
Hygeaii Opera. 2 Vol. Quarto. 9 3 12 13
    —— Planetary World, .., 11 5 22
Stone's Fluxions, ... 9 4 3
      —— Mathematical Dictionary, 9 4 9
Construction of Mapps, —— 9 4 4
Sturmey's Mathematics, —— 9 4 8
Wells of Shadows, ... 9 5 3
Miscellanea Curiosa, 2 Volumns, 9 5 4 5
Theodosii Sphericorum, —— 9 5 14
Hunt's Practical Gauging, ... 11 5 2
Gunter's Mathematics, —— 14 2 3
Vietæ Opera, ... 1 2 19

NATURAL PHILOSOPHY.

Rohaults Physicks, Latin, Eng. 9 5 21 23
   Keil Introductio ad veram Physicam, 9 4 21
Derham Physico-Theology, 5 6 4 & 9 5 11
the Religious Philosopher, 3 Vol. 5 6 1 to 3
Gravesandes Natural Phylosophy, 2 Vol. 5 6 7
                   Helk.

A Catalogue of the Library of Yale College in New Haven (1743)

C A T A L O G U E.

Nº.	FOLIO's.	No. of Vols.	Value, as near as can be estimated.	
			WHOLE SET.	EACH BOOK.
			Dollars	Dollars.
1	FATHERS PAUL's Council of Trent,	1	4	
2	Blair's Chronology, *(not to issue,)*	1	35	
3	Helvicus's Chronological Tables, -	1	3	
4	Booth's Diodorus Siculus, - - -	1	10	
5	Appian's History of the Civil Wars of the Romans, - - - - -	1	4	
6	Machiavel's Florentine History, -	1	3	
7	Duncan's Cæsar, - - - - - -	1	32	
8	Du Halede's History of China, -	2	24	12
10	De Soli's Conquest of Mexico, -	1	4	
11	Rapin's History of England, - -	5	50	10
16	Lord Herbert's Life of Henry VIII.	1	2	
17	Rushworth's Historical Collections,	8	24	3
25	Lord Clarendon's History of the Rebellion, - - - - - - - -	4	24	6
29	Guthrie's Geography, - - - -	1	13	
30	Bayle's Dictionary, - - - - -	5	30	6
35	Postlewayte's Dictionary of Commerce,	2	24	12
37	Beawes' Lex Mercatoria, - - -	1	12	
38	Domat's Civil Law, - - - - -	2	12	6
40	Grotius, by Barbeyrac, - - - -	1	14	
41	Puffendorf, by ditto, - - - - -	1	24	
42	Sidney on Government, - - - -	1	10	
43	Bacon's Works, - - - - - -	5	55	11

Catalogue of Books, Maps, and Charts, Belonging to The Library of the Two Houses of Congress (April, 1802)

CATALOGUE, &c.

AGRICULTURE, GARDENING, RURAL IMPROVE MENTS, AND DOMESTIC ECONOMY.

....

FOLIO.   **VOL.**

BAILEY's 106 Plates of Mechanical Machines and Im-
plements of Husbandry, approved and adopted
by the Society for the encouragement of Arts
and Manufactures   1
Complete Farmer; or A General Dictionary of Husbandry 1

QUARTO.

Columella (Lucius Moderatus) of Husbandry, in twelve
books; and his book concerning Trees: translated from the Latin   1
Communications to the Board of Agriculture of London,
on subjects relative to Husbandry, from 1797
to 1808   5
Dundonald's Treatise, showing the intimate connection,
that subsists between Agriculture and Chemistry, addressed to the cultivators of the soil, &c.   1
Evelyn's Silva; or A Discourse of Forest-trees, and the
Propagation of Timber; with Notes by A. Hun-
ter   2
Marshall's Minutes of Agriculture   1
———— Experiments and observations concerning Agri-
culture   1
Wildman's Treatise on the Management of Bees   1
Anderson's (James) Essays relating to Agriculture and ru-
ral Affairs   3
————On draining Bogs and swampy Grounds   1
————On Peat-moss   1

F.

A Catalogue of the Books . . . Library Company of
Baltimore (1809)

CATALOGUE, &c.

CLASS L

RELIGION, NATURAL THEOLOGY, DIVINITY, MYTHOLOGY,
AND ECCLESIASTICAL HISTORY.

A

353 ADDISON, Joseph: Evidences of the Christian Religion. d. Lond. 1763.
362 Age of Infidelity, in answer to the Second Part of the
Age of Reason. o. Phil. 1796.
6316 Animadversions upon a Book, entitled, Fanaticism
Fanatically imputed to the Catholics, Retorted by
S. C. d. Lond. 1674.

B

486 Baker, Miss Rachel: Devotional Somnium, or a Collection of Prayers and Exhortations. d. N. Y. 1815.
1296 Bates, Wm. Harmony of the Divine Attributes in the
Contrivance and Formation of Man's Redemption
by the Lord Jesus Christ. o. Lond. 1771.
333 Badin, S. T. Real Principles of Roman Catholics, in
Reference to God and the Country. d. Bardstown,
1805. *Donation of the Author.*
332 Barruel, Abbe: History of the Clergy during the
French Revolution. d. Burlington, 1794.
4449 Baptist Mission in India; containing a Narrative of its
Rise, Progress and present Condition ; a Statement of the physical and moral Character of the
Hindoos, their Cruelties, &c. with a very interesting Description of Bengal. d. Phil. 1811.
1305-6 Backus, Isaac: History of New England, with a
particular reference to the Denomination of Chris-
tians called Baptists. 2 vols. o. Boston, 1777.

B

CATALOGUE.

—◆—

DIVISION I.

ON THE INTELLECTUAL POWERS OF MAN.

1.—*Treatises on the Philosophy and Discipline of the Human Mind.*

—◆—

1. **A**NDERSON (Walter.) The Philosophy of Ancient Greece investigated in its origin and progress, to the eras of its greatest celebrity in the Ionian, Italian, and Athenian Schools, 1 vol. 4to. *Edinburgh,* 1791.

2. **A**RISTOTLE. The Metaphysics of Aristotle, translated from the Greek, with notes, in which the Pythagoric and Platonic dogmas respecting numbers and ideas, are unfolded from ancient sources: By Thomas Taylor, 1 vol. 4to. *London,* 1801.

3. **B**ROWN (Thomas.) Inquiry into the Relation of Cause and Effect, 1 vol. 8vo. *Andover,* 1822.

4. ———————— Lectures on the Philosophy of the Human Mind, 3 vols. 8vo. *Philadelphia,* 1824.

5. **B**URNET (James, Lord Monboddo.) Ancient Metaphysics, 6 vols. 4to. *Edinburgh,* 1779.

6. **D**RUMMOND (William.) Academical Questions, 1 vol. 4to. *London,* 1805.

7. **E**NSOR (George.) The Independent Man; or, an Essay on the formation and developement of those principles and faculties of the human mind which constitute moral and intellectual excellence, 2 vols. 8vo. *London,* 1806.

1

INDEX

To the Names of the AUTHORS *and the* TITLES *of Anonymous Books contained in the preceding Catalogue,*

(EXCEPTING Novels, which are already doubly entered.)

CHAPTER VII.

AGRICULTURE

AND

HORTICULTURE.

                                   Vols. Size

	Vols.	Size
Abu Zacaria Ebn el Awam. Book of Agriculture, Arabic & Spanish by Banqueri, *Madrid*, 1802	2	f
Christ, on the Cultivation of the Vine, German, *Frankfort*, 1800	1	8
Complete Body of Husbandry, *London*, 1756	2	f
Davy's Agricultural Chemistry. See Chem.		
Dickson's Agriculture, *Edinburgh*, 1770	2	8
Duhamel's Agriculture, Miller, *London*, 1764	2	8
Dundonald Treatise on Chem. & Agricul. *Lond.* 1803	1	4
Fellemberg, Views relative to the Agriculture of Switzerland French, *Geneva*, 1808	1	8
Gauteron's Letter to Picket on Agriculture, French, Pamphlet		
Kalb on the Cultivation of the Vine, German, *Stuttgart*, 1816	1	12
Kirwan on Manures, *London*, 1796	1	8
Knight on the Culture of the Apple and the Pear, *London*, 1818	1	8
Memoirs of the Society of Agriculture of the Seine, *Paris;*	9	8
Muller on the Cultivation of the Vine in Germany, German, *Leipsic*, 1803	1	12
Ray. Synopsis (Sterpium,) Latin, *London*, 1724	1	8
Serres, Theatre of Agriculture, by Gisors, French, *Paris*, 1802	4	8
Sichler's German Gardening, German,	3	8
" Manual of Gardening, Ger.	1	8
Sinclair's Code of Agriculture, *London*, 1821	1	8
Taylor's Arator *Petersburg*, 1818	1	8
Tull's Husbandry by Cobbett, *London*, 1822	1	8
Wheatly on Modern Gardening, " 1777	1	8

32

D

39 Dallas, R. C. Recollections of Lord Byron. Philadelphia, 1825. 8vo, 1 vol.

Dallas. See Poynder.

78 Dalzel, Andrew. Lectures on the Character and Literature of the Greeks, Edinburgh, 1821. 8vo, 2 vols,

Daniel, Samuel. See British Poets, vol. 2.

45 D'Anville, M. Compendium of Ancient Geography.— New-York, 1814. 8vo, 2 vols. and Atlas.

43 Darby, William. The Emigrant's Guide to the Western and South-western States and Territories. New-York, 1818. 8vo, 1 vol.

Darnley, a novel. See James, G. P. R.

Dartmouth College, Case of. See Farrar.

137 ——— ———, Tracts relating to. 8vo, 1 vol.

89 Darwin, Erasmus. The Botanic Garden, a poem in two parts London, 1795. 4to, 1 vol.

88 ———, ———. Zoonomia, or the Laws of Organic Life. London, 1796. 4to, 2 vols.

Davenant, Sir William. See British Poets, vol. 5.

23 David, Citoyen. Historie Chronologique des Operations de l'armee du Nord. Paris, 1795. 8vo, 1 vol.

Davies, Sir John. See British Poets, vol. 4.

35 Davies, Thomas. Life of David Garrick. London, 1781. 8vo, 2 vols.

24 Davila, H. C. History of the Civil Wars of France.— London, 1678. Folio, 1 vol.

———, —. —. See Adams, J.

86 Davy, Sir Humphrey. Agricultural Chemistry. Philadelphia, 1821. 8vo, 1 vol.

———, ———. Life of. See Paris.

49 Davy, John Account of Ceylon. London, 1821. 4to, 1 vl.

63 Dawson, Thomas. Defence of Christianity. London, 1733 8vo, 1 vol.

28 Deane, Samuel. History of Scituate, in Massachusetts, from its settlement to 1831. Boston, 1831. 8vo, 1 vol.

84 ———, ———. The New-England Farmer. Worcester, Ms. 1797. 8vo, 1 vol.

17 Debrett, John. Peerage of Great Britain and Ireland.— London, 1822. 12mo, 2 vols.

CATALOGUE.

THEOLOGY.

Form.		Edition.
8.	Acts of the Apostles, in modern Greek.	Malta 1827
F.	Ainsworth, H., Annotations on the five Books of Moses.	Lond. 1639
F.	Alesius, Alexander, super tertium sententiarum.	Venet. 1475
F.	Ambrose, Isaac, Works.	Lond. 1582
8.	American Preacher. 4 vols.	Elizabetht'n 1771
F.	Anselmus, Cantuar. archiepiscopus, opera.	Paris 1721
8.	Austin, Samuel, View of the Church.	Worcester 1807
8.	Backus, Isaac, History of the Church of N. England. 3 vols.	Bost. 1777-96
4.	Balduinus, F., Apostolica ministrorum, ecclesia institutio.	Wittenberg 1630
12.	Balguy, Thomas, Divine benevolence asserted.	Lond. 1803
	Ballou, H. Universalism.	
12.	Barclay, Robert, Catechism & Confession of Faith.	New York 1813
8.	——Apology for the true Christian Divinity.	Philad. 1805
F.	Bates, Wm. Works.	Lond. 1723
F.	Baxter, Richard, Works. 4 vols	ib. 1707
4.	Bebelius, B. Ecclesia antediluviana.	Argent. 1706
4.	Behmen, Jacob, Works, by Law. 4 vols.	Lond. 1764
8.	Bellamy, Joseph, Works. 3 vols.	New York, 1811

Catalogue of the Books belonging to the Library of the University
of Vermont (1836)

CATALOGUE.

CHAP. I.—(ALCOVE No. 4.)

Agriculture and Horticulture.

American Farmer, containing Original Essays &c , on Agriculture, Horticulture, Rural and Domestic Economy, and Internal Improvement, &c., edited by J. S. Skinner, 11 v., 4to; Baltimore, 1821—'29.

American Farmer, continued—Edited by G. Smith, 12th, 13 and 14th v., 4to; Baltimore, 1831—'33.

A Treatise on the Origin, Progressive Improvement and Present State of the Culture of Silk Manufacture, (the 14th v. of Lardner's Cabinet Cyclopædia) 12mo; Phil. 1832.

Chymistry Applied to Agriculture, by J. A. Chaptal, 8vo; Boston, 1836.

Culture of Silk. A Letter from the Secretary of the Treasury, Transmitting the information required by a Resolution of the House of Representatives, of May 11th, 1826, in relation to the Growth and Manufacture of Silk, 8vo; Washington, 1828. (present.)

Cultivator, a Monthly Publication, devoted to Agriculture, v., 4to; Albany, 1834-'35-'36-'37.

Farmers' and Graziers' Guide, in the Choice and Management of Neat Cattle and Sheep, &c, by B. Lawrence, 8vo; Phil. 1832.

ALPHABETICAL CATALOGUE.

ABBOT, Rev. A., Letters written in Cuba, 8vo. Boston, 1829.

—— Charles, Law of Merchant Ships and Seamen, 8vo. Lond. 1808.

*Abbreviatio Placitorum, Temp. Regum Ric. I., Johan., Hen. III., Ed. I, & II., fol. London, 1811.—*Gift of the British Government.*

Abeel, David, Journal of a Residence in China, from 1829 to 1833, 12mo. New-York, 1834.

Abeille Françoise, 8vo. Paris, l'an VII.

Abercrombie, James, Lectures on the Catechism, on Confirmation., &c., 8vo. Philadelphia, 1811.

—————— John, Gardener's Pocket Dictionary, 3 vols. 12mo. London, 1786.

————————————————————— Journal, 12mo. Lond. 1808.

—————— John, M. D., The Philosophy of the Moral Feelings, 18mo. New-York, 1833.

—————— John, Inquiries concerning the Intellectual Powers, and the Investigation of Truth, 18mo. New-York, 1832.

Abrantès, Duchess d', (Madam Junot,) Memoirs, 8vo. New-York, 1832.

*Abridgment of the Laws of the different Colonies of North America, 8vo. London, 1704.—*Gift of Jacob Radcliffe, Esq.*

Abulfeda. Annales Moslemici Latinos ex Arabicis, fecit J. J. Reiske, 4to. Lipsiæ, 1772. (1st volume.)

—— Descriptio Ægypti, Arabice et Latine, a J. D. Michælis, 8vo. Goettingæ, 1776.

Académie Royale des Inscriptions, et des Belles Lettres, Histoire de, 19 vols. 12mo. Paris, 1718—1785.

—— Mémoires de Littérature Tirés des Regístres de l'Académie, 81 vols. 12mo. Paris, 1772—1781.

Account of Jamaica, 8vo. London, 1808.

—————— the Island of St. Helena, with a Memoir of Buonaparte, 12mo. New-York, 1815.

Accum, Frederick, Chemical Amusements, 12mo. Philadelphia, 1818.

—————— On Adulteration of Food and Culinary Poisons, 12mo. Philadelphia, 1820.

—————— On gas lights, 8vo. London, 1815.

Acerbi, Joseph, Travels through Sweden, Finland and Lapland, 2 vols. 4to. London, 1802.

*Ackermann, R., Repository of Arts, Literature, Commerce, &c., 2 vols. 8vo. London, 1809.

---

* The asterisk prefixed to a title, indicates that the book is prohibited from circulation.

2

ANALYTICAL CATALOGUE.

THEOLOGY.

Sacred Writings, Philology and Criticism.

Alberti, J., Glossarium in N. Test.
Aquinas, T., In Epistolas.
Baker, R., Lord's Prayer.
Barradius, S., In Evangelicam.
———— Itinerarium ex Ægypto.
Becano, P. M., Analogia del Ant. y N. Test.
Bible, Old and New Testament, and parts thereof, in various languages.
Biblical Magazine.
Blackwall, A., Sacred Classics.
Blayney, B., Jeremiah and Lamentations.
Bloomfield, S. T., Recensio Synoptica.
———— Greek Testament.
Bochart, S. Phaleg, Canaan, &c.
Brentius, J., In Lucam.
Bryant, J., Plagues of Egypt.
Buchanan, G., Paraphrasis Psalmorum.
Burder, G., History of Bible.
Burkett, W., Exposition of N. Testament.
Butler, C., Horæ Biblicæ.
Bythnerus, V., Lyra Prophetica.
Calmet, A., Dictionary.
Calvin, J., In libros Mosis.
———— Jeremiam.
Campbell, G , Four Gospels.
Capellus, J., In N. Testamentum.
Chapman, E. J., Notes on N. Testament.
Chrysostomus, St., In Johannem.
Clarendon, E., On the Psalms.
Clemens, R., Epist.. ad Corinth. Interpret.
Coccejus, J., Proph., XII. Versione, &c.
———— In Joannis.
Concilliationes loc., V. Test., et Jonstonis de Festis.
Concordance of Scriptures.
Conversations on Bible.
Croly, G., On Apocalypse.
Crutwell, C., Concordance.
Del Rio, M., In Jeremiam.
De Ponte, L., In Cantica.
Desportes, P., Pseaumes de David.
Dialogues, Scriptural.
Duport, I., Metaphrasis Psalmorum.
Dyonisius, C., In Epistolas.
Eunarationes Evangeliarum.
Erasmus, D., In Epistolas Pauli.
———— Ecclesiastes.
Eusebius, P., Demonstratio Evangeliea.
Feri, In Libros Mosis.
———— Joannis.
———— Mathæium.
Geddes, A., On Scriptures.
Gell, R., Translation of Bible.
———— Remains.
Genebradius, G., In Psalmos.

Gleig, G. R., History of Bible.
Godeau, Pseaumes.
Good, J. M., Song of Songs.
Gray, R., Key to Old Testament.
Griesbach, J. J., N. Testamentum.
Grotius, H., In Evangelia.
Harmer, T., On Solomon's Song.
Harris, T. M., Natural Hist. of Bible.
Heinsius, D., In N. Testamentum.
Henry, M., On Bible.
Horne, G., On Psalms.
———— T. H., Study of Scriptures.
Hylaret, F. M., In Evangelia.
Index Biblicus.
Isidorus, St. P., De Scripturæ Interpret.
Jebb, J., Sacred Literature.
Joannem, Annotationes in.
Johnson, Rev. S., On Prophecies.
Jones, W., Figurative Language.
King, E., Morcels of Criticism.
Kortum, on Job.
Leigh, Critica Sacra.
Le Moyne, Jerem. xxiii.
L'Homond, Hist. Sacra.
Lieberkuhn, Hist. of J. C., in Delaware.
Lightfoot, In Joannis.
Locke, On St. Paul, and Le Clerc on Inspiration.
Lowth, Poesi Hebræorum.
———— Poetry of Hebrews.
———— Translation of Isaiah.
Luther, On Galatians.
Marckius, In Vet., et N. Testamentum.
McKnight, Harmony of Gospels.
Mey, On Proverbs.
Millhausen, On Reading Scriptures.
Newcome, Version of Ezekiel.
Newton, T., On Prophecies.
Nonnus, Poetæ Conv. Ev. Joannem.
Novum Testamentum, à Dakins.
Orton, Exposition of Old Testament.
Osiander, in Epist. ad Hebræos.
Ostervald, Arguments of Chapters.
Owen, C., On Septuagint Version.
Paley, Horæ Paulinæ.
Pareus, in Epist., ad Romanos.
———— Galatos.
Percy, Key to N. Testament.
Philo, Judæus, Opera.
Poole, Synopsis Criticorum.
Porteus, On St. Matthew.
Prideaux, Connections.
Psalms, by Gordon, with Music.
Psalterium, à Hessum.
Reeve, Hist. of the Bible.
Relandus, Analecta Rabbinica.
Roy, Key of Revelations.

N. B. The title in full will be found by referring to the *author's name, or initial word*, in the Alphabetical Catalogue.
32

Alphabetical and Analytical Catalogue of the New York Society Library (1838)

CATALOGUE.

A.

ABARBENEL, or ABRABANEL, or ABREBENEL, etc., ISAAC,
 a Rabbi ; b. at Lisbon 1437. *d.* 1508.

[1] פירוש על נביאים ראשונים. Commentarius in Prophetas
Priores ; Cura Augusti Pfeiffer. folio. Lipsiae, 1686.   27   17
> *Note.* See Wolf's Bibliotheca Hebraea. Vol. 1. Art. 1142.

ABBADIE, JAMES, D. D.
[2] [Mystery of Man's Salvation by Jesus Christ. 8vo. Lond. 1705.]   49   48
[3] Id. (Title changed to) A Treatise on the Div. of Christ. The
Translation revised and abr'd by Booth. 12mo. Lond. 1777.   37   26

ABBOT, ABIEL, D. D., *of Haverhill and Beverly, Mass.*
[4] Sermon at the Installation of Abiel Abbot, at Peterboro', N. H.
12mo. Boston, 1827. (Ord. Sermons, Vol. III.)   200   —

ABBOT, REV. JACOB, *of Hampton Falls.*
[5] Sermon at the Ordination of Jaazaniah Crosby ; with Bancroft's Ch. and Thayer's R't H'd. 8vo. Walpole, 1811. (Ord.
Serms. Vol. XXVII.)   200   —

ABERCROMBIE, JAMES, D. D.
[6] The Mourner Comforted. 2d ed. 8vo. Phila. 1821.   29   25

ABERCROMBIE, JOHN, M. D., F. R. S.
[7] Inquiries concerning the Intellectual Powers, and the Investigation of Truth. 12mo. N. York, 1839. (Fam. Lib.)   65   37
[8] Phil. of the Moral Feelings. 12mo. N. York, 1837. (Fam. Lib.)   65   58

ABERCROMBY, SIR RALPH.
[9] Life of Abercromby. (Gleig's Brit. Commanders, Vol. III. 197.)   12   24

ABRAHAM, or ABRAM, NICHOLAS, *a Jesuit.*
[10] Pharus Vet. Testamenti, sive Sacr. Quaestionum Libri XV.
Quibus acc. ejusd. Auth. de Veritate et Mendacio Lib. IV. folio.
Paris. 1648.   27   15

ABRAHAM SEBA, *a Rabbi of Lisbon ; flourished about A. D.* 1500.
[11] צרור המור. (Fasciculus Myrrhae, sive Commentarius in
Pentateuchum. fol. Venetiis, 1523.)   27   22
> *Note.* This book is called the " Bundle of myrrh," in allusion to
> Cant. 1: 13. See Wolf's Biblio. Hebraea. Vol. 1. Art. 127. p. 93.

ACCUM, FREDERICK.
[12] Theoretical and practical Chemistry. 2 vols. 8vo. 2d ed. (vol.
2 missing.) London, 1807.   136   19
[13] Id.   2 vols. 8vo. Philadelphia, 1808.   138   38
[14] Id. With an Appendix, by T. Cooper, Esq. 2 vols. 8vo. Philadelphia, 1814.   136   8

1

INDEX.

NOTE. The large figures refer to the pages of the Catalogue ; the small figures
to the figures in the left-hand margin.

CATALOGUE.

A.

ABBOT, Abiel, D. D., *of Haverhill and Beverly, Mass.; b.* 1770, *d.* 1828.

1 Letters, written in the interior of Cuba, in 1828. 8vo. Bost. 1829.   53   41

ABBOTT, Rev. Jacob, M. A., *late Principal of the Mt. Vernon Female School, Boston.*

2 The Young Christian. 12mo. Bost. 1832.   31   43

3 The Corner Stone; or a familiar Illustration of the elementary principles of Religious Truth. 12mo. Bost. 1834.   31   42

4 The Teacher. 12mo. Bost. 1833.   15   33

5 Edition of Abercrombie's Moral Philosophy. See ABERCROMBIE.   12   13

ABEEL, David.

6 Residence in China, from 1829 to 1833. 12mo. N. York, 1834.   43   63

ABERCROMBIE, John, M. D., F. R. S., *First Physician to his Majesty in Scotland.*

7 The Philosophy of the Moral Feelings; with Additions &c., by Jacob Abbott. 12mo. Bost. 1842.   12   13

ABERNETHY, Rev. John, *of Antrim, afterw. of Dublin; b.* 1680, *d.* 1740.

8 Sermons. 4 vols. 8vo. Lond. 1762.   34   16

ABRANTES, Duchess d' (Madame JUNOT).

9 Memoirs of Celebrated Women of all countries. 2 vols. 12mo. Phil. 1835.   40   38

10 Memoirs. 3 vols. 8vo. Lond. 1831.   43   17

ACHAINTRE, Nic. Lud.

11 Edition of Persius, whom see.   9   12

ADAM, Alexander, LL. D., *Rector of a High School, Edinburgh; b.* 1741, *d.* 1809.

12 Latin Grammar; with Rules for Pronunciation.

2

INDEX.

—

NOTE.—The large figures denote the page of the descriptive catalogue, and the small ones, the numeral prefixes in the left-hand margin.

CATALOGUE

OF THE

MERCANTILE LIBRARY.

A B A —— A B E

Abailard et Heloïse—Lettres, avec un Essai par Guizot. 2 v.	8vo. Paris.	1839
Abbott, Chas.—Law relative to Merchant Ships and Seamen	8vo. Lond.	1802
—— Jacob—China and the English	18o. N. Y.	1835
—— —— Corner Stone	12o. Bost.	1834
—— —— History of Alexander the Great	16o. N. Y.	1848
—— —— " King Alfred of England	16o. N. Y.	1849
—— —— " Julius Cæsar	16o. N. Y.	1849
—— —— " King Charles I.	16o. N. Y.	1848
—— —— " " Charles II.	16o. N. Y.	1849
—— —— " Cyrus the Great	16o. N. Y.	1850
—— —— " Queen Elizabeth	16o. N. Y.	1849
—— —— " Hannibal the Carthaginian	16o. N. Y.	1849
—— —— " Mary Queen of Scots	16o. N. Y.	1848
—— —— " William the Conqueror	16o. N. Y.	1849
—— —— Summer in Scotland	12o. N. Y.	1848
—— —— Teacher	12o. Bost.	1836
—— —— Way to do Good	12o. Bost.	1836
—— —— Young Christian	12o. N. Y.	1833
—— —— "	12o. N. Y.	1834
—— J. S. C.—History of Maria Antoinette	16o. N. Y.	1849
—— —— Kings and Queens; or, Life in the Palace	12o. N. Y.	1848
Abdy, E. S.—Residence and Tour in U. S., 1833–4. 3 v.	12o. Lond.	1835
Abeel, Dav.—Residence in China, &c., 1829–33	12o. N. Y.	1834
Abeillard and Heloisa, Hist. of the Lives of. [Title wanting.]	8vo.	
———————— See *Abailard*.		
Abell, Eliz.—Recollections of Napoleon at St. Helena	12o. Lond.	1845

2

Theology—Exegetical.

Kitto's Pictorial Hist. of Palestine and Jews.
Lectures on History of Christianity. *Burnap,*
Introduct. to History of the Church. *Jarvis.*
Strauss' Life of Christ.
Taylor's Life of Christ. (*Sac.* Classics),
Neander's Life of Christ.
Furness' Jesus and his Biographers.
Miracles of Our Lord. *Trench.*
Not Paul, but Jesus. *Bentham.*
Difficulties in Paul's Writings. *Whately.*

Stuart's Interpretation of Prophecy,
Explanat. of Script. Types & Proph. *Kinney.*
Apostles' School of Prophetic Interp. *Maitland.*
Dissertations on the Prophecies. *Faber.*
Nature and End of Prophecy. *Lee.*
Little Book Open ; of Christ's Coming.
Signs of the Times. *Keith,*
Dissertations on Prophecies. *Newton.*
Hyponoia ; Thoughts on Apocalypse. *Hurd.*
Lord's Exposition of the Apocalypse.
Wordsworth's Lectures on the Apocalypse.
Apocalypse of St. John. *Croly,*
Treatise on Millennium. *Bush,*
Bush's Anastasis ; Resurrection of the Body ;
" Anastasis" examined. *Fysh,*
Soul ; or, Scriptural Psychology. *Bush,*
Millennial Tidings. *Livermore,*
Second Appear. of Christ. *Darrow,* and others,
Second Advent. *Crosby,*

BIBLICAL AND EARLY CHURCH HISTORY.

History of Bible. *Stackhouse-*
History of Bible. *Gleig,*
Bible Narrative. *Zornlin,*
Sunday Evenings. (*Boys'* and Girls' Lib.),
Scripture Dialogues.
Scripture Characters. *Robinson,*
Sacred Biography. *Hunter.*
Family Pictures from the Bible. *Ellet,*
Lives of Apos. and Mar. (*Boys'* & Girls' Lib.)
Lives of Apostles. *Cave,*
Lives of the Apos. & John Baptist. *Greenwood,*
Apocryphal New Testament. (*Bible*).
Evangiles Apocryphes. *Brunet,*
Manual of Christian Antiquities. *Riddle.*
Compendium of Christian Antiquities. *Henry.*
Eusebius' Ecclesiastical History-
Neander's Hist. of Christian Relig. & Church.
Histoire du Gnosticisme. *Matter.*
History of the Christian Church. *Ruter.*
History of the Church of Christ. *Allen.*
Dowling's Introduction to Ecclesiastical Hist.
Seven Ages of the Church. *Cotterill.*
Stebbing's History of Christian Church,
Milner's History of Church of Christ.
Giesler's Ecclesiastical History.
Mosheim's Ecclesiastical History.
Milman's History of Christianity.
Compendium of Ecclesiast. Hist. *Palmer,*
Church of Saviour; Early Christ'y. *Bowring,*
Lives of the Fathers of the Church. *Blakey.*
Rome under Paganism and under Popes. *Miley.*
Causes of the Corrup. of Christianity. *Vaughan.*
Compendium of Ecclesiastical History. *Mason,*
Hist. of Church to Reformation. *Waddington.*

Theology—Devotional.

History of Success of the Gospel. *Gillies.*
Remarks on Ecclesiastical History. *Jortin.*
Cave's Primitive Christianity. (*Sac.* Classics),
Primitive Christianity Exemplified. *Mant.*
Early Conflicts of Christianity. *Kip,*
Early Progress of Christianity. *Hinds.*
Church in the Catacombs. *Maitland.*
Antiquities of Christian Church. *Bingham.*
Histoire des Conciles. *Guerin.*

DEVOTIONAL WORKS.

Christ is All. *Tyng.*
Martyr Lamb. *Krummacher,*
The Great Teacher. *Harris.*
Plan of the Founder of Christ'y. *Reinhard,*
Incarnation ; or, Virgin & her Son. *Beecher,*
Reflections on the Works of God. *Sturm,*
Oracles of God. *Irving,*
Letters to his Son on the Bible. *Adams,*
Boyle's Hum. Intel. & the Scrip. (*Sac.* Clas.),
Daily Scripture Readings. *Chalmers.*
Sabbath Scripture Readings. *Chalmers.*

Way of Life. *Hodge,*
Windings of the River of Life. *Cheever,*
Pleasantness of Religion. *Henry,*
Importance of Religion. *Foster,*
Importance of Religious Life. *Melmoth,*
Apples of Gold. *Brooks,*
Prize Letters to Students. *Dickinson,*
Letters to the Young. *Jewsbury,*
Anxious Enquirer. *James,*
Endeavors after Christian Life. *Martineau,*
Doddridge's Rise and Progress,
Regeneration and Salvation. *Doddridge,*
Abbott's Corner Stone,
Christian. the Deliv. of the Soul. *Mountford,*
Bunyan's Holy War,
Bunyan's Pilgrim's Progress ;
Cottage Lectures on Pilgrim's Progress,
Cheever's Lectures on Pilgrim's Progress.
Fountain of Living Waters,
True Happiness. *Pike,*
Heaven upon Earth. *Janeway,*
Bates' Spiritual Perfec. Unfolded. (*Sac.* Clas.),
Christian Piety. *M'Laurin,*
Live while you Live. *Griffith.*
Treatise on Religious Affections. *Edwards,*
Personal Declension & Revival. *Winslow,*
Harmony of Faith & Character. *Abercrombie,*
Progress of Christian Life. *Ware,*
Young Man's Closet Library. *Philip,*
No Cross, No Crown. *Penn.*
True Christian. *James,*
Pictures of Christian Life. *Willmott,*
Formation of Christian Character. *Ware.*
Traits of Christian Character. *Spring.*
Life of Faith. *Upham,*
Discourse concerning Prayer. *Patrick,*
Mt. of Olives; Lect. on Prayer. *Hamilton,*
Henry's Method for Prayer,
The Mercy Seat. *Spring.*
Sacra Privata. *Wilson,*
Daily Communion with God. *Henry,*
Guide to Devotion-
Pious Meditations. *Kirkpatrick,*

Catalogue of the Mercantile Library in New York (1850)

ALPHABETICAL CATALOGUE

OF THE

TENNESSEE STATE LIBRARY.

A.

ABBOTT, John S. C.
Life of Napoleon Bonaparte. 2 vols. 8vo. 6¾ by 10 in. 640 pp.
Harper & Brothers, New York, 1850.

ADAMS, John.
Life and Works of. By Charles Francis Adams. 2 copies: one not
complete. 9 vols. 8vo. 6 by 9¼ in. 634 pp. Little & Brown,
Boston, 1850.

ADAMS, John Quincy.
Life of Madison and Monroe, fourth and fifth Presidents of the United
States. 1 vol. 12mo. 5½ by 7¾ in. 440 pp. G. H. Derby,
Buffalo, 1850.

ADAMS, John Quincy, Life of. (See Seward, W. H.)

AGRICULTURE, Journal of.
Quarterly. 1828–55. New Series. 19 vols. 8vo. 5¾ by 8¾ in.
700 pp. W. Blackwood, Edinburgh, 1828–55.

Prize Essays of Highland Society, 1828–55, New Series, 14 vols. (See
Highland Society.)

AIDE MEMOIRE TO THE MILITARY SCIENCES.
Edited by a Committee of the Corps of Royal Engineers. Second edi-
tion. Plates. 3 vols. 8vo. 6½ by 10¼ in. 628 pp. J. Weale,
London, 1853.

2

GALVANISM.

HEAT.

ARNOTT, Neil.
On Warmth and Ventilation. 1 vol. 8vo.

METCALFE, Samuel L.
Caloric. Its Agencies in the Phenomena of Nature. 2 vols. 8vo.

LIGHT.

CHEMISTRY.

BRANDE, William Thomas.
Manual of Chemistry. Sixth edition. 2 vols. 8vo.

JOHNSTON, James F. W.
The Chemistry of Common Life. Illustrated. 2 vols. 12mo.

SMEDLEY, Thompson, Rich, etc.
The Occult Sciences. (Encyclopædia Metropolitana.) 1 vol. 12mo.

THOMPSON, Robert Dundas.
Cyclopædia of Chemistry. Illustrated. 1 vol. 8vo.

YOUMANS, Edward L.
Chemical Atlas. 1 vol. 4to.

(See Smithsonian Contributions.)

SOUND.

BREWER, Rev. Dr. E. Cobham.
Sound and its Phenomena. 1 vol. 16mo.

METEOROLOGY.

BASSNET, T.
Mechanical Theory of Storms. 1 vol. 12mo.

KÆMITZ, L. F.
On Meteorology. Translated by C. V. Walker. Illustrated. 1 vol.
12mo.

UNITED STATES EXPLORING EXPEDITION.
Vol. XI. Meteorology. By Capt. Wilkes. Illustrated. 1 vol. 4to.
(See Smithsonian Contributions.)

Catalogue of the Tennessee State Library (1855)

CATALOGUE

OF THE

Library of the Lyceum and Library Society.

ART.

AGRICULTURE, COMMERCE, PURE ART AND LANGUAGE.

	D.	S.	Book.
ALLAN's Agriculture—The American Farm Book...............	29	1	26
AN ARTIST on Oil Painting—A Treatise on Oil Painting; a hand-book of Young Painters............................	29	5	10
ARMSTRONG's Agriculture—A Treatise on Agriculture..........	29	1	33
ACADEMICIANS on Painting—Letters on Painting...............	29	5	7
ANONYMUS—Painters—The Modern Painter....................	29	5	8
do London Annual—An Illustrated Almanac from 1846 to 1852......................................	5	2	17
do English Worthies, with Portraits....................	5	6	17
do Athenæum—A Journal of English and Foreign Literature and Art, from 1849 to 1855, 18 vols....................	29	6	1—18
do United States—The Weakness and Inefficiency of the Government of the United States.....................	29	4	16
ARTISTS' Union—The Art Union......................	5	8	23
ACKERLY's Napoleon—Military Axioms of Napoleon.............	29	7	34
ALISON's Taste—A Treatise on Taste......................	29	7	36
ANONYMOUS—Husbandry—British Husbandry, 3 vols............	29	1	2—4
do Sheep—Their Breeds; their Management.............	29	1	5
ADDISON's Punctuation—A complete System of Punctuation......	29	7	22
BURN's Cotton Trade—Statistics of the Cotton Trade...........	29	1	17
BOUSSINGAULT's Rural Economy—Chemistry applied to Agriculture,	29	1	24
BEECHER's Domestic Economy—A Treatise on Family Economy...	29	1	30
BROWNE's Trees—A Description of the Trees of America........	28	5	28
BUEL's Instructor—Useful Knowledge for Young Farmers, 2 vols..	29	1	38—39
BOSANQUET's Currency—Metallic, Paper and Credit Currency; Means of Ascertaining their value...........................	29	4	7
BELL's Expression—Anatomy and Physiology of Expression, as connected with the Fine Arts..........................	29	5	14
do Italy—Observations on Italy, its Art and Architecture..	5	2	26
BARTLETT's Scenery—American Scenery, 2 vols................	5	2	20—21
BLAIR's Rhetoric—Lectures on Rhetoric, 2 copies..............	29	7	7—8
BURKE's Sublimity—A Treatise on the Nature of the Sublime and Beautiful, 3 copies..................................	29	7	18—20
BENNETT's Swimming—A Treatise on the Art of Swimming......	29	7	33

Catalogue of the Library of the Lyceum and Library Society, First District, City of New Orleans (1858)

CATALOGUE.

HISTORY.

HISTORY. § 1. *Philosophy of the Art.*

Bazin, L'Abbé :   The Philosophy of History, or a Philosophical and Historical Dissertation on the Origin, Manners, Customs and Religion of the different nations and people of antiquity, &c., &c.; translated by Henry Wood Gandell. 8vo. London, 1829. No. 7014.

Bolingbroke, St. John, Lord :   Letters on the Study and Use of History. Works, v. 2., p. 173. Polygraphs.

Herder, John -Godfrey :   Outlines of a Philosophy of the History of Man ; translated from the German, by T. Churchill. 4to. London, 1800. No. 10,122.

Montagu, Edward W. :   Reflections on the Rise and Fall of the Ancient Republics ; adapted to the present state of Great Britain. 12mo. Philadelphia, 1806. No. 8267.

[These are not the scape-grace's own, but written for him, by his tutor, the Rev. Mr. Foster. For the maternal opinion of his worthlessness, see Lady M. W. Montagu's Letters to her Husband. Works, polygraphs.]

Peabody, Elizabeth P. :   First steps to the study of History ; being part first of a Key-to History. 12mo. Boston, 1832. No. 15,612.

Schlegel, T. F. :   Philosophy of History, in a Course of Lectures delivered at Vienna ; translated, with a Memoir of the Author, by J. B. Robertson. 2d edition. 12mo. London, 1846. No. 1512.

Whateley, Richard :   Historic Doubts relative to Napoleon Bonaparte. 12mo. Boston, 1853. No. 15,075.

[The eldest treatise on the art of writing History, (and, it may be said, of studying it), is that of Lucian. It may be found in Franklin's Translation. It is, however, but the mere germ of the art of Critical History, of which the discovery is due to Vico, the Italian, a great genius, who, of himself, first devised the true idea of systematic and philosophic history, embodying it in his *Principii d'una Scienza nuova*, first published about 1725. Even then, his luminous conception slept almost unnoticed, until, about 1750, that piercing, though often ill-directed intelligence, Voltaire, begun to apply it, in his brilliant compositions, and drew to himself the credit of having invented it. His *Pyrrhonisme de l'Histoire* sets forth, as his *Siècle de Louis* XIV. exemplifies the new manner of historical investigation. He was followed by Beaufort, who, in his *Uncertainty of the first four centuries of the Roman History*, adopted the same methods ; and by Anselme, De Ponilly, Freret and De Burigny, in various papers that may be found in volumes IV, VI, XVIII, XIX, XL, of the *Mémoirs de l'Académie des Inscriptions et Belles Lettres.*

1

Catalogue Systematic and Analytical of the Books of the Saint Louis Mercantile Library Association (1858)

CATALOGUE

OF THE

OTIS LIBRARY.

ABBOTT, Jac. American History. (v. 1. Ab-
original America; v. 2. Discovery of
America.) 2 v. 12°. N. Y. n. d.
129a. 14.

—— China and the English. 18°. N. Y. 1835.
(2 copies.)   146. 8.8a.

—— Corner Stone. 12°. N. Y. n. d.
315. 18.

—— History of Alexander the Great. 16°. N.
Y. 1848.   535. 14.

——   "   Alfred the Great. 16°. N. Y.
1849.   535. 11.

——   "   Charles I. 16°. N. Y. 1848.
(2 copies.)   535. 16,17.

——   "   Charles II. 16° N. Y. 1849.
535. 6.

——   "   Cyrus the Great. 16°. N. Y.
1850. (2 copies.)   535. 13,17.

——   "   Darius the Great. 16°. N. Y.
1850.   535. 12.

——   "   Queen Elizabeth. 16°. N. Y.
1849. (2 copies.)   535. 8,9.

——   "   Hannibal the Carthaginian.
16°. N. Y. 1849.   535. 14.

——   "   Julius Cæsar. 16°. N. Y.
1849.   535. 10.

——   "   Mary, Queen of Scots. 16°.
N. Y. 1848. (2 copies.)
535. 9,16.

——   "   Nero 16°. N. Y. 1853.
535. 13.

ABBOTT, Jac. History of Pyrrhus. 16°. N. Y.
1854.   535. 15.

—— History Romulus. 16°. N. Y. 1852.
535. 15.

——   "   William the Conqueror. 16°.
N. Y. 1849. (2 copies.)
535. 10,11.

——   "   Xerxes the Great. 16°. N. Y.
1850.   535. 12.

—— Young Christian. 12°. N. Y. n. d. (2
copies.)   { 325. 7.
                          { 326. 18.

ABBOTT, Jno. S. C. Empire of Austria. r. 12°.
N. Y. 1859.   142. 16.

—— Empire of Russia. r. 12°. N. Y. 1860.
(2 copies.)   143. 2. 2a.

—— History of Maria Antoinette. 16°. N. Y.
1849. (2 copies.)   535. 6,7.

——   Madame Roland. 16°. N. Y.
1850. (2 copies.)   535. 7,8.

—— Italy, from Earliest Period. 12°. N. Y.
n. d.   143. 12.

—— Kings and Queens: or Life in the Palace.
12°. N. Y. 1855.   545. 3.

—— Mother at Home; or Principles of Maternal Duty, Familiarly Illustrated. 12°. N.
Y. 1852.   426. 11.

—— South and North: Impressions received
during a trip to Cuba and the South.
12°. N. Y. 1860.   230. 19.

Catalogue of Books in the Otis Library of the City of Norwich (1867)

ARTS.

General Treatises.

Address before American Institute. *Everett.*
                                            (P.)
Dictionary of Arts, Manufactures and Mines.
    Ure.   244. a1.
Eighty Years' Progress of the United States.
    (2 copies.)   241. 3, 3a.
Enterprise, Industry and Art of Man.
                                  938. 21.
Hand-Book of Useful Arts. *Antisell.*
                                  927. 7.
Manufacture of Porçelain and Glass.
                                  939b. 12.
New York Crystal Palace. *Richards.*
                                  245. 12.
Register of Arts. *Fessenden.*   243. 7.
Register of Arts. *Hebert.*   243. 8.
Rural Essays. *Downing.*   243. 5.
Technological Repository. *Gill.* 243. 9.
Useful Arts. *Martin.*   247. 8.

Mechanical Arts.

Art of Book-Binding. *Walker.* (2 copies.)
                                  243. 6, 6a.
Arts and Artisans. *Symons.*   245. 17.
Book of Illustrious Mechanics. *Foucaud.*
                                  246. a1.
Cabinet Maker and Upholsterer's Companion.
    Stokes.   247. 1.
History of American Manufactures, from 1608
    to 1860. *Bishop.*   241. 12.
Journal of the *Franklin* Institute. 242. 15.
Mechanic's Companion. *Nicholson.* 242. 7.
Mechanics' Institute, San Francisco. Report of
    Second Industrial Exhibition.   (P.)
United States. Manufactures, from Returns of
    8th Census.   (P. D.)

Machinery and Inventions.

Appleton's Dictionary of Machines and Engi-
    neering.   241. 2.
History of Inventions, Discoveries, etc. *Beck-
    mann.*   934. 2.
History of Inventions and Discoveries. *Wil-
    liams.*   244. 4.
History of Wonderful Inventions.   246. 7.
Hydraulics and other Machines. *Ewbank.*
                                  243. 2.

Price List and Description of Machinist's Tools.
    Gage, Warner and Whitney.   242. a3.
World of Waters. *Zornlin.*   247. 4.
Young Millwright and Miller's Guide. *Evans.*
                                  244. 10.

Civil Engineering.

Cadet Engineer. *Long and Buel.*   244. 7.
Construction and Management of Railways.
    Jervis.   246. 3.
United States. Inter-Oceanic Canals and Rail-
    Roads.   (P. D.)

Architecture and Carpentry.

American House Carpenter. *Hatfield.*
                                  244. 5.
Architecture in England. *Rose.*   244. 6.
Architecture of Country Houses. *Downing.*
    (2 copies.)   241. 9, 10.
Carpenter's New Guide. *Johnston.*
                                  110. 17.
Cottages and Cottage Life. *Elliott.* 242. 3.
Elements of Architecture. *Benjamin.*
                                  242. 5.
Gothic Ecclesiastical Architecture. *Bloxam.*
                                  246. 11.
Hints on Building in the Country. *Downing.*
                                  241. 8.
Hints on Public Architecture. *Owen.* 110. 15.
Hints to Young Architects. *Wightwick.*
                                  241. 8.
History of Propellers and Steam Navigation.
    MacFarlane.   245. 10.
Homes for the People. *Wheeler.* 246. 2.
Introduction to Gothic Architecture. 247. 11.
Model Architect. *Sloan.*   110. 9.
Practical Architecture. *Bartholomew.* 243. 3.
Principles of Architecture. *Nicholson.*
                                  241. 4.
Rudiments of Architecture and Building. *Bul-
    lock.* (Ed'r.)   244. 15.
Rural Homes. *Wheeler.* (2 copies.)
                                  245. 13, 13a.
Rural Studies. *Mitchell.*   246. b1.
School Architecture. *Barnard.*   242. 4.
Seven Lamps of Architecture. *Ruskin.*
                                  244. 13.
Smeaton and Lighthouses.   938. 1.

58   CATALOGUE.

SCIENCE AND ARTS.

A

	NO. VOLS.
AGASSIZ AND GOULD—	
Principles of Zoology	1
ALLEN, R. S.—	
American farm book	1
APPLETON'S—	
Dictionary of mechanics	1
AUDUBON, JOHN J.—	
Synopsis of the birds of America	1

B

BARRY, B.—	
Treatise on fruit garden	1
BALFOUR, J. H.—	
Class book of botany	1
BAKER, T.—	
Railway engineering and earth works	1
BERZELIUS—	
On the flower	1
BOOTH AND MORFITS—	
Recent improvement in chemical arts	1
BOURNE, JOHN—	
Catechism of the steam engine	1
BOUSSINGAULT, J. B.—	
Rural economy	2

Catalogue of Books, Maps, Charts, etc., Belonging to the
[Washington] Territorial Library (1867)

DARTMOUTH COLLEGE.   **111**

	Dep.	Shelf
Dumoriez. Gemalde von Portugal.	H	25
Dunbarton, N. H. His. of, Stark. 8°	G	12
Duncan, A. Dispensatory. 1806. 8°	C	21
" J. M. Lectures on Genesis. 1832. 8°	N	8
" W. Elements of Logic. Phila. 1792. 16°	F	14
" W. Tr. Cicero's Orationes. 1801. 8°	N	8
" W. Tr. of Caesar. 8° 2.	D	67
Dunlop. His. of Roman Literature. 8° 2.	O	2
" W. Sermons. Glasgow. 1747. V. 2. 16°	A	
Dupin, C. Mathematics. 8°	C	23
Dupuis, C. F. Works of, 8° 7.	P	17,18
Du Pan, J. M. Destruction of the Helvetic Union. 12°	F	11
Durfee, C. History of Williams College. 1860. 8°	G	10
Durham, J. An Exposition of Apocalypse. 1658. 4°	A	10
" Sermons. 2 copies. 12° 2.	A	57
" University, The Calendar of.	K	6
Duxbury, Mass. History of, Winsor, J. 1849. 8°	N	2
Duyckinck. Cyclopædia of Am. Literature. 1856. 8° 2.	T	1
Dwight, B. W. Modern Philosophy. N. Y. 1859. 8° 2.	F	5
" Timothy, Travels. 1821. 8° 4.	N	5
" T. Jr. New Gazeteer of the N. Y. 1832. 8°	H	3
" T. W. Inaugural Addresses of Columbia College. N. Y. 1859. 8°	K	3
Dymond, J. Essays on the Principles of Morality. N. Y. 1845. 12°	A	50
Dynamics. Whewell, W.	Q	10

E

Earth and Man. A. Guyot. 1853. 12°	C	28
East, E. H. Treatise on Pleas of the Crown. 1803. 8° 2.	L	46
" Reports. 1817. 8° 16.	L	39
" Tour in the, Lord Baltimore.	H	3
Eaton, Amos, Botany, Manual of, 1818. 8°	C	40
" A Geology. 1831. 12°	C	38
" An Index to the Geology of the Northern States. 1820. 12°		
" John, Honeycomb of Free Justification by Christ alone. 1666. 12°	A	49
Eberle, F. and others, Trial of, 1817. 8°		

PORTLAND INSTITUTE AND PUBLIC LIBRARY.

FINDING LIST OF BOOKS.

APRIL 1, 1869.

NOTE.—Persons wishing any book in this Catalogue, will please give the number, alcove, and shelf of such book, and the number of the volume if there is more than one.

	No.	Alcove.	Shelf.
ABBOT, The. Scott, *Sir* W.	2519	J 6, 3521 O	2
ABBOTT, A. O.			
— Prison life in the South	121	H	3
— - Same	1365		3
ABBOTT, J.			
— Franconia stories. 10 v., viz.:			
vol. 1. Malleville	2304	L	5
2. Wallace	2305		5
3. Mary Erskine	2306		5
4. Mary Bell	2308		5
5. Beechnut	2307		5
6. Rodolphus	2313		5
7. Ellen Lynn	2312		5
8. Stuyvesant	2311		5
9. Caroline	2309		5
10. Agnes	2310		5
— Harper's story books. 12 v., viz.:			
vol. 1. Bruno; Willie and the mortgage; The strait gate	2321	L	6
2. Little Louvre; Prank; Emma	2319		6
3. Virginia; Timboo and Joliba; Timboo and Fanny	2320		6
4. Harper establishment; Franklin; The studio	2322		6
5. Stories of History; Ancient; English; American	2323		6
6. John True; Elfred; Museum	2324		6
7. Engineer; Rambles among the Alps; Three gold dollars	2325		6
8. Gibraltar gallery; Alcove; Dialogues	2326		6
9. The great elm; Aunt Margaret; Vernon	2327		7
10. Carl and Jacko; Lapstone; Orkney	2328		9
11. Judge Justin; Minigo; Jasper	2329		6
12. Congo; Viola; Little Paul	2330		6
— Illustrated histories. 22 v., viz.:			
Hist. of Alexander the great	2291	L	5

	No.	Alcove.	Shelf.
ABBOTT, J., *continued.*			
Hist. of Alfred of England	2295	L	5
" Charles I. of England	2280		5
" Charles II. of England	2284		5
" Cleopatra	2294		5
" Cyrus the great	2276		5
" Darius the great	2279		5
" Queen Elizabeth	2287		5
" Genghis Khan	2282		5
" Hannibal the Carthaginian	2297		5
" Margaret of Anjou	2293		5
" Mary, queen of Scots	1452		5
" - Same	2283		5
" Nero	2281		5
" Peter the great	2286		5
" Pyrrhus	2206		5
" Richard I. of England (Cœur de lion)	2277		5
" Richard II. of England	2292		5
" Richard III. of England	2278		5
" Romulus	2289		5
" William the conqueror	2288		5
" Xerxes the great	2290		5
— Marco Paul series. 6 v., viz.:			
vol. 1. Marco Paul's adventures in New York	2285	L	5
2. on the Erie canal	2317		5
3. in the forests of Maine	2318		5
4. in Vermont	2315		5
5. in Boston	2316		5
6. at the Springfield armory	2314		5
— The young Christian	3594	S	1
ABBOTT, J. S. C.			
— The empire of Russia	2205	Z	3
— Illustrated histories. 6 v., viz.:			
Hist. of Henry IV. of France	1301	L	5
" Hernando Cortez	2299		5
" Josephine	2300		5
" King Philip	2303		5
" Madame Roland	2302		5
" Maria Antoinette	2278		5
ABELARD and Heloise, Romance of. Wight, O. W.	1446	N	2
ABERCROMBIE, J.			
— The intellectual powers	792	G	1

1

12   CATALOGUE OF THE

Alroy. B. Disraeli. Leipzig, 1846. 16° 364. 35
Alston, A. II. Seamanship and its Associated Duties in the Royal
    Navy. London, 1860. 16° 630. 6
Althaus, J. Treatise on Medical Electricity. Philadelphia, 1870. p. 8° 616.11
Alton Locke. C. Kingsley. New York, 1854. 12° . . . . . . ·. . 351. 36
Alune. M. M. Sherwood. New York, n. d. 12° . . . . . .v. 7 of 326. 1
Amateur Dramas. G. M. Baker. Boston, 1867. 12° 282. 10
Amazon River. Herndon, W. L. Exploration of Valley of the. (2 cop)480. 38
    Warren, J. E., Scenes and Adventures on the Banks of the. . 480. 28
Amazon, The. F. Dinglestedt. New York, 1868. 12° 410 36
Amber Gods and other Stories. II E. P. Spofford. Boston, 1863. 12° 405. 19
Amelia. II. Fielding. London, 1852. 8° 200. 41
        Same. London, 1775. 12° . . . . . . .v. 10, 11 of 200. 40
Amelie Mansfield. S. R. Cottin. Paris, 1811. 3v. 12° 835. 14
America.   Biography.
    Belcher, J., Clergy of. 572. 13
    Clement, J., Ed., Noble Deeds of American Women. 572. 15
    Cooper, J. F., Lives of American Naval Officers. v. 1. . . . .572. 16
    Ellet, E. F., Queens of American Society. 573. 18
    Fowler, II., American Pulpit, The. 573. 16
    Frost, J., American Naval Biography. . . . . · 573. 10
    Headley, J. T., Washington and his Generals. 2 v. 570. 54
    Hunt, F., Lives of American Merchants. v. 1. . . . . 373. 6
    Parker, T., Historic Americans. 572. 5
    Parton, J., Famous Americans of Recent Times. 572. 1
    Sparks, J Ed., Library of American Biography. 25 v. . . . 571. 1
        Same. v. 1–10. . . . . 571. 2
    Tuckerman, H. T., Book of the Artists. 573. 2
                            Coins.
    *Dickeson, M. W., American Numismatical Manual. 610. 49
                Description and Travels.
    Bryant, W. C., Notes of Things seen in. 421. 22
    *Castle, W., Coast and Continent of. . . . . . . .v. 2 of R. 11. 2
    Coxe, W., Russian Discoveries between Asia and. 441. 3
    Humboldt, F. II. A. von, Travels to the Equinoctial Regions
        of. 3 v. 480. 64
    Martineau, II., Society in . . . . · 40. 13
    *Nova Francia ; Description of that Part of New France which
        is One Continent with Virginia. . . . . .v. 2 of R. 11. 2
    Ossoli, S. M. F., Things and Thoughts in. 421. 20
    Pumpelly, R., Across America. 420. 3
    *Smith, J., Travels and Adventures in. . . . . . . .v. 2 of R. 16. 2
    Tytler, P. F., Discoveries on the Northern Coasts of. 800. 2
    See also: North-West Passage, and the Names of Various Countries, Lakes,
        Mountains, Rivers, States, etc., of America.
                            History.
    Abbott, J., American History. 3 v. 513. 22
    Banvard, J., Romance of American History. 573. 23

Catalogue of the Library of the Peabody Institute (1872)

CATALOGUE OF AUTHORS.

———◆◆———

ABERCROMBIE, J. Philosophy of the Moral Feelings. With introduction by Abbott. Boston, 1846. 12°. (330) **96.18**

ABLES, W. Gedanken ueber Natur- und ⎸Wortpoesie der Russischen Sprache. Berlin, 1861. 8°. (1346) **172.17**

ABOUT, E. Greece and the Greeks of the present day. New York, 1857. 12° (652) **226.12**

ABREGE de l'histoire ancienne, en particulier de l'histoire grecque. London, 1802. 12°. (1025) **266.19**

ACERBI, Joseph. Travels through Sweden, Finland, and Lapland, to the North Cape, in the years 1798 and 1799. London, 1802. 2v. sm. 4°. (256) **131.10**

ACHILLI, G. Dealings with the Inquisition. London, 1851. 8°. (2698) **336.6**

ADAMS, A. Travels of a Naturalist in Japan and Manchuria. London, 1870. 8°. (1564) **202.14**

ADAMS, E. The Elements of the English Language. New Edition. London, 1869. 16. (2568) **325.1**

ADAMS, H. G. Beautiful Butterflies described and illustrated, with the History of a Butterfly through all its changes and transformations. London, 1871. 16°. (1791) **315.14**

——Cyclopædia of Female Biography. London, 1869. sm. 8°. (1160) **66.10**

——Humming Birds described and illustrated. London. n. d. 16°. (1789) **315.13**

ADAMS, John, Letters of, addressed to his wife. Edited by Charles Francis Adams. Boston, 1841. 2 v. in 1. 16°. (632) **126.2**

ADAMS, J. Q. Letters on Silesia, written during a tour through that country in 1800--1801. London, 1804. 8°. (1767) **224.4**

DICTIONARY CATALOG

"A. B. C." guide to the making of autotype prints in permanent pigments. Sawyer, J. R.
WRS 773

A B C of bee culture. Root, A. I. RJJ 638

A B C of the foreign exchanges. Clare, George.
HME 332

"A. L. A." index. American library association.
AI 040

ABAILARD, PIERRE, 1079–1142. Compayré, Gabriel. Abelard and the origin and early history of universities. 1893. Ix 378

McCabe, Joseph. Peter Abélard. 1901.
E 921

Abbé Constantin. Halévy, Ludovic. YF 843

ABBEYS. See Cathedrals. Also names of abbeys, cathedrals, churches, minsters, etc., e. g. Bath abbey, Beverley minster, etc., etc. (Complete list of references under Cathedrals)

Abbot, Alice Balch. A frigate's namesake. 1901.
19cm Century $1 n 1,2 jYF y813

Abbot, Willis John. American merchant ships and sailors. 1902. 21cm Dodd $2 n 2,3
UU 387

Abbott, Alexander Crever. The hygiene of transmissible diseases. 2d ed. 1901. 24cm Saunders $2.50 n 3,3 QH 614

Abbott, Evelyn. A history of Greece. 1895–1901. 3 v. 22cm Putnam $2.25 ea 4,2
F32 938

Pericles and the golden age of Athens. 1897. 20cm (Heroes of nations) Putnam $1.50
5,3 F32A 938

ed. Heroes of the nations.

—— & Campbell, Lewis. The life and letters of Benjamin Jowett. 3d ed. 1897. 2 v. 23cm Murray 32/ 6,3 E 923

Abbott, George Frederick, ed. & tr. Songs of modern Greece. 1900. 17 x 13½cm Camb. univ. 5/ n 7,3 YP34 889

Abbott, Jacob. The Franconia stories. [190–?] 10 v. in 5. 17½cm Harper $5 8,2
jYF y813

Stories of Rainbow and Lucky. [1887–88] 5 v. 17cm Harper 75 cts ea 9,3
jYF y813

Abbott, John Stevens Cabot. Christopher Carson, known as Kit Carson. [1901] 19cm Dodd 75 cts 10,2 jE y923

Daniel Boone, pioneer of Kentucky. 1898. 19cm Dodd $1 11,2 jE y923

Abbott, Lyman. Christianity and social problems. 1896. 18½cm Houghton $1.25
12,3 H 304

The evolution of Christianity. [2d ed.] 1893. 18½cm Houghton $1.25 13,3 Cc 201

Henry Ward Beecher. 1903. 20cm Houghton $1.75 n 14/2 E 922

The life and letters of Paul the Apostle. 1898. 20½cm Houghton $1.50 15,3 CBW 225

The life and literature of the ancient Hebrews. 1901. 20cm Houghton $2 16,3
CBG 221

The rights of man; a study in twentieth century problems. 1901. 20½cm (Lowell inst. lect. 1901) Houghton $1.25 17,5
J 304

Abel, Mrs Mary W. (Hinman) Practical sanitary and economic cooking, adapted to persons of moderate and small means. Pub. by the American public health association. 1890 [1900?] 19cm Rochester, E. R. Andrews, pr. 40 cts 18,3 Rz 641

ABÉLARD, PIERRE. See Abailard, Pierre.

Abney, Sir William de Wiveleslie. Instantaneous photography. 1895. 18½cm (Phot. prim.) Low 1/ 19,3 WR 770

Instruction in photography. 10th ed. 1900. 19cm Low (Lippincott) $2 20,2
WR 770

A treatise on photography. 10th ed. 1901. 18cm (Text-bks. of sci.) Longmans $1.75 21/2 WR 770

—— & Clark, Lyonel. Platinotype: its preparation and manipulation. 2d Amer. ed. 1898. 18½cm (Scovill phot. ser.) Scovill (Low) 2/6 22/4 WRRY 772

About old story-tellers. Mitchell, D. G.
jZY y928

About Paris. Davis, R. H. G39P 914.4

About the weather. Harrington, M. W. MH 551

Abrahams, Israel. Jewish life in the middle ages. 1896. 21cm Macmillan $1.75 23,2
F61 296

(11)   AAA

APPENDIX C

LIBRARY OF CONGRESS CLASSIFICATION SCHEDULES

Outline of the Library of Congress Classification. 1942. (Reprinted 1958)

Classes A to Z:		§	§§
A	General works: Polygraphy. 3d ed., 1947. (Reprinted 1953)	47	
B	Philosophy and Religion:		
	Part I, B-BJ: Philosophy. 2d ed., 1950. (*Reprinted 1960)	166	45
	Part II, BL-BX: Religion. 1927. (Reprinted 1954)	337	
C	History: Auxiliary Sciences. 2d ed., 1948. (Reprinted 1953)	167	
D	History: General and Old World. 2d ed., 1959	747	
E-F	History: America. 3d ed., 1958.	607	
G	Geography, Anthropology, Folklore, etc. 3d ed., 1954	502	
H	Social Sciences. 3d ed., 1950. (*Reprinted 1959)	614	123
J	Political Science. 2d ed., 1924. (*Reprinted 1956)	434	123
K	Law (In preparation)		
L	Education. 3d ed., 1951. (*Reprinted 1960)	200	43
M	Music. 2d ed., 1917. (*Reprinted 1957)	157	85
N	Fine Arts. 3d ed., 1922. (*Reprinted 1955)	165	63
P	Philology and Literature:		
	P-PA: Philology. Classical Philology and Literature. 1928. (*Reprinted 1955)	447	25
	PA Supplement: Byzantine and Modern Greek Literature. Medieval and Modern Latin Literature. 1942. (*Reprinted 1956)	25	
	PB-PH: Modern European Languages. 1933. (Reprinted 1957)	226	27
	PG: Russian Literature. 1948. (*Reprinted 1955)	256	7
	PJ-PM: Languages and Literatures of Asia, Africa, Oceania, America; Mixed Languages; Artificial Languages. 1935. (*Reprinted 1956)	246	91
	P-PM: Supplement: Index to Languages and Dialects. 2d ed., 1957	71	
	PN, PR, PS, PZ: Literature — General, English, American. Fiction and Juvenile Literature. 1915. (*Reprinted 1956)	272	235
	PQ, Part 1: French Literature. 1936. (*Reprinted 1957)	185	11
	PQ, Part 2: Italian, Spanish, Portuguese Literatures. 1937. (*Reprinted 1955)	223	9
	PT, Part 1: German Literature. 1938 (*Reprinted 1957)	312	11
	PT, Part 2: Dutch and Scandinavian Literatures. 1942. (*Reprinted 1955)	102	15
Q	Science. 5th ed., 1950. (*Reprinted 1957)	215	21
R	Medicine. 3d ed., 1952. (*Reprinted 1960)	240	25
S	Agriculture, etc. 3d ed., 1948. (*Reprinted 1959)	101	37
T	Technology. 4th ed., 1948. (Reprinted 1953)	325	
U	Military Science. 3d ed., 1952. (*Reprinted 1960)	86	15
V	Naval Science. 2d ed., 1953	115	
Z	Bibliography and Library Science. 4th ed., 1959	226	

*Reprint with supplementary pages of additions and changes adopted since publication of latest edition.
§Number of pages in latest edition.
§§Number of pages in supplement to latest edition.

NUMBER OF VOLUMES IN THE CLASSIFIED COLLECTIONS OF THE LIBRARY OF CONGRESS BY CLASS (JUNE 30, 1959)

A	Polygraphy	231,465
B-BJ	Philosophy	82,016
BL-BX	Religion	266,017
C	History, Auxiliary Sciences	104,123
D	History (except American)	407,239
E-F	American History	343,319
G	Geography-Anthropology	123,188
H	Social Sciences	1,074,759
J	Political Science	435,479
L	Education	235,889
M	Music	242,812
N	Fine Arts	131,469
P	Language and Literature	830,856
Q	Science	415,290
R	Medicine	177,226
S	Agriculture	195,715
T	Technology	466,510
U	Military Science	97,398
V	Naval Science	54,177
Z	Bibliography	250,124
	Incunabula	445
	Total	6,165,516